⋐ CATO ⋑
SUPREME COURT
REVIEW
2 0 0 8 — 2 0 0 9

⤝ C A T O ⤜
SUPREME COURT
REVIEW
2 0 0 8 — 2 0 0 9

CENTER FOR CONSTITUTIONAL STUDIES
CATO
INSTITUTE
Washington, D.C.

THE CATO SUPREME COURT REVIEW (ISBN 978-1-935308-15-7) is published annually at the close of each Supreme Court term by the Cato Institute, 1000 Massachusetts Ave., N.W., Washington, D.C. 20001-5403.

CORRESPONDENCE. Correspondence regarding subscriptions, changes of address, procurement of back issues, advertising and marketing matters, and so forth, should be addressed to:

Publications Department
The Cato Institute
1000 Massachusetts Ave., N.W.
Washington, D.C. 20001

All other correspondence, including requests to quote or reproduce material, should be addressed to the editor.

CITATIONS: Citation to this volume of the Review should conform to the following style: 2008-2009 Cato Sup. Ct. Rev. (2009).

DISCLAIMER. The views expressed by the authors of the articles are their own and are not attributable to the editor, the editorial board, or the Cato Institute.

INTERNET ADDRESS. Articles from past editions are available to the general public, free of charge, at www.cato.org/pubs/scr.

Contents

CONTENTS

FOREWORD

Facial v. As-Applied Challenges: Does It Matter?

*Roger Pilon**

The Cato Institute's Center for Constitutional Studies is pleased to publish this eighth volume of the *Cato Supreme Court Review*, an annual critique of the Court's most important decisions from the term just ended, plus a look at the cases ahead—all from a classical Madisonian perspective, grounded in the nation's first principles, liberty and limited government. We release this volume each year at Cato's annual Constitution Day conference. And each year in this space I discuss briefly a theme that seemed to emerge from the Court's term or from the larger setting in which the term unfolded.

Although the Court heard several important cases over the past year, the term was not marked by high-profile, landmark decisions. Accordingly, as we are still taking the measure of the unfolding Roberts Court, I am going to turn this year to one of the more abstract and abstruse questions that has emerged over its brief tenure, drawing the attention of a number of Court watchers in the process: namely, whether the Court is making it more difficult to bring constitutional claims because it is increasingly favoring "as-applied" instead of "facial" challenges.

As we have often said to our readers, we try in this *Review* to make the work of the Court accessible to the educated layman, even when the Court offers us little help in that endeavor, as here. In this matter, however, I am afraid that the complexity is more than the Roberts Court's doing; it is inherent in the subject itself, although the Court's post-New Deal jurisprudence has exacerbated it—or so

* Roger Pilon is vice president for legal affairs at the Cato Institute, director of Cato's Center for Constitutional Studies, and publisher of the *Cato Supreme Court Review*.

I will argue. Nevertheless, I will try to shed such light as I can on the subject in the brief discussion that follows.

To give the issue something of an ideological hue, however, let me note that the American Constitution Society, the modern liberal answer to the older conservative and libertarian Federalist Society, thought the subject important enough to devote a session to it at its recent national convention. And two quite thoughtful articles on the issue have just appeared, one by Columbia's Gillian E. Metzger in the *Fordham Urban Law Journal*, the other by DePaul's David L. Franklin in a symposium devoted to the subject in the *Hastings Constitutional Law Quarterly*. I will draw on both.

Interestingly, both authors conclude, correctly I believe, that substantive constitutional doctrine is what ultimately drives the Court in treating claims as either facial or as-applied. Their particular focus, however, is on the question many liberals have raised: Is the Roberts Court, through its as-applied approach, making it more difficult to bring constitutional claims about individual rights? Responding to that question more generally, Professor Metzger writes: "The real question in the end is whether the Court is developing specific constitutional doctrines in ways that expand or contract the substantive scope of individual rights." My concern, by contrast, will be rather less with rights—or powers, for that matter—than with whether the Court is faithfully interpreting and applying the Constitution, and how the facial/as-applied distinction plays into that process.

To better place the issue in context, I will start with the barest sketch of what I take to be the appropriate methodology for judicial review. The Constitution, at bottom, authorizes federal powers and then limits both federal and state powers. Through the legitimating doctrine of enumerated powers it limits the objects Congress may pursue. State constitutions do the same, variously, which is for state courts to police. Moreover, under the last of Congress's 18 enumerated powers, the Necessary and Proper Clause, the means Congress may employ toward those enumerated ends must be both necessary and proper—"proper" implying respectful of the powers of the other branches and the states, and of the rights of individuals as well, enumerated and unenumerated alike. States too, since the Civil War Amendments were ratified, must respect those rights.

Article III's implicit provision for judicial review, made explicit in *Marbury v. Madison*, empowers federal courts to hear challenges to government measures. There are several doctrines that enable courts to avoid reviewing complaints, however. Because courts decide only "cases or controversies" and do not issue "advisory opinions," they can find that a complaint before them is not "ripe," or is "moot," or that the complainant has no "standing" because no particularized damages. Moreover, two years ago in *Bell Atlantic v. Twombly* and just this term in *Ashcroft v. Iqbal* the Supreme Court tightened pleading requirements, making it more difficult to bring claims.

But assuming those obstacles can be overcome, judicial review, at bottom, entails determining, first, whether a statute or regulation, or its execution, is authorized, and, second, whether the means Congress or the government employs are necessary and proper. To challenge a measure, individuals can bring either a facial or an as-applied challenge or both. A successful facial challenge finds the measure, or the part at issue, unconstitutional per se, and it is no more. A successful as-applied challenge, as the name implies, finds the measure or its part unconstitutional as applied to the individual, leaving it otherwise intact. But that brief outline only begins the discussion, which is made more difficult because the Court has never articulated a consistent theory of the matter. So we turn now to a bit more detail.

For three main reasons the Court for years has shown a preference for as-applied challenges. First, since the New Deal "constitutional revolution" the Court has accorded the actions of the political branches and the states a fairly robust presumption of constitutionality, a point I will return to later. Second, and closely related, a concern for judicial restraint has rendered the Court deferential to those branches and the states and hence reluctant to find their measures wholly unconstitutional. But third, even with a weaker presumption of constitutionality—and there must be some such presumption if a complaint is to be brought—there is a fairly heavy burden for anyone bringing a facial challenge. As the Court put it in 1987 in the seminal case of *United States v. Salerno*, a facial challenge requires that there be "no set of circumstances" under which the measure is constitutional. Given all of that, it is understandable, as the Court has said, that "as-applied challenges are the basic building blocks of constitutional adjudication."

Before taking up that approach, however, let us look at three successful and fairly simple facial challenges, one claiming no power, the other two claiming a right. In 1995, in *United States v. Lopez*, the Court for the first time in 58 years found that Congress had exceeded its power to regulate interstate commerce when, purportedly under that grant, it enacted the Gun Free School Zones Act of 1990. In deciding that facial challenge, the Court needed to take only the first step mentioned above: it needed to find only that Congress was not regulating commerce, much less interstate commerce, and so had exceeded its authority. "Under no circumstances," therefore, could the statute be saved.

Turning now to a simple rights case, where the Court must take that second step, in 2002, in *Lawrence v. Texas*, the Court upheld a facial challenge to a state statute that criminalized homosexual sodomy in the privacy of one's home. Here, the Court could not deny that the state had a general police power to regulate health, safety, and, to some extent, morals; but the means employed went too far, implicating the unenumerated right of the plaintiff to sexual freedom in that context, the exercise of which implicated the rights of no one else. As in the 1965 case of *Griswold v. Connecticut*, which overturned a state statute that criminalized the sale and use of contraceptives by married couples, this use of the police power was not protecting rights, its main function, but violating them. No set of circumstances could justify the law.

Finally, in a somewhat more complicated rights case decided a year ago, *Davis v. FEC*, the Court upheld a facial challenge to the so-called Millionaire's Amendment to the far more complex McCain-Feingold campaign finance law. (More on that law below.) Because the Court had previously upheld the *power* of Congress to regulate federal campaign financing, the question here was the narrower one about the constitutionally of section 319 of the bill, which tripled the contribution limits for House candidates facing opponents who spent their own money beyond the statutory threshold while keeping opponents' contribution limits at the lower level. In effect, the provision amounted to a "categorical burden" on the self-financed candidate's First Amendment speech *rights*, as Professor Metzger put it, so the entire provision had to be severed from the larger bill, not just found unconstitutional as it applied to the plaintiff before the Court.

To complicate matters, however, and return to the powers side, facial challenges can sometimes *validate* measures, argues Professor Franklin, pointing to the 2005 case of *Gonzales v. Raich*, which he calls an example of "facial adjudication in as-applied clothing." The plaintiff here, seeking to use home-grown medical marijuana under California law, brought an *as-applied* challenge to the federal Controlled Substances Act (CSA), claiming that the Act, passed pursuant to Congress's power to regulate interstate commerce, did not apply to her because there was no "commerce" to regulate, much less interstate commerce. Unlike in *Lopez*, that is, Congress had been held previously to have the *power* to regulate the subject—controlled substances in interstate commerce—but that power did not reach home-grown medical marijuana. Thus, we're back to the first step of judicial review, but asking only if Congress's power "applies" here. The Court reasoned, however, that when Congress creates a comprehensive regulatory scheme for a product in interstate commerce, it can regulate any subclass of activities that are an essential part of that scheme, even when those activities are entirely noncommercial and local. With that, Professor Franklin believes, the Court "*facially validated* the CSA for Commerce Clause purposes," for given the character of the activities reached, "it is not too far a stretch to conclude that the Court has in effect outlawed as-applied constitutional challenges under the Commerce Clause."

Thus, while the Court disfavors facial challenges, neither are they rare. In fact, in two areas of the law—concerning the First Amendment and abortion—there has been a presumption favoring them. Regarding speech, the idea seems to be that case-by-case adjudication would produce uncertainty, would require repeated and costly litigation, and would generally chill speech, so better to find a speech regulation facially unconstitutional, even if there might be a few situations that would justify regulation. In abortion litigation, however, it seems that obverse concerns have been at play. Thus, in 1992, in *Planned Parenthood of Southern Pennsylvania v. Casey*, the Court upheld a facial challenge to the spousal notification provision of a state abortion law even though it would impose an "undue burden" on only a few of the women seeking abortions. And in 2000, in *Stenberg v. Carhart*, the Court upheld a facial challenge to Nebraska's "partial-birth abortion" statute because it lacked a health exception for those few women who might need such a procedure.

More recently, however, the Court has issued two as-applied abortion decisions, and that has caught the attention of liberals. In 2006, in *Ayotte v. Planned Parenthood of Northern New England*, a facial challenge was brought against a New Hampshire statute that required parental notice even when an immediate abortion was needed to preserve the minor's health. But a unanimous Court held, as Professor Metzger summarized it, "that this constitutional infirmity need not lead to the statute's being 'invalidated . . . wholesale,' given that 'only a few applications' of the statute 'would present a constitutional problem.'" And in 2007, in *Gonzales v. Carhart*, a 5-4 Court rejected a facial challenge to the federal Partial-Birth Abortion Ban Act, which sought to prohibit intact D&E abortions, notwithstanding that the act was virtually identical to the Nebraska statute the Court had overturned in 2000 in *Stenberg*.

Casey and *Ayotte* can be reconciled, Professor Franklin argues, since the spousal notification provision in *Casey* "was unconstitutional on its face and had to be struck entirely," whereas the parental notification provision in *Ayotte* was "unconstitutional on its face for want of a health exception, but this time the Court concluded that the infirmity could be cured by judicial surgery." In other words, "the plaintiffs' sought-after remedy was narrowed but not denied."

Reconciling *Stenberg* and *Gonzales*, however, is another matter. Writing for the majority in *Gonzales*, Justice Anthony Kennedy argued that the federal ban was more carefully drawn to apply only to the intact D&E procedure. And he held that medical uncertainty about the necessity of the procedure enabled the federal ban to survive a facial challenge despite the absence of a health exception. Yet in *Stenberg* that same medical uncertainty had made a health exception necessary—and its absence proved fatal, facially. Perhaps more telling, in *Gonzales* Kennedy contended that "these facial attacks should not have been entertained in the first instance." Rather, an as-applied challenge was "the proper manner to protect the health of the woman if it could be shown that in discrete and well-defined instances a particular condition has or is likely to occur in which the procedure . . . must be used." All of which prompted Professor Franklin to conclude that, after *Gonzales*, "it is hard to resist the conclusion that the Court has abandoned . . . [the] facial approach from *Casey* and has assimilated abortion rights to the traditional model in which as-applied challenges hold sway."

Returning to the First Amendment, at least in the election law context, here too we seem to see movement in that direction—a year ago we saw two decisions rejecting facial in favor of as-applied challenges. Relying on a 1966 case that found a state poll tax facially unconstitutional, the plaintiffs in *Crawford v. Marion County Election Board* brought a facial challenge to Indiana's recently enacted voter ID law, claiming among other things that the law was politically motivated and burdened discrete classes of potential voters. The Court plurality rejected the challenge, citing the weak evidentiary record plus the state's interest in combating voter fraud, but it hinted at the (remote) possibility that the law might be subject to an as-applied challenge.

And in *Washington State Grange v. Washington State Republican Party* the Court rejected a facial challenge to the state's "blanket primary" system, where primary candidates self-identify by party, regardless of the party's preference. Writing for a majority of five, Justice Clarence Thomas cited judicial restraint and the need to avoid broad or premature constitutional rulings based on "factual assumptions about voter confusion that can be evaluated only in the context of an as-applied challenge."

A final case brings us back to the complex McCain-Feingold campaign finance regime—the Bipartisan Campaign Reform Act of 2002 (BCRA)—section 203 of which prohibits "electioneering communications" financed from the general treasuries of corporations and labor unions during designated periods before elections. Senator Mitch McConnell and others brought a facial challenge immediately after BCRA's passage, charging that section 203 was overbroad under the First Amendment because it prohibited funding not only campaign ads but issue ads as well. The Court rejected the challenge in 2003 in *McConnell v. Federal Election Commission*. With that, Wisconsin Right to Life (WRTL), a non-profit corporation, brought an as-applied challenge, resulting in a 2006 *per curium* opinion (*WRTL I*) that made clear what had been unclear after *McConnell*, namely, that as-applied challenges could be brought against section 203. A year later the case made it back to the Court: In *Federal Election Commission v. Wisconsin Right to Life* (*WRTL II*) a 5-4 Court upheld WRTL's as-applied challenge. But the opinion also strongly implied that *all* as-applied issue-advocacy challenges would succeed, leading Professor Franklin to call this an example of facial invalidation in as-applied clothing.

But the unwillingness of the Court to go all the way and find section 203 facially unconstitutional prompted a sharp concurrence by Justice Antonin Scalia, joined by Justices Kennedy and Thomas. The provision is overbroad, Scalia said, and should have been struck on its face because it chills political discourse. And he added, given that seven justices of widely divergent views all agree that the Court's opinion, written by Chief Justice John Roberts and joined by Justice Samuel Alito, "effectively overrules *McConnell* without saying so," the Court has engaged in "faux judicial restraint" amounting to "judicial obfuscation." To that, Alito responded in his own concurrence:

> [B]ecause §203 is unconstitutional as applied to the advertise-ments before us, it is unnecessary to go further and decide whether §203 is unconstitutional on its face. If it turns out that the implementation of the as-applied standard set out in the principal opinion impermissibly chills political speech, we will presumably be asked in a future case to reconsider the holding in *McConnell* that §203 is facially constitutional.

Because the Court decides questions only properly before it, properly briefed and argued, Alito is probably right. Since this was an as-applied challenge, that judicial restraint leaves open the possibility that an as-applied challenge might fail.

Yet Scalia is right too—if the chance of such a challenge failing, given the opinion in *WRTL II*, is vanishingly thin. And so we come as a practical matter to that thin line, in many cases at least, between facial and as-applied adjudication. And in the issue at hand, it may not be long before the thinness of the line is demonstrated. For the "future case" Alito contemplated, *Citizens United v. FEC*, was just now before the Court; but in a surprise move in its final week the Court held the case over for re-argument on September 9, directing the parties to brief the Court on whether not only section 203 but the Court's closely related 1990 decision in *Austin v. Michigan Chamber of Commerce* should be overturned. Although the government is contending that Citizens United abandoned its facial challenge, it is not likely that the Court took the step it did simply to make another as-applied decision in a matter that arises so often with so far-reaching implications. We shall see.

Stepping back, we need to ask whether the Court's choice between facial and as-applied adjudication matters, and whether, as some liberals fear, the Roberts Court is making it more difficult to bring constitutional claims by increasingly favoring as-applied over facial adjudication. The first question cannot be answered in the abstract. Increasing as-applied adjudication would certainly matter to prospective plaintiffs, since even if the holdings in such litigation reached beyond the case itself to "classes of contexts," a point Professor Metzger notes, there would still be room for much more litigation, uncertain and costly, than if the challenged measure were to fall completely. But as she also notes, while as-applied rather than facial invalidation may reflect greater judicial restraint, severing parts of statutes can amount to its own brand of judicial activism, upsetting the careful balance of competing interests the legislature may have struck. Better, perhaps, to strike the whole statute and let the legislature go back to the drawing board. And of course the distinction matters insofar as clarity and certainty are legal virtues: as-applied adjudication leaves it open whether the next case brought before a court, with its own set of facts, will or will not be covered by the prior as-applied decision under the statute. Still, there are statutes that cannot be adjudicated facially until experience shows more fully how they will work in practice. Judicial modesty entails limiting judicial speculation.

Regarding the factual predicate to the question whether the Roberts Court is making it more difficult to bring constitutional claims, Professor Metzger concludes that although "resistance to facial challenges is a recurring theme of the Roberts Court, . . . close analysis of the Court's decisions suggests that its approach to facial and as-applied challenges is largely consistent with prior practice." There is some evidence, of course, that the distinction matters in areas of particular interest to liberals—abortion and voting, especially, but campaign finance as well, which implicates the First Amendment, at least among conservatives and libertarians. And that brings us to a conclusion that Professors Metzger and Franklin both stress, that what matters most in determining whether the Court takes a facial or an as-applied approach is its substantive constitutional doctrine. As Professor Metzger puts it, "it is substantive constitutional law that determines not just the availability of facial challenges, but in addition the extent to which as-applied challenges represent a meaningful mechanism for asserting constitutional rights."

If that is so, then attention should be directed ultimately to those substantive doctrines upon which the choice between facial and as-applied adjudication rests. The point emerges nicely in Professor

Franklin's brief discussion of a four-sentence concurrence by Justice Kennedy, joined by Justice Scalia, in the 2004 case of *Sabri v. United States*. There, Franklin observes, the two "pointedly declined to join the section of the majority opinion throwing cold water on facial challenges" in cases like *Lopez*, where the Court decided basic questions about whether Congress "had exceeded its legislative power under the Constitution. . . . For Justices Kennedy and Scalia," Franklin continues, "when 'basic questions' concerning 'legislative power' are at issue, the traditional preference for as-applied challenges ought to give way."

In other words, facial challenges are paradigmatically called for when the Court has before it something of a "First Principle," a "basic question" about whether Congress has the power at all to enact what it has enacted. That is certainly clear in a simple case like *Lopez*. But why not beyond that? The answer to that is clear too. It is because, with the New Deal constitutional revolution, the Court abandoned the doctrine of enumerated powers—and with it the limited presumption of constitutionality, necessary simply to get litigation off the ground, after which the presumption might easily be rebutted, and the burden would shift to the government to justify its action as both authorized, because in furtherance of an enumerated end, and necessary and proper. And the same is true with the scope of state police power, *mutatis mutandis*, which was once understood as granted mainly to secure rights, not to violate them, as with the statutes at issue in *Lawrence* and *Griswold*, two other simple and straightforward cases.

But the Progressive Era, culminating in the New Deal and modern liberalism, ended that simple and straightforward constitutionalism, replacing it with a broad conception of federal and state power, a political bifurcation of rights into "fundamental" and "nonfundamental," a robust presumption of constitutionality, a heavy burden to rebut that presumption, and judicial deference to the political branches to boot—all to facilitate the very social engineering the Constitution was otherwise written to prevent. As Rexford Tugwell, one of the principal architects of the New Deal, once put it: "To the extent that these [New Deal policies] developed, they were tortured interpretations of a document intended to prevent them."

And the great irony, of course, is that the liberals today who are concerned about the difficulties they imagine in bringing facial challenges to protect rights are the very class of people who promoted and still promote the expansive governmental powers that threaten those rights. To be sure, government is appropriately involved in setting the rules for voting or drawing the lines between the rights of expectant women and unborn children. But when government is presumed to have authority over all that it touches today, then the principal restraint on overweening government that the Framers infused in the Constitution is lost, and with it our rights as well. The issue is thus far deeper than whether the Court is taking a facial or an as-applied approach to the case before it. It is about the substance of the matter—whether the Court has grasped the true Constitution.

Introduction

*Ilya Shapiro**

This is the eighth volume of the *Cato Supreme Court Review*, the nation's first in-depth critique of the Supreme Court term just ended. We release this journal every year on September 17, Constitution Day, about two and a half months after the previous term concludes and two weeks before the next one begins (though this year we will already have had the *Citizens United* campaign finance case reargument in early September). We are proud of the speed with which we publish this tome—authors of articles about the last-decided cases have little more than a month to provide us full drafts—and of its accessibility, at least insofar as the Court's opinions allow for that. This is not a typical law review, after all, whose prolix submissions use more space for obscure footnotes than for article text. Instead, this is a book about law intended for everyone from lawyers and judges to educated laymen and interested citizens.

And we are happy to confess our biases: We approach our subject matter from a classical Madisonian perspective, with a focus on individual liberty, property rights, and federalism, and a vision of a government of delegated, enumerated, and thus limited powers. We also try to maintain a strict separation of politics (or policy) and law; just because something is good policy doesn't mean it's legal, and vice versa. Similarly, certain decisions must necessarily be left to the political process: We aim to be governed by laws, not lawyers, so just as a good lawyer will present all plausibly legal options to his client, a good public official will recognize that the ultimate buck stops with him.

Having said that, let's take a quick survey of the term that was. October Term 2008 produced more divisions but fewer headlines than the previous term. Of the 79 cases with opinions after argument,

* Senior Fellow in Constitutional Studies, Cato Institute and Editor-in-Chief, *Cato Supreme Court Review*.

23 went 5-4 (29.1 percent, up from 20 percent last year) and 26 had no dissenters (32.9 percent, up from 30 percent last year but down significantly from previous years). More interestingly, the total number of dissenting votes across all cases was notably high, with an average decision producing 2.04 justices in dissent, up from an average of 1.66 over the preceding 10 years. Justice Anthony Kennedy regained his usual status as the justice most often in the majority (92.4 percent of cases and 16 of 23 5-4 decisions), while Justice John Paul Stevens was most likely to dissent (35.4 percent of cases and an incredible 52.8 percent in cases that had dissenters). Chief Justice John Roberts and Justice Samuel Alito were the justices most likely to agree, voting the same way at least in part in 73 of 79 cases (92 percent, followed by six different pairings at 86-87 percent), while Justices Stevens and Clarence Thomas voted together in only 36 cases (46 percent).[1]

Looking beyond the statistics, this was of course the final term for Justice David Souter. Souter did not write any notable opinions, but buried in his dissent in *District Attorney's Office v. Osborne* was a meditation on the wisdom of judicial minimalism—or incrementalism—regarding the recognition of new rights in light of changes in "societal understandings of the fundamental reasonableness of government actions."[2] Some have suggested that this passage reflects the retiring justice's views on gay marriage,[3] but more broadly it was a sort of valedictory address on the nature of the judicial process.

Replacing Souter, of course, will be Justice Sonia Sotomayor, late of the Second Circuit Court of Appeals. While her confirmation was never in any serious doubt, Sotomayor faced strong criticism from legal analysts and Republican senators on issues ranging from property rights and the use of foreign law in constitutional interpretation to *Ricci v. DeStefano*—noted below is our article on the case—and

---

[1] All statistics taken from SCOTUSblog, Summary Memo and Super Stack Pack (Updated), June 30, 2009, available at http://www.scotusblog.com/wp/end-of-term-super-stat-pack/.

[2] District Attorney's Office for the Third Judicial District v. Osborne, 557 U.S. ____, 129 S. Ct. 2308, 2341 (2009) (Souter, J., dissenting).

[3] See, e.g., Walter Dellinger, Souter: A Last Lecture on Gay Marriage?, Slate, June 29, 2009, available at http://www.slate.com/id/2220927/entry/2221719.

the "wise Latina" speeches that led people to question her commitment to judicial objectivity.[4] Only time will tell what kind of a justice Sotomayor will be now that she is unfettered from higher court precedent.

Turning to the *Review*, we begin, as always, with the previous year's B. Kenneth Simon Lecture in Constitutional Thought, which in 2008 was delivered by Professor Randy Barnett of the Georgetown University Law Center. Prof. Barnett poses the provocative question—evoking Justice Oliver Wendell Holmes's infamous *Lochner* dissent—"Is the Constitution Libertarian?" Barnett confronts Holmes's dismissal of Herbert Spencer's "law of equal freedom"—which affirmed that each man "has freedom to do all that he wills provided that he infringes not the equal freedom of any other"—and finds that the Constitution "may be the most explicitly libertarian governing document ever actually enacted into law." While we have lost much of that libertarian understanding, we can regain it if we elect presidents who will appoint and senators who will confirm judges who interpret the Constitution properly—giving effect to its original public meaning, applying a "presumption of liberty," and construing vague terms in a way that enhances constitutional legitimacy.

We move then to the 2008 Term, beginning with provocative essays on the big civil rights cases of the year. Roger Clegg, president of the Center for Equal Opportunity, tackles *Bartlett v. Strickland* and *NAMUDNO v. Holder*, which challenged sections 2 and 5, respectively, of the Voting Rights Act. He discusses Section 2's internal contradictions—prohibiting racially disparate treatment but requiring racial gerrymandering—and Section 5's violation of federalism, questioning their continuing constitutionality. Notably, the *NAMUDNO* decision avoided the constitutional questions at the heart of our voting rights regime, an unsatisfying result that Clegg

---

[4] This editor was one of the critics. See, e.g., Ilya Shapiro, The Sotomayor Vote, Washington Times, August 7, 2009, available at http://www.washingtontimes.com/news/2009/aug/07/all-americans-should-take-pride-in-seeing-our-firs; Ilya Shapiro, Sotomayor Doesn't Deserve a Supreme Court Seat, Cato@Liberty, July 22, 2009, available at http://www.cato-at-liberty.org/2009/07/22/sotomayor-doesnt-deserve-a-supreme-court-seat; Ilya Shapiro, Five Questions for Sotomayor, Christian Science Monitor, June 9, 2009, http://www.csmonitor.com/2009/0609/p09s01-coop.html; Ilya Shapiro, Sotomayor Pick Not Based on Merit, CNN.com, May 27, 2009, available at http://www.cnn.com/2009/POLITICS/05/27/shapiro.scotus.identity/index.html.

laments. He concludes, "The Act should be refocused on fulfilling—not undermining—the Fifteenth Amendment's purpose: ensuring that the right to vote is not denied or abridged on account of race."

Ken Marcus of the City University of New York's Baruch College School of Public Affairs writes on *Ricci v. DeStefano*, the New Haven firefighters' case that figured so prominently in Justice Sotomayor's confirmation hearings. *Ricci* exposed the long-simmering tension between the disparate impact provisions of Title VII of the Civil Rights Act and the Fourteenth Amendment's Equal Protection Clause—which Justice Scalia pointed out in his concurrence. Disparate impact is constitutionally dubious, Marcus argues, because it is "sometimes used to level racial disparities that do not arise from intentional or unconscious discrimination," a purpose for which the Equal Protection Clause "does not permit state actors to take race-conscious actions." The Court will surely revisit this issue, and Congress may be forced to act.

Roger Pilon—director of Cato's Center for Constitutional Studies—dives into the biggest business case of the year, *Wyeth v. Levine*, where the Court had to decide whether a pharmaceutical company that satisfied the FDA's labeling requirements could nevertheless be held liable under state law for the harm that followed when a physician's assistant ignored the label's warnings. It's a tricky issue, not least because normally libertarians and conservatives support limited federal power and the role of states as "laboratories of democracy." Yet here it is the reverse, with (modern) liberals arguing that state law is the ultimate guarantor of individual rights. Pilon argues that "if the text of a constitutionally authorized statute or regulation implies the purposes or objectives of the measure . . . and a state law conflicts with the administrative execution of those purposes or objectives . . . then the effect of the Supremacy Clause is clear: the state law must yield."

Next, the University of Michigan's Dan Crane provides a page-turning look at the state of antitrust law—you read that right—through the lens of this term's price-squeeze case, *Pacific Bell v. link-Line*. It turns out that this spring's announcement of a change in policy on monopolization offenses by Christine Varney, the new Antitrust Division head at the Department of Justice, renewed a rift between the Chicago and Harvard Schools of antitrust. And as re-regulation comes to the political fore, the Court's antitrust jurisprudence may come under attack. "Only a deliberate and patient strategy that addresses the two schools' institutionalist concerns," Crane explains, "stands a chance of advancing the new administration's ambitious agenda."

We then have two articles on the term's Fourth Amendment cases. *Herring v. United States* asked whether evidence should be excluded when it is found as a result of a search based on a warrant that was erroneously listed in a police database. *Arizona v. Gant* explored the power to search incident to arrest in a case where police searched an arrestee's car after its owner had been secured in the back of a patrol car. *Arizona v. Johnson* probed the scope of the "stop and frisk" doctrine in the context of a patdown of a car's passenger by an officer who believed him to be armed and dangerous but had no reasonable grounds to believe he committed a crime. *Pearson v. Callahan* presented the Court with a police entry into a home based on consent given to an undercover informant. And *Safford v. Redding*, which got the most headlines, inquired into school officials' liability for strip-searching a middle school student. Law professors Erik Luna and Michael O'Neill give their nuanced takes on where the Court is going in this vital area.

Luna, of Washington and Lee, criticizes the Court's *Herring* decision as continuing "the movement toward constitutional rights without remedies, allowing law enforcement to infringe upon an individual's Fourth Amendment rights and then present the fruits of that violation against him at trial." He supports *Gant*'s result but notes his agreement with the dissent in that case regarding the Court's disingenuousness in its treatment of precedent. More broadly, Luna identifies "a sort of doctrinal creep-and-crawl" in constitutional criminal procedure, eroding our civil liberties as citizens place greater demands on law enforcement.

O'Neill, of George Mason, surveys the two big battlegrounds in Fourth Amendment jurisprudence: the warrant requirement and the exclusionary rule. He gleans several interesting insights from how each justice—including the newly arrived Sotomayor—will vote in these cases but also expresses frustration at a lack of judicial clarity about the meaning of "(un)reasonableness." O'Neill ultimately suggests that Congress "consider providing greater privacy protections for individuals and better guidance for law enforcement."

Mark Chenoweth of the Pacific Research Institute similarly surveys the Court's Sixth Amendment jurisprudence, focusing on *Oregon v. Ice* and *Melendez-Diaz v. Massachusetts*. *Ice* queried whether a sentencing judge may find facts apart from the jury verdict to determine whether a defendant will serve consecutive or concurrent sentences. *Melendez-Diaz* considered whether a defendant has the right to demand the live testimony of a lab technician when the prosecution wants to present forensic evidence. The latter-stage Rehnquist Court decisions in *Apprendi v. New Jersey* and *Crawford v. Washington* threw this area of law into a flux, but Chenoweth helps make sense of the current state of play.

Switching to the First Amendment, University of South Dakota law professor Patrick Garry examines the quixotic *Pleasant Grove City v. Summum*. Does a city displaying a privately donated Ten Commandments monument in a public park have to also display the monument an obscure religious sect wants to donate? Curiously, the Court refrained from addressing the obvious Establishment Clause issue here—the government endorsement of one religion's symbol over another's—and ruled for the city because the Free Speech Clause doesn't apply to government speech. Garry delves into those Establishment Clause implications, however, arguing that this sort of monument refusal may well violate the doctrine of "nonpreferentialism."

Communications and media law guru Robert Corn-Revere, also a Cato adjunct scholar, contributes a piece on yet another case where the Court declined to address the more interesting constitutional issue: *FCC v. Fox*. Here the Court reviewed the FCC's policies regarding broadcast indecency for the first time in 30 years. It ended up affirming the agency's new ban on "fleeting expletives"—following several celebrated incidents where, for example, Cher told us what she thought of her critics and Nicole Richie explained how difficult it was to get manure out of a designer purse—on administrative law grounds. Corn-Revere predicts that the Court will not long avoid the inherent First Amendment issues—representing CBS, he may know something about this—and sketches the parameters of that future litigation.

In a fascinating confluence of the First and Fourteenth Amendments—political speech and the right to unbiased judges—Center for Competitive Politics co-founders Steve Hoersting and Brad Smith (also former FEC chairman) cover *Caperton v. Massey Coal*. In this case, Massey Coal's CEO spent three million dollars to unseat a state supreme court justice unfriendly to the company's interests—without coordinating with his preferred candidate's campaign—which his legal adversary later claimed required judicial recusal under the Due Process Clause. Hoersting and Smith contend that *Caperton* "typifies the old maxim that hard cases make bad law," with the Court here creating a "new, largely unworkable standard" for recusals and then constitutionalizing it. Interestingly, the Court's decision on whether to overrule *Austin v. Michigan* and a related portion of *McConnell v. FEC*—via the reargued *Citizens United v. FEC*—will control *Caperton*'s broader ramifications on independent political speech.

At this point we normally would've had an article on *Citizens United* itself, the case about the regulation of *Hillary: The Movie* as "electioneering communication" under McCain-Feingold. The Court chose to hold the case over, however, and ask for briefing and rearguement relating to the regulation of corporate and union speech generally. This is a positive development for the First Amendment, we hope—but alas we'll have to wait till next year for an analysis in these pages.

In any event, this volume concludes with a look ahead to October Term 2009—and what we can expect from Justice Sotomayor—by Jan Crawford Greenburg, ABC News legal correspondent and author of the best recent history of the modern court.[5] Continuing its trend from this past term, the Court has further front-loaded its caseload—with 46 arguments on its docket before the term has even started. Fortunately, unlike last year, we should see many blockbuster constitutional cases, including: First Amendment challenges to national park monuments and a statute criminalizing the depiction of animal cruelty; an Eighth Amendment challenge to life sentences for juveniles; a potential revisiting of *Miranda* rights; federalism concerns over legislation regarding civil commitment of "sexually dangerous" persons; a separation-of-powers dispute concerning the agency enforcing Sarbanes-Oxley; and judicial takings of beachfront property. Cato has filed amicus briefs in many of these cases, so I will be paying extra-close attention.

[5] Supreme Conflict: The Inside Story of the Struggle for Control of the United States Supreme Court (2007).

*   *   *

This is the second volume of the *Cato Supreme Court Review* that I have edited. While the learning curve was steeper last year, the amount of work has not decreased—and so I have many people to thank for their contributions to this endeavor. I first need to thank our authors, without whom there would obviously not be anything to edit or read. My gratitude also goes to my colleagues at Cato's Center for Constitutional Studies, Bob Levy and Tim Lynch, who continue to provide valuable counsel in areas of law with which I'm less than familiar. A big thanks to research assistant Jonathan Blanks for making the trains run on time and keeping me honest, as well as to legal associate Travis Cushman and interns Matthew Aichele, Christian Brockman, Will Hild, and Jeff Widmayer, for doing the more thankless (except here) tasks. Neither the *Review* nor our Constitution Day conference would be the successes they are without them. Finally, thanks to Roger Pilon, the founder and *éminence* not-so-*grise* of this now well-established journal, without whom I would now be fretting about my role in the new legal economy.

I reiterate our hope that this collection of essays will deepen and promote the Madisonian first principles of our Constitution, giving renewed voice to the Framers' fervent wish that we have a government of laws and not of men. In so doing, we hope also to do justice to a rich legal tradition—now eclipsed by the modern regulatory state—in which judges, politicians, and ordinary citizens alike understood that the Constitution reflects and protects the natural rights of life, liberty, and property, and serves as a bulwark against the abuse of state power. In this uncertain time of "bailout," "stimulus," "public options," and general government overreach, it is more important than ever to remember our humble roots in the Enlightenment tradition.

We hope you enjoy this eighth volume of the *Cato Supreme Court Review*.

Is the Constitution Libertarian?

*Randy E. Barnett**

I am honored to be delivering the Seventh Annual B. Kenneth Simon Lecture. I have been philosophically close to the Cato Institute since its founding. And one of the fringe benefits of moving to the Georgetown University Law Center is that now I am physically close to Cato as well. As a public policy shop, the work of Cato touched only tangentially on my own scholarship. But ever since the establishment of its Center for Constitutional Studies, under the extraordinary leadership of my old friend Roger Pilon, I have enjoyed a much closer relationship to Cato than ever before. That I might be invited to deliver the prestigious Simon Lecture is, for me, a wonderful validation of a beautiful friendship.

In this lecture, I want to address a topic that goes to to the heart of the mission of the Cato Institute and its Center for Constitutional Studies: Is the Constitution libertarian?

Libertarians and the Constitution: A Love-Hate Relationship

Truth be told, libertarians have a love-hate relationship with the Constitution. On the one hand libertarians, like most Americans, revere the Constitution. Libertarians particularly appreciate its express guarantees of individual liberty and its mechanisms to preserve limited government. If being American is to subscribe to a creed, then the Constitution and the Declaration of Independence that gave rise to it are the foundational statements of this creed. It is no coincidence, then, that the Cato Institute is famous for distributing millions of copies of its little red books containing the Declaration and Constitution so that the public, both here and abroad, might read and appreciate the actual words of these singular texts.

* Carmack Waterhouse Professor of Legal Theory, Georgetown University Law Center. Senior Fellow, Cato Institute. An abbreviated version of this article was delivered as the Seventh Annual B. Kenneth Simon Lecture at the Cato Institute on Constitution Day, September 17, 2008. Permission to copy for classroom use is hereby granted.

But some libertarians have issues with the Constitution as well. And here I speak for myself, as well as others. There was a reason I eschewed writing about and teaching constitutional law when I became a law professor in favor of teaching contracts. After taking constitutional law in law school, I considered the Constitution an experiment in limiting the powers of government that, however noble, had largely failed. Every time we got to one of the "good parts" of the text, we then read a Supreme Court opinion that explained why it did not really mean what it appeared to mean.

Nor was only one branch of the government to blame. The judicial passivism of the Supreme Court has combined with activism by both Congress and presidents to produce the behemoth federal and state governments that seem to render the actual Constitution a mere relic, rather than the governing document it purports to be. This fundamental failure of the Constitution to limit the size and scope of government has even led some libertarians to contend that the enactment of the Constitution represented a coup d'état by big government Federalists against the more preferable regime defined by the Articles of Confederation and favored by the Anti-Federalists.

Yet libertarians are genuinely torn—one might go so far as to say schizophrenic—about how the Constitution has actually worked out. Big and intrusive as government is today, it could be much worse. Few can point to other countries where individuals are freer in practice than in the United States. Many libertarians might be willing to move there, if such a place existed; yet no such exodus has occurred. And, in important respects, life as an American feels freer than it once did. We seem to have more choices than ever before and are freer to live the sorts of lives we wish. Libertarians still refer to the United States as a "free country," maybe still the freest on earth, even as the Cato Institute documents the many ways in which our freedoms are unnecessarily restricted. That the Constitution deserves at least some of the credit for this freedom seems likely.

So is the Constitution libertarian or not? It turns out that this is not an easy question to answer.

What I Mean by "Libertarian"

For one thing, we need to settle on what is meant by "libertarian." The most obvious meaning of "libertarian" is a belief in or commitment to individual liberty. In my experience, the world is divided between Lockeans and Hobbesians: between those for whom individual liberty is their first principle of social ordering, and those who give priority to the need for government power to provide social order and pursue social ends. Yet most Americans, like Locke himself, harbor a belief in *both* individual liberty *and* the need for government power to accomplish some ends they believe are important.

However, a general sympathy for individual liberty shared by most Americans should be distinguished from the modern political philosophy known as "libertarianism." A libertarian, in this sense, favors the rigorous protection of certain individual rights that define the space within which people are free to choose how to act. These fundamental rights consist of (1) the right of *private property*, which includes the property one has in one's own person; (2) the right of *freedom of contract* by which rights are transferred by one person to another; (3) the right of *first possession*, by which property comes to be owned from an unowned state; (4) the right to *defend oneself and others* when fundamental rights are being threatened; and (5) the right to *restitution* or compensation from those who violate another's fundamental rights.[1]

If modern libertarianism is defined by the commitment to these rights, it is not defined by the *justifications* for this commitment. Some libertarians are consequentialists, others are deontologists, while still others adopt a compatablist approach that straddles the line between moral and consequentialist justifications. It is useful to emphasize that libertarianism is not a moral philosophy; it is a political philosophy that rests upon certain moral conclusions that can be supported in a variety of ways.[2]

Modern libertarianism can be viewed as a subset of classical liberalism, in the following way: All classical liberals believe in respecting and protecting these five rights, which distinguishes classical liberals from others who would deny some or all of these rights. Yet some classical liberals might add other rights to this list—such as an enforceable right to some minimum level of material support—or

---

[1] See Randy E. Barnett, The Structure of Liberty: Justice and the Rule of Law (1998) (explaining how these five fundamental rights solve the pervasive social problems of knowledge, interest, and power).

[2] See Randy E. Barnett, The Moral Foundations of Modern Libertarianism, in Varieties of Conservatism in America 51 (Peter Berkowitz, ed. 2004).

might sometimes favor limiting the scope of these fundamental rights to achieve other important social objectives.

In contrast, modern libertarians are distinctive for their tendency to limit the set of fundamental rights to these five, and their reluctance ever to restrict the exercise of these rights to achieve other worthy objectives. They view these rights as "side-constraints"[3] on the pursuit of any personal and collective ends. Their working thesis is that all genuinely desirable social objectives can be achieved while respecting these rights—the more rigorously, the better. Hereafter, I will consider the degree to which the Constitution is "libertarian" insofar as it respects and protects the fundamental rights to which modern libertarians and classical liberals generally adhere.

Holmes's Denial that the Constitution Is Libertarian

Now for some, asking whether the Constitution is libertarian in either the classical liberal or modern sense may seem completely inappropriate. In one of the most famous lines in any Supreme Court opinion, Justice Oliver Wendell Holmes Jr., in his dissent in the 1905 case of *Lochner v. New York*,[4] proclaimed that "[t]he Constitution does not enact Mr. Herbert Spencer's *Social Statics*."[5] Because modern academics know so little about Spencer, and what they think they know is a distortion, Holmes's exact meaning here is not always appreciated. Holmes was not rejecting the so-called social Darwinism that has been falsely associated with Spencer. Indeed, Holmes was himself a social Darwinist, as were most political progressives of his day.

No, Holmes was referring to Spencer's "law of equal freedom," the principle made so famous by Spencer that Holmes could be confident that his readers would not miss his reference. In *Social Statics*, Spencer affirmed "that every man may claim the fullest liberty to exercise his faculties compatible with the possession of like liberty to every other man."[6] Or, in another formulation, each "has freedom to do all that he wills provided that he infringes not

---

[3] The term "side-constraints" was coined by Robert Nozick. See Robert Nozick, Anarchy, State, and Utopia 33-35 (1974).

[4] 198 U.S. 45 (1905).

[5] *Id.* at 75 (Holmes, J. dissenting).

[6] Herbert Spencer, Social Statics: or, The Conditions essential to Happiness specified, and the First of them Developed 239 (1851).

the equal freedom of any other."[7] That this was Holmes's target was made clear just before his reference to Spencer when he referred to: "The liberty of the citizen to do as he likes so long as he does not interfere with the liberty of others to do the same," which Holmes dismissed as "a shibboleth for some well-known writers."[8]

Holmes took on Spencer in this way because the majority opinion in *Lochner* came as close as the Supreme Court ever has to protecting a general right to liberty under the Fourteenth Amendment. In his opinion for the Court, Justice Rufus Peckham affirmed that the Constitution protected "the right of the individual to his personal liberty, or to enter into those contracts in relation to labor which may seem to him appropriate or necessary for the support of himself and his family."[9] For this reason, ever since law school, Peckham's opinion in *Lochner* has been my favorite majority opinion in any Supreme Court case. (Justice Scalia's opinion in *District of Columbia v. Heller*[10] has recently become number two!)

Holmes's pithy dissent offered two influential arguments against recognizing a general constitutional right to liberty. First, he claimed that Supreme Court precedents were inconsistent with a general right to liberty. A citizen's liberty, he wrote, "is interfered with by school laws, by the Post Office, by every state or municipal institution which takes his money for purposes thought desirable, whether he likes it or not."[11] And any constitutional right to freedom of contract was belied by previous decisions upholding vaccination laws and maximum hours laws for miners, and prohibitions on "combinations" and the sale of stock on margins or for future delivery.

Second, apart from precedent, Holmes offered a claim about the Constitution's meaning. "[A] Constitution is not intended to embody a particular economic theory," he contended, "whether of paternalism and the organic relation of the citizen to the State or of *laissez faire.*"[12] Rather, in Holmes's view, the Constitution "is made for people of fundamentally differing views, and the accident of our

[7] *Id.* at 337.

[8] Lochner, 198 U.S. at 75 (Holmes, J., dissenting).

[9] *Id.* at 56 (Peckham, J.).

[10] 554 U.S., ____, 128 S.Ct. 2783 (2008).

[11] Lochner, 198 U.S. at 75 (Holmes, J., dissenting).

[12] *Id.*

finding certain opinions natural and familiar, or novel, and even shocking, ought not to conclude our judgment upon the question whether statutes embodying them conflict with the Constitution of the United States."[13]

Both of these objections to a constitutional right to liberty have become deeply embedded in constitutional discourse. For example, the first of Holmes's arguments was echoed by Ronald Dworkin in his book *Taking Rights Seriously*.[14] Dworkin denied there was a general right to liberty on the ground that no one has a "political right to drive up Lexington Avenue" (which is a one-way street running downtown, not uptown).[15] Holmes's second argument was echoed by John Rawls in *Political Liberalism*, when Rawls contended that, because of "the fact of reasonable pluralism,"[16] a constitution was best conceived as a second-order process for handling political disagreement in a pluralist society rather than dictating a first-order answer to political disagreements.

Yet neither objection is compelling. Holmes contended that previous decisions accepting restrictions on liberty refute the existence of a constitutional right to liberty, but this does not follow. For one thing, prior decisions may have been mistaken to uphold these restrictions on liberty. Even if correct, however, such decisions do not refute the existence of a right to liberty. Instead, they could simply be "exceptions." An exception presupposes the existence of a general rule (to which it is the exception).

Law professors have long derided what they call "slippery slope" arguments.[17] This is an objection to a particular law or ruling because it makes more likely an even more objectionable law or ruling in the future. Once you take a single step on a slippery slope, you are likely to slide all the way down. Restricting liberty in one case is likely to lead to other restrictions down the road. Law professors

---

[13] *Id.* at 76.

[14] See Ronald Dworkin, What Rights Do We Have?, in Taking Rights Seriously 266–272 (discussing why there is "no right to liberty").

[15] *Id.* at 269.

[16] John Rawls, Political Liberalism 36 (1996).

[17] See Eugene Volokh, The Mechanisms of the Slippery Slope, 116 Harv. L. Rev. 117 (2003) (examining the logic of and defending slippery slope arguments from critics).

respond that the law makes distinctions all the time and each decision should be made on its own merits. If you don't want to go farther
in a future situation, then that is the time to make one's objection.
The wide acceptance of Holmes's use of exceptions to deny the
existence of a rule, however, supports skepticism about the feasibility
of making exceptions in a common-law system in which any exception is thereafter transformed into a *precedent* for more of the same.
Assuming the Constitution really does protect a general right to
liberty, as the majority in *Lochner* appear to have believed, perhaps
it was a mistake to recognize any of the exceptions on which Holmes
rested his argument. On the other hand, how can the existence of
all these approved constraints on liberty be consistent with a general
right of liberty? Perhaps Holmes is correct that the existence of so-
called exceptions is evidence that the purported rule is unsound. At
a minimum, they would seem to be precedent for upholding further
restrictions on liberty.

Holmes's argument assumes that a constitutional right to liberty
must be absolute to be a right. If, however, a right to liberty is
viewed as presumptive rather than absolute, then the existence of
"exceptions" is not a bug, it is a feature. Take, for example, the
freedom of speech. In practice, this right is presumptive rather than
absolute. No one thinks that the constitutionality of "time, place,
and manner" regulations of speech refutes the existence of the right.
Holmes himself repeatedly asserted a general right to freedom of
speech, notwithstanding his opinion that no one has a right to falsely
shout fire in a crowded theater.[18] That freedom of speech is a constitutional right places the burden on the government to justify its restriction as necessary and proper. It may not burden speech merely
because it thinks it is a nifty idea. A court must pass upon its
necessity.

Likewise, if a general right to liberty is conceived as a "presumption of liberty,"[19] this does not automatically render all restrictions
on actions unconstitutional. It merely means that, as with speech,
any restriction on other types of conduct must be justified. The type

[18] See Schenck v. United States, 249 U.S. 47, 52 (1919) (Holmes, J.) ("The most
stringent protection of free speech would not protect a man falsely shouting fire in
a theater and causing a panic.").

[19] See generally Randy E. Barnett, Restoring the Lost Constitution: The Presumption
of Liberty (2004).

of justification will vary depending on whether a law is a prohibition of wrongful conduct or a regulation of rightful conduct.

Prohibiting wrongful conduct is perfectly consistent with a right to liberty. By "wrongful," I mean conduct that violates the rights of others.[20] As Spencer's law of equal freedom maintains, no one has the rightful liberty to violate the equal rights of others. The prohibition of wrongful acts constitutes a protection of the rightful liberty of others, rather than an infringement on the liberty of the wrongdoer. One has no right to do wrong to another.

Nor are all legal regulations of rightful conduct inconsistent with a general right to liberty. A "regulation" is a law that specifies *how* a liberty may be exercised. It takes the form, "If you want to do X— make a contract, carry a gun, drive a car—then here is how you do it." Legal regulations are consistent with liberty because the fundamental rights that define liberty are too abstract to be applied directly to all but the simplest of cases. For example, what constitutes a sufficient provocation to justify self-defense? What constitutes consent to a contract? How do we measure damages for breaches of contracts or torts? Rules of law are needed to answer these and countless other such questions. As Locke observed, in the state of nature: "There wants an established, settled, known law, received and allowed by common consent to be the standard of right and wrong, and the common measure to decide all controversies between them. . . ."[21]

Whether a particular regulation is consistent with liberty depends on the justification offered on its behalf. Regulations are not inimical to liberty if they coordinate individual conduct as do, for example, traffic regulations mandating driving on one side of the street or the other. They may also be consistent with liberty if they prevent irreparable tortious accidents before they occur, as speed limits do. True, you could sue someone for negligently driving too fast after he crashes into you, but given the bodily harm caused by an accident, it might be better to reduce incidents of negligence by specifying in advance how fast one should drive on a particular stretch of road.

---

[20] As I am using the term, "wrongful" or *unjust* conduct that violates the rights of others is a subset of "bad" or *immoral* conduct that may or may not be rights violating.

[21] John Locke, Second Treatise of Government, ch. IX, § 124.

Although many libertarians object to government ownership of highways, no libertarian objects in principle to a highway owner regulating its use to enhance the speed and safety of driving. Similarly, contract law is a body of rules regulating the making and enforcing of agreements, and libertarians are not opposed to contract law.

For libertarians, the issue is often not whether conduct should be regulated but who should regulate, the government or property owners? Property owners typically have greater incentives for more efficient regulations than government. And, even where this is not the case, the fact that governments typically exert ownership powers over all the streets, sidewalks, and parks in a given territory makes their regulatory powers far more susceptible to abuse.

A law restricting conduct is consistent with a right to liberty, therefore, if it is *prohibiting wrongful* acts that violate the rights of others or *regulating rightful* acts in such a way as to coordinate conduct or prevent the violation of rights that might accidentally occur. A law is inconsistent with liberty if it is either prohibiting rightful acts, or regulating unnecessarily or improperly. A regulation is improper when it imposes an undue burden on rightful conduct, or when its justification is merely a pretext for restricting a liberty of which others disapprove. And one way of identifying a regulation as pretextual is to assess whether the regulatory means it employs do not effectively fit its purported health and safety ends.

Here is how the majority in *Lochner* distinguished a constitutional exercise of the police power from an unconstitutional restraint on liberty:

> In every case that comes before this court, therefore, where legislation of this character is concerned, and where the protection of the Federal Constitution is sought, the question necessarily arises: Is this a fair, reasonable and appropriate exercise of the police power of the state, or is it an unreasonable, unnecessary and arbitrary interference with the right of the individual to his personal liberty, or to enter into those contracts in relation to labor which may seem to him appropriate or necessary for the support of himself and his family?[22]

---

[22] 198 U.S. at 56 (Peckham, J.).

We may conclude from all this that, if a general right to liberty is presumptive, not absolute, and if the presumption may be rebutted by a showing that a law is prohibiting wrongful or properly regulating rightful acts, then the fact that regulations of liberty have been upheld as constitutional is no evidence that the general constitutional right to liberty does not exist. It may merely be a sign that the government has met its properly defined burden of proof.

But does the Constitution protect a general right to liberty of this type? This brings us to the second of Holmes's objections: that the Constitution does not "embody a particular economic theory, whether of paternalism and the organic relation of the citizen to the State or of *laissez faire*,"[23] or the modern version of this argument that the Constitution establishes second-order decision mechanisms by which first-order political disagreements are hashed out. In *Lochner*, who was right about the Constitution, the majority or Holmes? The answer depends on what the Constitution means, and to figure this out requires a method of constitutional interpretation.

Originalism and Liberty

As a political philosophy, libertarianism does not specify how the Constitution should be interpreted. Should a libertarian simply favor any interpretation of the text that enhances liberty? I think not. The Constitution is the law that governs those who govern us. That those who govern may be restrained in the exercise of their power, it was put in writing. As John Marshall explained in *Marbury v. Madison*, "the powers of the legislature are defined and limited; and that those limits may not be mistaken, or forgotten, the constitution is written."[24] A written constitution performs this restraining function because it has a semantic meaning that is independent of the desires of those who are called to interpret it.

This implication of a written constitution was clearly identified by Lysander Spooner, one of America's earliest constitutional theorists. In his 1847 book, *The Unconstitutionality of Slavery*, Spooner observed:

> [T]he constitution, *of itself, independently of the actual intentions of the people,* expresses some certain fixed, definite, and legal

---

[23] *Id.* at 75 (Holmes, J. dissenting).

[24] Marbury v. Madison, 5 U.S. 137, 176 (1803) (Marshall, C.J.)

intentions; else the people themselves would express no intentions by agreeing to it. The instrument would, in fact, contain nothing that the people *could* agree to. Agreeing to an instrument that had no meaning *of its own*, would only be agreeing to nothing.[25]

In other words, the meaning of a written constitution is the semantic meaning of its words in context.[26] We adopt a written constitution because it has a semantic meaning that defines the limits of the powers of those who govern, and thereby helps keep these powers within proper bounds. And we adhere to the semantic meaning at the time of enactment because a written constitution would fail to perform its purpose if legislatures, executives, or courts could, whether alone or in combination, alter the meaning of these constraints on their powers.[27] The name we use today to describe this approach to constitutional interpretation is "original public meaning originalism," or "originalism" for short. An originalist is simply a person who believes that the semantic meaning of the Constitution must be followed until it is properly changed.

But there is a limit to the guidance provided by the original public meaning of the Constitution. Often the text is specific enough to be applied directly to most controversies it was meant to govern. For example, each state is to have two senators, and the president is to be 35 years of age. These are the provisions of the Constitution that are not usually disputed or litigated. But other provisions of the text are more general or vague.

The Eighth Amendment bans "cruel and unusual" punishments, not specific types of punishment; it also bans "excessive" bail and fines, not a specific sum of money. The Fourth Amendment bans "unreasonable" searches and seizures, and the Fifth and Fourteenth Amendments require the "due" process of law. Even seemingly more specific provisions, such as the prohibition on laws "abridging

---

[25] Lysander Spooner, The Unconstitutionality of Slavery 222 (rev. ed. 1860) (emphasis added). Part I of this work was published 1845. The quoted passage comes from Part II, which first appeared in 1847.

[26] See Lawrence B. Solum, Semantic Originalism, (July 2, 2008), Illinois Public Law Research Paper No. 07-24. Available at SSRN: http://ssrn.com/abstract=1120244.

[27] See Barnett, *supra* note 19, at 89–117.

the freedom of speech" require further specification of what constitutes "speech" given changing technology and what constitutes an "abridgment."

That the original meaning of provisions like these are vague does not mean that they provide no guidance at all. For one thing there are core or paradigm cases to which they clearly apply, and peripheral cases to which they clearly do not. A text is vague when it is unclear whether a borderline case is included or excluded by its meaning. In this situation, the original meaning of the text must be supplemented. Constitutional interpretation is the activity of identifying the original meaning of the text; constitutional construction is the activity of supplementation when the meaning is too vague to settle a dispute.[28]

This does not entail that constitutional construction is an entirely open-ended affair. A construction of the text that violated the original public meaning would be improper. You can think of constitutional interpretation as providing a frame within which choices must be made; but any choices that are outside the frame are unconstitutional.

Let me illustrate this by the Second Amendment, the original public meaning of which the Court in *Heller* correctly found to protect an individual right. Given that the D.C. statute prohibited the exercise of this right, it was a paradigm case of a statute that "infringed" the Second Amendment "right of the people to keep and bear Arms." But what about laws that regulate rather than prohibit the exercise of this right? Suppose a law allows the concealed carrying of a firearm, but only by those adults who take an approved firearms safety course: Is this regulation reasonable? Because whatever answer to this question is given will not be deduced directly from the original meaning of the Second Amendment, a construction of the Constitution in addition to an interpretation is required.

How constitutional construction should be done is a bigger issue than I can address here, so let me simply summarize the conclusion I defend in *Restoring the Lost Constitution*: constitutional construction

---

[28] See Barnett, *supra* note 19, at 118–130. Constitutional construction is also needed when the original meaning of the text is irreducibly ambiguous in the sense that its words in context have multiple meanings and evidence is insufficient to establish a unique original semantic meaning. See Solum, *supra* note 26; Randy E. Barnett, The Misconceived Assumption About Constitutional Assumptions, 103 Nw. U.L. Rev. 615 (2009).

should be done in such a manner as to enhance the legitimacy of the Constitution.[29] By "legitimacy" I mean whatever quality makes the Constitution binding.

How people construe vagueness in the text will often depend on what they believe makes the Constitution legitimate. Some believe that the legitimacy of the Constitution rests on the original consent of the people. Others think its legitimacy rests on the consent of the people today.

I agree with Lysander Spooner that both original and contemporary consent is a fiction.[30] Laws enacted pursuant to the Constitution are imposed on those who do not consent to it, every bit as much as they are applied to those who do. If so, a constitution is legitimate, only if it provides adequate assurances that the laws it imposes on nonconsenting persons do not violate their rights and are necessary to protect the rights of others. When the text is too vague to resolve a dispute, the text should be construed to ensure that the rights retained by the people are not being denied or disparaged.

What the Constitution Says

With this analysis in mind, we are now in a position to refine the question, "Is the Constitution Libertarian?" to this: "Does the original meaning of the Constitution, as amended, respect and protect the fundamental individual rights that define the core of both classical liberalism and modern libertarianism?" To assess this, we must now briefly examine the original meaning of what the Constitution says and how it may fairly be construed.

Except for the prohibition of involuntary servitude in the Thirteenth Amendment, the Constitution does not apply directly to the people. Instead it creates a process by which laws are made, applied, and enforced. So when asking whether the Constitution is "libertarian," we are really asking whether the laws that are applied to and enforced against particular persons pursuant to the Constitution respect their fundamental rights.

The Original Constitution. The original Constitution protected the rights to life, liberty, and property against infringement by the federal government in two ways. First and foremost, Congress was not

---

[29] See Barnett, *supra* note 19, at 32–52, 125–28.

[30] See *id.* at 11–31; Lysander Spooner, No Treason VI: The Constitution of No Authority (1870).

given a general legislative power but only those legislative powers "herein granted,"[31] referring to those powers enumerated in Article I, section 8. It is striking how these powers avoid expressly restricting the rightful exercise of liberty. The power "to raise and support Armies"[32] does not include an express power of conscription, which would interfere with the property one has in one's own person. The power to establish the post office does not expressly claim a power to make the government post office a monopoly,[33] which would interfere with the freedom of contract of those who wish to contract with a private mail company of the sort founded by Lysander Spooner. (By contrast, the Articles of Confederation *did* accord the power in Congress to establish a postal monopoly.[34])

There are only three powers that might be construed as restricting the rightful exercise of liberty. First is the Necessary and Proper Clause granting Congress the power "to make all laws which shall be necessary and proper for carrying into Execution"[35] its other powers. Even here, a law must not only be necessary, it must also be *proper*, which suggests that a law that violates the rights retained by the people might well be improper.

Second, is the power of Congress "to promote the Progress of Science and useful Arts, by securing for limited Times to Authors and Inventors the exclusive Right to their respective Writings and Discoveries."[36] Libertarians are divided about whether granting patents or copyrights to some violates the rights of others. But even this provision does not mandate the creation of a patent or copyright system; it merely allows Congress to do so if it chooses.

---

[31] U.S. Const. art. I, § 1 ("All legislative Powers herein granted shall be vested in a Congress of the United States").

[32] U.S. Const. art. I, § 8.

[33] U.S. Const. art. I, § 8 ("The Congress shall have power . . . To establish Post Offices and post Roads").

[34] See Art. of Confederation art. IX ("The United States in Congress assembled shall also have the sole and exclusive right and power of . . . establishing or regulating post offices from one State to another, throughout all the United States, and exacting such postage on the papers passing through the same as may be requisite to defray the expenses of the said office. . . .").

[35] U.S. Const. art. I, § 8.

[36] *Id.*

Finally, I leave aside the question of whether the power "To lay and collect Taxes, Duties, Imposts and Excises"[37] is a violation of fundamental rights. This is a more complex issue than I can tackle here. Whether or not a general tax violates the fundamental right to property, however, it does not restrict liberty in the same way that a prohibition or regulation does. Compare the impact of conscription on a person's liberty as compared with imposing a tax to pay others to enlist in the military.

Of course, the Supreme Court has upheld countless federal laws restricting liberty, primarily under the power of Congress "To regulate Commerce . . . among the several States"[38] combined with an open-ended reading of the Necessary and Proper Clause. Further it has upheld the power of Congress to spend tax revenue for purposes other than "for carrying into execution" its enumerated powers, thereby exceeding the scope of the Necessary and Proper Clause. This shows only that, with respect to federal power, the text of the original Constitution is far more libertarian than the redacted constitution enforced by the Supreme Court.

But the original Constitution is not all we have.

The Amendments to the Constitution. Two years after its enactment, the Constitution was amended by the Bill of Rights. These 10 amendments included several express guarantees of such liberties as the freedom of speech, press, assembly, and the right to keep and bear arms. The Bill of Rights barred takings for public use without just compensation. It also provided additional procedural assurances that the laws would be applied accurately and fairly to particular individuals.

All of the rights enumerated in the Bill of Rights are consistent with modern libertarian political philosophy. And to this list of rights was added the Ninth Amendment that said, "The enumeration in the Constitution of certain rights shall not be construed to deny or disparage others retained by the people." In this way, even liberty rights that were not listed were given express constitutional protection.[39] Finally, the Tenth Amendment reaffirmed that Congress could

---

[37] *Id.*

[38] *Id.*

[39] See Randy E. Barnett, The Ninth Amendment: It Means What It Says, 85 Tex. L. Rev. 1 (2006).

exercise only those powers to which it was delegated "by this Constitution."

Despite the efforts of James Madison, the first 10 amendments restricted only federal power—or so the Supreme Court held in *Barron v. Baltimore*.[40] States retained their virtually unlimited powers to restrict the liberties of their residents, subject only to their own constitutions as interpreted by their own courts. And the Eleventh Amendment further expanded state powers by rendering them immune from suits in federal court by citizens of other states.

Article I, section 9 of the original Constitution placed some restrictions on the power of state governments, but these constraints were few. So great were their reserved powers that states could sanction the enslavement of some persons within their jurisdiction. And, unless one accepts the interpretive claims of such abolitionists as Lysander Spooner, William Goodell, Gerrit Smith, Joel Tiffany, and Frederick Douglass, the original Constitution also protected slavery by mandating the return of runaway slaves who managed to escape to free states. Because it allowed states to violate the rights of their citizens with near impunity, the original Constitution was deeply flawed from a libertarian perspective. Fortunately, it has been amended in ways that made it more libertarian.

While the Thirteenth Amendment's ban on involuntary servitude expanded the Constitution's protection of individual liberty against abuses by states, it was the Fourteenth Amendment that radically altered the federalism of the original Constitution. After the Fourteenth Amendment, Congress and the courts could invalidate state laws that "abridge[d] the privileges or immunities of citizens of the United States." The original meaning of "privileges or immunities" included the same natural rights retained by the people to which the Ninth Amendment referred, but also the additional enumerated rights contained in the Bill of Rights.[41] The Fourteenth Amendment's Due Process Clause required that any deprivation of the fundamental rights to life, liberty, or property be authorized by a valid state "law" and placed a federal check on the procedures by which such laws are applied to particular persons. The Equal Protection Clause

---

[40] See Barron v. Mayor of Baltimore, 32 U.S. (7 Pet.) 243 (1833).
[41] See Barnett, *supra* note 19, at 60–68.

imposed a duty on state executive branches to provide the protection of the law to all persons without discrimination.

Although some libertarians are uncomfortable with what they view as a weakening of states' rights, the Fourteenth Amendment only expanded the power of the Congress and courts to protect against state infringements of individual rights. Libertarians might well favor some mechanism by which state courts could protect individual rights from federal infringements. Still, the federal government's power to combat what constitutional lawyer and Institute for Justice co-founder Clint Bolick has called "grassroots tyranny"[42] represented a significant enhancement of the protection of individual liberty afforded by the Constitution. When the Privileges or Immunities Clause of the Fourteenth Amendment is combined with the Ninth, the unenumerated rights retained by the people are expressly protected against infringement by both federal and state governments.

But constitutional construction is required to put these protections of liberty into effect. Beginning in the 1930s,[43] the Supreme Court reversed its approach in *Lochner* and adopted a presumption of constitutionality whenever a statute restricted unenumerated liberty rights. In the 1950s, it made this presumption effectively irrebuttable.[44] Now it will protect only those liberties that are listed, or a very few unenumerated rights such as the right of privacy. But such an approach violates the Ninth Amendment's injunction against using the fact that some rights are enumerated to deny or disparage others because they are not.[45] Like the presumption of constitutionality, a presumption of liberty that places the burden on the government to show that its restriction on any liberty is both necessary and proper is also a constitutional construction. Neither is mentioned in the text, but a presumption of liberty is far more compatible with

---

[42] See Clint Bolick, Grassroots Tyranny: The Limits of Federalism (1993).

[43] See O'Gorman & Young, Inc. v. Hartford Fire Ins. Co., 282 U.S. 251, 257–58 (1931) (Cardozo, J.) ("the presumption of constitutionality must prevail in the absence of some factual foundation of record for overthrowing the statute.").

[44] See Williamson v. Lee Optical of Oklahoma, 348 U.S. 483 (1955) (Douglas, J.) ("the law need not be in every respect logically consistent with its aims to be constitutional. It is enough that there is an evil at hand for correction, and that it *might be thought* that the particular legislative measure was a rational way to correct it." [emphasis added]).

[45] See Randy E. Barnett, Scrutiny Land, 106 Mich. L. Rev. 1479, 1495–1500 (2008).

the original meaning of what the Constitution says in the Ninth and Fourteenth Amendments.

Of course, the protection of liberty afforded by the Constitution is not limited to the protection of liberty rights by courts. It includes as well the "checks and balances" provided by the separation of powers at the federal level and the division of powers between the national and state governments. In addition, the Constitution contains popular checks on legislative and executive power. These include the power of the electorate to remove legislators and presidents from office during regular elections and, eventually, term limits for the president. The constitutional guarantee of a jury trial originally included not only the power of citizen juries to pass upon both the facts of case to acquit the innocent, but also the power to refuse to convict persons charged with violating unjust laws.[46]

It is worth noting that none of these structural and procedural protections is dictated by libertarian political philosophy. Instead, all are to be assessed pragmatically by whether, on balance, they serve to protect fundamental rights. With the weakening or loss of other liberty-protecting clauses of the Constitution, these structural constraints are responsible for preserving the liberty Americans still enjoy.

The Foreign Policy Powers

To this point, I have confined my analysis to the domestic powers of the federal and state governments that restrict the liberties of the people. I have not mentioned, much less analyzed, the foreign policy powers created by the Constitution. In this final section, I want to explain why libertarianism tells us very little about either the conduct of foreign policy or how the foreign policy powers of the national government should be allocated among the different branches. Not coincidentally, perhaps, neither does the original meaning of the Constitution.

Modern libertarianism is based on the recognition and protection of the five fundamental human rights of private property, freedom of contract, first possession, defense of self and others, and restitution. My thesis is that (1) a constitution is libertarian to the extent it creates a political order that respects and protects these rights,

---

[46] See Clay S. Conrad, Jury Nullification: The Evolution of a Doctrine (1998).

and (2) the original meaning of the amended Constitution is far more libertarian than the redacted version applied by the Supreme Court today. In this sense, the Constitution should be considered libertarian, at least relative to the status quo.

In the realm of foreign policy, however, the libertarian commitment to these individual fundamental rights complicates matters in ways that many libertarians do not appreciate. Some libertarians try to apply the same principles of self-defense and aggression to states that they apply to individuals. But doing so is a category mistake that results, ironically, in the reification of nation states in a way that should make libertarians uncomfortable. In the realm of foreign policy, libertarians need to think more carefully about the concept of sovereignty.

To reduce the likelihood of religious wars, the Peace of Westphalia in the seventeenth century gave every monarch a "sovereign" control over the lives and property of all within its territory. Every monarch could establish the religion of his realm to which all must adhere and no monarch was to interfere with the internal affairs of any other sovereign, for example, to aid persons being persecuted for their religious beliefs. In effect, each sovereign monarch became the recognized legal "owner" of his territory and the people residing thereon, and each sovereign was obliged to respect the ownership rights of the other sovereign monarchs.

Whatever the practical advantages of this system of nation-state sovereignties, the founding of the American republic greatly complicated the theory on which it rested. Lacking a monarch or aristocracy, Americans were skeptical of the very notion of sovereignty. Consider the 1793 case of *Chisholm v. Georgia*,[47] the Supreme Court's first great constitutional case.[48] In *Chisholm*, the Court rejected the state of Georgia's claim of sovereign immunity against a suit for breach of contract, which had been brought against it in federal court by a citizen of South Carolina. Justice James Wilson began his opinion by observing: "'To the Constitution of the United States the term

[47] 2 U.S. (2 Dall.) 419 (1793).

[48] For a more detailed discussion of the concept of individual sovereignty articulated in Chisholm, see Randy E. Barnett, The People or the State? Chisholm v. Georgia and Popular Sovereignty, 93 U. Va. L. Rev. 1729 (2007); and Randy E. Barnett, Kurt Lash's Majoritarian Difficulty, 60 Stan. L. Rev. 937, 954–960 (2008).

SOVEREIGN, is totally unknown."[49] For Wilson, "[t]here is but one place where it could have been used with propriety. . . . They might have announced themselves 'SOVEREIGN,' people of the United States: But serenely conscious of the fact, they avoided the ostentatious declaration."[50]

It is worth noting that, as a delegate to the Constitutional Convention from Pennsylvania, Wilson—perhaps our most neglected Founder—was a member of the Committee of Detail that produced the first draft of the actual wording of the Constitution.[51] He was also the first professor of law at the University of Pennsylvania. In his lengthy opinion in Chisholm, Wilson rejected both the feudal notion of monarchical sovereignty and the Blackstonian notion of parliamentary sovereignty in favor of the concept of individual sovereignty.

According to Wilson, governments were not sovereigns themselves, but aggregates of individual sovereigns. "The only reason, I believe, why a free man is bound by human laws, is, that he binds himself. Upon the same principles, upon which he becomes bound by the laws, he becomes amenable to the Courts of Justice, which are formed and authorised by those laws."[52] Wilson then identifies what can only be called an individualist notion of popular sovereignty: "If one free man, an original sovereign, may do all this; why may not an aggregate of free men, a collection of original sovereigns, do this likewise? If the dignity of each singly is undiminished; the dignity of all jointly must be unimpaired."[53] Likewise, in his own Chisholm opinion, Chief Justice John Jay referred to "fellow citizens and joint sovereigns."[54]

---

49 2 U.S. (2 Dall.) at 454 (Wilson, J.).

50 Id.

51 See James Wilson (1742–1798), in Joseph C. Morton, Shapers of the Great Debate at the Constitutional Convention of 1787, at 301, 304–07, 307 n.1 (2006) (describing Wilson's contributions to and influence at the Constitutional Convention); Julian P. Boyd, James Wilson, in Dictionary of American Biography 326, 329 (Dumas Malone ed., 1936) (describing Wilson's contributions to and influence at the Pennsylvania ratification convention).

52 2 U.S. (2 Dall.) at 456 (Wilson, J.).

53 Id. (emphases added).

54 Id. at 479 (Jay, C.J.).

James Wilson was a forceful proponent of natural rights[55] and the notion of individual sovereignty he articulated in *Chisholm* is indistinguishable from the libertarian view that each person is sovereign with respect to what is properly hers as defined by the five fundamental rights. Like a monarch within her realm, she may do or refrain from doing anything with what she rightfully possesses. Any forcible interference with this individual sovereignty constitutes an aggression that may be resisted by force, if necessary, in self-defense. Furthermore, others may justly come to the assistance of a person whose rights are being violated.

Indeed, the close relationship between natural rights and individual sovereignty is reflected in the pairing of the Ninth Amendment's protection of the natural "rights . . . retained by the people" with the Tenth Amendment's reservation "to the states respectively, or to the people," of any powers that were not delegated to the federal government.

While *Chisholm* concerned the assertion of state sovereign immunity within a federal system, the libertarian concept of individual sovereignty also complicates and qualifies the Westphalian notion of unfettered state sovereignty in international relations. If the people are the true joint sovereigns, then no ruler may justly deprive them of their inalienable fundamental rights. Since the horrors of the Holocaust, the Westphalian concept of sovereignty has been qualified in international law by the recognition of "human rights" that no state may violate—though it is far from clear when one state, or group of states, may intervene to protect these rights.

Individual-empowering technology has also undermined the neat Westphalian picture of sovereign nation states with the power to control what takes place within their borders. Transnational globalization is a liberating upside of empowered individuals; the newfound power of nongovernmental terrorist organizations to wage wars against the populations of nation states is a most unfortunate downside.

This erosion of the Westphalian nation state system requires new and more careful theoretical analysis by libertarians. The first

---

[55] See James Wilson, Of the Natural Rights of Individuals, in 2 The Collected Works of James Wilson 1051–1083 (Kermit L. Hall & Mark David Hall, eds. 2007) (part of Wilson's lectures on law originally delivered at the University of Pennsylvania in 1790–91).

instincts of collectivists have been to create and empower international organizations that resemble governments writ large. For them, the New World Order requires one world government. Libertarians know this is a bad idea, but they have yet to develop their own coherent approach to the protection of individual rights from abuses by nation states.

Libertarians need to look beyond the Westphalian system of sovereignty, and explore how existing governments and their militaries might evolve within a polycentric regime of competitive private ordering that arises spontaneously across national boundaries. In both the domestic and international spheres, the respect for and protection of individual sovereignty defined by the fundamental rights of all persons provides the ends against which the performance of government can be assessed.

The foreign policy of noninterventionism to which the Cato Institute is committed is, by and large, the most workable approach to the preservation of the liberties enjoyed by Americans and the avoidance of the unanticipated consequences of initiating or provoking foreign wars. But a policy of nonintervention should not be equated with the fundamental human rights that define modern libertarianism. It is a policy that must be evaluated pragmatically, and one in which exceptions are sometimes warranted, for example when the protection of the rights of Americans is best served by protecting the individual sovereignty of foreigners.

By no means am I proposing that any single nation state, such as the United States, should take it upon itself to go to the rescue of all those whose fundamental rights are being systematically violated by their own governments. I am merely noting that a nation state is not violating libertarian fundamental rights when, for reasons of its own national interest, it protects those whose individual sovereignty is being systematically violated by a government that claims jurisdiction over them. When the French government provided military assistance to the American revolutionaries, for example, it did so after the Declaration of Independence specified how the British government had systematically violated the rights of Americans. That the French government interfered with British "sovereignty" does not, by itself, entail any transgression of libertarian fundamental rights and individual sovereignty.

In foreign policy matters, the text of the Constitution provides much less guidance than it does with respect to domestic powers.

While the proper scope of the domestic powers of the federal government is limited, the scope of its foreign policy powers is not. While its allocation of domestic powers among the three branches of government is specified to some degree, its allocation of foreign policy powers is far more open-ended.

For example, the Constitution says Congress has the power "to declare War,"[56] but the original meaning of this term had a technical sense of altering the legal relationship of two nations under international law from a state of peace to a state of war. It did not purport to govern the use of the armed forces of the United States in response to a "state of war" initiated by the aggression of a foreign power against Americans, whether at home or abroad. One can declare war without firing a shot, but when shots are fired a state of war may nevertheless exist even without a declaration.

The Constitution says that the president is "Commander in Chief"[57] of the armed forces, but does not specify the degree to which his powers can be constrained by statutes enacted by Congress, which the Constitution says the president has a duty to "take Care"[58] are faithfully executed. The Constitution gives Congress the enumerated power to "make Rules for the Government and Regulation of the land and naval Forces"[59] but is unclear as to whether these regulations apply to the president himself, or to the minute details of a military campaign. The Constitution also empowers Congress "To regulate Commerce with foreign nations"[60] and provides procedures to govern the making of treaties. And only Congress has the power to commit funds "to raise and support Armies."[61]

In short, the text of the Constitution provides little guidance on the proper separation of powers with respect to the conduct of foreign policy and no guidance whatsoever on the substance of foreign policy. As wrong as Holmes was to claim a lack of constitutional constraints on the domestic powers of government, his description might well be accurate with respect to the realm of

---

[56] U.S. Const. art. I, § 8.
[57] U.S. Const. art II, § 2.
[58] U.S. Const. art II, § 3.
[59] U.S. Const. art. I, § 8.
[60] *Id.*
[61] *Id.*

foreign policy. For better or worse, the Constitution may well be "made for people of fundamentally differing views"[62] about foreign policy, whether these views be interventionist or noninterventionist. While the domestic powers of the federal government are constitutionally limited, its foreign policy powers are, for all intents and purposes, limited only by political mechanisms.

Conclusion

So is the Constitution libertarian? Even with all the caveats and qualifications, the answer is clear. As written, the original Constitution of the United States, together with its amendments, may be the most explicitly libertarian governing document ever actually enacted into law. The Supreme Court says that only the liberties that are listed in the Bill of Rights, plus a right of privacy, merit judicial protection.[63] But the Constitution says that the enumeration in the Constitution of certain rights shall not be construed to deny or disparate others retained by the people. The Supreme Court says that the states must respect a mere handful of liberties. But the Constitution says that no state shall make or enforce any law which shall abridge the privileges or immunities of citizens of the United States.

Why then have these and other libertarian protections been excised from constitutional law and lost from our conception of the Constitution? Tempting as it is to blame the Court, the Founders understood how unrealistic it is to expect judges to withstand majoritarian pressures for very long. After all, justices are typically chosen by presidents from among those who share the zeitgeist of their day. The Constitution has been redacted precisely because its across-the-board protection of liberty stood in the way of the politically popular growth of government that culminated in the New Deal and the Great Society. Once grown, these powers are very difficult to pare back even when they become less popular.

The lost provisions that make the Constitution libertarian will be restored only when the constitutional imperatives of individual liberty are as well understood today as they were by those who wrote the Constitution, the Bill of Rights, and the Thirteenth and

---

[62] Lochner, 198 U.S. at 76 (Holmes, J., dissenting).

[63] See Barnett, *supra* note 45.

Fourteenth Amendments. All who read these words have a role to play in bettering their own understanding of individual liberty so they may explain the blessings of liberty to others. These lost parts of the Constitution will not be restored by erudite legal arguments or clever litigation strategies until the public's demand for individual liberty and limited government produces a president who will appoint faithful originalist justices who believe in the power of courts to nullify unconstitutional laws and senators who will confirm them. And when that day arrives, the libertarian Constitution will be waiting.

The Future of the Voting Rights Act after *Bartlett* and *NAMUDNO*

Roger Clegg*

According to my handy pocket copy of the U.S. Constitution (Cato edition), Section 1 of the Fifteenth Amendment provides: "The right of citizens of the United States to vote shall not be denied or abridged by the United States or by any State on account of race, color, or previous condition of servitude." Section 2 provides: "The Congress shall have power to enforce this article by appropriate legislation."[1]

It's hard to fault either provision. Of course nobody should be kept from voting because he or she is the wrong color; and, given the historical context, it makes perfect sense to give the national legislature the authority to pass statutes that make the guarantee a reality.

The trouble is that the principal statutes that Congress has passed in the name of the Fifteenth Amendment go far beyond enforcing this guarantee. Worse, in many respects the statutes passed are used to encourage racial segregation of voting districts through racial gerrymandering—a result quite at odds with the underlying constitutional guarantee.

In its 2008–2009 term, the Supreme Court handed down decisions in two cases that involved the Voting Rights Act. One, *Bartlett v. Strickland*,[2] involved Section 2 of the Act; the other, *Northwest Austin Municipal Utility District Number One v. Holder*, involved Section 5.[3]

---

* President and General Counsel of the Center for Equal Opportunity, which joined amicus briefs in the two cases discussed in this article.

[1] Useful histories of the passage of the Fifteenth Amendment can be found in Alexander Keyssar, The Right to Vote 93–104 (2000), and The Heritage Guide to the Constitution 409–11 (Edwin Meese III et al. eds., 2005). Neither suggests, however, that the amendment means or was intended to mean anything more or less than what its text actually says.

[2] Bartlett v. Strickland, 129 S. Ct. 1231, 556 U.S. _____ (2009).

[3] Nw. Austin Mun. Util. Dist. No. One v. Holder, 129 S. Ct. 2504, 557 U.S. _____ (2009).

The focus of this article will be on those two decisions; its theme is the abyss between those two sections of the Voting Rights Act and the important but precise guarantee of the Fifteenth Amendment.

I. The Problem with the Voting Rights Act

A. The Devolution of Sections 2 and 5 of the Voting Rights Act

One's suspicion that there is an abyss between the statutory provisions and the constitutional language is aroused by the disconnect between the prolixity of the Voting Rights Act and the short and simple guarantee of the Fifteenth Amendment.

Section 2 of the VRA, which deals with the "[d]enial or abridgement of right to vote on account of race or color through voting qualifications or prerequisites; establishment of violation," contains over 200 words.[4] Section 5, which covers the "[a]lteration of voting qualifications; procedure and appeal; purpose or effect of diminishing the ability of citizens to elect their preferred candidates," contains over 650 words.[5]

---

[4] 42 U.S.C. 1973 (2006). Section 2 provides:

(a) No voting qualification or prerequisite to voting or standard, practice, or procedure shall be imposed or applied by any State or political subdivision in a manner which results in a denial or abridgement of the right of any citizen of the United States to vote on account of race or color, or in contravention of the guarantees set forth in section 1973b(f)(2) of this title, as provided in subsection (b) of this section.

(b) A violation of subsection (a) of this section is established if, based on the totality of circumstances, it is shown that the political processes leading to nomination or election in the State or political subdivision are not equally open to participation by members of a class of citizens protected by subsection (a) of this section in that its members have less opportunity than other members of the electorate to participate in the political process and to elect representatives of their choice. The extent to which members of a protected class have been elected to office in the State or political subdivision is one circumstance which may be considered: Provided, That nothing in this section establishes a right to have members of a protected class elected in numbers equal to their proportion in the population.

[5] 42 U.S.C. 1973c (2006). Section 5 provides:

(a) Whenever a State or political subdivision with respect to which the prohibitions set forth in section 1973b(a) of this title based upon determinations made under the first sentence of section 1973b(b) of this title are in effect shall enact or seek to administer any voting qualification or prerequisite to voting, or standard, practice, or procedure with respect to voting different from that in force or effect on November 1, 1964, or whenever a State or political subdivision with respect to which the prohibitions set forth in section 1973b(a) of this title based upon determinations made under the second sentence of section

Now, what is going on here? One could understand how a constitutional provision "[t]o provide and maintain a Navy"[6] might necessitate

1973b(b) of this title are in effect shall enact or seek to administer any voting qualification or prerequisite to voting, or standard, practice, or procedure with respect to voting different from that in force or effect on November 1, 1968, or whenever a State or political subdivision with respect to which the prohibitions set forth in section 1973b(a) of this title based upon determinations made under the third sentence of section 1973b(b) of this title are in effect shall enact or seek to administer any voting qualification or prerequisite to voting, or standard, practice, or procedure with respect to voting different from that in force or effect on November 1, 1972, such State or subdivision may institute an action in the United States District Court for the District of Columbia for a declaratory judgment that such qualification, prerequisite, standard, practice, or procedure neither has the purpose nor will have the effect of denying or abridging the right to vote on account of race or color, or in contravention of the guarantees set forth in section 1973b(f)(2) of this title, and unless and until the court enters such judgment no person shall be denied the right to vote for failure to comply with such qualification, prerequisite, standard, practice, or procedure: Provided, That such qualification, prerequisite, standard, practice, or procedure may be enforced without such proceeding if the qualification, prerequisite, standard, practice, or procedure has been submitted by the chief legal officer or other appropriate official of such State or subdivision to the Attorney General and the Attorney General has not interposed an objection within sixty days after such submission, or upon good cause shown, to facilitate an expedited approval within sixty days after such submission, the Attorney General has affirmatively indicated that such objection will not be made. Neither an affirmative indication by the Attorney General that no objection will be made, nor the Attorney General's failure to object, nor a declaratory judgment entered under this section shall bar a subsequent action to enjoin enforcement of such qualification, prerequisite, standard, practice, or procedure. In the event the Attorney General affirmatively indicates that no objection will be made within the sixty-day period following receipt of a submission, the Attorney General may reserve the right to reexamine the submission if additional information comes to his attention during the remainder of the sixty-day period which would otherwise require objection in accordance with this section. Any action under this section shall be heard and determined by a court of three judges in accordance with the provisions of section 2284 of title 28 and any appeal shall lie to the Supreme Court.

(b) Any voting qualification or prerequisite to voting, or standard, practice, or procedure with respect to voting that has the purpose of or will have the effect of diminishing the ability of any citizens of the United States on account of race or color, or in contravention of the guarantees set forth in section 1973b(f)(2) of this title, to elect their preferred candidates of choice denies or abridges the right to vote within the meaning of subsection (a) of this section.

(c) The term "purpose" in subsections (a) and (b) of this section shall include any discriminatory purpose.

(d) The purpose of subsection (b) of this section is to protect the ability of such citizens to elect their preferred candidates of choice.

[6] U.S. Const. art. I, § 8.

an enacting statute of more than a few words, but why does a bar on racial discrimination in voting require all this verbiage? There is a different answer for each provision.

With regard to Section 2, it is instructive to begin by noting that the original 1965 version was much shorter: "No voting qualification or prerequisite to voting, or standard, practice, or procedure shall be imposed or applied by any State or political subdivision to deny or abridge the right of any citizen of the United States to vote on account of race or color."[7] The longer version was enacted in 1982 in order to overturn a Supreme Court decision—*Mobile v. Bolden*[8]— that had determined this shorter language was coextensive with the Constitution and prohibited only racially disparate *treatment*, and not voting practices and procedures that a judge or bureaucrat determined had a racially disparate *result*.[9] In other words, Congress decided to use its enforcement power under Section 2 of the Fifteenth Amendment to ban actions that aren't illegal under Section 1 of the Fifteenth Amendment. Hmmm.

With regard to Section 5, there is a more sympathetic answer. Certain jurisdictions in the South had played a cat-and-mouse game with federal voting rights enforcement, and so Congress decided to require them to get permission from the U.S. Department of Justice or a District of Columbia—no hometowning allowed—court before making any voting changes. Fair enough, although it is problematic that Congress has outlawed not only actions with a racially disparate "purpose" but also those with a racially disparate "effect"—so once more what is permitted by the Constitution is not permitted under a statute supposedly passed to enforce it.[10] Hmmm again.

B. Why Sections 2 and 5 Are Objectionable

If a voting practice or procedure is racially nondiscriminatory on its face, is applied equally and nondiscriminatorily, and was not

---

[7] Voting Rights Act of 1965, Pub. L. No. 89-110, 79 Stat. 437 (codified as amended at 42 U.S.C. 1973 (2006)). For anyone interested in the Voting Rights Act, its history, and its abuses, see Abigail Thernstrom, Voting Rights and Wrongs: The Elusive Quest for Racially Fair Elections (2009). Thernstrom's work in this area over the years has been and continues to be invaluable.

[8] Mobile v. Bolden, 446 U.S. 55 (1980).

[9] 42 U.S.C. 1973 (2006).

[10] *Id.* § 1973c.

adopted with any discriminatory intent, then can it be said to be racial discrimination? For example, suppose that a state does not allow prison inmates to vote. Suppose further that this law applies to all inmates without regard to color, was adopted without a desire to disenfranchise African Americans (indeed, perhaps when the state had very few African Americans, or when most of the African Americans there were slaves and thus were never expected to vote anyhow), and has always been applied to all inmates without regard to race. But it turns out that, in 2009, there is now a substantially higher percentage of African Americans in the prison population than in the general population. Are African Americans now being denied the right to vote "on account of race" (to quote the Fifteenth Amendment)?

If you said yes, you may have a future in this-or-that Legal Defense and Education Fund. The correct answer is that this is *not* racial discrimination, and so such laws are not fairly within Congress's enforcement authority under Section 2 of the Fifteenth Amendment.

What's more, whenever the government bans actions (public or private) that merely have racially disparate impact, two bad outcomes are encouraged that would not be encouraged, or would at least be encouraged less, if the government stuck to banning actions that are actually racially discriminatory. First, actions that are perfectly legitimate will be abandoned. Second, if the action is valuable enough, then surreptitious—or not so surreptitious—racial quotas will be adopted so that the action is no longer racially disparate in its impact.[11]

In employment, for example, an employer who has required each of his employees to have a high school diploma, and who does not want to be sued for the racially disparate impact this criterion creates, has two choices: He can abandon the requirement (thus hiring

---

[11] My criticisms of the disparate-impact approach are set out in Disparate Impact in the Private Sector: A Theory Going Haywire (2001). This monograph elaborates on my article, The Bad Law of "Disparate Impact," Public Interest (Winter 2009), at 79. Even under a disparate impact/effects/results approach, the defendant can prevail if he can show a sufficiently strong reason for the challenged practice. Thus, for example, I've argued that the disenfranchisement of felons ought to be lawful under Section 2 of the Voting Rights Act, even if it has racially disproportionate results. See, e.g., Roger Clegg, The Case against Felon Voting, 2 U. St. Thomas J.L. & Pub. Pol'y 1, 12 (2008). But the pressure to abandon criteria with racially disproportionate results, or to overlay them with quotas, remains.

employees he believes to be less productive) or he can keep the requirement but instruct his managers to meet racial hiring quotas (thus, perversely, engaging in the very discrimination that the statute supposedly is designed to ban). This latter tension—between the anti-race-conscious mandate of prohibiting disparate treatment and the race-conscious mandate of prohibiting disparate impact—was at the forefront of another civil rights case the Supreme Court decided last term, *Ricci v. DeStefano*.[12] Justice Antonin Scalia's concurrence in that case noted that, indeed, the tension is so strong that disparate impact statutes may violate the Constitution's equal-protection guarantee.[13]

We see the same phenomenon with respect to the Voting Rights Act. Some legitimate voting practices—for example, making sure that voters can identify themselves as registered-to-vote, U.S. citizens—will be challenged if they have a racially disparate impact; this problem is beyond the scope of this article. The other problem is central to it: Jurisdictions will be pressed to use racial gerrymandering—racially segregated districting—to ensure racially proportionate election results and thus, perversely, to engage in the very discrimination that is at odds with the underlying law's ideals.

Let me emphasize and elaborate on that last point, because otherwise the *Bartlett* decision, to which I turn next, is incomprehensible— and so are the high stakes regarding the constitutionality *vel non* of Section 5, which I discuss thereafter: *The principal use of Sections 2 and 5 in 2009 is to coerce state and local jurisdictions into drawing districts with an eye on race, to ensure that there are African American (and, in some instances, Latino) majorities who will elect representatives of the right color.*

Note also that the VRA literally denies the equal protection of the laws by providing legal guarantees to some racial groups that it denies to others. A minority group may be entitled to have a racially gerrymandered district, or be protected against racial gerrymandering that favors other groups. At the same time, other groups are not entitled to gerrymander and indeed may lack protection against gerrymandering that hurts them. This is nothing if not treating people differently based on their race. Under the Constitution, no racial

---

[12] Ricci v. DeStefano, 129 S. Ct. 2658, 555 U.S. _____ (2009).

[13] *Id.* at 2681–83 (Scalia, J, concurring).

group should be guaranteed "safe" districts or districts where it has "influence" or some combination thereof unless all other groups are given the same guarantee—a guarantee that is impossible to give (even if it were a good idea to encourage racial obsession).

The racial gerrymandering Sections 2 and 5 foster is pernicious. The Supreme Court has warned about the unconstitutionality of racial gerrymandering in a number of decisions, because the practice encourages racial balkanization and identity politics.[14] In addition, the segregated districts that gerrymandering creates have contributed to lack of competitiveness in elections, districts that are more polarized (both racially and ideologically), the insulation of Republican candidates and incumbents from minority voters and issues of particular interest to them—to the detriment of both Republicans and minority communities—and, conversely, the insulation of minority candidates and incumbents from white voters (making it harder for those politicians to run for statewide or other larger-jurisdiction positions).[15] As Chief Justice John Roberts wrote, it is, indeed, "a sordid business, this divvying us up by race."[16]

II. The Court's Decisions

A. Bartlett v. Strickland

North Carolina's state constitution contains a "Whole County Provision" that prohibits the General Assembly from dividing counties when it draws its own legislative districts.[17] The issue in *Bartlett v. Strickland* was whether, nonetheless, Section 2 of the Voting Rights

---

[14] Among the Supreme Court's anti-racial-gerrymandering pronouncements, see especially Shaw v. Reno, 509 U.S. 630 (1993); and Miller v. Johnson, 515 U.S. 300 (1995).

[15] Regarding these bad side-effects of racial gerrymandering, see generally Roger Clegg & Linda Chavez, An Analysis of the Reauthorized Sections 5 and 203 of the Voting Rights Act of 1965: Bad Policy and Unconstitutional, 5 Geo. J.L. & Pub. Pol'y 561 (2007) (citing, inter alia, Christopher M. Burke, The Appearance of Equality: Racial Gerrymandering, Redistricting, and the Supreme Court 32–33 (1999); Katharine Inglis Butler, Racial Fairness and Traditional Districting Standards: Observations on the Impact of the Voting Rights Act on Geographic Representation, 57 S.C. L. Rev. 749, 780–81 (2006)). See also Jim Sleeper, Liberal Racism 43–66 (1997); Sheryll D. Cashin, Democracy, Race, and Multiculturalism in the Twenty-First Century: Will the Voting Rights Act Ever Be Obsolete?, 22 Wash. U. J.L. & Pol'y 71, 90 (2006).

[16] League of United Latin American Citizens v. Perry, 548 U.S. 399, 511 (2006) (Roberts, J., concurring in part and dissenting in part).

[17] Bartlett v. Strickland, 129 S. Ct. 1231, 1239 (2009).

Act required that this be done, when the resulting, racially gerrymandered district would not be majority African American, but would nonetheless have given African American voters the potential to join with like-minded white voters to elect the black voters' candidate of choice.[18]

A majority of the justices say "no." Three of them—Chief Justice Roberts and Justice Samuel Alito joining an opinion by Justice Anthony Kennedy—apply the Court's seminal ruling on Section 2 after it had been amended in 1982, *Thornburg v. Gingles.*[19] There the Court had identified three "necessary preconditions" for a Section 2 malapportionment claim, the first of which was that the relevant minority group be "sufficiently large and geographically compact to constitute a majority in a single-member district."[20] Thus, if there was no majority, there was no possible Section 2 malapportionment claim. Two of the justices—Scalia joining an opinion by Justice Clarence Thomas—concur in the *Bartlett* judgment but because, in their view, "[t]he text of Section 2 . . . does not authorize any vote dilution claim, regardless of the size of the minority population in a given district."[21] They reject the *Gingles* framework "because it has no basis in the text of Section 2"; that framework, they added, has produced "'a disastrous misadventure in judicial policymaking.'"[22]

Four justices dissent—Justices John Paul Stevens, Ruth Bader Ginsburg, and Stephen Breyer all joining an opinion by Justice David Souter,[23] with Breyer and Ginsburg also adding separate dissenting opinions of their own.[24] Souter's dissent centers on the right way to interpret and apply *Gingles,* as a matter of both logic and policy. Breyer writes to explain why, even if bright lines are needed, he has a better idea than the majority's 50 percent rule, namely a "2-to-1 rule"—that is a 2-to-1 ratio "of voting age minority population to necessary non-minority crossover votes."[25] Ginsburg's dissent is

---

[18] *Id.* at 1231.

[19] Thornburg v. Gingles, 478 U.S. 30 (1986).

[20] *Id.* at 50. See also Growe v. Emison, 507 U.S. 25 (1993).

[21] Bartlett, 129 S. Ct. at 1250.

[22] *Id.* (citing Holder v. Hall, 512 U.S. 874, 893 (1994)).

[23] Bartlett, 129 S. Ct. at 1250.

[24] *Id.* at 1260.

[25] *Id.* at 1262.

simply a paragraph inviting Congress to overturn the Court's ruling.[26]

B. Northwest Austin Municipal Utility District Number One ("NAMUDNO") v. Holder

NAMUDNO is a small utility district in Texas that is covered by Section 5 of the Voting Rights Act. It filed suit seeking relief under the "bailout" provision of Section 4(a), which allows a "political subdivision" to be released from Section 5's preclearance requirements if certain conditions are met. But it also argued in the alternative that Section 5 is unconstitutional. The three-judge District of Columbia district court ruled that NAMUDNO was ineligible for bailout, and then upheld the constitutionality of Section 5.[27] The Supreme Court noted probable jurisdiction over the utility district's appeal, ruled that in fact NAMUDNO was eligible for bailout, and therefore did not rule on Section 5's constitutionality.[28]

1. The Majority Opinion

Part I.A of the Court's decision—written by Chief Justice Roberts and joined by every justice except Thomas—recounts the history of the Voting Rights Act, particularly Sections 4 and 5, and part I.B briefly summarizes the litigation below. Part II provides the critical discussion for those pondering the future of the Voting Rights Act and will be discussed at greater length later, but can be summarized in the opinion's conclusion:

> More than 40 years ago, this Court concluded that "exceptional conditions" prevailing in certain parts of the country justified extraordinary legislation otherwise unfamiliar to our federal system. . . . In part due to the success of that legislation, we are now a very different Nation. Whether conditions continue to justify such legislation is a difficult constitutional question we do not answer today.[29]

---

[26] *Id.* at 1260.

[27] Nw. Austin Mun. Util. Dist. No. One v. Mukasey, 573 F. Supp. 2d 221 (D.D.C. 2008).

[28] Nw. Austin Mun. Util. Dist. No. One ("NAMUDNO") v. Holder, 129 S. Ct. 2504 (2009).

[29] *Id.* at 2516.

Part III explains how the Court concluded that the utility district is eligible to invoke Section 4's bailout provision, acknowledging: "Were the scope of §4(a) considered in isolation from the rest of the statute and our prior cases, the District Court's approach might well be correct. But here specific precedent, the structure of the Voting Rights Act, and underlying constitutional concerns compel a broader reading of the bailout provision."[30] All in all, concludes the Court, "It is unlikely that Congress intended the provision to have such limited effect."[31]

As noted above, Part II is the part of the opinion of most interest for this article. The Court begins by acknowledging that "[t]he historic accomplishments of the Voting Rights Act are undeniable" in fighting discrimination,[32] but then turns to the constitutional problems that the VRA raises. For starters, Section 5, "which authorizes federal intrusion into sensitive areas of state and local policymaking, imposes substantial federalism costs."[33] What's more, "Section 5 goes beyond the prohibition of the Fifteenth Amendment by suspending *all* changes to state election law—however innocuous—until they have been precleared by federal authorities in Washington, D.C."[34] The Court warns: "Past success alone . . . is not adequate justification to retain the preclearance requirements."[35]

The Court expresses concern that the VRA "also differentiates between the States."[36] This state-discrimination problem is aggravated by the fact that the statute's coverage formula is dated and may no longer correctly target the worst offenders.[37] Most telling with regard to the concerns expressed in this article is this paragraph in Part II:

> These federalism concerns are underscored by the argument that the preclearance requirements in one State would be unconstitutional in another. See *Georgia* v. *Ashcroft*, 539 U.S.

---

[30] *Id.* at 2514.
[31] *Id.* at 2516.
[32] *Id.* at 2511.
[33] *Id.* (internal quotation marks and citations omitted).
[34] NAMUDNO, 129 S. Ct. at 2511 (emphasis in the original).
[35] *Id.*
[36] *Id.* at 2512.
[37] *Id.*

461, 491-492 (2003) (Kennedy, J., concurring) ("Race cannot be the predominant factor in redistricting under our decision in *Miller* v. *Johnson*, 515 U. S. 900 (1995). Yet considerations of race that would doom a redistricting plan under the Fourteenth Amendment or §2 seem to be what save it under §5"). Additional constitutional concerns are raised in saying that this tension between §§2 and 5 must persist in covered jurisdictions and not elsewhere.[38]

The Court does not resolve the question of what degree of scrutiny was appropriate, but noted that the "Act's preclearance requirements and its coverage formula raise serious constitutional questions" in any event.[39]

But then the Court shifts gears again, acknowledging the gravity of determining the constitutionality of an act of Congress, "a coequal branch of government whose Members take the same oath we do to uphold the Constitution of the United States," and the one which the Fifteenth Amendment empowers "in the first instance" to determine "what legislation is needed to enforce it."[40] The Court further acknowledges that "Congress amassed a sizable record" to justify the legislation and that this record had impressed the district court.[41]

Still, says the Court, it is a well-established principle that the Court will avoid constitutional pronouncements if there is some other way to dispose of the case, and NAMUDNO had acknowledged in its brief and at oral argument that, if it prevailed on the bailout issue, the constitutional issue need not be reached.[42] And so, *pace* Justice Thomas's partial dissent, the Court doesn't reach it.

2. Justice Thomas's Partial Dissent

Indeed, only Justice Thomas does not join the Court's opinion, and only he writes separately, concurring in the judgment in part and dissenting in part. Part I of his opinion explains why he thinks the "doctrine of constitutional avoidance" should not apply in this case and why the Court should have reached the issue of Section

[38] *Id.*

[39] *Id.* at 2513.

[40] *Id.* (quoting Rostker v. Goldberg, 453 U.S. 57 (1981) (internal quotation marks omitted)).

[41] NAMUDNO, 129 S. Ct. at 2513.

[42] *Id.*

5's constitutionality.[43] In Part II, Justice Thomas explains why Section 5 is, in fact, unconstitutional.[44]

Here he first provides the historical and legal backdrop, noting that voting law is generally a state matter but then reviewing the blatant racial discrimination that prompted Section 5's initial passage in 1965.[45] He next turns to the Court's decision in *South Carolina v. Katzenbach*,[46] which upheld Section 5 against an early constitutional challenge, and highlights that "[s]everal important principles emerge from *Katzenbach* and the decisions that followed it":[47] (a) Section 5 "prohibits more state voting practices than those necessarily encompassed by the explicit prohibition on intentional discrimination found in the text of the Fifteenth Amendment";[48] (b) thus, Section 5 "pushes the outer boundaries of Congress' Fifteenth Amendment enforcement authority";[49] and so (c) "to accommodate the tension between the constitutional imperatives of the Fifteenth and Tenth Amendments . . . the constitutionality of Section 5 has always depended on the proven existence of intentional discrimination so extensive that elimination of it through case-by-case enforcement would be impossible."[50]

In the last part of his opinion, Justice Thomas applies these principles and concludes, "The extensive pattern of discrimination that led the Court to previously uphold Section 5 as enforcing the Fifteenth Amendment no longer exists."[51] This is confirmed by both broad historical and "current statistical evidence"[52]—"[i]ndeed, when reenacting §5 in 2006, Congress evidently understood that the emergency conditions which prompted §5's original enactment no longer exist,"[53] given the weaker evidence it was able to marshal.[54] And

---

[43] *Id.* at 2517 (Thomas, J., dissenting).

[44] *Id.* at 2519–27.

[45] *Id.* at 2519–23.

[46] 383 U.S. 301 (1966).

[47] NAMUDNO, 129 S. Ct. at 2523.

[48] *Id.* at 2523.

[49] *Id.* at 2524.

[50] *Id.*

[51] *Id.* at 2525.

[52] *Id.*

[53] *Id.* at 2526.

[54] *Id.* at 2525.

cheer up: "Admitting that a prophylactic law as broad as §5 is no longer constitutionally justified based on current evidence of discrimination is not a sign of defeat. It is an acknowledgment of victory."[55] Justice Thomas concludes his opinion on a decidedly upbeat note: "An acknowledgment of §5's unconstitutionality represents a fulfillment of the Fifteenth Amendment's promise of full enfranchisement and honors the success achieved by the VRA."[56]

C. A Word on "Judicial Activism" and NAMUDNO

Were the Court to strike down Section 5 as unconstitutional, would this be judicial activism? A number of people said so in the run-up to the Court's decision, perhaps the most prominent of whom was Senator Patrick Leahy, chairman of the Senate Judiciary Committee.[57] But the correct answer is "no."

Judicial activism, properly defined, is a court's substitution of its own policy preferences for what the text of the Constitution—or other law—actually says. The classic instance involves inventing a limitation on a legislature that doesn't actually exist in the Constitution, but it also includes ignoring a limitation that actually *does* exist.

The problem with Section 5 is that it prohibits many state actions that are not unconstitutional because, as discussed, it employs an "effects" test while the Fifteenth Amendment prohibits only disparate treatment, namely actions taken "on account of race." Indeed, its principal use today is applying this effects test to *require states to engage in disparate treatment*: the racial segregation of voting districts by racial gerrymandering. In addition, Section 5 supplants state authority in matters committed to them by the Constitution and substitutes federal judicial and bureaucratic supervision. (This could be justified if necessary to stop states from violating the Constitution but, as just noted, Section 5 goes far beyond that.) Finally, Section 5 applies to some states and not others—without any existing factual basis for doing so—which is likewise inconsistent with the Constitution's federalist structure.

---

[55] *Id.*

[56] *Id.* at 2527.

[57] See Patrick Leahy, Senator, UDC David A. Clarke School of Law Annual Rauh Lecture: The Supreme Court and the Nomination of Judge Sonia Sotomayor (June 16, 2009).

So, in reauthorizing Section 5 in 2006, Congress exceeded its constitutional authority. Striking it down would honor the Constitution's text and would not be judicial activism. Indeed, upholding it would mean *ignoring* constitutional text and would thus be true judicial activism.[58]

What about the argument that the Court cannot legitimately conclude that Section 5 might once have been constitutional but, because of changes in the facts, isn't any longer—because such fact-finding is up to Congress? The answer is that courts determine facts all the time and changes in factual circumstances may mean that what once met an *unchanging* constitutional standard no longer does.

For example, if a policeman asks a court for a search warrant and produces no evidence, he won't get it; if he produces good evidence, he will. That's hardly judicial activism. Likewise, as the evidence of severe discrimination peculiar to the South diminishes, so will the defensibility of Section 5 before the courts. That's not judicial activism either.

The Fifteenth Amendment says that legislation passed by Congress to enforce the Amendment is to be "appropriate." There is nothing in the text to suggest that Congress intended to insulate such legislation from judicial review to make sure it is.[59]

III. What Next?

A. Good News and Bad News

Given the tension between racial gerrymandering and the ideals of the Voting Rights Act—to say nothing of the Fifteenth Amendment itself—it makes sense to limit Section 2 in the way that the Court

---

[58] I testified before both the House and the Senate in 2006, urging them not to reauthorize Section 5 on the grounds that to do so was both bad policy and unconstitutional. See Reauthorization of the Voting Rights Act Before the H. Comm. Subcomm. on the Constitution, 110th Cong. (2006) (statement of Roger Clegg); Reauthorization of the Voting Rights Act Before the S. Comm. on the Judiciary, 110th Cong. (2006) (statement of Roger Clegg). See also Clegg & Chavez, *supra* note 15. Alas, they did not listen.

[59] It is interesting that in both cases discussed in this article the Court interpreted the Voting Rights Act in a particular way to avoid having to reach a constitutional question. This principle led to a more "conservative" result in *Bartlett,* but it need not always do so. Indeed, "constitutional avoidance" might have saved the Act in *NAMUDNO*—if a majority of justices were willing to strike it down had the case not been disposed of on statutory (bailout) grounds.

did in *Bartlett v. Strickland.* The question in *Bartlett* could not be clearly answered by the statute's text. Accordingly, the three-justice plurality—and, implicitly, the two-justice concurrence—was correct in adopting an interpretation that limited the requirement of constitutionally dubious race-based redistricting.[60] Given that tension, however, as well as the federalism problems recognized by all nine justices, it is disappointing that the Court left Section 5 intact in *NAMUDNO*—although we can take solace in the warning shot it fired.

The good news—and it is *very* good news—is that the problem of systemic exclusion of racial minorities from the polls no longer exists. This is not to say that there are not still occasional instances of such discrimination, but they are aberrant: The problem that the framers of the Fifteenth Amendment undoubtedly had foremost in their minds—and that, unconscionably, had festered until 1965— has been addressed. In this respect, then, Sections 2 and 5 of the Voting Rights Act can be hailed as stunningly successful.

But there is bad news, too. First, there is no longer any rhyme or reason to the jurisdictions that are covered by Section 5. And given the intrusiveness of the statute, this problem is not simply an aesthetic one: It raises serious federalism concerns. Second, both Sections 2 and 5—by incorporating "results" and "effects" tests, respectively—have banned much that is *not* illegal under the Fifteenth Amendment. Further, not only have they required something that is not required by the Fifteenth Amendment, but the requirement itself undermines the Amendment's guarantees and voting integrity generally. This in turn is objectionable not just as a matter of federalism and federal overreach, but because state laws that might be objectively good are discouraged or struck down (e.g., anti-voter-fraud measures that might have a disparate impact, or long-standing laws preventing criminals from voting), and because state practices

---

[60] Bartlett, 129 S. Ct. at 1247–48. The amicus brief filed by Pacific Legal Foundation and joined by the author's Center for Equal Opportunity had urged this approach. After all, if the line is not drawn at 50 percent, then it is hard to see why the line should be drawn anywhere, and every jurisdiction in the country that has a minority resident will be subject to racial gerrymandering requirements. In this regard, while *Bartlett* received much less publicity than *NAMUDNO,* had it had come out differently then its impact would have been dramatic and lamentable. Thus, one hopes Congress will not accept Justice Ginsburg's dissenting invitation to overturn the majority opinion.

that are bad are now required (in particular, racial segregation of voting districts through racial gerrymandering).

What's more, Section 2 and Section 5 *are* the Voting Rights Act: They are by far its most important provisions. Realizing the deep flaws at the heart of the VRA leads one to wonder whether it wouldn't be better to scrap the law altogether and start anew.[61]

B. Concluding Libertarian Postscript

Because this is an article in a Cato Institute publication, a decent respect to the opinions of one's host suggests that I end by posing and answering this question: What's a libertarian to think of all this?

Libertarians ought to oppose government policies that racially discriminate in voting; there is no issue here, really, of private discrimination. But whom ought we to trust to make sure this discrimination doesn't happen? The federal government or state and local entities? The political branches or the judiciary?

Given American history, it is easy to recognize, to borrow Clint Bolick's phrase, the problem of "grassroots tyranny" here[62]—that, as James Madison discussed in *Federalist* No. 10, the federal government might be needed to prevent abuses by state and local governments. On the other hand, the federal government is also perfectly capable of abusing its power in this area, and, as an unintended (perhaps) consequence, this is what's happened. As is often the case, in this abuse there has been collaboration between liberal federal bureaucrats and activist judges. As is also often the case, this collaboration has replaced a colorblind ideal with politically correct color-consciousness. Adding to the problem is that partisans from both parties have happily supported the abuse.

Bottom line: Friends of liberty—and opponents of racial discrimination in voting—should now favor less of a federal role than could have been justified in 1965. This aim of lessening the federal role

---

[61] And let me add that another provision, Section 203, is at least as objectionable and even more unconstitutional than Sections 2 and 5. Section 203 requires some jurisdictions to print ballots and other election materials in foreign languages. 42 U.S.C. 1973b(f) and 1973aa-1a. This is bad policy because it balkanizes our country, facilitates voter fraud, and wastes state and local government resources. And it is unconstitutional because it lacks all congruence and proportionality to the end of stopping purposeful racial and ethnic discrimination by state and local jurisdictions. See Clegg & Chavez, *supra* note 15, at 575–80.

[62] Clint Bolick, Grassroots Tyranny: The Limits of Federalism (1993).

should be pursued both through the political branches and through litigation, because the current text of the Voting Rights Act exceeds Congress's power. The Act should be refocused on fulfilling—not undermining—the Fifteenth Amendment's purpose: ensuring that the right to vote is not denied or abridged on account of race.

The War between Disparate Impact and Equal Protection

*Kenneth L. Marcus**

Title VII of the Civil Rights Act of 1964 forbids job discrimination based on race, color, religion, sex, or national origin.[1] Title VII was originally enacted as a regulation of interstate commerce and applied only to private employers. In 1972, however, the Act was extended to the public sector pursuant to Congress's Fourteenth Amendment authority to ensure that "[n]o State shall . . . deny to any person within its jurisdiction the equal protection of the laws." Because the Equal Protection Clause was intended to guarantee equal opportunities rather than equal outcomes, the Supreme Court's application of that clause has focused on intentional discrimination. Title VII initially barred only disparate treatment, which encompasses only such intentional discrimination and, under some interpretations, also unconscious bias. But under Title VII, Congress expanded the reach of anti-discrimination litigation: Employers may be held accountable not only for disparate treatment, but also for disparate impact, which refers to discriminatory effects arising out of workplace policies or procedures, even when an intent to discriminate cannot be proven.

On its face, the New Haven firefighters' case, *Ricci v. DeStefano*, is about the tension between these two sides of Title VII.[2] At root, however, the real war is between disparate impact and the Equal Protection Clause.

* Lillie & Nathan Ackerman Chair in Equality & Justice in America, The City University of New York, Bernard M. Baruch College School of Public Affairs; Director, Initiative on Anti-Semitism & Anti-Israelism in American Educational Systems, Institute for Jewish & Community Research; J.D., University of California at Berkeley; B.A. in Moral and Political Philosophy, Williams College. The author submitted an amicus brief, together with several other scholars, on behalf of the plaintiffs in Ricci v. DeStefano, 557 U.S. ___, 129 S. Ct. 2658.

[1] 78 Stat. 253, as amended, 42 U.S.C. § 2000e et seq.

[2] 557 U.S. ___, 129 S. Ct. 2658 (2009).

I. Introduction

"The way to stop discrimination on the basis of race," Chief Justice John Roberts recently wrote, "is to stop discriminating on the basis of race."[3] In other words, state actors can best achieve equal treatment by eliminating all governmental racial preferences. This notion builds upon Justice John Marshall Harlan's dissent in *Plessy v. Ferguson*, which proclaimed that "our Constitution is colorblind, and neither knows nor tolerates classes among its citizens."[4] It contrasts, however, with Justice Harry Blackmun's equally canonical view that "in order to get beyond racism, we must first take account of race."[5] To the extent that anti-discrimination jurisprudence now adopts—or shuttles between—these conflicting views, a difficult question emerges for disparate-impact doctrine: Under what circumstances, if any, can state actors intentionally discriminate in order to avoid the unintended discrimination that might otherwise result from facially neutral policies?

The question is whether such race-conscious actions are consistent with the constitutional guarantee that no person will be denied "the equal protection of the laws." Although posed in *Ricci*, the issue is not resolved there. As Justice Antonin Scalia observed in his concurrence to that decision, the Court's narrow resolution of *Ricci* "merely postpones the evil day" the Court will have to decide the central, looming question: "Whether, or to what extent, are the disparate-impact provisions of Title VII of the Civil Rights Act of 1964 consistent with the Constitution's guarantee of equal protection?"[6] As Scalia acknowledges, "The question is not an easy one."[7] It is, however, both important and timely. Because "the war between disparate impact and equal protection will be waged sooner or later . . . it behooves us to begin thinking about how—and on what terms—to make peace between them."[8]

---

[3] Parents Involved in Cmty. Sch. v. Seattle Sch. Dist. No. 1, 551 U.S. 701, 748 (2007).

[4] Plessy v. Ferguson, 163 U.S. 537, 559 (1896).

[5] Regents of the University of California v. Bakke, 438 U.S. 265, 407 (1978) (Blackmun, J., concurring).

[6] Ricci, 129 S. Ct. at 2682 (Scalia, J., concurring).

[7] *Id.*

[8] *Id.* at 2683.

Although *Ricci* does not resolve this conflict, it does identify the problem clearly and suggests that a future case will resolve it. *Ricci* holds that employers may not subject employees to disparate treatment without a strong basis in evidence to believe that facially neutral application of their employment policies would entail liability for disparate impact.[9] Writing for a five-justice majority, Justice Anthony Kennedy based the Court's opinion entirely on Title VII. Significantly, Kennedy emphasized that the Court does not address "the constitutionality of the measures taken here in purported compliance with Title VII," nor does it "hold that meeting the strong-basis-in-evidence standard would satisfy the Equal Protection Clause in a future case."[10] In other words, the Court explicitly reserved the option to hold, in a later case, that the prospect of disparate-impact liability is never a sufficient justification, under the Equal Protection Clause, for the use of racially preferential employment measures.

This article will argue that equal protection is consistent with disparate impact only when the latter provision is narrowly construed. Disparate impact plays an important role in identifying and eliminating intentional and unconscious discrimination that cannot be proved through other means. Even under strict scrutiny, state actors may take narrowly tailored race-conscious actions to avoid creating such discriminatory impacts.[11] On the other hand, disparate impact is also sometimes used to level racial disparities that do not arise from intentional or unconscious discrimination. Equal protection does not permit state actors to take race-conscious actions for this purpose. Because Title VII's disparate-impact provision is based in significant part on this less-than-compelling rationale, this article will argue that it must be narrowed or struck down. Finally, disparate impact may also be used to eliminate systemic racial biases that do not arise from an institution's present or prior discriminatory actions. Equal protection may permit state actors to conduct certain

---

[9] *Id.* at 2675 (Kennedy, J.) (majority opinion).

[10] *Id.* at 2676.

[11] Under the Equal Protection Clause, courts will strictly scrutinize state laws that discriminate on the basis of race. Strict scrutiny requires the state to show that the law is, first, justified by a compelling governmental interest and, second, narrowly tailored to achieve that interest.

narrowly tailored race-conscious actions to avoid disparate impacts of this sort, although Congress cannot constitutionally require them.

II. Background

Ricci is a challenge to the New Haven Civil Service Board's decision not to certify the results of a promotional examination in the city's fire department brought by 18 white and Hispanic firefighters who likely would have been promoted based on their strong performance on the test. CSB had come to its decision after finding that very few African American or Hispanic firefighters scored highly enough on the examination to be promoted. CSB had been advised by counsel that certifying the results could render New Haven liable to minority candidates under Title VII's disparate-impact provision.

Firefighting is a field in which, as Justice Ruth Bader Ginsburg observed in her dissent, "the legacy of racial discrimination casts an especially long shadow."[12] Congress took note of this history in 1972 when it extended Title VII to state and local government employers. Specifically, Congress took note of a U.S. Commission on Civil Rights report that found that racial discrimination in municipal employment was even "more pervasive than in the private sector."[13] In particular, the USCCR had criticized fire and police departments for "[b]arriers to equal employment . . . greater . . . than in any other area of State or local government," finding that African Americans held "almost no positions in the officer ranks."[14] The USCCR had reported that intentional racism was partly responsible, but that the problem was exacerbated by municipalities' failure to apply merit-based hiring and promotion principles. Instead, government agencies often relied on nepotism, political patronage, and other practices that reinforced long-standing racial disparities.

Historically, New Haven's fire department has been characterized by stark racial disparities similar to what the USCCR had observed nationwide. In the early 1970s, for example, African Americans and Hispanics composed 30 percent of New Haven's population, but only 3.6 percent of the city's 502 firefighters. In recent years, African

---

[12] Ricci, 129 S. Ct. at 2690 (Ginsburg, J., dissenting).

[13] Id. at 2690 (quoting H. R. Rep. No. 92-238, p. 17 (1971)).

[14] Id. at 2690–91.

Americans and Hispanics have remained significantly under-repre-sented among New Haven's senior firefighting officers. For example, only one of the fire department's 21 captains is black. New Haven did not present any evidence, however, to demonstrate that New Haven's fire department had previously engaged in racial discrimination.[15]

In 2003, 118 firefighters took New Haven's promotional examina-tions to qualify for advancement to lieutenant or captain.[16] New Haven conducted these examinations infrequently, so the results would dictate which applicants would be considered for promotion during the following two years. The examination had both written and oral components. New Haven's contract with its firefighters' union required that the written exam would account for 60 percent and the oral exam 40 percent of an applicant's total score. The CSB's charter established a "rule of three," under which municipal hiring authorities must fill any vacancy by selecting a candidate from the top three scorers.

New Haven contracted with Industrial/Organizational Solutions, Inc. to develop and administer the tests. IOS specializes in designing examinations for fire and police departments. IOS began its test-design process by conducting analyses to identify the knowledge, skills, and abilities that are essential for the positions. IOS inter-viewed incumbents and their superiors, conducted ride-alongs and observed on-duty officers. Based on these practices, IOS prepared questionnaires and administered them to most incumbent depart-ment officers. At every stage, IOS over-sampled minority officers so that the results would not be biased towards white applicants. In order to prepare the oral examination, IOS used its job analysis data to develop hypothetical situations that would test relevant job requirements. Candidates were given the hypotheticals and asked to address them before a three-person panel of assessors. Sixty-six percent of the panelists were minority group members, and every assessment panel had two minorities.

Seventy-seven firefighters took the lieutenant examination: 43 whites, 19 blacks, and 15 Hispanics. Only 34 candidates passed:

---

[15] Amicus Br. of Claremont Inst. Center for Const. Jurisprudence, Ricci v. DeStefano, 2009 WL 507011 at *19, citing Pet. App. 938a–945a, 1013a–1037a.

[16] Ricci, 129 S. Ct. at 2664.

25 whites, 6 blacks, and 3 Hispanics. When the examination was conducted, eight lieutenant positions were vacant. Under New Haven's "rule of three," the top ten candidates were eligible for promotion. All 10 of them were white. Subsequent vacancies would have allowed at least three black candidates to be considered for promotion to lieutenant. Forty-one firefighters took the captaincy examination: 25 whites, 8 blacks, and 8 Hispanics. Twenty-two passed: 16 whites, 3 blacks, and 3 Hispanics. Because seven captain positions were vacant, nine candidates were immediately eligible for elevation: 7 whites and 2 Hispanics. In other words, if the CSB had certified the results, no black firefighters could have been considered for any of the then-vacant promotional opportunities.

When the racial disparities in the test results were revealed, a heated public debate ensued. Some firefighters threatened to sue New Haven for disparate-impact discrimination if the department made promotions based on the examinations. Others threatened to sue if New Haven discarded the test results because of the racial composition of the candidates who would otherwise be promoted. New Haven's attorney, Thomas Ude, counseled the city that under federal antidiscrimination law, "a statistical demonstration of disparate impact," in and of itself, "constitutes a sufficiently serious claim of racial discrimination to serve as a predicate for employer initiated, voluntar[y] remedies—even . . . race-conscious remedies."[17] The test-maker, meanwhile, insisted that there was "nothing in those examinations . . . that should cause somebody to think that one group would perform differently than another group."[18] At Ude's urging, New Haven sided with the protesters and discarded the examinations.

The plaintiff firefighters alleged that New Haven (and various officials) discriminated against them based on their race by disregarding the test results, in violation of both Title VII's disparate-treatment provision and the Fourteenth Amendment's Equal Protection Clause. New Haven defended its actions, arguing that it had refused to certify the examination results based on a good-faith belief that, had it certified the results, it would have been liable under Title VII's disparate-impact provision for adopting a practice that adversely affected minority firefighters.[19]

[17] Id., 129 S. Ct. at 2666–67 (quoting App. to Pet. for Cert. in No. 07-1428, p. 443a).

[18] Id., 129 S. Ct. at 2668 (quoting App. in No. 06-4996-cv (CA2), at A961).

[19] Id. at 2661.

III. The Supreme Court's Opinion

Justice Anthony Kennedy, writing for the Court, reversed the Second Circuit and held in favor of the plaintiffs. Justice Kennedy began with the observation that New Haven's actions would violate Title VII's disparate-treatment prohibition absent some valid defense.[20] This is important, because the district court had characterized New Haven's actions as involving "the use of race-neutral means to improve racial and gender representation."[21] After all, New Haven had discarded all test results, rather than treating results differently based on the race of the test-taker.

In *Parents Involved in Community Schools v. Seattle School District No. 1*, Justice Kennedy had appeared to argue that such race-neutral measures do not trigger strict scrutiny under the Equal Protection Clause. But here, Kennedy emphasized that New Haven decided not to certify the results because of racial disparities in performance. Quoting the district court, Kennedy characterized New Haven's view as that "too many whites and not enough minorities would be promoted were the lists to be certified."[22] Absent sufficient justification, Kennedy explained, such "race-based decisionmaking violates Title VII's command that employers cannot take adverse employment actions because of an individual's race."[23]

Kennedy next considered whether the intent to avoid disparate-impact liability justified disparate-treatment discrimination that would otherwise be prohibited. He rejected the firefighters' argument that it can never be permissible under Title VII for an employer to "take race-based adverse employment actions in order to avoid disparate-impact liability—even if the employer knows its practice violates the disparate-impact provision."[24] As Kennedy explained, this approach would ignore Congress's decision when codifying the disparate-impact provision in 1991 to expressly prohibit both forms of discrimination. Apparently, in a situation where either disparate treatment or disparate impact could be avoided, but not both, Kennedy surmised that Congress wanted the courts to establish relevant standards rather than categorically prohibit one or the other.

[20] *Id.* at 2664.

[21] Ricci, 554 F. Supp. 2d at 157.

[22] Ricci, 129 S. Ct. at 2673 (quoting Ricci, 554 F. Supp. 2d at 152).

[23] *Id.* (citing 42 U.S.C. § 2000e-2(a)(1)).

[24] *Id.* at 2674.

Similarly, Kennedy rejected the argument that an employer must violate the disparate-impact provision before it can use the fear of a disparate-impact suit as a defense to a disparate-treatment claim. Forbidding employers from undertaking race-based action unless they know, with certainty, that their conduct violates the disparate-impact provision would "bring compliance efforts to a near standstill."[25]

On the other hand, Kennedy also rejected New Haven's argument that race-based employment decisions can be justified by an employer's mere good-faith belief that its actions are necessary for compliance with Title VII's disparate-impact provision.[26] Kennedy explained that allowing employers to violate the disparate-treatment prohibition based on a mere showing of "good-faith" would encourage race-based decisionmaking at "the slightest hint of disparate impact."[27] This would, Kennedy aptly observed, "amount to a *de facto* quota system, in which a 'focus on statistics . . . could put undue pressure on employers to adopt inappropriate prophylactic measures.'"[28] Moreover, it could encourage employers to manipulate employment practices in order to engineer the employer's "preferred racial balance." "That operational principle," Kennedy wrote, "could not be justified, for Title VII is express in disclaiming any interpretation of its requirements as calling for outright racial balancing."[29]

Triangulating between these two absolute positions, Kennedy adopted a new standard based on Equal Protection Clause jurisprudence. In the past, the Court had held that some race-conscious state remedial actions are constitutionally permissible, but only if there is a "'strong basis in evidence'" that such remedial actions were necessary.[30] Applying the strong-basis-in-evidence standard to Title VII, Kennedy argued, would give effect to both disparate treatment

---

[25] *Id.* at 2674.

[26] *Id.*

[27] *Id.* at 2675.

[28] Ricci, 129 S. Ct. at 2675, (citing Watson v. Fort Worth Bank & Trust, 487 U.S. 977, 992 (1988) (plurality opinion)).

[29] Ricci, 129 S. Ct. at 2675 (citing 42 U.S.C. §2000e-2(j)).

[30] Richmond v. J. A. Croson Co., 488 U. S. 469, 500 (1989) (plurality opinion by O'Connor, J., joined by Rehnquist, C.J., and White and Kennedy, JJ.) (quoting Wygant v. Jackson Board of Education, 476 U.S. 267, 277 (1986)).

and disparate impact, allowing violations of the former in the name of compliance with the latter only in limited circumstances. Employers would not be barred from race-based decisionmaking unless and until there were a provable disparate-impact violation, but they would be required to demonstrate strong evidence of disparate-impact liability.

Applying this standard, Kennedy found that New Haven lacked a strong basis in evidence for its actions. He acknowledged that the racially adverse impact here was significant and that New Haven indisputably faced a prima facie case of disparate-impact liability. On the captain's examination, white candidates had a 64 percent pass rate compared to 37.5 percent for black and Hispanic candidates. On the lieutenant's exam, 58.1 percent of the white candidates passed while only 31.6 percent of black candidates and only 20 percent of Hispanic candidates passed. The pass rates for minorities were approximately half those for white candidates and thus fell significantly below the Equal Employment Opportunity Commission's 80-percent threshold, which triggers the disparate-impact provision of Title VII.[31] As Kennedy put it, based on the degree of adverse impact reflected in the results, "respondents were compelled to take a hard look at the examinations to determine whether certifying the results would have had an impermissible disparate impact."[32]

Nevertheless, Kennedy insisted that "a prima facie case of disparate-impact liability—essentially, a threshold showing of a significant statistical disparity . . . and nothing more—is far from a strong basis in evidence that the city would have been liable under Title VII had it certified the results."[33] Kennedy reasoned that New Haven could have defended against a disparate-impact claim if the examinations were job-related and consistent with business necessity, and there were no equally valid, less discriminatory alternative that New Haven had rejected even though it served the city's needs.

IV. Discussion

A. The Nature and Extent of the Conflict

Ricci is significant as the first case to identify the conflict between equal protection and disparate impact. Title VII's disparate-impact

---

[31] See 29 CFR §1607.4(D) (2008).

[32] *Ricci*, 129 S. Ct. at 2678.

[33] *Id.*

provision provides that employment practices with adverse ethnic or racial impacts violate Title VII unless (i) the practices are job-related and based upon business necessity and (ii) there are no adequate, less-discriminatory alternatives.[34] Like other governmental actions, this provision conflicts with the Equal Protection Clause to the extent that it (or a state actor implementing it) classifies people by racial groups, has an illicit motive, or allocates benefits on the basis of race.

Justice Ginsburg denies the existence of any conflict in her *Ricci* dissent, arguing that the Court's decision "sets at odds" two "core directives" which, properly interpreted, advance the same objectives: ending workplace discrimination and promoting genuinely equal opportunity."[35] Ironically, it was one of Ginsburg's former clerks, Professor Richard A. Primus, who first identified and explored the conflict in a seminal *Harvard Law Review* article, "Equal Protection and Disparate Impact: Round Three."[36] The conflict is best understood when broken down into the three areas in which disparate-impact doctrine and practice would violate equal protection: racial classifications, illicit motives, and racially allocated benefits.

1. Racial Classifications

Under the Equal Protection Clause, the courts subject all state actors' racial classifications to strict scrutiny, regardless of whether minority groups are helped or harmed by the classification.[37] Disparate impact may entail suspect racial classifications in two respects: first, in the legislation itself, which would subject the congressional enactment to strict scrutiny; second, in actions taken by public employers to comply with the legislation. Equal protection concerns are particularly acute where disparate-impact compliance entails preferential treatment or the use of quotas by public employers.[38]

---

[34] 42 U.S.C. § 2000e-2(a), (k)(1)(A). In addition to race and national origin, this provision also covers disparate impacts on the basis of color, sex and religion.

[35] Ricci, 129 S. Ct. at 2699 (Ginsburg, J., dissenting) (citing McDonnell Douglas Corp. v. Green, 411 U. S. 792, 800 (1973)).

[36] Richard Primus, Equal Protection and Disparate Impact: Round Three, 117 Harv. L. Rev. 493 (2003).

[37] See Croson, 488 U.S. at 494 (1989) (plurality opinion) (citing Wygant, 476 U.S. at 279–80); see also *id.* at 520, 527–28 (Scalia, J., concurring).

[38] See, e.g., Watson, 487 U.S. at 992 (O'Connor, J., plurality).

Title VII's disparate-impact provision does not expressly discuss particular racial groups. If a race-based cause of action is pursued, however, agencies, litigants and courts will have to classify people according to their race.[39] As *Ricci* illustrates, employers may be driven by compliance concerns to classify their employees and candidates by race in order to avoid the prospect of disparate-impact liability. Worse, as Justice Kennedy observes, employers may also use the prospect of disparate-impact liability as a pretext to justify their efforts to achieve a particular ethno-racial balance in their workforce.

As long ago as *Watson v. Fort Worth Bank & Trust* (which predated the 1991 Civil Rights Act), Justice O'Connor recognized "that the inevitable focus on statistics in disparate impact cases could put undue pressure on employers to adopt inappropriate prophylactic measures."[40] This is a potentially widespread problem because racial disparities are ubiquitous in every realm of social encounter—if only because, as O'Connor observed, "It is completely unrealistic to assume that unlawful discrimination is the sole cause of people failing to gravitate to jobs and employers in accord with the laws of chance."[41] Despite Title VII's nominal aversion to the use of racial preferences,[42] an employer faced with the resulting disparities may find it cheaper to use racial preferences than to determine whether the disparities arise from policies that are job-related and consistent with business necessity. As Justice O'Connor noted, it would be "unrealistic to suppose that employers can eliminate, or discover

---

[39] Primus, *supra* note 36 at 508.

[40] See Watson, 487 U.S. at 992 (O'Connor, J., plurality).

[41] See *id.*

[42] See 42 U. S. C. § 2000e-2(j):

> Nothing contained in [Title VII] shall be interpreted to require any employer . . . to grant preferential treatment to any individual or to any group because of the race, color, religion, sex, or national origin of such individual or group on account of an imbalance which may exist with respect to the total number or percentage of persons of any race, color, religion, sex, or national origin employed by any employer . . . in comparison with the total number or percentage of persons of such race, color, religion, sex, or national origin in any community, State, section, or other area, or in the available work force in any community, State, section, or other area.

and explain, the myriad of innocent causes that may lead to statistical imbalances in the composition of their work forces."[43]

Hence the "Hobson's choice" for public employers: "If quotas and preferential treatment become the only cost-effective means of avoiding expensive litigation and potentially catastrophic liability, such measures will be widely adopted."[44] Naturally, the "prudent employer" will take care to discuss such programs "in euphemistic terms," but "will be equally careful to ensure that the quotas are met."[45] An employer seeking to achieve a particular racial outcome need only identify a racial disparity, locate a selection mechanism that achieves the desired demographic mix, and identify whatever business necessities best justify the mechanism. The tendency of disparate-impact law is to pressure employers to effectuate quotas in just this manner: Employers increasingly understand that disparities will not survive a disparate-impact challenge except to the extent that existing processes can be tied to business necessities. Justice O'Connor argued that various evidentiary mechanisms can counteract this tendency, including the requirements of the prima facie case, causation requirements, and burdens of proof.[46] Whether they have done so is an empirical question, but *Ricci* provides new reasons for concern.

Ironically, this point is well illustrated in Justice Ginsburg's dissent. As Ginsburg reveals, New Haven's fire department could have designed the racial composition of its senior officers fairly precisely by altering the respective weights assigned to the written and oral components of its promotional examinations. Because minorities had a comparative advantage on the oral component, New Haven could increase the minority pass rate by overweighting that section. Indeed, the city's failure to do so is subject to precisely the attack that Ginsburg levels—that written examinations cannot properly evaluate certain important professional competencies (e.g., complex

---

[43] See Watson, 487 U.S. at 992 (O'Connor, J., plurality) (citation omitted).

[44] See *id.* at 993 (1988) (O'Connor, J., plurality); see also Roger Clegg, Disparate Impact in the Private Sector: A Theory Going Haywire, Briefly . . . Perspectives on Legislation, Regulation, and Litigation v.9 no.12 (Dec. 2001) at 11 ("And so—surprise—many defendants will simply ensure that the disparate impact does not occur in the first place, by taking steps to guarantee that their numbers come out right.").

[45] See *id.* at 993 (1988) (O'Connor, J., plurality).

[46] See *id.* at 994–98 (1988).

behaviors, interpersonal skills, and ability to succeed under pressure). Given the ability to determine the likely racial outcome of alternative testing protocols, New Haven would always be subject to disparate-impact liability except to the extent that the city adopts promotional mechanisms that yield no adverse statistical outcomes on racial minorities—tests that achieve rigid quotas based on demographic racial balancing.

2. Illicit Motives

Since *Village of Arlington Heights v. Metropolitan Housing Development Corp.,* the Supreme Court has subjected governmental actions motivated by discriminatory intent to strict scrutiny.[47] The Court has consistently applied this principle, not only to statutes that contain express racial classifications, but also to facially race-neutral statutes that are motivated by a racial purpose. Clearly, intentional discrimination is the core concern both Title VII and the Equal Protection Clause. Disparate impact, say its proponents, is a means of uncovering surreptitious intentional discrimination. For this reason, the Court has considered the "'correction of past discrimination to be a compelling government interest [when] eliminat[ing] the discriminatory effects of the past as well as [barring] like discrimination in the future.'"[48] Indeed, to the extent that the disparate-impact provision serves the "prophylactic" function of preventing intentional discrimination, it can be seen as a means of enforcing equal protection.[49]

a. Congressional motives

The problem is that the purpose of Title VII's disparate-impact provision is not limited to ascertaining hidden discriminatory intent or unconscious bias. If this were its sole purpose, as Justice Scalia noted in his concurrence, then employers would be permitted to assert a defense of "good faith."[50] The unavailability of that defense suggests that something other than discriminatory intent is at issue.

---

[47] Vill. of Arlington Heights v. Metro. Hous. Dev. Corp. 429 U.S. 252 (1977).

[48] Freeman v. Pitts, 503 U.S. 467, 511 (1992) (quoting Green v. County Sch. Bd. 391 U.S. 430, 438 n. 4 (1968)).

[49] See Tennessee v. Lane, 541 U.S. 509, 520 (2004) ("When Congress seeks to remedy or prevent unconstitutional discrimination, § 5 authorizes it to enact prophylactic legislation proscribing practices that are discriminatory in effect, if not in intent, to carry out the basic objectives of the Equal Protection Clause.").

[50] 129 S.Ct. at 2682.

Professor Primus adds that other technical features, such as the unavailability of damages in disparate-impact litigation, further demonstrate that Congress viewed disparate-impact as addressing something more and perhaps less than intentional discrimination.[51] This in turn raises a fundamental question: If Congress intended the disparate-impact provision to address something other than intentional discrimination, what exactly was Congress trying to address?

Congressional motives may have included a desire to increase racial diversity in the workforce other than by reducing discrimination. Former White House counsel Boyden Gray has disclosed that a "principal motivation" for the Civil Rights Act of 1991, which codified the disparate-impact provision, was to achieve racial balancing.[52] Some critics opposed the disparate-impact provision of the 1991 Act on the ground that it was a "government mandate for proportional quotas."[53] Indeed, law professor Nelson Lund has written that nearly all of the congressional debate leading up the Civil Rights Act of 1991 concerned "whether and to what extent" Title VII's disparate-impact provision encouraged employers to implement quotas or to discriminate in favor of minorities in other ways.[54] It has been observed that public resistance to quotas led Congress to strip from the 1991 Act many of the provisions that would have significantly increased the pressure on employers to achieve proportional representation.[55] The resulting compromise did not, however,

[51] Primus, *supra* note 36 at 521–522. To the extent that disparate-impact litigation reveals intentional discrimination, there is no reason why wrongdoers should not have to repay the victims of their discrimination to the same extent as in disparate-treatment cases. Congress's failure to provide for damages in disparate-impact cases suggests a tacit recognition that liable employers may be responsible for something less onerous than intentional discrimination.

[52] See Boyden Gray, The Civil Rights Act of 1991: A Symposium: Disparate Impact: History and Consequences, 54 La. L. Rev. 1487, 1491 (Jul. 1994) (quoting William Coleman, a prominent advocate for the disparate impact provision, as announcing his motivation during a White House meeting: "What I need is a generation of proportional hiring, and then we can relax these provisions.").

[53] Michael Carvin, Disparate Impact Claims Under the New Title VII, 68 Notre Dame L. Rev. 1153, 1153 (1993).

[54] Nelson Lund, The Law of Affirmative Action in and after the Civil Rights Act of 1991: Congress Invites Judicial Reform, 6 Geo. Mason L. Rev. 87, 88 (Fall 1997).

[55] See Kingsley R. Browne, Civil Rights Act of 1991: A "Quota Bill," a Codification of Griggs, a Partial Return to Wards Cove, or All of the Above?, 43 Case W. Res. L. Rev. 287, 380–381 (1993).

eliminate the use of statistical evidence to pressure employers to alter the demographic composition of their workforces.

b. Public employer motives

The other potentially problematic governmental motivations are those of public employers who rely upon disparate impact to justify their adoption of race-conscious practices. As the *Ricci* case illustrates, governmental employers rely on the disparate-impact provision when undertaking significant employment decisions. After all, Equal Employment Opportunity Commission regulations emphasized that Congress, in passing Title VII, "strongly encouraged employers . . . to act on a voluntary basis to modify employment practices and systems which constituted barriers to equal employment opportunity, without awaiting litigation or formal government action."[56] Employees who disfavor nonminority applicants by canceling promotions to avoid creating a disparate impact, as in *Ricci*, are likely engaged in race-based actions. Even before *Ricci*, the Court had rejected as "flawed" the argument that strict scrutiny did not apply because of the need to consider race for purposes of compliance with antidiscrimination law.[57]

3. Allocation of Benefits on the Basis of Race

With characteristic bluntness, Justice Scalia describes the allocation problem as a conflict between two legal principles. On the one hand, the disparate-impact provision "not only permits but affirmatively requires" race-based actions "when a disparate-impact violation would otherwise result."[58] On the other hand, "if the Federal Government is prohibited from discriminating on the basis of race, then surely it is also prohibited from enacting laws mandating that third parties (e.g., employers, whether private, State, or municipal) discriminate on the basis of race."[59] To Scalia, the facts of *Ricci* and other disparate-impact cases illustrate that the disparate-impact provision "place[s] a racial thumb on the scales, often requiring employers to evaluate the racial outcomes of their policies, and to make decisions

---

[56] 29 C.F.R. § 1608.1(b).

[57] Shaw v. Reno, 509 U.S. 630, 653 (1993).

[58] 129 S. Ct. at 2682 (2009).

[59] *Id.* (citations omitted).

based on (because of) those racial outcomes."[60] Such "racial decision-making," Scalia observes, is "discriminatory" under *Ricci*. Equal protection recognizes a "personal right[] to be treated with equal dignity and respect" which may be affronted by state actions that treat people less as individuals than as ethnically determined racial members.[61] This right reflects the "ultimate goal" of "eliminating entirely from governmental decisionmaking such irrelevant factors as a human being's race."[62] "The idea is a simple one: 'At the heart of the Constitution's guarantee of equal protection lies the simple command that the Government must treat citizens as individuals, not as simply components of a racial, religious, sexual or national class.'"[63] This command is violated when any individual "is disadvantaged by the government because of his or her race."[64] More broadly, strict scrutiny is applicable "when the government distributes burdens or benefits on the basis of individual racial classifications."[65] It was for this reason that the Court struck down the undergraduate admissions policy at the University of Michigan,[66] which failed to provide an individualized process of review, while upholding the law school admissions policy at that same institution.[67]

The firefighters argued with some plausibility that New Haven's actions more heavily emphasized racial labeling than the University of Michigan had in *Gratz v. Bollinger*. The allocation of benefits at issue here, it must be emphasized, is not merely that minorities disproportionately benefit from antidiscrimination laws because they are disproportionately subjected to discrimination. Instead, the concern here is that public employers, pressured by the prospect of disparate-impact liability, will employ preferences or quotas to

---

[60] *Id.*

[61] See City of Richmond v. J.A. Croson Co., 488 U.S. 469, 493 (1989) (plurality opinion).

[62] See *id.* at 495 (plurality opinion) (quoting Wygant v. Jackson Board of Education, 476 U.S. 267, 320 (1986) (plurality opinion)).

[63] Miller v. Johnson, 515 U.S. 900, 911 (1995), (quoting Metro Broadcasting, Inc. v. FCC, 497 U.S. 547, 602 (1990) (O'Connor, J., dissenting) (internal quotation marks and citations omitted)).

[64] Adarand v. Pena, 515 U.S. 200, 230 (1995).

[65] Parents Involved, 551 U.S. at 719.

[66] Gratz v. Bollinger, 539 U.S. 244, 271 (2003).

[67] Grutter v. Bollinger, 539 U.S. 306, 339 (2003).

groups disfavored by existing statistical disparities. The problem is not the existence or size of the resulting reallocation—which would be unobjectionable if it resulted from the elimination of intentional or subconscious discrimination—but rather the means employed.

Allocation of public benefits must be made on an individual basis, rather than on the basis of racial group membership. Failure to do so, the Court has instructed, may reflect racial prejudice,[68] perpetuate pernicious stereotypes,[69] foster social balkanization, and frustrate the goal of achieving a "political system in which race no longer matters."[70] As the *Adarand* Court said, "whenever the government treats any person unequally because of [his] race, that person has suffered an injury that falls squarely within the language and spirit of the Constitution's guarantee of Equal Protection."[71]

4. Ginsburg's Claim of Illusoriness

Justice Ginsburg's dissent denies the very existence of this conflict, arguing that "Title VII's disparate-treatment and disparate-impact proscriptions must be read as complementary." Before *Ricci*, Ginsburg argued, there had been not "even a hint of 'conflict' between an employer's obligations under the statute's disparate-treatment and disparate-impact provisions." It is only the *Ricci* opinion itself that "sets at odds the statute's core directives."

According to Professor Primus, thinking about the possibility "that equal protection might affirmatively prohibit the use of statutory disparate impact standards departs significantly from settled ways of thinking about antidiscrimination law."[72] Indeed, other

---

[68] See Palmore v. Sidoti, 466 U.S. 429, 432 (1984).

[69] Metro Broadcasting, 497 U.S. at 604 (O'Connor, J., dissenting) (citation omitted).

[70] Shaw, *supra* note 57 at 657.

[71] Adarand, 515 U.S. at 229–230.

[72] Primus, *supra* note 36 at 495. Indeed, *Davis* appeared to bless Congress's use of disparate impact in federal civil rights statutes. See Davis, 426 U.S. at 248. Primus, however, points out that this language was merely dicta. Primus, *supra* note 36 at 497–98. Moreover, as Primus observed, "equal protection has changed a great deal since *Davis* was decided, and the changes raise questions about a statute that places people in racial categories and measures liability in part by reference to the allocation of employment opportunities among those racial groups." *Id.* at 495. In Primus's provocative formulation, "Pre-*Davis*, many courts and commentators believed that state actions creating disparate impacts violated equal protection; post-*Adarand*, one could well ask whether state actions prohibiting disparate impact violate equal protection." *Id.* at 496 (internal citations omitted).

scholars had also observed that disparate-impact theory was widely accepted before *Ricci*.[73] In this sense, there is some truth to Ginsburg's argument. Moreover, to the extent that the disparate-impact provision is narrowly construed as a means to limit intentional or even unconscious discrimination, the conflict dissolves. The problem is that disparate impact has grown in ways that exceed that core purpose, and that is the source of its conflict with both disparate treatment and equal protection.

It may be true, as Ginsburg argued, that before *Ricci* the Supreme Court had never explicitly questioned the conformity of Title VII's disparate-impact component with equal protection. The Court's prior failure to recognize this conflict does not, however, prove that the conflict did not exist. What Ginsburg apparently means is that, before *Ricci*, conflicts between the two provisions were largely decided in favor of disparate impact—and disparate treatment had been construed narrowly enough to avoid the appearance of discord.

B. Ricci's Contribution to the Resolution of the Conflict

In a dark prophesy or curse, Ginsburg argues that the majority's opinion "will not have staying power."[74] Beyond its identification of the disconnect between disparate impact and equal protection, *Ricci* provides three potentially important contributions towards a resolution: the Court's treatment of race-neutral diversity policies, its discussion of disparate-impact quota-tendencies, and its establishment of a strong-basis-in-evidence standard.

1. Treatment of Race-Neutral Diversity Policies

The key fact in *Ricci* is that disparate-treatment analysis was triggered by an employment decision that arguably had race-conscious intent and effects, even though it treated employees of all races in an identical manner—by discarding their test scores. The intent of the employment decision could be characterized either as race-neutral (anti-discrimination compliance) or as race-conscious (altering the racial composition of promoted candidates). While both factors were undoubtedly in play, the separate opinions of Justices Kennedy, Scalia, and Samuel Alito all reflect the majority's conclusion that

---

[73] See, e.g., Deborah Malamud, Values, Symbols, and Facts in the Affirmative Action Debate, 95 Mich. L. Rev. 1668, 1693 (1997).

[74] Ricci, 129 S. Ct. at 2690.

race-conscious motivations predominated. The most salient lesson from Justice Kennedy's majority opinion is that facially neutral employment decisions will trigger disparate-treatment analysis when they are motivated by a predominantly race-conscious intent. After *Ricci*, one can draw a parallel lesson from Kennedy's *Parents Involved* concurrence: Facially neutral educational decisions will trigger strict scrutiny when they are motivated by a predominantly race-conscious intent. That link between the two opinions has broad implications.

The lower courts had decided that New Haven's decision to discard its examination results should not even trigger disparate-treatment analysis, because the action was facially neutral. As the district court reasoned, "all the test results were discarded, no one was promoted, and firefighters of every race will have to participate in another selection process to be considered for promotion."[75] Justice Ginsburg was similarly convinced that "New Haven's action, which gave no individual a preference, was simply not analogous to a quota system or a minority set-aside where candidates, on the basis of their race, are not treated uniformly.'"[76]

Some thought that this argument would appeal to Justice Kennedy. In *Parents Involved*, Kennedy had insisted that school boards could pursue diversity objectives through the way in which they select new school sites; draw attendance zones; allocate resources for special programs; recruit students and faculty; and track enrollments, performance, and other statistics.[77] Significantly, Kennedy argued, "These mechanisms are race conscious but do not lead to different treatment based on a classification that tells each student he or she is to be defined by race, so it is unlikely any of them would demand strict scrutiny to be found permissible."[78] Some commentators interpreted this language as a signal that race-neutral diversity plans would not trigger strict scrutiny even if they are motivated by a racial intent.[79] If this interpretation had been correct, however,

[75] Ricci v. DeStefano, 554 F. Supp. 2d 142, 158 (Conn. 2006), aff'd, 530 F.3d 87 (2d Cir. 2008) (per curiam).

[76] Ricci, 129 S. Ct. at 2696 (Ginsburg, J. dissenting) (quoting 554 F. Supp. 2d at 157).

[77] Parents Involved, 551 U.S. at 788 (Kennedy, J., concurring).

[78] *Id.*

[79] See, e.g., Samuel Estreicher, The Non-Preferment Principle and the "Racial Tiebreaker" Cases, 2006–2007 Cato Sup. Ct. Rev. 239, 249–50 (2007).

then Kennedy should have ruled with New Haven in *Ricci*. After all, if school districts can redraw school boundary lines in order to achieve diversity goals, then employers should be able to rewrite examinations in order to achieve antidiscrimination goals.

Viewed through the lens of *Ricci*, *Parents Involved* now takes on a different complexion. In light of *Ricci*, it now appears that some commentators' initial interpretation was incorrect. Kennedy's *Parents Involved* concurrence may now be better understood as arguing that facially neutral state actions should be subjected to strict scrutiny whenever racial considerations are the "predominant" governmental motivation. Kennedy prefers this standard, adopted from voting rights cases, to the less stringent "but for" standard, under which defendants might be held liable if they would not have engaged in the challenged conduct "but for" the impermissible motivation.[80] This is consistent with the position, established in *Ricci*, that facially race-neutral governmental practices that are motivated by racial purposes should be treated judicially in the same manner as if their race-consciousness were overt.[81] Taking *Ricci* and *Parents Involved* together, the Court has established that racially neutral governmental actions with a predominant racial motive trigger both strict scrutiny and disparate-treatment analysis.

The scope of decisions covered by this new rule is potentially broad, encompassing racially motivated decisions by school districts to redraw school boundaries or employ socioeconomic factors in student assignment decisions, state universities to institute percent-rank plans, and private universities to give admissions or financial

---

[80] Kennedy's point is that government bodies sometimes have mixed motives for the questionable decisions that they make. A school board, for example, may redraw school boundary lines because it reduces overcrowding, simplifies bus routes, and increases each school's student body diversity in terms of both family income and race. Under the predominant-motivation approach, the school board's decision would trigger strict scrutiny only if racial diversity is the board's predominant motivation. If the board's other goals figured equally in its decisionmaking, then race is not the predominant motivation, even if they would not have been sufficient to support the decision without the added factor of race.

[81] Some commentators interpreted *Parents Involved* in this manner from the start. See George La Noue & Kenneth L. Marcus, "Serious Consideration" of Race-Neutral Alternatives in Higher Education, 57 Cath. U. L. Rev. 991, 1012–13 (Sum. 2008); Brian Fitzpatrick, Essay, Can Michigan Universities Use Proxies for Race After the Ban on Racial Preferences?, 13 Mich. J. Race & L. 277, 290 (2007).

aid preferences on the basis of either student economic status or such factors as whether a student is the first person in his family to attend college. In all of these cases, strict scrutiny and disparate-treatment analysis are both triggered.

This should have significant ramifications for policies like the University of Texas's former "Ten Percent Plan," under which UT guaranteed admissions to students graduating within the top 10 percent of their high school class.[82] There is considerable evidence, including contemporaneous admissions, which suggest that Texas policymakers adopted this plan in order to diversify the racial composition of UT's student body, in the face of a judicial decision which precluded the explicit consideration of race. As in *Ricci*, the government used a facially neutral policy to pursue a racially conscious agenda. Under *Ricci* and *Parents Involved*, the Ten Percent Plan should trigger strict scrutiny to the extent that Texas's racial motivations predominated in the institution of the plan.[83]

Where strict scrutiny applies, the defendant not only must proffer a compelling governmental interest but also must satisfy the stringent demands of narrow tailoring: Have less racially intrusive alternatives been subjected to the rigors of "serious, good-faith consideration"?[84] Is the program limited by explicit sunset provisions?[85] Does the institution regularly monitor the program to determine its continuing necessity?[86]

[82] See Brian T. Fitzpatrick, Strict Scrutiny of Facially Race-Neutral State Action and the Texas Ten Percent Plan, 53 Baylor L. Rev. 289, 291–93 (2001).

[83] See, e.g., Kenneth L. Marcus, Diversity & Race-Neutrality, 103 Nw. U. L. Rev. Colloquy 163, 166–67 (2008), available at http://ssrn.com/abstract=1284652.

[84] See Grutter v. Bollinger, 539 U.S. 306, 339 (2003) (requiring "serious, good faith consideration of workable race-neutral alternatives").

[85] See *id.* at 342 (articulating the principles that "all governmental use of race must have a logical end point" and that "the durational requirement can be met by sunset provisions in race-conscious admissions policies and periodic reviews to determine whether racial preferences are still necessary to achieve student body diversity"); Croson, 488 U.S., at 510 (plurality opinion) (discussing the importance of the principle that any "deviation from the norm of equal treatment of all racial and ethnic groups is a temporary matter. . ."); Stephanie Monroe, Guidance Letter, Use of Race in Student Admissions, (Aug. 28, 2008) at 2, available at http://www.ed.gov/about/offices/list/ocr/letters/raceadmissionpse.html (reminding postsecondary institutions that "the use of race must have a logical end point").

[86] See *id.* (reminding postsecondary institutions that "[p]eriodic reviews are necessary" when race is used as a factor in college admissions).

2. The Tendency of Disparate Impact Towards Quotas

Ricci is also important for its recognition, particularly in the Scalia concurrence, that disparate-impact compliance can lead to quotas. The question of quotas is significant because the Court had long established that "[p]referential treatment and the use of quotas by public employers subject to Title VII can violate the Constitution, and it has long been recognized that legal rules leaving any class of employers with 'little choice' but to adopt such measures would be 'far from the intent of Title VII.'"[87] *Ricci* reiterates *Watson's* concern that disparate impact, when not sufficiently constrained by evidentiary standards, will tend to pressure employers to establish quotas. "Even worse," *Ricci* adds, is the prospect that employers could reengineer employment practices in order to achieve a "preferred racial balance."[88] Thus, the *Ricci* Court held that anything less than the strong-basis-in-evidence standard creates the risk of "a *de facto* quota system, in which . . . an employer could discard test results . . . with the intent of obtaining the employer's preferred racial balance."[89]

Justice Kennedy's majority opinion insists that quota-seeking designed for disparate-impact compliance offends Title VII's express language, which does not call for outright racial balancing.[90] Justice Scalia deftly pierces this conceit: While disparate-impact laws may not require employers to impose racial quotas, neither do such laws provide a "safe harbor."[91] Yet, in effect, disparate impact forces employers to impose quotas when quotas are the most cost-effective way to satisfy the requirements of disparate impact. Under these circumstances, Scalia argues, Congress is as liable for the employer's imposition of a quota as if Congress had established the quota itself. By analogy, he hypothesizes a private employer who refrains from imposing a racial quota but who deliberately designs hiring practices to reach the same result. Such an employer, Scalia points out, would be liable for employment discrimination, "just one step up the

---

[87] Watson, 487 U.S. at 993 (internal citations omitted).

[88] Ricci, 129 S. Ct. at 2675.

[89] *Id.*

[90] *Id.* at (citing § 2000e–2(j)).

[91] Ricci, 129 S. Ct. at 2681 (Scalia, J., concurring).

chain."[92] From this analogy, Scalia reasons that governmental pressure to alleviate disparate impact "would therefore seemingly violate equal protection principles."[93] It does not matter that race is considered only "on a wholesale, rather than retail, level" because equal protection requires the government to treat citizens as individuals.[94]

3. The Strong-Basis-in-Evidence Test

As *Ricci*'s Kennedy-Scalia dialogue on the topic of quotas suggests, public employers must be held to a standard that can ferret out disparate-impact concerns that are merely pretextual. Thus, when the Court addresses the conflict between disparate impact and equal protection, it may be tempted to rely upon *Ricci*'s strong-basis-in-evidence test. Unfortunately, the new standard is problematic in several respects: its inappropriate focus on the government's interest in liability-avoidance (as opposed to its interest in nondiscrimination), its apparent unworkability, and the unlikelihood that it is sufficiently well-considered to endure over time.

a. Incorrect focus on liability-avoidance

The first concern is that *Ricci*'s discussion of the government's interest in avoiding disparate-impact liability is, at best, a circuitous articulation of the government's proper interest. To the extent that disparate impact is a trustworthy device for identifying actual discrimination, state actors who are sincere about compliance should be less concerned about the prospect of liability than they are about the violation itself. In other words, they should be more concerned about doing the right thing than they are about being sued for doing wrong. The government's proper interest, then, is to provide equal protection, not to avoid liability for discrimination. The fact that New Haven articulates its interest primarily in terms of liability-avoidance merely confirms that the city was driven by the *ex post* disparate impact of the promotional examination, not by an *ex ante* conviction that certification of the examination would actually have been discriminatory. This is a distressing symptom of the pathology of disparate-impact doctrine.

---

[92] *Id.* at 517.

[93] *Id.*

[94] *Id.*

The focus on liability-avoidance generates subsidiary problems for the strong-basis-in-evidence standard. For example, should the public employer's basis in evidence depend on factors unrelated to the presence of actual discrimination, such the credibility of witnesses, the availability of evidence, the sympathetic qualities of the likely plaintiffs, or its own unsympathetic qualities? To the extent that the government's requisite interest is defined in terms of the basis in evidence for its calculation of potential liability, the answer to all these questions must be yes. Of course, none of these questions addresses the prospect that the government is engaged in discrimination sufficient to justify actions that would otherwise violate equal protection. Obviously, the government's interest is in avoiding conduct that would actually be discriminatory, regardless of whether it would be found to be such by a court. The strong-basis-in-evidence standard should support the government's determination that the practices in question are intentionally discriminatory or at least that they are motivated by unconscious bias.

b. Ineffectiveness of the standard

Justice Ginsburg argues that the strong-basis-in-evidence standard is inapposite, vague, and yet perhaps more stringent than the majority acknowledges. With some justification, she argues that "[o]ne is left to wonder what cases would meet the standard and why the Court is so sure this case does not." Ginsburg is probably correct to complain that the majority "stacks the deck . . . by denying respondents any chance to satisfy the newly announced strong basis-in-evidence standard." As she argues, the proper course would have been to remand the case for a determination of New Haven's compliance.[95]

Indeed, Justice Kennedy is flatly wrong when he states, in defense of the Court's preemptory ruling, that New Haven's evidence of disparate-impact liability was "nothing more" than "a significant statistical disparity." New Haven had also presented less statistically discriminating alternatives that would have promoted important business objectives, such as underweighting the written component

---

[95] See, e.g., Johnson v. California, 543 U. S. 499, 515 (2005).

of the examination or eliminating it altogether—as the nearby town of Bridgeport had with marked success.[96]

Given the findings that the lower courts had already made, it is likely that they would have found that New Haven did in fact have a strong basis in evidence to believe that it faced probable disparate-impact liability. This would in turn have led to another Second Circuit decision in favor of New Haven, which the Court could have reversed only by deciding the constitutionality of Title VII's disparate-impact provision. Justice Alito responds to Ginsburg's dissent by presenting copious evidence to show that New Haven discarded its examination results in order to satisfy a politically powerful constituency, rather than to avoid unintentional discrimination. Alito's evidence is quite convincing: New Haven's supposed fear of disparate-impact liability may well have been a pretext to engage in politically driven racial balancing. This does not, however, address Ginsburg's underlying point.

Regardless of New Haven's motives, a strong case can be made that the city would have been liable under existing disparate-impact law to the extent that it had failed adequately to consider alternative procedures that would have generated less racially disparate results. It is not clear whether Kennedy and Alito's failure to acknowledge this point demonstrates the unworkability of the substantial-basis standard or merely that it was incorrectly applied. Even if the latter were the case, however, it does not speak well of a newly created judicial standard when the issuing court cannot apply it properly.

c. Likely impermanence of the standard

Will the strong-basis-in-evidence test endure even in the context in which *Ricci* presents it—as a standard for determining when state actors may legitimately take race-conscious action to avoid disparate-impact liability? Ginsburg predicts that it will not. She is likely correct but not necessarily for the reasons that she has in mind. Ginsburg clearly yearns for the day when an ideologically

---

[96] Ginsburg was also concerned by testimony that some exam questions were not relevant to New Haven's firefighting procedures and that firefighters had unequal access to study materials which fell in part along racial lines. That is because many white candidates could get materials and assistance from family members in the fire department, while most minority candidates were "first generation firefighters" who lacked such support networks. Ricci, 129 S. Ct. at 2693 (Ginsburg, J., dissenting).

reconstructed Court will overturn *Ricci* and embrace a vigorous conception of disparate impact. Depending on the timing of future Supreme Court vacancies, that is certainly a possibility. It is also possible, however, that a Court substantially similar in composition to the present one will continue the work that *Ricci* began. That Court would likely narrow the scope of the disparate-impact provision in order to conform it to the requirements of the Equal Protection Clause. Interestingly, *Ricci*'s strong-basis standard would no better survive the ruling of a sympathetic Court than it would an unsympathetic one.

In one respect, this point may belabor the obvious. Suppose the Court interprets the Equal Protection Clause expansively and strikes down or substantially limits the disparate-impact provision. In that case, the *Ricci* strong-basis-in-evidence standard would no longer be applicable to state actors who fear that their employment practices have a disparate impact. Even with a strong basis, the use of race-conscious measures would be a constitutionally forbidden non-starter. The more interesting question is how this equal protection result would affect non-state actors who are subject to Title VII. Would the *Ricci* standard apply to a large private employer that contemplated race-conscious action to address potential disparate-impact liability? Probably not. After all, Congress cannot require employers to engage in conduct that, if federally conducted, would violate the Equal Protection Clause. If the equal protection bars state actors from engaging in race-conscious activity in order to avoid a disparate impact, then it also bars Congress from requiring private employers to do so. For this reason, further deliberations on the issues underlying *Ricci* will likely doom the *Ricci* standard, whether the reviewing Court is sympathetic to *Ricci*'s premises or not.

C. The Proper Resolution

1. Anti-Discrimination Device

The core purpose of the disparate-impact provision is the government's compelling interest to identify and eliminate intentional or unconscious discrimination that cannot be proved through the disparate-treatment provision.[97] Given the difficulty of proving conscious

---

[97] See, e.g., Griggs v. Duke Power Co., 401 U.S. 424, 431 (1971) ("Discriminatory preference for any group, minority or majority, is precisely and only what Congress has proscribed.").

intent, let alone the near-impossibility of demonstrating implicit bias, disparate impact provides a means of enforcing antidiscrimination laws in an age when bigots seldom announce their prejudices.[98] Employers seldom leave behind direct evidence of discriminatory animus.[99] This is particularly true in the case of large corporate employers, whose intent must be gleaned from their various agents, who may have differing motivations, overlapping authority, and practices that differ from formal policy. For this reason, the disparate-impact provision permits plaintiffs to prove discrimination by presenting evidence of the discriminatory effects of employment practices and by demonstrating that the employer's justification offered for these practices is pretextual.[100] As discussed above, the narrowly tailored use of disparate-impact analysis to effect this purpose is constitutionally unproblematic.

In practice, the constitutionality of applying disparate impact will turn on the question of narrow tailoring. Difficult problems arise, as arguably occurred in the *Ricci* case, when public employers shift the allocation of employment benefits in order to avert racial disparities that cannot be justified by business necessity. The government should not be in the position of requiring actual, present, intentional discrimination as a means of averting the prospect of potential, perhaps unconscious, discrimination. Even when disparate-impact analysis is employed as a prophylactic device to avert intentional discrimination, it should be used in a way that does not generate other forms of discrimination. The use of racially preferential practices, quotas or double standards, for example, will seldom—if ever—be the least intrusive means of achieving the government's antidiscrimination interest. Courts will likely need to address this issue on a case-by-case basis to ensure that the method chosen to avert discrimination is least likely to exacerbate the problem it is intended to redress.

---

[98] See, e.g., Washington v. Davis, 426 U.S. 229, 253 (1976) (Stevens, J., concurring) ("Frequently the most probative evidence of intent will be objective evidence of what actually happened.").

[99] U.S. Postal Service Bd. of Governors v. Aikens, 460 U.S. 711, 716 (1983) ("There will seldom be 'eyewitness' testimony to the employer's mental processes.").

[100] George Rutherglen, Disparate Impact Under Title VII: An Objective Theory of Discrimination, 73 Va. L. Rev. 1297, 1309–10 (1987).

2. Leveling Device

Beyond its role in combating intentional and unconscious discrimination, disparate impact has also been used more broadly as a means of redistributing employment opportunities. As the Court explained in *Watson v. Fort Worth Bank & Trust*, "the necessary premise of the disparate-impact approach is that some employment practices, adopted without a deliberately discriminatory motive, may in operation be functionally equivalent to intentional discrimination."[101] The idea is that employers who lack discriminatory animus may nevertheless, and for no good reason, adopt practices that have the effect of limiting employment opportunities for women and minorities. As *Griggs* instructed, "Congress directed the thrust of the Act to the consequences of employment practices, not simply the motivation."[102] The government's motive in redistributing employment opportunities, however, absent intentional or unconscious discrimination, is on weaker ground than its motive in avoiding actual discrimination.

Because this latter strand of disparate-impact law is on much weaker footing constitutionally, one potential approach is to interpret the disparate-impact provision as serving only the purpose of combating intentional or unconscious discrimination.[103] As Justice Scalia and Professor Primus have pointed out, however, this interpretation is difficult to maintain in light of various statutory provisions, such as the absence of a good-faith defense. Given this problem, the Court may be forced to strike down the disparate-impact provision and encourage Congress to reenact it without its problematic features.[104] This will ensure that disparate impact is grounded on a compelling governmental interest.

---

[101] Watson, 487 U.S. at 987 (1988).

[102] Griggs, 401 U.S. 424, 432 (1971); see also Watson v. Fort Worth Bank & Trust, 487 U.S. 977, 987 (1988) ("[T]he necessary premise of the disparate impact approach is that some employment practices, adopted without a deliberately discriminatory motive, may in operation be functionally equivalent to intentional discrimination.").

[103] Primus, *supra* note 36.

[104] Roger Clegg has floated legislative language to produce this result. See Clegg, *supra* note 44, at 34–35:

> In any action brought under 42 U.S.C. 2000e–2(k), no respondent shall be found liable if it can demonstrate that the challenged practice was neither adopted with the intent of discriminating on the basis of race, color, religion, sex, or national origin nor applied unequally on the basis of race, color, religion, sex, or national origin.

Professor Primus argues that limiting disparate impact to its role in addressing intentional discrimination fails to address what he considers to be a larger purpose of antidiscrimination law: eradicating "historically embedded hierarchies."[105] As a practical matter, Primus concedes that disparate-impact litigation no longer plays a significant role in creating opportunities for large numbers of nonwhite workers. However, Primus argues that disparate impact's "symbolic or expressive functions" are nevertheless important because they shape the way in which the public understands antidiscrimination law and policy.[106] For this reason, Primus urges the courts not to perpetuate "a worldview on which racial inequity is primarily the product of present bad actors rather than largely a matter of historically embedded hierarchies."[107]

These arguments, however, provide a less-than-compelling rationale for abiding conduct that violates the fundamental right to equal protection of the laws. Symbolic or expressive functions may be important, but they cannot outweigh the harms of actual discrimination. Moreover, disparate impact's symbolic and expressive functions are not entirely benign. When it degenerates into preferential treatment, dual standards, and racial quotas, disparate impact may affect the institutionalization of race-consciousness and, with it, the entrenchment of pernicious stereotypes, social division, resentment, and stigmatization.[108] Nevertheless, there may be some truth to the notion that governmental agencies must be permitted to address— in a race-conscious but not racially preferential manner—those structural forms of bias that, although not supported by current discriminatory intent, nevertheless affect the demographic compositions of the workforce. This issue is best understood in terms of disparate impact's function as a "diversity management device."

3. Diversity Management Device

A third function of disparate impact is to identify practices that, while not supported by present discriminatory intent, have the function of restricting employment opportunities by gender or race. This

---

[105] Primus, *supra* note 36 at 499.

[106] *Id.*

[107] *Id.*

[108] See, e.g., Clegg, *supra* note 44 at 11–14.

might be described as a "diversity management" device in the sense that it is intended to address frictions that arise from human differences, rather than to address present intentional or subconscious discrimination or to advance particular racial outcomes.[109] For example, an agency may have a dominant culture—a "body of unspoken and unexamined assumptions, values, and mythologies"—which historically developed around a predominantly white male workforce and to which white males can more easily adapt than members of other groups.[110] Certain practices within this culture (e.g., advancing employees who seem to be a good "fit") may have an adverse impact on minorities and women.

The requirement that employers use less-disparity-producing alternatives can break down practices that "operate as 'built-in headwinds' for minority groups and are unrelated to measuring job capability."[111] One example is the use of height and weight requirements for prison guards that may exclude most women, rather than directly measuring strength or other job-relevant variables.[112] In *Griggs,* for example, the Court held that Title VII prohibits disparate impact regardless of an employer's intentions, announcing that Title VII "proscribes not only overt discrimination but also practices that are fair in form, but discriminatory in operation."[113]

The last two sections explained, however, why Congress cannot statutorily disassemble such cultural obstacles to equal opportunity. Investigating and responding to the racial impacts of institutional culture are, after all, race-conscious activities that require some degree of racial categorization. Strict judicial scrutiny, which applies in this situation, cannot be satisfied by a government interest in disassembling employment obstacles—unless they result from conscious or unconscious discriminatory animus. On the other hand, it is troublesome to suggest that government actions to address such cultural issues—for example, auditing agency practices to identify nondiscriminatory obstacles to equal advancement—cannot be

---

[109] See Gill Kirton and Anne-Marie Greene, The Dynamics of Managing Diversity: A Critical Approach, 2d ed. (2005) at 123–127.

[110] See R. Roosevelt Thomas Jr., From Affirmative Action to Affirming Diversity, in Harvard Business Review on Managing Diversity (2001) at 16–17.

[111] Griggs v. Duke Power Co., 401 U.S. 424, 432 (1971).

[112] See Dothard v. Rawlinson, 433 U.S. 321 (1977).

[113] Griggs, 401 U.S. at 426 n.1.

undertaken proactively by state actors without offending equal protection. While Congress may not be able to mandate such activities, it seems that public employees must be permitted to voluntarily undertake them.

V. Conclusion

There is one point on which Justice Ginsburg agreed with her former clerk's "Equal Protection and Disparate Impact" analysis in the *Harvard Law Review.* "The very radicalism of holding disparate impact doctrine unconstitutional as a matter of equal protection," Primus insisted (and Ginsburg approvingly quoted) "suggests that only a very uncompromising court would issue such a decision."[114] This may be true. At the same time, it is no less true that the very incompatibility of current disparate-impact doctrine with equal protection suggests that only a very irresponsible court could uphold the former in a challenge based on the latter. At any rate, it is not clear that "compromising" is the best attribute that we can expect from a court enforcing equal protection nor that we should prefer our jurisprudence in this area to be "compromised."

This article has explained why Title VII's disparate-impact provision, as currently drafted, cannot survive a challenge based on the Equal Protection Clause. Congress can best save the provision by providing an exception for good-faith employer behavior that is not motivated by any form of discriminatory animus. Even when limited in this manner, however, disparate impact is still susceptible to various forms of abuse when it provides the basis for race-conscious state actions. This can be curtailed by judicious enforcement of the narrow-tailoring requirement. Specifically, the courts should look with great skepticism at state actions that entail any form of racial or ethnic preference or quota. On the other hand, equal protection does not prohibit—and indeed its underlying values may encourage—the voluntary, non-preferential efforts by public or private employers to eliminate policies and practices that tend to limit equal employment opportunities without adequate business or public policy justification.

---

[114] Primus, *supra* note 36 at 585.

Into the Pre-emption Thicket: *Wyeth v. Levine*

Roger Pilon*

Introduction

One is easily entangled in a thicket. That seems the condition of the Supreme Court after *Wyeth v. Levine*[1]—entangled in a thicket of its own making, its pre-emption jurisprudence. Pre-emption flows from the Constitution's Supremacy Clause.[2] Stated simply, given the Constitution's provisions for dual sovereignty, its division of powers between the federal and state governments, pre-emption stands for the idea that, in a conflict between the two, federal law trumps state law.[3] Yet for all that simplicity—"conflict" is deceptively simple—the Court over the years, as one seasoned litigator has put it, "has issued a confusing, erratic succession of fragmented tort preemption decisions involving various types of federally regulated products and state-law causes of action. . . . Practicing attorneys, as well as judges and legal scholars, have found it virtually impossible to reconcile these decisions."[4]

Undaunted, I shall wade into this thicket to try to make such sense as I can of *Wyeth*, where the Court found that federal law

---

* Roger Pilon is vice president for legal affairs at the Cato Institute, director of Cato's Center for Constitutional Studies, and publisher of the *Cato Supreme Court Review*.

[1] 555 U.S. ____, 129 S. Ct. 1187 (2009).

[2] "The Constitution, and the Laws of the United States which shall be made in Pursuance thereof . . . shall be the supreme Law of the Land; and the Judges in every State shall be bound thereby, any Thing in the Constitution or Laws of any State to the Contrary notwithstanding." U.S. Const. art. VI, cl. 2.

[3] For a useful overview of the subject in these pages, analyzing the six pre-emption cases the Court considered in its 2007 term, see Daniel E. Troy and Rebecca K. Wood, Federal Preemption at the Supreme Court, 2007–2008 Cato Sup. Ct. Rev. 257 (2008).

[4] Lawrence S. Ebner, Four Myths About Federal Preemption of State Tort Claims, 24 (19) Washington Legal Foundation Legal Backgrounder, June 5, 2009. Although I will be focusing on the operation of pre-emption in the area of pharmaceuticals, pre-emption issues arise in virtually every area of federal activity.

regulating a drug warning label did not protect pharmaceutical giant Wyeth against a failure-to-warn claim under state common law. I will begin by setting forth the facts of the case, then summarize, critically, Justice John Paul Stevens's opinion for the Court. Next, using as a springboard Justice Clarence Thomas's concurrence in the judgment alone, I will set forth some first principles of the matter to reach a quite different judgment than he did. Finally, I will turn to Justice Samuel Alito's dissent, joined by Chief Justice John Roberts and Justice Antonin Scalia, which gets it largely right, I believe, and should have been the opinion for the Court.

Before beginning, however, three preliminary points need noting. First, as with so many complex and confused areas of the modern Court's jurisprudence, the problems surrounding the Court's pre-emption jurisprudence stem in significant part from the felt imperatives of *stare decisis*, which is all the more reason to return to first principles, as Justice Thomas attempts to do, rather than try to square current cases with past mistakes.

Second, and following closely, something of a cottage industry has arisen around this matter, with its own nomenclature, not surprisingly. It would be useful, therefore, to repeat the outline of the subject that Daniel Troy and Rebecca Wood set forth here a year ago:

> [F]ederal pre-emption may be "expressed or implied" in the pertinent federal regime. Express pre-emption involves discerning the meaning of an explicit preemption provision. There are at least two types of implied pre-emption: field pre-emption . . . and conflict pre-emption. Field pre-emption recognizes limited, but exclusive, areas of federal domain even in the absence of an explicit preemption provision from Congress. Conflict pre-emption tends to paint with a narrower brush and applies to particular issues where it is impossible for a private party to comply with both state and federal law, or where state law stands as an obstacle to the accomplishment and execution of the full purposes and objectives of Congress or of a federal agency acting within the scope of its congressionally delegated authority.[5]

---

[5] Troy and Wood, Federal Preemption, *supra* note 3 at 258–260 (internal quotation marks and citations omitted) (four spellings of "preemption" changed to "pre-emption" for consistency within block quote).

Wyeth involved a claim by the company, defending against the plaintiff's failure-to-warn claim, of implied conflict pre-emption, which the Court rejected.

Finally, the "politics" of this issue are not straightforward. One ordinarily thinks of conservatives and libertarians as supporting limited federal power, especially police power over health and safety matters, a power that belongs mainly with the states. Yet here, for constitutional reasons discussed below, most such people believe that in many if not most cases federal power should trump state power.[6] By contrast, modern liberals are ordinarily thought to favor federal power, especially federal regulatory power over economic affairs under Congress's power to regulate interstate commerce. Yet many of those liberals, in the tort bar and among consumer advocates and state officials, will be found arguing for the supremacy of state law as providing more protection for individual "rights" than federal law may provide.[7] My concern here is less with politics, however, than with what the Constitution requires. Accordingly, I turn now to the case.

"Tragic Facts Make Bad Law"[8]

In brief, on April 7, 2000, plaintiff-respondent Diana Levine, seeking relief for the second time that day from severe migraine headaches and nausea, suffered irreversible gangrene followed by amputation of her right forearm after her physician's assistant administered defendant-petitioner Wyeth's drug Phenergan by the "IV-push" method. The injectable form of the drug could be administered either intramuscularly or intravenously. And intravenous administration could be performed by either the slow "IV-drip" method or the faster, but more risky, IV-push method, where inadvertent intra-*arterial* injection would lead to the tragic results that followed here.

---

[6] See Review & Outlook, Pre-empting Drug Innovation, Wall St. J., Mar. 5, 2009, at A16.

[7] See Supreme Court Decision in Wyeth v. Levine Victory for Consumers, Alliance for Justice Press Release, March 4, 2009, available at http://www.afj.org/about-afj/press/03042009.html ("The six justices who stood up for accountability sent a clear message that FDA approval does not necessarily grant a corporation a license to hit and run," said AFJ president Nan Aron.).

[8] Thus does Justice Alito begin his dissent. Wyeth, 129 S. Ct. at 1217 (Alito, J., dissenting).

The risks of inadvertent intra-arterial injection from using the IV-push method were well known. In fact, Phenergan's labeling contained both detailed instructions about the procedure and no fewer than six separate warnings about its risks, warnings that had evolved over the years and been approved by the federal Food and Drug Administration (FDA). Notwithstanding those warnings, Levine and her physician decided to employ the procedure to obtain the benefits it promised.

Levine brought and won a negligence action in Vermont state court against the clinic, her doctor, and the doctor's assistant, who "disregarded Phenergan's label and pushed [a double dose of] the drug into the single spot on [Levine's] arm that is *most* likely to cause an intra-arterial injection."[9] She then sued Wyeth, alleging

> that the labeling was defective because it failed to instruct clinicians to use the IV-drip method of intravenous adminis- tration instead of the higher risk IV-push method. More broadly, she alleged that Phenergan is not reasonably safe for intravenous administration because the foreseeable risks of gangrene and loss of limb are great in relation to the drug's therapeutic benefits.[10]

The trial court rejected Wyeth's motion for summary judgment, which argued that Levine's failure-to-warn claims were preempted by federal law, holding that there was no merit in either Wyeth's field pre-emption argument or its conflict pre-emption argument. Regarding Wyeth's conflict argument, the court found no evidence that the company had tried to strengthen the warning or that the FDA had disallowed a stronger warning. After reviewing FDA's 45-year history of Phenergan regulation, the trial judge instructed the jury that Wyeth's compliance with FDA requirements "did not estab- lish that the warnings were adequate."[11] The jury found "that Wyeth was negligent, that Phenergan was a defective product as a result of inadequate warnings and instructions, and that no intervening cause had broken the causal connection between the product defects and the plaintiff's injury."[12] It awarded Levine $6.7 million.

[9] *Id.* at 1226 (original emphasis).

[10] *Id.* at 1191–1192.

[11] *Id.* at 1193.

[12] *Id.*

In a "comprehensive opinion," the court denied Wyeth's motion for judgment as a matter of law and determined further "that there was no direct conflict between FDA regulations and Levine's state-law claims because those regulations permit strengthened warnings without FDA approval on an interim basis."[13] The Vermont Supreme Court affirmed, with a dissent by its chief justice. It found that the jury verdict did not conflict with FDA's labeling requirements and that "federal labeling requirements create a floor, not a ceiling, for state regulation."[14]

Justice Stevens for the Court

Justice Stevens began his opinion for the Court by noting that Wyeth raised two separate pre-emption arguments: first, that it would have been impossible for the company to comply with the state-law duty to modify Phenergan's label without violating federal law; and, second, that recognizing the state-law duty creates an unacceptable "obstacle to the accomplishment and execution of the full purposes and objectives of Congress."[15] As discussed below, those two arguments are more closely connected than the Court seemed to appreciate. Before it addressed them, however, the Court offered a "preface"—identifying two factual propositions decided at trial, emphasizing two legal principles that guided its analysis, and reviewing the history of the controlling federal statute.

The two factual propositions are: first, "that Levine's injury would not have occurred if Phenergan's label had included an adequate warning about the risks of the IV-push method of administering the drug;" and, second, "that the critical defect in Phenergan's label was the lack of an adequate warning about the risks of IV-push administration."[16] It's hard to know what to make of those "factual propositions:" as Justice Alito wrote in dissent, "it is unclear how a 'stronger' warning could have helped respondent; after all, the physician's assistant who treated her disregarded at least six separate warnings that are already on Phenergan's labeling, so respondent

[13] *Id.*

[14] *Id.* (internal quotation marks and citations omitted).

[15] *Id.* at 1193 (quoting Hines v. Davidowitz, 312 U.S. 52, 67 (1941) (internal quotation marks omitted)).

[16] *Id.* at 1194.

would be hard pressed to prove that a seventh would have made a difference."[17] Since the jury found only that the six warnings were insufficient, not what additional or different warnings would have been sufficient, one suspects that *no* warning would have been found sufficient if the result warned against had materialized.

The two guiding legal principles are: first, that "the purpose of Congress is the ultimate touchstone in every pre-emption case;"[18] and, second, that "the historic police powers of the States were not to be superseded by the Federal Act unless that was the clear and manifest purpose of Congress."[19] Reviewing the history of the Federal Food and Drug Act and the later Federal Food, Drug, and Cosmetic Act (FDCA), the Court took note of the 1962 amendments that shifted the burden of proof for drug safety and efficacy from the FDA to the manufacturer and, in addition, "added a saving clause, indicating that a provision of state law would only be invalidated upon a 'direct and positive conflict' with the FDCA."[20] Moreover, the Court noted that "when Congress enacted an express pre-emption provision for medical devices in 1976, it declined to enact such a provision for prescription drugs."[21]

Wyeth's Impossibility Argument

Its preface completed, the Court turned to Wyeth's first argument, that it would be impossible for the company to comply with the state-law duty to modify Phenergan's label without violating federal law. But rather than address the substantive purposes and objectives that Congress may have had, which implicitly underpin Wyeth's impossibility argument, the Court offered what in the end is a vacuous analysis of regulatory changes and inferences to be drawn from them: Generally speaking, the Court said, after FDA approval of a label, subsequent changes require FDA approval; but, FDA "changes being effected" (CBE) regulations allow *strengthening* a warning "to reflect newly acquired information" or "new analyses of previously

[17] *Id.* at 1217–1218.

[18] *Id.* at 1219 (quoting Medtronic, Inc. v. Lohr, 518 U.S. 470, 485 (1996) (internal quotation marks omitted)).

[19] *Id.* at 1194–1195 (quoting Lohr, 518 U.S. at 485) (internal quotation marks and citation omitted).

[20] *Id.* at 1196.

[21] *Id.*

submitted data" prior to receiving FDA approval;[22] and the burden remains on the manufacturer to make such changes.

Plainly, the implication of the Court's analysis is that Wyeth did not strengthen its label "to reflect newly acquired information" or "new analyses of previously submitted data." The issue turns, then, on whether there was any such information or data. And on that, the Court was vague, at best:

> The record is limited concerning what newly acquired information Wyeth had or should have had about the risks of IV-push administration of Phenergan because Wyeth did not argue before the trial court that such information was required for a CBE labeling change. Levine did, however, present evidence of at least 20 incidents prior to her injury in which a Phenergan injection resulted in gangrene and an amputation.[23]

Absent further information, however, we have no way of knowing whether 20 incidents over 45 years is an acceptable number—all drugs and drug administration procedures entail risk, after all. The Court noted that the first incident came to Wyeth's attention in 1967, and it added that Wyeth notified FDA and worked with the agency to change Phenergen's label. But it then said that in later years (which years we're not told), "as amputations continued to occur, Wyeth could have analyzed the accumulating data and added a stronger warning about IV-push administration of the drug."[24] And it concluded that, "when the risk of gangrene from IV-push injection of Phenergan became apparent"—again, just what point in time that was we don't know—"Wyeth had a duty to provide a warning that adequately described that risk."[25]

Wyeth responded, of course, that it did just that, that it did provide warnings that adequately described the risk, but that the physician's assistant ignored them. Given that failure, the dissent raised the crucial question—whether yet another warning would have made any difference at all. Indeed, we don't know how many of the 20 other incidents over the years arose from a similar cause, from a

[22] 73 Fed. Reg. 49603, 49609.

[23] *Id.* at 1197.

[24] *Id.*

[25] *Id.* at 1198.

failure to heed the warnings that were given. In the end, clearly, the Court's conclusion is little more than a prescription for ever more failure-to-warn rulings, because it flows not from any independent risk assessment based on costs and benefits, but simply from the occurrence of the untoward incident. In sum, the Court's analysis is circular: if there is an incident, the warning, ipso facto, will be deemed inadequate.

Wyeth's Purposes and Objectives Argument

Thus, as noted above, the Court failed to recognize that Wyeth's "impossibility" or "conflict" argument is intimately connected to its second argument, that recognizing a state-law duty to modify Phenergan's label creates an unacceptable "obstacle to the accomplishment and execution of the full purposes and objectives of Congress." The connection stems from the fact that the FDA, pursuant to Congress's purposes and objectives in enacting the FDCA, provides that independent cost-benefit risk assessment, at least in principle if not in fact. To be sure, incidents such as the Levine case factor into such assessments. But it is the FDA's cost-benefit assessment, not some jury verdict, *ex post*, that is the standard for deciding whether a warning is adequate. Here, the warning was to give notice about the risk involved in the procedure, not to discourage all use of the procedure and the benefits it provided.

We come, then, to the first of the Court's two "guiding principles," that "the purpose of Congress is the ultimate touchstone in every pre-emption case," and to the Court's analysis of Wyeth's second argument. Unfortunately, the analysis all but ignores that first principle, focusing instead on the *second* of its guiding principles, that "the historic police powers of the States were not to be superseded by the Federal Act unless that was the clear and manifest purpose of Congress"—the so-called presumption against pre-emption. In fact, the Court appears to read the first principle's "purpose of Congress" as denoting simply Congress's *pre-emptive* purpose, or lack thereof, not its *substantive* purpose in enacting the statute in the first place. The closest the Court comes to the latter is in its characterization of Wyeth's claim: quoting from Wyeth's brief, the Court says that Wyeth maintains that Levine's tort claims are pre-empted "because they interfere with 'Congress's purposes to entrust an expert agency to make drug labeling decisions that strike a balance between competing objectives.'"[26]

Well what are those "competing objectives"? The Court never grapples with that substantive question, with Congress's "purposes and objectives" in enacting the FDCA and establishing the FDA. Yet, absent an express pre-emption provision, understanding those substantive purposes and objectives is absolutely crucial to understanding whether and how pre-emption operates in the FDCA context. In brief, to be discussed a bit more fully below, Congress's objective clearly was to ensure that drugs and the procedures for administering them are safe and effective. But "safe" and "effective" are sometimes themselves competing objectives. In fact, that precisely is the case here. The IV-drip method of administering Phenergan is safer but less effective than the IV-push method—that's why, on her second visit to the clinic that day, Levine and her physician decided to pursue the less safe but more effective IV-push method. Yet the Court is oblivious to this trade-off. It is as if the Court were trying to eliminate all risk. If the IV-push method is effectively prohibited, so too will be the risk associated with it—and the benefits from its availability.

Thus deprived of the issues required for a full and proper implied pre-emption analysis—issues found in Congress's *substantive* purposes and objectives—the Court narrowed its focus, looking only to "secondary" sources, so to speak. Responding to Wyeth's contention that the FDA's labeling requirements establish both a floor and a ceiling, for example, the Court found the evidence all to the contrary. Congress's silence constituted the bulk of that evidence, however: in particular, the Court noted that Congress had not provided a federal remedy for consumers harmed by unsafe or ineffective drugs. "Evidently, it determined that widely available state rights of action provided appropriate relief for injured consumers."[27] That may be so, but how probative is that evidence of the question at issue? After all, many claims are properly adjudicated under state law—perhaps claims about adulterated or mislabeled drugs, or about design or manufacturing defects more generally. But if among such claims is the language of drug warnings—which follows, under the FDCA,

---

[26] *Id.* at 1999 (citation omitted).

[27] *Id.*

only from extensive FDA testing—then what is the point of FDA testing? If 50 states remain free, in effect, to draft that language themselves, then in any given adjudication the FDA "floor" will be meaningless. (More on this in the next section.)

It appears, however, that the FDA did eventually become concerned about the problem state common-law decisions might pose for the drug labeling part of its mission. Thus, in 2000 it issued a notice of proposed rulemaking pertaining to the content and format of prescription drug labels, saying that the rule "did not propose to preempt State law."[28] But when the agency finalized the rule in 2006—"without offering States or other interested parties notice or opportunity for comment,"[29] the Court notes—the preamble to the rule, on which Wyeth relied before the Court, declared that the FDCA establishes "both a 'floor' and a 'ceiling,'" so that "FDA approval of labeling . . . preempts conflicting or contrary State law."[30]

Thus, the question for the Court was how much weight to give "an agency's mere assertion that state law is an obstacle to achieving its statutory objectives."[31] Not much, it seems, since the Court found that the FDA's views on this point were "inherently suspect" in light of its notice-and-comment "procedural failure[s]."[32] Moreover, the Court continued, the preamble "reverses the FDA's own long-standing position" that state law not only posed no obstacle but, in fact, complemented its statutory mission by uncovering "unknown drug hazards and provid[ing] incentives for drug manufacturers to disclose safety risks promptly."[33] To be sure, there are cases in which state law suits have uncovered unknown hazards, but where were the unknown hazards here, and what was not disclosed by the FDA-approved labeling? On its facts, this is not a complicated case: Wyeth gave a proper warning; the physician's assistant ignored it.

Clearly, to have properly determined whether state law like this is an obstacle to the FDA's mission, the Court would have had to consider evidence beyond Congress's silence and the agency's

---

[28] 71 Fed. Reg. 3922, 3969.

[29] Wyeth, 129 S. Ct. at 1201.

[30] Id. at 1200.

[31] Id. at 1201.

[32] Id.

[33] Id. at 1202.

evolving views. It would have had to engage with the substance of the matter, with Congress's "purposes and objectives" in passing the FDCA in the first place—at least sufficiently to take notice of the two sides of this issue, the costs *and* the benefits. That it did not do. Like the jury, it saw only costs, which it attributed to an inadequate warning. And even then it did not see all of the costs: it was oblivious to the costs of *over*warning, for example, which discourages and may even eliminate the use of efficacious drugs and effective procedures for administering them. The FDA's mission is two-fold: to ensure the safety of drugs; but to ensure their availability as well.

Justice Thomas and First Principles

It may be noteworthy that in his 6,000-word opinion for the Court, not once did Justice Stevens use the word "Constitution" or any of its cognates. Justice Thomas made up for that, grounding his concurrence with the Court's judgment in the Constitution's provisions for dual sovereignty, but taking strong exception to the Court's "implicit endorsement of far-reaching implied pre-emption doctrines," especially its "'purposes and objectives' jurisprudence. Under this approach," he wrote, "the Court routinely invalidates state laws based on perceived conflicts with broad federal policy objectives, legislative history, or generalized notions of congressional purposes that are not embodied within the text of federal law."[34] Taking thus a narrow textualist approach to the pre-emption question, he concurred only with the Court's judgment.

Beginning with First Principles

Thomas began his concurrence by drawing from the theory of Federalist No. 51 and from recent cases invoking its argument that dual sovereignty was meant to provide "a double security . . . to the rights of the people."[35] Although the Constitution provides for concurrent federal and state power, the power of the states, he noted, is "subject only to limitations imposed by the Supremacy Clause."[36] That clause gives the federal government a decided advantage, however: "[a]s long as it is acting within the powers granted it under

---

[34] *Id.* at 1205.

[35] *Id..*

[36] *Id.* (quoting Taffin v. Levitt, 493 U.S. 455, 458 (1990) (internal quotation marks omitted)).

the Constitution, Congress may impose its will on the States."[37] But there, precisely, is a fundamental limitation on federal power, which Thomas stressed: as James Madison wrote in Federalist No. 45, "[t]he powers delegated by the proposed constitution to the federal government, are few and defined," while "[t]hose which are to remain in the state governments, are numerous and indefinite."[38] And there is a second limitation as well: if this "delicate balance" is to be preserved, "the Supremacy Clause must operate only in accordance with its terms,"[39] which means that the clause must give "supreme" status "only to those [federal laws] that are 'made in Pursuance' of '[t]his Constitution.'"[40]

There are thus "two key structural limitations in the Constitution that ensure that the Federal Government does not amass too much power at the expense of the States:" the doctrine of enumerated and thus limited federal powers, and "the complex set of procedures that Congress and the President must follow to enact 'Laws of the United States'"[41]—in particular, the bicameral and Presentment Clause requirements. In sum, pre-emptive effect can be given only to those federal laws that flow from Congress's enumerated powers and those "federal standards and policies that are set forth in, or necessarily follow from, the statutory text that was produced through the constitutionally required bicameral and presentment procedures."[42]

Given those constitutional principles, "[c]ongressional and agency musings . . . do not satisfy the Art. I, § 7 requirements for enactment of federal law and, therefore, do not pre-empt state law under the Supremacy Clause."[43] Emphasizing his textualism, Thomas added that when analyzing statutes or regulations, "'[e]vidence of pre-emptive purpose [must be] sought in the text and structure of the [provision] at issue' to comply with the Constitution."[44] And again:

---

[37] *Id.* (quoting Gregory v. Ashcroft, 501 U.S. 452, 460 (1991) (internal quotation marks omitted)).

[38] *Id.* at 1206 (internal quotation marks omitted).

[39] *Id.*

[40] *Id.,* citing the Supremacy Clause, *supra* n.2.

[41] *Id.* at 1206–1207, citing INS v. Chadha, 462 U.S. 919, 945–946 (1983).

[42] *Id.* at 1207.

[43] *Id.*

[44] *Id.* (quoting CSX Transp., Inc. v. Easterwood, 507 U.S. 658, 664 (1993)).

"Pre-emption must turn on whether state law conflicts with the text of the relevant federal statute or with the federal regulations authorized by that text."[45]

Those constitutional and interpretive principles established, Thomas turned at last to the Court's *Wyeth* analysis, again distinguishing the Court's two categories of implied conflict pre-emption—where compliance with both federal and state law is "impossible," and where state law stands as an obstacle to Congress's "purposes and objectives." He would be focusing his fire on the second, he explained, since "[t]he Court has generally articulated a very narrow 'impossibility standard'—in part because the overly broad sweep of the Court's 'purposes and objectives' approach has rendered it unnecessary for the Court to rely on 'impossibility' preemption."[46]

Largely agreeing with the Court's impossibility analysis in the case at hand, and concerned more about the Court's broader pre-emption jurisprudence, Thomas reflected first on the Court's less-than-clear distinction between a narrow "physical impossibility" standard and its more general "direct conflict" standard. Under either, however, "[t]he text of the federal laws at issue [here] do [sic] not require that the state-court judgment at issue be pre-empted."[47] It was not physically impossible for Wyeth to strengthen its label and still comply with federal law. And "there is no 'direct conflict' between the federal labeling law and the state-court judgment."[48] Of particular importance for the discussion of first principles just below, Thomas concluded that "the text of the statutory provisions governing FDA drug labeling, and the regulations promulgated thereunder, do not give drug manufacturers an unconditional right to market their federally approved drug at all times with the precise label initially approved by the FDA,"[49] a conclusion he summarized succinctly as: "the relevant federal law did not give Wyeth a right that the state-law judgment took away."[50]

---

[45] *Id.* at 1208.

[46] *Id.* at 1209 (internal citation omitted).

[47] *Id.*

[48] *Id.* at 1210.

[49] *Id.*

[50] *Id.* at 1211.

Turning finally to his larger concern, the Court's "entirely flawed" purposes and objectives jurisprudence, Thomas's main objections were threefold: first, constitutional fidelity; second, the Court's reliance on extra-textual materials such as legislative history, divined notions of congressional purpose, and even congressional inaction; and, third, the implications of such reliance for judicial review and its proper limits.

He located the origins of this "flawed" approach in *Hines v. Davidowitz*,[51] then turned to *Geier v. American Honda Motor Co.*[52]—distinguished by the *Wyeth* majority, but relied on by the dissent—where the statute contained an express pre-emption provision, but also a seemingly contradictory saving clause. In his analysis of the two cases, Thomas charged the Court with "look[ing] far beyond the relevant federal statutory text and instead embark[ing] on its own freeranging speculation about what the purposes of the federal law must have been."[53] In *Hines* the Court looked at statements by members of Congress, public sentiment, and other things; in *Geier* its inquiry included agency comments made when promulgating its regulation and statements made by the government in its brief to the Court.

Turning to *Wyeth*, Thomas faults the Court for relying on Congress's silence—its failure here to exempt drug labeling from state tort judgments—which may be pertinent, he said: "But the relevance is in the fact that no statute *explicitly* pre-empts the lawsuits, and not in any inferences that the Court may draw from congressional silence about the motivations or policies underlying Congress' failure to act."[54] Indeed, he added, the Court's willingness to guess about the inferences to be drawn from Congress's silence could just as easily be used to give unduly broad pre-emptive effect to federal law.[55]

Drawing his argument to its conclusion, Thomas returned to the Constitution: "[O]ur federal system in general, and the Supremacy Clause in particular, accords pre-emptive effect to only those policies

---

[51] 312 U.S. 52 (1941).

[52] 529 U.S. 861 (2000).

[53] Wyeth, 129 S. Ct. at 1212.

[54] *Id.* at 1216 (emphasis added).

[55] *Id.* at 1216–1217.

that are actually authorized by and effectuated through the statutory text."[56] That being so, the Court's "purposes and objectives" pre-emption jurisprudence takes it "beyond the scope of proper judicial review."[57] The Court's role "is merely 'to interpret the language of the statute[s] enacted by Congress.'"[58]

In sum, like the *Wyeth* majority, but for more searching reasons, Thomas did not grapple with the substantive issues underlying the FDCA and their implications for the pre-emption question at issue here. Drawing on fundamental constitutional and interpretive principles, he argued even more narrowly than did the majority, emphasizing textualism and seeming to say that only explicit or express pre-emption will do. The question for us is whether his is a true account of the First Principles of the matter.

First Principles Reconsidered

Justice Thomas is to be commended for his willingness, without embarrassment, to turn frequently to the Constitution's First Principles—modern "constitutional law" notwithstanding.[59] And his insistence on textualism and judicial restraint (or modesty) are virtues as well. In his concurrence he has raised serious issues that need to be addressed. In the end, however, one must ask whether so narrow a textualism is appropriate when the Court is wrestling with pre-emption, one of the Constitution's more difficult because more textually underdetermined matters. Not even express pre-emption provisions, after all, are invariably unambiguous.[60] Thus, the Court will

[56] *Id.* at 1216.

[57] *Id.*

[58] *Id.* at 1217 (citing Barnhart v. Sigmon Coal Co., 534 U.S. 438, 461 (2002)).

[59] See, e.g., United States v. Lopez, 514 U.S. 549, 584 (1995) (Thomas, J., concurring).

[60] See, e.g., Michael Greve, Preemption Strike, National Review Online, March 23, 2009 (available at http://article.nationalreview.com/?q = YTE0N2ZjNDEyYmQ3 MTAxYTQ0Y2I2Y2I4MmFiOGJlMmQ =) (original emphasis):

> Because Congress cannot possibly foresee [all state] stratagems, it cannot "clearly" preempt them. For example, the clearest federal preemption provision of all prohibits states from administering "a law or regulation related to fuel economy standards." California's proposed greenhouse-gas standards do not simply "relate to" fuel economy; they *are* fuel-economy standards. Even so, federal courts have upheld them against preemption challenges because California describes them as emission standards instead.

For examples of courts rejecting pre-emption challenges of this type, see, e.g., Central Valley Chrysler-Jeep v. Goldstene, 529 F. Supp. 2d 1151 (E.D. Cal. 2007) and Green Mountain Chrysler-Plymouth-Dodge v. Crombie, 508 F. Supp. 2d 295 (D. Vt. 2007).

often have to turn to extra-textual materials to properly understand and interpret even those texts—and will have to do so *a fortiori* when the claim is one of implied pre-emption.

The question, then, is whether the Court's interpretive responsibilities in any pre-emption case are executed well or poorly. And given the range of subjects over which pre-emption may be at issue, that is no easy question to answer, which is one reason why this is such a legal thicket. It may be, in fact, that general principles will take one only so far in a given case, after which the facts take over. Still, it is important to begin with the principles of the matter, as Thomas did, and take them as far as possible.

And the place to start as a general matter is with the theory of dual sovereignty, as Thomas rightly saw. But immediately upon doing so we're taken to the "purposes and objectives" of dual sovereignty, namely, to provide "a double security ... to the rights of the people."[61] And that takes us to more fundamental "First Principles," to questions about "the rights of the people," and to our founding document, the Declaration of Independence, where the Founders, in the name of those rights, set forth the theory of government that the Framers would institute through the Constitution 11 years later.

In a nutshell,[62] the Declaration, grounding the nation in the natural rights strain of natural law, makes it clear that we're born with our rights, we don't get them from government, and we institute government mainly to secure those rights through powers "derived from the consent of the governed." By implication—given the wide variety of ways individuals might exercise their right to pursue happiness, and the considerable difficulties, accordingly, of achieving the kind of broad consent the theory requires for political legitimacy—the scope of the governmental powers envisioned is decidedly limited, leaving us free to pursue happiness as we wish, mostly in our private capacities.

The Constitution captures that vision of individual liberty and limited government in several ways: the Preamble, like the Declaration, invoking the tradition of state-of-nature theory, wherein the

---

[61] Federalist No. 51; see also *supra*, note 35 and accompanying text.

[62] I have discussed these issues more fully in Roger Pilon, The Purpose and Limits of Government, Cato's Letters No. 13 (1999).

people, by right, "do ordain and establish this Constitution" and hence the government authorized by it; the doctrine of delegated, enumerated, and thus limited federal powers; the separation of powers, defined functionally; the division of powers, leaving most power with the states; provision for a bicameral legislature, a unitary executive, an independent judiciary, and periodic elections to fill the offices set forth in the document—those were among the ways the people at once both empowered and limited the government they created.

As a practical legal charter, the Constitution was of course far more detailed and specific than the Declaration, even as it sought to secure, institutionally, the Declaration's vision.[63] Yet the 18 powers delegated to Congress and enumerated in Article I, section 8, were still aimed largely at securing our rights—the function of government set forth in the Declaration—either directly (the war powers, the power to establish lower courts, to secure intellectual property) or instrumentally (the power to tax and to borrow to support those other powers).

But most of our right-securing power[64] was left with the states in the form of the general police power—the power to define and enforce our substantive and procedural rights through either common-law adjudication or statutory declaration. Ideally, those adjudicative and declaratory functions would be grounded in reason, not mere political will.[65] But objective reason goes only so far before subjective values have to be brought into the process. That occurs

---

[63] With the Constitution's oblique recognition of slavery, failing which there would have been no "united" states, the Declaration's vision was imperfectly secured, to be sure. It would take the ratification of the Civil War Amendments to "complete" the Constitution, at least in principle. See Robert J. Reinstein, Completing the Constitution: The Declaration of Independence, Bill of Rights and Fourteenth Amendment, 47 Temple L. Rev. 361 (1993).

[64] John Locke, the philosophical father of the nation, called that the "Executive Power"—the power each of us has in the state of nature to secure his rights, which we yield up to government to exercise on our behalf when we enter the state of civil society. John Locke, The Second Treatise of Government, in Two Treatises of Government § 13 (1690).

[65] On the evolution of those processes, see Edward S. Corwin, The "Higher Law" Background of American Constitutional Law (1955), at 26 ("[T]he notion that the common law embodied right reason furnished from the fourteenth century its chief claim to be regarded as higher law.").

in at least four areas in particular: nuisance, risk, remedies, and enforcement. Regarding nuisances like noise, particulate matter, odors, and the like, "public lines" need to be drawn defining where one man's right to the active enjoyment of his rights ends and his neighbor's right to the quiet enjoyment of his rights begins. Likewise, the remedial value of a life or a limb is not a matter for pure reason; nor are the second-order investigative and prosecutorial rights that arise when first-order substantive rights are violated, as is evidenced by such evaluative words as "unreasonable" and "probable" in the Fourth Amendment.

Our focus here, however, is on risk, which arises in infinite variety. As with those other categories, there is no bright line, rooted in reason, defining how much risk one may put one's neighbor to before his right to be free from such risk is implicated. On one hand, a risk-free world is a world without action and hence without life. On the other hand, we don't allow people to drive down city streets at any speed they wish. Obviously, people have different tastes for risk. Mutual consent can accommodate many of those differences. But where consent is not an option, for whatever reason, *notice* serves to reduce risk. Some risks are "open and obvious," to use an old common-law term. Others are hidden, at least to strangers, and need to be made open and obvious by giving notice so that strangers, by being made aware of the risk, may adjust their behavior accordingly.

Pharmaceutical drugs provide extraordinary benefits but entail risks as well. As the manufacturers of those drugs learn about the benefits and risks, through FDA testing procedures or otherwise, they can reduce the risks to users by giving notice about use, dosages, administration, and the like. That is what labeling is all about. Proper labeling does not eliminate the risk. It simply makes it known to the physician or user. Just how much or what kind of notice (or warning) is "proper" is not a matter written in stone or subject to determination by pure reason. The "reasonable man" standard comes to the fore here. Again, too little notice may introduce more risk than is desirable. Too much may reduce the availability of benefits that are desirable.

But once a balance is struck, and a public line has been drawn, the parties know their respective rights and obligations in this otherwise uncertain domain. Drug manufacturers know the kind of notice they must give to discharge their obligation not to put users at too great a risk. Potential users now know the risk associated with the drug and, accordingly, can decide whether and how to approach it.

What if there is no public line, however? Or what if there are many—say, 50—ever-changing public lines? In that case, our rights and obligations are uncertain and unstable. On one hand, juries could tell injured drug consumers that they used at their peril (not likely). On the other hand, they could tell drug manufacturers that they sold at their (legal) peril. Since the second is the far more likely scenario—certainly under our current tort law—the regime of strict (absolute?) manufacturer liability that follows either discourages the research, development, and sale of drugs or vastly raises the prices for all concerned, including consumers. It is, in short, an uncertain and inefficient world.

In fact, *mutatis mutandis,* that scenario is not entirely unlike the one the Framers faced at the time they drafted the Constitution, and so we return to that story, which sheds light on the question of who gets to draw the public lines the theory of rights requires if "the rights of the people" are to be fleshed out fully. Under the Articles of Confederation, states had erected tariffs and related measures to protect local merchants and manufacturers from out-of-state competitors. That was leading, in turn, to the breakdown of trade among the states—not unlike the scenario envisioned if 50 different sovereigns require, in effect, 50 different risk warnings. (And even then the warning may not be deemed "adequate" if the risk materializes.) In fact, one of the main reasons a new Constitution was thought necessary was to enable the federal government to check that growing state protectionism.[66] Thus, *Congress* was given the power to regulate—or "make regular"—commerce among the states—essentially, a power to negate state actions that frustrated free interstate trade and to do the few other things that might be needed to facilitate that commerce.[67]

Properly understood, then, Congress's commerce power, notwithstanding its use today as an instrument of virtually unbounded

---

[66] The other main reason was the need for a stronger national government and a stronger federal executive to deal with foreign affairs. See John Yoo, The Powers of War and Peace, ch. 3 (2005).

[67] See, e.g., Randy E. Barnett, The Original Meaning of the Commerce Clause, 68 U. Chi. L. Rev. 101 (2000). Cf. Richard A. Epstein, The Proper Scope of the Commerce Power, 73 Va. L. Rev. 1387 (1987).

federal policy, is at bottom a limited federal police power. Aimed mainly at ensuring a national market free from invidious state interference, it enables Congress not only to negate such interference but also, affirmatively, to facilitate free trade by regularizing otherwise potentially balkanized markets. As one aspect of that function, Congress may need to draw the "public lines" just discussed to more surely define the rights and obligations of parties engaged in interstate commerce. That, in fact, is one of the basic "purposes and objectives" of the FDA, at least as its functions have evolved. Here, it is to determine, after extensive testing, just what warning label is "adequate" such that drug manufacturers can meet their obligation to give notice about the risks associated with their products and users can have that notice so they can then act accordingly.

In this context, then, the FDA's function—pursuant to Congress's "purposes and objectives" in enacting the FDCA—is to assess both the risks and the benefits of a drug and, with labeling, to set both a "floor" and a "ceiling." It is to draw that line, in this inherently line-drawing context, that defines the rights and obligations of the respective parties. Through the *positive* law that emerges, manufacturers can meet their inherently unclear *natural* law obligation to give adequate notice to users about the risk. Having done so, having respected the right of the user to be given such notice, the manufacturer has a right to immunity from suit for damages if the user decides to approach the risk and the outcome warned against materializes—to say nothing of the case here, where the user's assistant ignored the warning.

By contrast, for the Court to treat the FDA-determined warning as a "floor," on which states may add further warnings, is to render Congress's responsibility under the Commerce Clause and the agency's function under the statute all but pointless. Further, by rendering that federal "check" on state power pointless, the Court compromises the "purposes and objectives" of dual sovereignty—to provide "a double security ... to the rights of the people," in this case, the rights of manufacturers. In effect and in fact, the Court creates an unfounded "right" in users, at the expense of the manufacturer's genuine rights. For having been warned of the risk, the user here, now informed, has a right to pursue the risky procedure and enjoy the benefits that flow from it. But if the untoward outcome warned against materializes, then the user has yet a second "right," at the expense of the manufacturer, to be made whole. It's a "risk-free" scenario for the user.

Finally, recasting this with reference to the so-called presumption against pre-emption, given that our system of dual sovereignty leaves the general police power over health and safety with the states, that presumption is sound, for rights are initially defined and enforced by the states. And in the absence of federal regulation, state common-law decisions based on *rational* tort law might very well draw reasonable and fairly uniform lines concerning adequate and inadequate warnings such that all parties have a fairly clear understanding of their respective rights and obligations. But whatever the original impetus for Congress's having decided to exercise its commerce power and regulate drug safety and efficacy, there is today, given the tort law we see at play in cases like *Wyeth,* ample support for federal regulation under the *original* rationale for that power—to cure the inefficiencies of regulatory balkanization. But given that rationale plus the Supremacy Clause, there is no constitutional support for adding state regulation on top of federal regulation. On the contrary, the very "purposes and objectives" that justify federal regulation justify pre-empting state regulation.

None of that is to say that FDA regulation has been flawless, of course. The agency has been too risk-averse, if anything, keeping efficacious drugs off the market for too long and denying access to potentially life-saving drugs when individuals would be only too willing to assume the risk.[68] (Allowing state tort law to regulate labeling would only exacerbate that problem, of course.) But the question here is whether, absent an express pre-emption provision, FDA labeling regulations should be read as implicitly pre-empting state common-law judgments. Given Congress's substantive "purposes and objectives" in enacting the FDCA in the first place, the answer is yes.

In sum, then, express pre-emption is not necessarily valid: as Thomas noted, the underlying regulation may be beyond Congress's authority under the doctrine of enumerated powers, assuming there is anything left of that doctrine after *Gonzales v. Raich;*[69] or the scope

---

[68] See Roger Pilon, New Right to Life, Wall St. J., Aug. 10, 2007, at A11 (discussing Abigail Alliance v. von Eschenbach, 495 F.3d 695 (D.C. Cir. 2007)).

[69] 545 U.S. 1 (2005).

of the pre-emption may not reach the issue before the Court. But neither is implied pre-emption necessarily invalid, especially if Congress is pre-empting a field or, as here, if state regulation would be inconsistent with the substantive objects and purposes of Congress.

It seems, therefore, that Justice Thomas's understandable concern for text-based adjudication and judicial restraint led him to a narrower vision of the Constitution's First Principles than is needed when pre-emption is before the Court. Often, laws "made in Pursuance" of "[t]his Constitution" cannot be understood properly on their text alone, without inquiry into the "purposes and objectives" of Congress in enacting them and of agencies in executing them. Moreover, when one factors in the true "purposes and objectives" of the Commerce Clause, under which so much federal regulation is enacted, and adds the Supremacy Clause as well, a richer conception of dual sovereignty emerges, protecting "the rights of the people" against both federal *and* state power.

Interestingly, as the dissent notes, the Court's first great Commerce Clause case, *Gibbons v. Ogden*, was arguably an implied conflict preemption case, where the Court found that a federal coasting statute, enacted under the commerce power, trumped a state law that restricted the rights of would-be entrepreneurs.[70] For present purposes, however, what is more interesting about the case is how Chief Justice John Marshall, in deciding it, went out of his way to emphasize that constitutional text must be interpreted in light of its "purposes and objectives." Thus, he was concerned to avoid not only "an enlarged construction" but a "narrow construction, which would cripple the government, *and render it unequal to the object for which it is declared to be instituted* . . . ."[71] Marshall's focus, plainly, was on the very purpose of the government the Constitution created. He continued in that vein: "If . . . there should be serious doubts respecting the extent of any given power, it is a well settled rule, *that the objects for which it was given . . . should have great influence in the construction.*"[72] Finally, to the same effect: "We know of no rule for construing the extent of such powers [as the commerce power],

---

[70] Wyeth, 129 S. Ct. at 1229, n.14 (Alito, J., dissenting) (citing Gibbons v. Ogden, 22 U.S. 1 (1824)).

[71] Gibbons, 22 U.S. at 233–234 (emphasis added).

[72] *Id.* at 234 (emphasis added).

other than is given by the language of the instrument which confers them, *taken in connexion with the purposes for which they were conferred.*"[73] Today, of course, the commerce power is used promiscuously to run roughshod over the powers of states and "the rights of the people" alike. But it has its uses to protect those rights, and they need to be rediscovered.

Justice Alito's Dissent

In his trenchant dissent, Justice Alito made it clear from the start that this was not a complicated case. (Accordingly, I will simply summarize the dissent.) Its tragic facts aside, it was a simple medical malpractice case. Ignoring that conclusion, drawn from the facts, the Court turned "a common-law tort suit into a 'frontal assault' on the FDA's regulatory regime for drug labeling,"[74] Alito charged. In so doing, it upset "the well-settled meaning of the Supremacy Clause and [the Court's] conflict pre-emption jurisprudence," holding "that a state tort jury, rather than the ... FDA, is ultimately responsible for regulating warning labels for prescription drugs."[75]

Showing no reluctance to examine Congress's "purposes and objectives," Alito began his argument by going not to Congress's pre-emptive but straight to its substantive purpose in enacting the FDCA: "Congress made its 'purpose' plain in authorizing the FDA—not state tort juries—to determine when and under what circumstances a drug is 'safe.'"[76] After reviewing several relevant statutory and regulatory provisions and procedures—"spanning an entire part of the Code of Federal Regulations, with seven subparts and 70 separate sections"—he concluded that "a drug's warning label 'serves as the standard under which the FDA determines whether a product is safe and effective.' Labeling is '[t]he centerpiece of risk management,' as it 'communicates to health care practitioners the agency's formal, authoritative conclusions regarding the conditions under which the product can be used safely and effectively.'"[77] And

---

[73] *Id.* at 235 (emphases added).

[74] Wyeth, 129 S. Ct. at 1218 (Alito, J., dissenting) (quoting the brief for the United States as amicus curiae, at 21).

[75] *Id.* at 1217–1218.

[76] *Id.* at 1219.

[77] *Id.* (quoting 50 Fed. Reg. 7470 (1985) and 71 Fed. Reg 3934 (2006)).

he added that "[n]either the FDCA nor its implementing regulations suggest that juries may second-guess the FDA's labeling decisions."[78]

Turning to the cases, Alito found that once the FDA had decided that a drug was safe and effective, no state could countermand that decision.[79] Thus, "it is irrelevant in conflict pre-emption cases whether Congress 'enacted an express pre-emption provision at some point during the FDCA's 70-year history.' . . . Rather, the ordinary principles of conflict pre-emption turn solely on whether a State has upset the regulatory balance struck by the federal agency."[80] Analyzing conflict pre-emption, he continued, involves a simple "two-step process of first ascertaining the construction of the federal and state laws and then determining the constitutional question whether they are actually in conflict."[81] Likewise, "it is irrelevant [here] that the FDA's preamble does not 'bear the force of law,'" a charge the majority had made, "because the FDA's labeling decisions surely do."[82] Here, as in all such cases, "the sole question is whether there is an 'actual conflict' between state and federal law; if so, then pre-emption follows automatically by operation of the Supremacy Clause."[83]

Conclusion

In sum, even for textualists, if the text of a constitutionally authorized statute or regulation implies the purposes or objectives of the measure, as invariably it does after thoughtful analysis, and a state law conflicts with the administrative execution of those purposes or objectives, in the sense that the law upsets the balance the agency has struck between competing objectives, then the effect of the Supremacy Clause is clear: The state law must yield. It's no more complicated than that.

The pre-emption problem is prevalent today, of course, because regulations—federal, state, and local—are ubiquitous. The expansion of the commerce power beyond its original purpose is the main

---

[78] *Id.* at 1220.

[79] *Id.* (citing Buckman Co. v. Plaintiffs' Legal Comm., 531 U.S. 341, 348 (2001)).

[80] *Id.*

[81] *Id.* (internal quotation marks and citations omitted).

[82] *Id.* at 1228 (citing 21 U.S.C. § 355).

[83] *Id.*

source of the problem. But adding yet more conflicting regulations at the state and local level is no answer to that problem. After its decision in *Wyeth v. Levine,* however, it is the answer the Court has given us.

linkLine's Institutional Suspicions

Daniel A. Crane*

Antitrust scholars are having fun again. Not so long ago, they were the poor, redheaded stepchildren of the legal academy, either pining for the older days of rigorous antitrust enforcement or trying to kill off what was left of the enterprise.[1] Other law professors felt sorry for them, ignored them, or both.

But now antitrust is making a comeback of sorts.[2] In one heady week in May of 2009, a front-page story in the *New York Times*[3] reported the dramatic decision of Christine Varney—the Obama Administration's new Antitrust Division head at the Department of Justice—to jettison the entire report on monopolization offenses released by the Bush DOJ just eight months earlier.[4] In a speech before the Center for American Progress, Varney announced that the Justice Department is "committed to aggressively pursuing enforcement of Section 2 of the Sherman Act."[5] As if to prove that "shock and awe" enforcement against monopolists is still possible, two days later the European Commission released its decision fining Intel nearly $1.5 billion for beating up on AMD in the microprocessor

---

* Professor of Law, University of Michigan Law School.

[1] This is merely a figure of speech and is not intended to disparage the poor, redheads (which I used to be when I had hair), or stepchildren.

[2] For an insightful description of antitrust's comeback in the legal academy, see Joshua Wright, Don't Call It a Comeback, Truth on the Market Blog, available at http://www.truthonthemarket.com/2009/04/11/dont-call-it-a-comeback/ (April 11, 2009).

[3] Stephen Labaton, Administration Plans to Strengthen Antitrust Rules, N.Y. Times May 11, 2009.

[4] Press Release, USDOJ, Competition and Monopoly: Single-Firm Conduct Under Section 2 of the Sherman Act, available at http://www.usdoj.gov/atr/public/reports/236681.pdf.

[5] Christine A. Varney, Vigorous Antitrust Enforcement in This Challenging Era (May 11, 2009), available at http://www.usdoj.gov/atr/public/speeches/245711.htm.

market.[6] Suddenly, the antitrust community felt an electric current that it hadn't felt for many years.[7]

A point of note for those who checked out of antitrust law when Ronald Reagan was president: What is significant about this recent surge is not so much that the prospect of public antitrust enforcement has reemerged. Some areas of public antitrust enforcement have endured despite ideological shifts between administrations.[8] For example, the Reagan, Bush I, and Bush II administrations were very active in anti-cartel enforcement and even brought some merger challenges.[9] What is notable is the prospect that monopolization law—the branch of antitrust dealing with unilateral exclusionary conduct by dominant firms—may enjoy a revival.

Monopolization law was always the Chicago School's bête noire.[10] Certainly, Chicago Schoolers critiqued the Warren Court-era precedents in other areas such as vertical or conglomerate mergers or horizontal mergers in unconcentrated markets, but they saved their strongest fire for interventionist antitrust norms on unilateral exclusionary conduct such as tying, predatory pricing, and related practices. When Aaron Levi and Aaron Director wrote their influential "Law and the Future" article in 1956, their primary target was "monopoly leveraging" theory—the argument that monopolists frequently seek to spread their monopoly power to adjacent markets.[11]

---

[6] Press Release, European Commission, Commission Imposes Fine of €1.06 Bn on Intel for Abuse of Dominant Position; Orders Intel to Cease Illegal Practices, (May 13, 2009), available at http://europa.eu/rapid/pressReleasesAction.do?reference=IP/09/745&format=HTML&aged=0&language=EN&guiLanguage=en.

[7] Of course, the jettisoning of the monopolization report and Intel decisions were highly controversial in the antirust community. Nonetheless, as Herbert Hovenkamp has noted, members of the antitrust community generally gain from enhanced enforcement. See Labatan, *supra* n. 3 (quoting Professor Herbert Hovenkamp: "People aligned with plaintiffs will rejoice. Those aligned with defendants will wring their hands. A lot of law firms will be indifferent because they take money from both sides.").

[8] See Daniel A. Crane, Technocracy and Antitrust, 86 Tex. L. Rev. 1159, 1175–80 (2008).

[9] *Id.*

[10] For a brief sketch of the Chicago School of antitrust—not to be confused with the Chicago School of economics—as opposed to the Harvard School, see Part II.A *infra*.

[11] Aaron Director & Edward H. Levi, Law and the Future: Trade Regulation, 51 Nw. U. L. Rev. 281 (1956).

Now the antitrust enforcement agencies in Europe and the United States—buttressed by a new wave of post-Chicago economic scholarship[12]—are rallying against the monopolists. In the United States, they face but one major obstacle: the courts. The Supreme Court in particular has become very conservative on antitrust cases in general and monopolization cases in particular.[13] Since 1993, defendants are 15-0 in antitrust cases in the Supreme Court.[14] Six of those cases involved claims of monopolization or exclusionary conduct.[15] Defendants have won the last nine exclusionary conduct cases in the Supreme Court since 1992.[16] The writing on the wall suggests that we are about to witness a clash between the new wave of anti-monopolization sentiment in the federal antitrust enforcement agencies and the Chicago School-dominated federal courts.

Yet to understand the coming clash simply as a courts versus agencies showdown would be to miss a much richer tapestry of institutional interactions. The evolving story of monopolization law involves a complex set of relationships among a number of different institutional actors (broadly speaking) including judges, juries, the Department of Justice, the Federal Trade Commission, industry regulators, the private plaintiffs' bar, dominant firms, and markets. The interaction of these institutions—and their mutual trust and, more to the point, mistrust—molds modern monopolization law.

[12] See Daniel A. Crane, Chicago, Post-Chicago, and Neo-Chicago, 76 U. Chi. L. Rev. ___ (forthcoming 2009).

[13] The Court has not heard a substantive merger case since 1974. United States v. Marine Bancorporation, Inc., 418 U.S. 602 (1974); United States v. Gen. Dynamics Corp., 415 U.S. 486 (1974).

[14] Plaintiffs last prevailed in Hartford Fire Ins. Co. v. California, 509 U.S. 764 (1993).

[15] Pacific Bell Tel. Co. v. linkLine Commc'ns, Inc., 129 S.Ct. 1109 (2009) (price squeeze); Weyerhaeuser Co. v. Ross-Simmons Hardwood Lumber Co., 549 U.S. 312 (2007) (predatory overbidding); Illinois Tool Works Inc. v. Independent Ink, Inc., 547 U.S. 28 (2006) (tying); Volvo Trucks of North America, Inc. v. Reeder-Simco GMC, Inc., 546 U.S. 164 (2006) (price discrimination); Verizon Commc'ns Inc. v. Law Offices of Curtis V. Trinko, L.L.P., 540 U.S. 398 (2004) (refusal to deal); Nynex Corp. v. Discon, Inc., 525 U.S. 128 (1998) (boycott).

[16] In addition to the six cases listed in the previous footnote, defendants won in Brooke Group Ltd. v. Brown & Williamson Tobacco Corp., 509 U.S. 209 (1993) (predatory pricing), Spectrum Sports, Inc. v. McQuillan, 506 U.S. 447 (1993) (retailer termination), and Professional Real Estate Investors Inc. v. Columbia Pictures Industries, Inc., 508 U.S. 49 (1993) (anticompetitive litigation). The last plaintiff win was Eastman Kodak Co. v. Image Technical Services, Inc., 504 U.S. 451 (1992) (tying).

In this essay, I review the Supreme Court's most recent monopolization decision—*Pacific Bell v. linkLine*[17]—with a focus on the suspicions between the various institutions that had a hand in the case. In Part I, I review *linkLine*'s facts and locate it within the sweep of recent monopolization decisions. I then compare *linkLine* to another recent monopolization case—the D.C. Circuit's decision in *Rambus v. FTC*[18]—that involved a different set of institutional actors. Taken together, *linkLine* and *Rambus* provide a comprehensive introduction to the cast of instructional players who shape monopolization law and to their nexus of mutual suspicions. In Part II, I show the mutual suspicions of the various institutional actors shape monopolization law. Finally, in Part III, I offer some observations on the implications of these institutional suspicions for the Obama administration's ambitions to reinvigorate antitrust enforcement.

I. *linkLine* and *Rambus*

A. linkLine

The *linkLine* decision continues the lengthy historical saga concerning the relationship between regulation and antitrust in the telecommunications industry. In 1982, the Reagan administration resolved the long-standing AT&T antitrust litigation with a consent decree that split AT&T from its local telephone service subsidiaries.[19] Then, in 1996, President Bill Clinton signed into law the Telecommunications Act ("Telecom Act"), which fundamentally restructured the telephone industry by requiring incumbent local exchange carriers (ILECs) to share their telephone networks with competitors.[20] Since then, three of the Supreme Court's most important antitrust decisions have involved implications of the Telecom Act for antitrust enforcement.

---

[17] Pacific Bell Tel. Co. v. linkLine Communs., Inc., 555 U.S. ___, 129 S. Ct. 1109 (2009).

[18] Rambus, Inc. v. FTC, 522 F.3d 456 (D.C. Cir. 2008).

[19] U.S. v. American Tel. & Tel. Co., 552 F.Supp. 131 (D.D.C. 1982), aff'd. sub nom. Maryland v. U.S., 460 U.S. 1001, 103 S.Ct. 1240, 75 L.Ed.2d 472 (1983).

[20] Telecommunications Act of 1996 (1996 Act or Act), Pub.L. 104-104, 110 Stat. 56. See generally AT & T Corp. v. Iowa Utilities Bd., 525 U.S. 366, 372-73 (1999) (explaining that requesting carriers can access the ILEC's network in one of three ways: "It can purchase local telephone services at wholesale rates for resale to end users; it can lease elements of the incumbent's network 'on an unbundled basis'; and it can interconnect its own facilities with the incumbent's network").

In the first case, *Verizon Communications v. Trinko*,[21] the plaintiffs were local phone company subscribers who alleged that Verizon— the incumbent local exchange carrier—in New York City had shirked its interconnection obligations with competitive local exchange carriers (CLECs) like AT&T, thus delaying the advent of local phone service competition in the New York area.[22] There was no dispute in that case that Verizon had, in fact, violated its Telecom Act obligations by stalling when requested to fill the CLECs' interconnection requests, and the Federal Communications Commission fined Verizon $3 million (through a consent decree).[23] The question was whether Verizon's failure to cooperate with AT&T could also give rise to monopolization liability under Section 2 of the Sherman Act.[24] The Supreme Court unanimously ruled for Verizon (although three justices—John Paul Stevens, David Souter, and Clarence Thomas— would have decided the issue on standing grounds and did not opine on the merits). It held that Section 2 of the Sherman Act generally does not impose on monopolists a duty to deal with their rivals and therefore does not impose an obligation to provide a "sufficient" level of service.[25] That the Telecom Act imposed a duty to deal did not strengthen the case for an antitrust duty to deal. If anything, held the Court, the power of the FCC to impose fines weakened the case for an antitrust duty to deal, since there was already an administrative mechanism in place to police the interconnection obligations. As we shall see, *Trinko* forms the critical backdrop to *linkLine*.

The second case, *Bell Atlantic v. Twombly*,[26] was less directly relevant to *linkLine* but crucially important to pleading private antitrust cases, pleading civil cases generally, and the story of institutional suspicions in antitrust (as we shall see in a moment). In *Twombly*, a putative class action consisting of local telephone and/or high-speed internet subscribers alleged that the ILECs had conspired to stay

---

[21] Verizon Communications Inc. v. Law Offices of Curtis V. Trinko, 540 U.S. 398, 410 (2004).

[22] 540 U.S. at 403.

[23] 15 FCC Rcd. 5415, 5421, & ¶ 16 (2000).

[24] 15 U.S.C. § 2.

[25] 540 U.S. at 410.

[26] Bell Atlantic Corp. v. Twombly, 550 U.S. 544 (2007).

out of each other's territories and therefore to divide markets in contravention of the Telecom Act's purposes. By a 7–2 vote, the Supreme Court held that the plaintiffs had failed to allege sufficient facts to survive a motion to dismiss and obtain discovery on the alleged cartel.[27]

That brings us to *linkLine*. AT&T (for short, because the petitioners consisted of a number of affiliated companies whose names changed over time) owns much of the fiber-optic infrastructure for local telephone services in California.[28] In particular, it holds the keys to the "last mile"—the lines connecting residences and business to the telephone network.[29] Until 2005, the FCC required the ILECs to sell transmission services to independent digital subscriber line ("DSL") suppliers so that the independents could provide DSL internet service in competition with the ILECs.[30] In 2005, the FCC largely abandoned this requirement, finding that DSL faces vigorous competition from other forms of internet access including cable, wireless, and satellite.[31] AT&T remains bound to a mandatory interconnection obligation, however, as a condition of the AT&T/BellSouth merger that created the modern AT&T.[32] Specifically, AT&T is required to provide "DSL transport" services to independent DSL providers at a price no greater than AT&T's own DSL retail prices.[33]

The plaintiffs in *linkLine* were four independent DSL providers who alleged that AT&T engaged in an exclusionary "price squeeze." Specifically, plaintiffs alleged that AT&T set a high wholesale price to them but then a low retail price to its own customers and that the effect of this squeeze was that they could not profitably compete against AT&T.[34] Initially, at least, plaintiffs did not allege that AT&T's retail price was predatory—that is to say, set below marginal cost.[35]

---

[27] *Id.* at 571.

[28] linkLine, 129 S. Ct. at 1115.

[29] *Id.*

[30] See In re Appropriate Framework for Broadband Access to Internet Over Wireline Facilities, 20 FCC Rcd. 14853, 14868 (FCC 2005).

[31] *Id.* at 14879–14887.

[32] In re AT&T Inc. and BellSouth Corp., 22 FCC Rcd. 5662, 5814 (FCC 2007).

[33] *Id.*

[34] linkLine, 129 S. Ct. at 1115.

[35] Under U.S. predatory pricing principles, the plaintiff usually must show that the defendant priced below some measure of incremental or marginal cost, although the Supreme Court still has not decided exactly what measure of cost should be employed.

The District Court for the Central District of California declined to dismiss the complaint but certified to the U.S. Court of Appeals for the Ninth Circuit the question whether "*Trinko* bars price squeeze claims where the parties are compelled to deal under the federal communications laws."[36] On interlocutory appeal, the Ninth Circuit affirmed the district court's denial of AT&T's motion for judgment on the pleadings, finding *Trinko* inapposite since it did not involve a price-squeeze claim.[37] Judge Ronald Gould, however, filed a dissenting opinion presaging the Supreme Court's ultimate decision. In his view, a price-squeeze claim without allegations of below-cost pricing by the vertically integrated monopolist was merely the marriage of two previously rejected theories—that a monopolist has a duty to deal in the wholesale market (rejected in *Trinko*) and that a defendant can be found liable for predatory pricing without pricing below cost (rejected in *Brooke Group*[38] and earlier cases).

When the Supreme Court granted certiorari, it was clear to most informed observers that *Trinko* and *Brooke Group* presented a perfect Scylla and Charybdis to price-squeeze claims. Plaintiffs tried to avoid an adverse Supreme Court decision by suddenly proclaiming an affinity for Judge Gould's dissenting opinion and asking to be allowed to file an amended complaint alleging predatory pricing.[39] Various pro-enforcement amici curiae, fearful of anything the Roberts Court might say in a monopolization case, asked the Court to dismiss the case as moot. But the Court had already sunk its teeth into the case and would not let go without tasting some blood. It rejected the mootness arguments, declined to pass on whether the plaintiffs should be allowed to (or even needed to) amend, dove into the price-squeeze issue, and unanimously rejected price-squeeze claims.

---

[36] linkLine, 129 S. Ct. at 1116.

[37] 503 F.3d 876 (9th Cir. 2007).

[38] Brooke Group Ltd. v. Brown & Williamson Tobacco Corp., 509 U.S. 209 (1993). To be clear, plaintiff in Brooke Group accepted that it would have to show below-cost pricing to win on a predatory pricing theory, but the Court nonetheless took the opportunity to reaffirm what it had said in a line of cases since the 1980s—that there is no predatory pricing liability unless prices are below an "appropriate measure of cost." Id. at 222. The Court reaffirmed this principle in Weyerhaeuser Co. v. Ross-Simmons Hardwood Lumber Co., 549 U.S. 312 (2007), a case that involved "predatory overbidding" allegations.

[39] 129 S. Ct. at 1117.

The five most conservative justices (John Roberts, Antonin Scalia, Anthony Kennedy, Clarence Thomas, and Samuel Alito) joined together in an opinion by Chief Justice Roberts. The core of this opinion is relatively formalistic and narrowly applicable (although not necessarily wrong or inappropriate for those reasons). Price-squeeze claims, reasoned the Court, necessarily involve defendants who operate in two markets—an upstream and downstream market—and a plaintiff that operates in only the downstream market. The plaintiff must buy from the defendant in the upstream market in order to compete with the defendant in the downstream market. The plaintiff alleges that the defendant misbehaved in both markets. First, the defendant charged too high a price in the upstream market. That claim is foreclosed by *Trinko*. Since the defendant has no anti-trust duty to deal at all in the upstream market, if it does choose to deal it can charge whatever price it wants.[40] Second, the plaintiff alleges that defendant priced too low in the downstream market. But unless plaintiff alleges that defendant priced below cost in the downstream market, it runs into *Brooke Group*, which immunizes low prices from liability unless they are below cost. To summarize:

> Plaintiffs' price-squeeze claim, looking at the relation between retail and wholesale prices, is thus nothing more than an amalgamation of a meritless claim at the retail level and a meritless claim at the wholesale level. If there is no duty to deal at the wholesale level and no predatory pricing at the retail level, then a firm is certainly not required to price both of these services in a manner that preserves its rivals' profit margins.[41]

The Court then turned from this juridical analysis to an institution-alist analysis. Per Chief Justice Roberts, "[i]nstitutional concerns counsel against recognition of such [price-squeeze] claims."[42] In *Trinko*, the Court had found that "[c]ourts are ill suited to act as central planners, identifying the proper price, quantity, and other

---

[40] This is purely from an antitrust perspective. In *Trinko*, the Court had distinguished between regulatory duties to deal (for example, those created by the Telecom Act) and antitrust duties to deal (those created—if ever—by antitrust law).

[41] 129 S. Ct. 1120.

[42] *Id.* at 1120-21.

terms of dealing."[43] In *Trinko*, the Court had quoted extensively from Philip Areeda's repudiation of the essential facilities doctrine, and it did so again: "No court should impose a duty to deal that it cannot adequately explain or adequately and reasonably supervise. The problems should be deemed irremedia[ble] by antitrust law when compulsory access requires the court to assume the day-to-day controls characteristic of a regulatory agency."[44]

For extra measure, or perhaps to tweak a recalcitrant colleague, Roberts tossed in a lengthy quote from *Town of Concord*,[45] an opinion written by now-Justice Stephen Breyer while he was chief judge of the First Circuit Court of Appeals. In that case, Breyer rejected a price-squeeze claim against a vertically integrated electrical company that was rate-regulated at both the wholesale and retail levels.[46] He wrote:

> [H]ow is a judge or jury to determine a "fair price?" Is it the price charged by other suppliers of the primary product? None exists. Is it the price that competition "would have set" were the primary level not monopolized? How can the court determine this price without examining costs and demands, indeed without acting like a rate-setting regulatory agency, the rate-setting proceedings of which often last for several years?[47]

The Court then considered, and rejected, a few tests proposed by amici (the plaintiff DSL providers didn't propose any, since they were now in full retraction mode, asking to be allowed to assert a predatory pricing claim). It reversed the Ninth Circuit decision and remanded the case, leaving open the possibility that plaintiffs would be granted leave to amend and assert a predation claim.

Breyer, joined by the Court's more liberal members, Stevens, Souter, and Ginsburg, filed a brief opinion concurring in the judgment. We will revert to this opinion in a moment, but its nub suggests accepting plaintiffs' concession that the price squeeze claim was

[43] *Id.* (quoting Trinko, 540 U.S. at 408).

[44] *Id.* (quoting Phillip Areeda, Essential Facilities: An Epithet in Need of Limiting Principles, 58 Antitrust L. J. 841, 853 (1989)).

[45] Town of Concord v. Boston Edison Co., 915 F.2d 17 (1st Cir. 1990).

[46] *Id.* at 29.

[47] linkLine, 129 S. Ct. at 1121 (quoting Town of Concord, 915 F.2d at 25).

erroneous and remanding to allow the district court to determine whether plaintiffs should be allowed to replead.

B. Rambus

The D.C. Circuit's recent decision in *Rambus* probably received more attention than the Supreme Court's decision in *linkLine* because of its implications for high-tech product standardization—a hot topic in antitrust and intellectual property circles.[48] Rambus creates computer memory technology which it licenses to computer hardware manufacturers. During the 1990s, Rambus participated in the Joint Electron Device Engineering Council, which was then in the process of formulating new computer memory standards.[49] At some point before the finalization of the new standards, Rambus withdrew from JEDEC. According to the FTC's subsequent administrative complaint, Rambus failed to disclose that it had various patents or patent applications on technologies that would be essential to practicing the new standard. After the standard's adoption, Rambus began to demand royalties from firms practicing the standard.

The FTC decided that Rambus violated Section 2 of the Sherman Act (as enforced through Section 5 of the FTC Act) by deceiving JEDEC about its patents and patent applications. The FTC then determined that Rambus should be compelled to license certain of its computer memory patents on reasonable and nondiscriminatory ("RAND") terms (as set by the FTC in a separate order on remedy)[50] because its participation in JEDEC without disclosure of its patents and patent applications gave Rambus a monopolistic holdout position after the standard was irretrievably adopted.[51]

On appeal, the D.C. Circuit vacated the FTC decision. Relying on Section 2 monopolization precedents, the court found that the FTC

---

[48] In the interests of full disclosure, I was the primary author of an amicus curiae brief on behalf of 20 law professors and economists urging the Supreme Court to grant certiorari in *Rambus*. The Supreme Court denied certiorari. FTC v. Rambus, 129 S. Ct. 1318 (2009).

[49] Rambus, Inc. v. FTC, 522 F.3d 456, 458–60 (D.C. Cir. 2008).

[50] In re Rambus, Inc., No. 9302 (Final Order Feb. 5, 2007), http://www.ftc.gov/os/adjpro/d9302/070205opinion.pdf.

[51] In re Rambus, Inc., No. 9302 (Order Reversing and Vacating Initial Decision August 2, 2006), http://www.ftc.gov/os/adjpro/d9302/060802rambusorder.pdf.

had failed to prove anticompetitive behavior. In particular, the Commission had failed to establish the causation necessary to demonstrate that Rambus's conduct had suppressed competition. In its liability decision, the Commission had observed that the but-for world was not fully knowable. In the event that Rambus had disclosed its patent applications, one of two things might have happened. One possibility was that JEDEC would have chosen an alternative technology that did not tread on Rambus's patents. The other possibility was that JEDEC would have negotiated with Rambus for a commitment to license its patents at lower rates than it demanded after sneaking through the standardization process.

Judge Stephen F. Williams's decision conceded that the first path—the choice of a different technology—might show monopolistic conduct.[52] But the second path—JEDEC's failure to negotiate a better price—would not.[53] The court relied heavily on the Supreme Court's 1998 decision in *NYNEX v. Discon*[54]—a Stephen Breyer opinion for a unanimous Court. In that case, a provider of obsolete telephone equipment removal services alleged that the NYNEX—an ILEC—conspired with a competitor of Discon's to give the competitor all of its removal service work at inflated prices. After regulators approved NYNEX's tariffs, the competitor secretly rebated money to NYNEX. Justice Breyer's opinion held that such cheating on rate regulators was not a monopolization offense, since it did not involve a diminution in the competitiveness of the market. The *Rambus* court took *NYNEX* to mean that mere deception that gives dominant firms the power to charge higher than competitive prices does not rise to antitrust liability.[55] Because the second possible path found by the FTC merely reflected the possibility that Rambus deceived JEDEC into allowing it to charge a higher-than-competitive price, path two did not describe an antitrust violation.[56]

---

[52] 522 F.3d at 463.

[53] *Id.*

[54] NYNEX Corp. v. Discon, Inc., 525 U.S. 128 (1998).

[55] 522 F.3d at 466.

[56] This reasoning is questionable. While it is true that mere deception that gives a monopolist the ability to charge a higher price is not an antitrust violation, when the deception results in the suppression of competition and *that* creates the ability to charge a higher price, there is an antitrust violation.

A barrage of high-tech industry groups, academics, and antitrust advocacy groups urged the Supreme Court to hear *Rambus*.[57] The stakes for antitrust enforcement in product standardization contexts—where billions of dollars in patent royalties and the path of innovation are at issue—are very high. Nonetheless, the Court declined to hear the case without even seeking the views of the solicitor general. The Court denied certiorari on February 23, 2009, barely a month after President Barack Obama's inauguration.[58] It is uncertain what position the Bush Justice Department would have taken if asked for its views. There is little doubt that the Obama Justice Department would have strongly pushed for the grant of certiorari and reversal.[59]

II. The Institutions and Their Suspicions

In the antitrust community, most of the commentary about the *linkLine* and *Rambus* decisions has focused on the merits of the decisions as a matter of law or economics. Could price squeezes be more anticompetitive than simple refusals to deal and above-cost retail pricing? Did the D.C. Circuit misapply the relevant monopolization precedents on misrepresentation and deception? These questions are important, but it is impossible to understand either decision without considering the institutional context that influenced the decisions. Antitrust law is not created in an intellectual vacuum. It is the product of clashing and mutually suspicious institutions. The clash of those institutions has far more explanatory power than economic or legal arguments on the merits.

A. linkLine's *Institutions*

A conventional account of U.S. antitrust jurisprudence views U.S. courts as captured by a Chicago School ideology that is committed

---

[57] The amici supporting the FTC included Hewlett-Packard, Cisco Systems, Inc., Sun Microsystems, Inc., Oracle Corporation, Advanced Media Workflow Association, Consumer Electronics Association; Globalplatform Inc., IMS Global Learning Consortium, Inc., International Imaging Industry Association, Inc., IPC, Association Connecting Electronics Industries; Linux Foundation, Midi Manufactures Association; Mobile Printing and Imaging Consortium, Open Geospatial Consortium, and OpenSAF Foundation.

[58] FTC v. Rambus, 129 S. Ct. 1318 (2009).

[59] One of the signatories of the academics' amicus curiae brief urging the Supreme Court to grant certiorari and reverse in *Rambus* was Carl Shapiro, who is currently the Deputy Assistant Attorney General for Economics in the Antitrust Division.

to laissez faire principles and hence seeks to roll back antitrust enforcement.[60] But, as a number of prominent scholars have recently argued,[61] the real story is considerably more complicated. Modern U.S. antitrust law can be understood as the product of two different schools—the Chicago School of Richard Posner, Frank Easterbrook, Robert Bork, Antonin Scalia, et al., and the Harvard School of Phillip Areeda, Donald Turner, Herbert Hovenkamp, and Stephen Breyer, who often leads the Court's four liberal justices in antitrust cases. Each of these schools deeply mistrusts various of the other institutional actors in the antitrust system. Although the two schools also mistrust each other—which explains why in cases like *linkLine* the Chicago and Harvard Schoolers reach the same result but decline to join each other's opinions—more often than not they reach common ground on outcomes.

The Harvard School's interplay with Chicago School themes is encapsulated in an intriguing passage in Justice Breyer's concurring opinion in *linkLine*. Breyer begins: "A 'price-squeeze' claim finds its natural home in a Sherman Act § 2 claim where *the Government* as plaintiff seeks to show that a defendant's monopoly power rests, not upon 'skill, foresight and industry'," but upon exclusionary conduct."[62] Breyer does not explain why it should matter to the viability of a price-squeeze claim that the government, rather than a private party, is the plaintiff. After all, the government and private plaintiffs would be enforcing the same statute.[63] Yet Breyer's aim seems to be to rehabilitate the Justice Department's successful price-squeeze claims in *Alcoa*, snubbed by Chief Justice Roberts et al. as overridden by subsequent "developments in economic theory and antitrust jurisprudence."[64] Breyer argues that price squeezes could

---

[60] I explore these themes at greater length in Daniel A. Crane, Chicago, Post-Chicago, and Neo-Chicago, 76 U. Chi. L. Rev. (forthcoming 2009).

[61] See, e.g., William E. Kovacic, The Intellectual DNA of Modern U.S. Competition Law for Dominant Firm Conduct: The Chicago/Harvard Double Helix, 2007 Colum Bus L Rev 1; Einer Elhauge, Harvard, Not Chicago: Which Antitrust School Drives Recent U.S. Supreme Court Decisions, 3 Comp Policy Intl 59 (2007).

[62] 129 S. Ct. at 1124 (Breyer, J., concurring) (citing United States v. Aluminum Co. of America, 148 F.2d 416, 430 (2d Cir. 1945) ("Alcoa")) (emphasis added).

[63] At least this is true of actions by the Justice Department, which was the party in all of the examples that Justice Breyer gives.

[64] linkLine, 129 S. Ct. at 1120.

theoretically be exclusionary even if the simple refusal to deal upstream would not be exclusionary.[65] However, the FCC's regulatory presence obviates the difficulty of this issue. "During the time covered by the complaint, [AT&T was] required to provide [DSL] transport service as a common carrier, charging 'just and reasonable rates' that were not 'unreasonably discriminatory.'"[66] Then, sounding one of the Harvard School's frequent refrains, Breyer notes: "When a regulatory structure exists to deter and remedy anticompetitive harm, the costs of antitrust enforcement are likely to be greater than the benefits."[67]

Within these few lines are packed, and partly hidden, a set of ideological commitments about various institutional players. First, there is the juxtaposition between private enforcement and public enforcement. One mainstay of the Chicago School perspective is a deep suspicion of private antitrust plaintiffs—and their lawyers—as freeloaders on the treble damages bounty automatically afforded to successful plaintiffs in antitrust cases. A substantial body of scholarship views competitor-plaintiffs—the usual plaintiffs in monopolization cases—as strategic abusers of antitrust litigation.[68]

Here, Justice Breyer's Harvard School seems to concur in the Chicago School's suspicion. Juries are quirky, unpredictable, and emotional and inherently inferior to technocratic regulators.[69] What emerges from the convergence of suspicions is a body of antitrust precedents that expresses nearly unanimous hostility to private litigation.

---

[65] *Id.* at 1124 (Breyer, J., concurring).

[66] *Id.*

[67] *Id.* Justice Breyer then naturally cites his own *Town of Concord* decision from the First Circuit and the Areeda-Turner treatise, the intellectual repository of Harvard School ideas.

[68] William J. Baumol & Janusz A. Ordover, Use of Antitrust to Subvert Competition, 28 J.L. & Econ. 247 (1985); Frank H. Easterbrook, The Limits of Antitrust, 63 Tex. L. Rev. 1 (1984); Daniel A. Crane, The Paradox of Predatory Pricing, 91 Cornell L. Rev. 1, 5–32 (2005); R. Preston McAfee & Nicholas V. Vakkur, The Strategic Abuse of the Antitrust Laws, 2 J. Strategic Mgmt. Educ. 37, 37–38 (2005); Edward A. Snyder & Thomas E. Kauper, Misuse of the Antitrust Laws: The Competitor Plaintiff, 90 Mich. L. Rev. 551 (1991).

[69] Elsewhere, Justice Breyer has argued that neither judges nor juries are very good at making risk assessments. Stephen Breyer, Breaking the Vicious Circle: Toward Effective Risk Regulation 58–59 (1993).

A related institutional actor lurking in Justice Breyer's opinion is the jury. Here again, the Harvard and Chicago Schools' suspicions converge. Private antitrust cases are problematic not only because they involve untrustworthy private plaintiffs, but also because private lawsuits inevitably seek damages—which are the province of juries. For the Chicago School, antitrust juries are perhaps the primary institutional foe. Juries do not understand the economic complexities of antitrust cases and therefore fall back on populist ideas about "fair" competition and moral limitations on the behavior of dominant firms. Juries thus provide a natural check on the economic efficiency oriented trajectory of Chicago School antitrust law and (to Chicagoans) must be curbed through the use of procedural devices like motions to dismiss and for summary judgment, *Daubert* gatekeeping of expert witness testimony by judges,[70] and sharply contracted liability norms.

The Harvard Schoolers largely concur. They are primarily concerned with comparative institutional competence and prefer expert decisionmaking to lay decisionmaking. In several other antitrust opinions, Breyer has plainly called into question the competence of generalist judges and, in particular, juries.[71] In *Twombly*, Justice Stevens's dissenting opinion accused the majority (including Breyer and Souter) of erecting a high barrier to pleading antitrust cases because of a distrust of juries.[72] Although Breyer does not explicitly mention juries in *linkLine*, the jury's shadow is implicit in his allusion to a more favorable reception to governmentally initiated price squeeze claims. Government enforcement actions in equity—like the *Alcoa* case he refers to—are not tried before juries.

A third institutional actor singled out by Justice Breyer is the regulator. In *linkLine*, as in *Trinko* and *Credit Suisse*, Breyer authored or signed onto opinions that argue against antitrust intervention

---

[70] Daubert v. Merrell Dow Pharms., Inc., 509 U.S. 579 (1993).

[71] See, e.g., Credit Suisse Secs., (USA) LLC v. Billings, 551 U.S. 264, 281 (2007) (observing the risks of inconsistency entailed in entrusting decisional authority to "different nonexpert judges and different nonexpert juries"); Leegin Creative Leather Prods., Inc. v. PSKS, Inc., 551 U.S. 877, 917 (2007) (Breyer, J., dissenting) (arguing that "[o]ne cannot fairly expect judges and juries in [resale price maintenance] cases to apply complex economic criteria without making a considerable number of mistakes, which themselves may impose serious costs").

[72] 550 U.S. at 573 (Stevens, J., dissenting).

where a regulator already is active in the sector. Suspicious of juries and private plaintiffs, the Harvard Schoolers favor technocratic regulation to police market power problems.

This, of course, is a point of divergence between the two schools. The Chicago School surely does not favor regulators over market solutions. To be sure, in *Trinko*, *linkLine*, and *Credit Suisse*, the Chicago Schoolers were willing to give a nod to the active presence of the Federal Communications Commission or the Securities and Exchange Commission in the relevant sectors as a reason to withhold antitrust intervention. But in cases involving the reach of agency regulatory authority, the clash between Harvard and Chicago often becomes apparent.[73] The two schools agree, then, that antitrust solutions should be rejected when regulators are present. They disagree about whether *regulatory* solutions should be rejected when regulators are present—but those conflicts do not usually arise in antitrust cases.

The Chicago-Harvard divergence over regulators invokes another "institution," broadly speaking—the market. Chicagoans tend to trust the market to produce optimal outcomes.[74] In *Trinko*, Justice Scalia's opinion asserts that monopoly profits are not merely an unfortunate side effect of market systems but an affirmatively beneficial feature insofar as they spur innovation and investment in infrastructure.[75] The Harvard Schoolers have no such affinity for monopoly profits and no such trust of markets. They suspect markets as much as the Chicago Schoolers suspect regulators. However, the Harvard School suspicions of juries and private plaintiffs are almost always sufficient to overcome their suspicion of markets where a regulator is theoretically able to take care of business.

So Harvard and Chicago often combine to beat up on plaintiffs in private antitrust cases. Although the two schools diverge on the relative trust they have in dominant firms, unregulated markets,

---

[73] See generally FDA v. Brown & Williamson Tobacco Corp., 529 U.S. 120 (2000). In *Brown & Williamson*, the five conservative justices held that the FDA lacked authority to regulate tobacco, while the four liberal justices joined a Breyer dissent.

[74] Or at least that was historically the Chicago perspective. The economic crisis of 2008 has led to some Chicago School re-evaluations of market self-correction theory. See Richard A. Posner, A Failure of Capitalism: The Crisis of '08 and the Descent into Depression (2009).

[75] 540 U.S. at 407.

and regulators, they share a disdain for treble damages cases, juries, complaining competitors, and the antitrust plaintiffs' bar. In cases like *Trinko*, *Twombly*, and now *linkLine*, the two schools' grudging alliance served up unanimous or nearly unanimous defeats to the plaintiffs.

B. Rambus's *Institutions*

Rambus was an FTC case so there were no treble damages, jury, rent-seeking competitors, or greedy trial lawyers to worry about. Still, those "institutions" played a large shadow role in *Rambus*. The FTC explicitly stated that it was relying on general Sherman Act Section 2 law in bringing its challenge to Rambus's conduct.[76] The D.C. Circuit relied heavily on antitrust doctrines created in private cases. Those cases, which substantially contracted liability norms, reflect the full gamut of Harvard and Chicago School institutional suspicions. In *NYNEX*, for example, Justice Breyer's opinion worried that applying antitrust rules to "regulatory fraud . . . would transform cases involving business behavior that is improper for various reasons, say, cases involving nepotism or personal pique, into treble-damages antitrust cases."[77] Because private cases outweigh public cases by a margin of ten to one, most antitrust law today develops in private cases. When the agencies sue, they have to work with liability norms that have been substantially contracted in generation after generation of private lawsuit. Hence, the Harvard and Chicago School's suspicions of treble damages, juries, and private litigants often contribute significantly to the agencies' defeats, even though those factors have no direct role in a particular agency's enforcement action.

In a case in which the FTC itself was the plaintiff, the Harvard School might well echo Justice Breyer's *linkLine* concurrence and explain that private enforcement decisions should not apply with equal force when the Commission is the party. The FTC has reached the Supreme Court as a party to an antitrust case just once in the last two decades—in *California Dental*—and that case resulted in a 5-4 decision with a Chicago School majority rejecting the FTC's claim and Justice Breyer supporting it.[78] Notably, in *California Dental*,

---

[76] 522 F.3d at 462.

[77] 525 U.S. at 136–37.

[78] California Dental Ass'n v. FTC, 526 U.S. 756 (1999).

Justice Breyer invoked the FTC's expertise in false advertising cases as a reason to defer to the Commission's antitrust enforcement action against a dental association's advertising restrictions,[79] a classically Harvard School position on the comparative advantages of technocratic regulators over generalist judges.

Unfortunately for the FTC, the Chicago School has not looked particularly favorably on the Commission.[80] During the 1970s, when Chicago was ascendant, the FTC was the major bulwark of pro-enforcement sentiment. The Commission was thus on a collision course with Chicago. Thus, for example, while the Chicago School was urging the Supreme Court to roll back all antitrust policing of vertical restraints such as resale price maintenance, the FTC was seeking to overturn the *Colgate* doctrine—which allowed manufacturers to establish suggested resale prices and was thus the one exception to the Court's historic hostility to resale price maintenance.[81]

In recent times, the interventionist Commission has overtly clashed with the Chicago School-oriented Antitrust Division. The overt bickering began when the FTC asked the Supreme Court to reverse its defeat in the Eleventh Circuit Court of Appeals over the legality of pharmaceutical patent settlements while Justice Department recommended the denial of certiorari.[82] Payback time came in *linkLine*, when the Justice Department filed a brief arguing against price squeeze liability. The FTC issued a press release explaining why it did not join the Justice Department brief and urged the Supreme Court to deny certiorari.[83] The final straw came when the Justice Department issued its Section 2 report[84] and three FTC Commissioners issued a shrill dissenting statement, disagreeing with

[79] *Id.* at 787 (Breyer, J., dissenting) (noting that the FTC "is expert in the area of false and misleading advertising").

[80] See, e.g., Richard A. Posner, The Federal Trade Commission, 37 U. Chi. L. Rev. 47 (1969) (arguing that the FTC has no institutional advantage over Article III courts).

[81] See Russell Stover Candies, Inc. v. FTC, 718 F.2d 256, 257 (8th Cir. 1983) (citing United States v. Colgate & Co., 250 U.S. 300 (1919)).

[82] Brief for the United States as Amicus Curiae, FTC v. Schering-Plough Corp. (May 17, 2006), 2006 WL 1358441.

[83] Statement of the Federal Trade Commission, Petition for a Writ of Certiorari in Pacific Bell Tel. Co. d/b/a AT&T California v. linkLine Comms. Inc. (No. 07-512) (May 23, 2008), available at http://www.ftc.gov/os/2008/05/P072104stmt.pdf.

[84] Competition and Monopoly: Single-Firm Conduct Under Section 2 of the Sherman Act, available at http://www.usdoj.gov/atr/public/reports/236681.pdf.

almost everything in the report and warning that the FTC "stands ready to fill any Sherman Act enforcement void that might be created if the Justice Department actually implements the policy decisions expressed in its Report."[85]

This interagency hostility probably diminished the effectiveness of the two agencies in carrying on their antitrust missions, even when they were not directly squabbling. That is, it is hard to justify deference to the antitrust agencies' decisions based on their expertise when the supposed experts perpetually contradict each other. And even though the hostility has abated considerably since Obama's inauguration, the Chicago School courts are unlikely to give the FTC any quarter. *Rambus* is but the latest decision in which the full panoply of judicial suspicion of private antitrust litigation has led to the defeat of FTC enforcement actions as well.

Taken together, *linkLine* and *Rambus* demonstrate the feedback effects of the Harvard and Chicago Schools on the entire system of antitrust enforcement. Although mutually suspicious of one another, the two schools coalesce in suspicion of juries, generalist judges, treble damages, private plaintiffs, and the plaintiffs' bar. The Harvard School's suspicions of dominant firms and unregulated markets are muted in cases where a regulator could theoretically intervene— which is perhaps the majority of significant modern antitrust cases. Private antitrust actions thus face high hurdles in the Supreme Court. Although the two schools' grudging alliance should—and sometimes does—fray in government enforcement cases, the predominance of private litigation over public litigation results in the creation and then application of contracted liability norms to even public lawsuits. And the Chicago School has enough of an upper hand over the Harvard School on the Supreme Court and in many lower courts that even when the two schools diverge in public enforcement cases, the Chicago School's free marketeerism and distrust of the antitrust agencies often prevails. These are the realities facing President Obama's antitrust ambitions.

III. The Obama Aministration's Ambitions

With the benefit of hindsight, *linkLine* and *Rambus* may prove to represent monopolization law at its nadir in the United States. Under

---

[85] Press Release, FTC, FTC Commissioners React to Department of Justice Report, Competition and Monopoly: Single-Firm Conduct Under Section 2 of the Sherman Act, available at http://www.ftc.gov/opa/2008/09/section2.shtm.

Varney's leadership, the Antitrust Division appears to be headed in a more European direction. Almost across the board, the European Union is far more interventionist than the United States in monopolization cases. In the European Union, Pacific Bell and Rambus would have met or did meet very different fates. The European Commission's Guidance paper on abuses of a dominant position—the analog to the now-retracted DOJ report on unilateral exclusionary conduct—calls for policing of "margin squeezes" that prevent equally efficient firms from profitably trading in the downstream market "on a lasting basis."[86] In June of 2009, Rambus reached a tentative agreement with the EC to settle the EC's administrative complaint (known as a "Statement of Objections") by capping its royalty rates for dynamic random access memory for a five-year period.[87] And even while the FTC was continuing its own ponderous investigation of Intel, the EC issued its $1.5 billion fine. The new administration's antitrust enforcers are eyeing these and similar influences across the Atlantic and contemplating their replication in the United States.

Still, even in the post-economic-crisis environment, where markets are under suspicion and the Obama administration rides a pro-regulatory tide, it seems unlikely that U.S. monopolization law will come to resemble E.U. abuse of dominance law. The courts have the last word on antitrust cases and there is little indication that they are about to abandon their institutional suspicions.

Curiously, many members of the antitrust community—present or former enforcement officials, practicing lawyers, economists, and academics—continue to believe that the key to reinvigorated antitrust enforcement is convincing the courts that the balance has tipped too far in favor of dominant firms and that certain business practices really do harm consumers. On a number of occasions, I have heard senior antitrust enforcement officials (former and present) comment that no progress can be made until the composition of the Supreme

[86] Press Release, European Commission, Communication from the Commission: Guidance on the Commission's Enforcement Priorities in Applying Article 82 of the EC Treaty to Abusive Exclusionary Conduct by Dominant Undertakings ¶ 80 (February 9, 2009), available at http://ec.europa.eu/competition/antitrust/art82/guidance_en.pdf.

[87] See Press Release, European Commission, Antitrust: Commission Market Tests Commitments Proposed by Rambus Concerning Memory Chips, (June 12, 2009) available at http://europa.eu/rapid/pressReleasesAction.do?reference=MEMO/09/273&format=HTML&aged=0&language=EN&guiLanguage=en.

Court changes. But in the current context antitrust is not like abortion, where a one- or two-justice shift could radically alter the balance.

Modern antitrust law represents the alliance—albeit mutually suspicious—of Chicago and Harvard. Since Breyer joined the Court in 1994, the Supreme Court has decided 14 antitrust cases. In those cases, there have been 108 votes for the majority position and only 14 votes in dissent. Breyer has been on the losing side only twice, as often as Thomas. Many of the decisions most reviled by the pro-enforcement camp have been unanimous or nearly so. Even if the antitrust views of Supreme Court nominees mattered to presidents—and they don't—it would take decades to break the Chicago-Harvard "double helix," as former FTC Chair Bill Kovacic has called it.[88]

So the Obama administration's suspicions of unbounded markets are destined to run into the courts' suspicions of juries, generalist judges, treble damages, the plaintiffs' bar, and even the enforcement agencies themselves. Merely repealing the Section 2 report and calling for more aggressive enforcement—or even filing more aggressive lawsuits—will not get the administration very far. To be successful in its antitrust ambitions, the administration needs a calculated, nuanced strategy to address the courts' institutional suspicions head-on and, where possible, to draw out the Harvard School justices and their sympathizers in the lower courts.

The core of this strategy will have to be a clearly and convincingly articulated position on why the antitrust agencies should be accorded greater latitude than private plaintiffs to push the boundaries of antitrust liability. In legal briefs, enforcement guidelines, and public speeches the agencies need to acknowledge directly the impulses that have reduced antitrust liability norms—the suspicion of competitor plaintiffs, the chilling effect of the treble damages remedies and fee-shifting, the error costs of false positives, and the limited capacity of lay jurors. Whether or not they embrace these impulses as legitimate, the agencies need to accept them as presently unchangeable facts. Then they need to explain why they should not have to carry the baggage of private antitrust litigation, how the liability norms created in private litigation need not apply wholesale in public litigation, and how there is ample room within antitrust

---

[88] Kovacic, *supra* note 61.

law's statutory framework for treating public enforcers more generously than private ones. Finally, to be successful, they need to move beyond a "just trust us" framework for deference to agency decisions and offer concrete and judicially administrable principles to delimit the boundaries of agency enforcement discretion.

Having articulated their principles, the agencies will need to start testing them in litigated cases. Even with an institutionalist focus, the road ahead will be bumpy. Winning over the Harvard School nets only four justices on the Supreme Court and the occasional victory in the lower courts. The pay-off for an institutionally focused strategy will thus not be immediate. But it is much more likely to result in enhanced public antitrust enforcement over the next decade than a strategy that simply tries to establish the theoretical proposition that price squeezes, patent ambushes, or other business practices are harmful and should be condemned. To borrow from James Carville: It's the institutions, stupid.

Conclusion

Despite the pro-regulatory sentiment brought about by the financial crisis, the Obama administration's zeal for reinvigorated antitrust enforcement faces some serious obstacles. For one, although regulation may increase in times of financial crisis, antitrust enforcement has historically been a casualty of economic crises.[89] More fundamentally, cases like *linkLine* and *Rambus* reveal the courts' deep skepticism about the need for vigorous monopolization enforcement and, most of all, the immovable obstacle formed by the uneasy alliance of the Harvard and Chicago Schools. Only a deliberate and patient strategy that addresses the two schools' institutionalist concerns stands a chance of advancing the new administration's ambitious agenda.

---

[89] See Daniel A. Crane, Antitrust Enforcement During National Crises: An Unhappy History, Global Competition Policy (Dec. 2008).

Hydraulic Pressures and Slight Deviations

*Erik Luna**

> Though the proceeding in question is divested of many of the aggravating incidents of actual search and seizure . . . it contains their substance and essence, and effects their substantial purpose. It may be that it is the obnoxious thing in its mildest and least repulsive form; but illegitimate and unconstitutional practices get their first footing in that way, namely, by silent approaches and slight deviations from legal modes of procedure. This can only be obviated by adhering to the rule that constitutional provisions for the security of person and property should be liberally construed. A close and literal construction deprives them of half their efficacy, and leads to gradual depreciation of the right, as if it consisted more in sound than in substance. It is the duty of courts to be watchful for the constitutional rights of the citizen, and against any stealthy encroachments thereon. Their motto should be *obsta principiis.*
>
> —*Boyd v. United States*[1]

> To give the police greater power than a magistrate [could authorize] is to take a long step down the totalitarian path. Perhaps such a step is desirable to cope with modern forms of lawlessness. But if it is taken, it should be the deliberate choice of the people through a constitutional amendment. . . . There have been powerful hydraulic pressures throughout our history that bear heavily on the Court to water down constitutional guarantees and give the police the upper hand. That hydraulic pressure has probably never been greater than it is today. Yet if the individual is no longer to be

* Professor of Law, Washington and Lee University School of Law. Many thanks to Tim Lynch and Ilya Shapiro for their comments, and to Daniel Goldman and Thomas J. Moran for their research assistance.

[1] 116 U.S. 616, 635 (1886).

> sovereign, if the police can pick him up whenever they do
> not like the cut of his jib, if they can 'seize' and 'search' him
> in their discretion, we enter a new regime.
>
> —Justice William O. Douglas[2]

> It is, perhaps, a fact provocative of sour mirth that the Bill
> of Rights was designed trustfully to prohibit forever . . . the
> invasion of the citizen's liberty without justifiable cause and
> due process of law. It is a fact provocative of mirth yet more
> sour that the execution of these prohibitions was put into
> the hands of courts, which is to say, into the hands of lawyers,
> which is to say, into the hands of men specifically educated
> to discover legal excuses for dishonest, dishonorable and
> anti-social acts. The actual history of the Constitution, as
> everyone knows, has been a history of the gradual abandon-
> ment of all such impediments to government tyranny. Today
> we live frankly under a government of men, not of laws.
>
> —H.L. Mencken[3]

I. Introduction

The U.S. Supreme Court's most recent term included several
Fourth Amendment decisions of varying levels of popular and academic interest and jurisprudential import. The opinion that may
receive the most scholarly attention, *Herring v. United States*, further
curtailed the exclusionary rule as a remedy for search and seizure
violations.[4] In that case, the defendant was taken into custody after
a sheriff's agent was informed about an outstanding warrant for his
arrest, and a subsequent search revealed illegal drugs and a weapon.
As it turns out, however, the warrant had been recalled five months
earlier, but law enforcement employees had failed to update their
computer database. Relying upon a series of earlier decisions, especially those that created a "good faith" exception to the exclusionary
rule,[5] the Court held that suppression of incriminating evidence
is justified only when the deterrence of unconstitutional conduct
substantially outweighs the societal cost of a guilty person going
free. Where the Fourth Amendment violation results from police

---

[2] Terry v. Ohio, 392 U.S. 1, 38–39 (1968) (Douglas, J., dissenting).

[3] H.L. Mencken, Prejudices: A Selection 181–82 (James T. Farrell ed., 1958).

[4] See Herring v. United States, 555 U.S. ___, 129 S. Ct. 695 (2009).

[5] See *infra* notes 8–10 and accompanying text.

negligence, as was the case here, the exclusionary rule need not apply.

There are lots of reasons someone might dislike the *Herring* opinion. It continues the Court's movement toward constitutional rights without remedies, allowing law enforcement to infringe upon an individual's Fourth Amendment rights and then present the fruits of that violation against him at trial.[6] Drawing upon the lessons of tort law, it can be argued that placing a cost on law enforcement for negligent behavior does, in fact, create an important incentive for the state and its employees to act with greater care.[7] One might also criticize *Herring* for analyzing what would seem to be an empirical question, the level of deterrence from applying the exclusionary rule, without any reference to data or research. This deficiency is particularly striking when compared to the decision the *Herring* Court relied heavily upon, *United States v. Leon,* a case where both majority and dissenting opinions grounded their arguments in empirical evidence.[8]

But the Supreme Court's use of *Leon* and its progeny is jurisprudentially interesting irrespective of one's position on the exclusionary rule or the ultimate judgment in *Herring.* The *Leon* exception applied first in situations where law enforcement relied in "good faith" upon a judicial warrant later declared to be invalid.[9] The rule was then extended to warrantless searches based on information contained in a court database and maintained by judicial employees, as well as to searches executed in reliance upon a statute later declared to be unconstitutional.[10] To a large degree, *Leon* was premised on the idea that evidentiary suppression for mistakes made by actors outside of the executive branch cannot meaningfully deter law enforcement. A quarter-century later, however, the *Herring* Court would dismiss—via footnote—any distinction between errors of the judiciary and those of the police.[11] At this juncture, it is hard to tell

---

[6] See, e.g., Hudson v. Michigan, 547 U.S. 586 (2006).

[7] See Herring, 129 S. Ct. at 708–10 (Ginsburg, J., dissenting).

[8] Compare United States v. Leon, 468 U.S. 897, 907 n.6 (1984), with *id.* at 950–51 (Brennan, J., dissenting).

[9] See *id.* See also Massachusetts v. Sheppard, 468 U.S. 981 (1984).

[10] Arizona v. Evans, 514 U.S. 1 (1995); Illinois v. Krull, 480 U.S. 340 (1987).

[11] Herring, 129 S. Ct. at 701 n.3. But see *id.* at 710–11 (Breyer, J., dissenting).

how far the Supreme Court will extend the concept of "good faith" and abstract deterrence balancing, but we surely have not seen the last iteration.

Another case from this past term, *Arizona v. Gant*,[12] confronted a different Fourth Amendment doctrine that had been stretched beyond its original theoretical justification: the power to search incident to lawful arrests. Four decades ago in *Chimel v. California*, the Court held that law enforcement may search the area within the arrestee's immediate control—that is, where he "might reach in order to grab a weapon or evidentiary items"—with the goal of ensuring officer safety and preventing the destruction of evidence.[13] A few years after *Chimel*, the justices created a per se rule allowing a full search of an arrestee's person without any suspicion that weapons or evidence of crime might be uncovered.[14] In its 1981 decision in *New York v. Belton*, the Court fashioned an even broader rule for automobile searches incident to arrest.[15] In order to assist law enforcement and the lower courts, *Belton* propounded a "generalization" that the passenger compartment of a vehicle is within an arrestee's control, thereby drawing a bright-line rule permitting law enforcement to search the entire area incident to an arrest.[16]

In the years that followed, *Belton* generated considerable scholarly criticism.[17] More importantly, the case had been invoked in scenarios where it would have been silly to reference the original justifications for a search incident to arrest—protecting officers and preventing evidence destruction. Such cases were "legion" in the lower courts,[18] with searches upheld despite the fact that an arrestee had already been removed from his vehicle, handcuffed, and placed in the back of a patrol car.[19] A search might occur even though the handcuffed arrestee had been in the squad car for more than half an hour, or

[12] Arizona v. Gant, 556 U.S. ___, 129 S. Ct. 1710 (2009).

[13] Chimel v. California, 395 U.S. 752, 763 (1969).

[14] United States v. Robinson, 414 U.S. 218 (1973).

[15] New York v. Belton, 453 U.S. 454 (1981).

[16] See *id.* at 460.

[17] See, e.g., Wayne R. LaFave, The Fourth Amendment in an Imperfect World: On Drawing "Bright Lines" and "Good Faith," 43 U. Pitt. L. Rev. 307 (1982).

[18] Thornton v. United States, 541 U.S. 615, 625–29 (2004) (Scalia, J., concurring in the judgment).

[19] See 4 Wayne R. LaFave, Search and Seizure § 7.1(c) (4th ed. 2004).

worse yet, he was already being transported to jail.[20] The Supreme Court only exacerbated the problem with its 2004 decision in *Thornton v. United States*,[21] which extended the *Belton* rule to "recent occupants" of an automobile. It was of no consequence that law enforcement first confronted the driver after he had parked and exited his car. According to the Court, the police need for a clear, unvarying rule in this situation justified "the sort of generalization which *Belton* enunciated."[22] But *Thornton* offered little guidance as to the meaning of *recent occupant*, portending further extensions by later cases—or so it seemed.

This past April in *Arizona v. Gant*, the Supreme Court considered a fact pattern that was materially indistinguishable from *Thornton*: After a driver had exited his vehicle, law enforcement arrested and handcuffed the man, placed him in the back of a patrol car, and then searched his vehicle.[23] In ruling the search unconstitutional, the *Gant* Court began by reciting the fundamental rule of Fourth Amendment law—"searches conducted outside the judicial process, without prior approval by judge or magistrate, are per se unreasonable under the Fourth Amendment . . . subject only to a few specifically established and well-delineated exceptions"[24]—without mentioning that today this principle is more honored in the breach than in the observance. The majority opinion then described the limited nature of *Chimel*, emphasizing that the so-called "grabbing area" of an arrestee had been defined consistent with the justifications for a post-arrest search, protecting officers and safeguarding evidence. Turning to the context of vehicle occupants, however, the *Gant* Court struggled mightily to recast the rule propounded in *Belton*, which had been extended in *Thornton* only five years earlier. Among other things, the majority highlighted the fact that none of the party and amici briefs in *Belton* had advocated a mechanical approach. It even suggested that Justice William Brennan's *dissenting* opinion in *Belton*

---

[20] See United States v. McLaughlin, 170 F.3d 889, 894–95 (9th Cir. 1999) (Trott, J., concurring).

[21] 541 U.S. 615 (2004).

[22] *Id.* at 623–24.

[23] Arizona v. Gant, 129 S. Ct. 1710 (2009).

[24] *Id.* at 1716 (quoting Katz v. United States, 389 U.S. 347, 357 (1967)).

was to blame for subsequent cases that understood the decision as adopting a bright-line rule.[25]

Ultimately, the *Gant* Court rejected this rule, claiming that the nearly three decades "since we decided *Belton* has shown that the generalization underpinning the broad reading of that decision is unfounded."[26] Instead, the doctrine should be read as allowing a car search incident to a recent occupant's arrest only if he is within reaching distance of the passenger compartment at the time of the search or if there is reason to believe that the automobile contains evidence of crime. Four dissenting justices took the *Gant* majority to task for ignoring principles of *stare decisis*.[27] Although one may disagree with the dissenters about the pros and cons of ditching the *Belton* rule, it is hard to quarrel with their interpretation of the Court's precedents and their conclusion that *Gant* overruled both *Belton* and *Thornton*. The majority attempted to distinguish the present case on the facts: *Belton* involved a single officer, for instance, and the arrestees had not been handcuffed or placed in a patrol car, while *Thornton* concerned an arrest for a drug offense. Such distinctions are less than convincing, however, given the language of the precedents themselves.[28] Even concurring Justice Antonin Scalia recognized that *Belton* and *Thornton* stood for a bright-line rule and that the narrowing of those decisions was "artificial."[29]

Both *Gant* and *Herring* are important opinions that deserve, and will receive, detailed scholarly attention in their own right. What I would like to suggest here, however, is that these cases have elements of a broader phenomenon—a sort of doctrinal creep-and-crawl—seen in constitutional criminal procedure and, in particular, Fourth Amendment law. The demands placed on police are unrelenting, as is the widely held belief that the Constitution inordinately hinders the efforts of officers to prevent, detect, and solve crimes. Law

---

[25] See *id.* at 1716–19.

[26] *Id.* at 1723.

[27] See *id.* at 1725–26 (Breyer, J., dissenting); *id.* at 1726–32 (Alito, J., dissenting, joined by Roberts, C.J., and Kennedy, J.).

[28] See Belton, 453 U.S. at 460; Thornton, 541 U.S. at 620. See also Thornton, 541 U.S. at 625 (Scalia, J., concurring in judgment).

[29] Gant, 129 S. Ct. at 1725 (Scalia, J., concurring).

enforcement presses the judiciary for change, which is understandable in light of the difficult duties of police officers and the adversarial nature of their profession. The courts may accede to such demands by recognizing limited exceptions to the exclusionary rule or the Fourth Amendment's command of warrants and probable cause. The original decisions might be tolerable, allowing small constitutional variations delimited by their alleged justifications. Over time, however, the courts can be pushed to extend an exception—sometimes in small increments, each case founded upon the last—until the point that the rationale for the original decision can no longer justify the doctrine.

One might argue that *Leon* and *Belton* were well-intentioned, the former premised on the futility (if not unfairness) of punishing law enforcement for judicial errors, and the latter concerned about the safety of officers who have just conducted an arrest as well as the preservation of incriminating evidence. But the cases that followed *Belton* allowed searches where the arrestee could be dangerous or destroy evidence only if he were "possessed of the skill of Houdini and the strength of Hercules."[30] The *Gant* Court may have ended such tomfoolery, but only through some disingenuous recasting of precedents. In turn, *Leon* now stands as a forerunner of the Court's new exception to the exclusionary rule, where law enforcement cannot be held responsible for the constitutional violations of *law enforcement*. The case spinoffs from *Herring* are limited only by the legal imagination. During this past term, however, the most enlightening example of doctrinal deviations under enforcement pressure was not *Herring*'s new exception or *Gant*'s erasure of a bright-line rule. Instead, it was the Court's decision in *Arizona v. Johnson*[31] concerning a seemingly minor and arguably preordained extension of the so-called "stop and frisk" doctrine.

As will be discussed in greater detail below, the Supreme Court's 1968 decision in *Terry v. Ohio* authorized police to respond to suspicious behavior with brief detentions and limited patdowns in the absence of a warrant or even probable cause.[32] Few doubt that the

---

[30] United States v. Frick, 490 F.2d 666, 673 (5th Cir. 1973) (Goldberg, J., concurring in part and dissenting in part).

[31] See Arizona v. Johnson, 555 U.S. ____, 129 S. Ct. 781 (2009).

[32] Terry v. Ohio, 392 U.S. 1 (1968).

Terry Court had good intentions, trying to balance the interests of law enforcement and the public through an opinion containing restrictive language on the permissible scope of police practice. But Justice William O. Douglas, the sole dissenter in *Terry*, spoke of the longstanding "hydraulic pressures" to dilute individual rights in favor of law enforcement prerogatives. The Court's decision, he believed, would usher in a new regime where police could search and seize at will.[33] Several years later, Justice Thurgood Marshall admitted that Douglas had been prescient, "that the delicate balance that *Terry* struck was simply too delicate, too susceptible to the 'hydraulic pressures of the day,'" portending a future where innocent people may be detained and their bodies searched without any suspicion of wrongdoing.[34] Despite such admonitions, the succeeding years would witness the Court deferring to government claims under the *Terry* rubric, expanding police authority with each decision and moving further and further away from the original justification.

To be sure, the Supreme Court has found constitutional violations in *Terry* cases, and one could point to any number of lower court decisions in favor of the defense.[35] But the overall trend is unmistakable, toward a general police power to search and seize. This was not the intent of *Terry*, which might be characterized as a mild reworking of existing jurisprudence. But to use the words of Fourth Amendment law's great chestnut, "illegitimate and unconstitutional practices get their first footing in that way, namely, by silent approaches and slight deviations from legal modes of procedure."[36] Some forty years after the stop and frisk doctrine was first announced, the *Johnson* Court held that police may pat down an individual without any suspicion of criminal activity, a now-predictable decision but one that only Justice Douglas foresaw in 1968.[37] The potential consequences are manifest and disquieting. Soon enough, we may see whether the Court will assent to further extensions or instead try to correct a doctrine cut loose from its theoretical moorings.

---

[33] *Id.* at 38–39 (Douglas, J., dissenting).

[34] Adams v. Williams, 407 U.S. 143, 162 (1972) (Marshall, J., dissenting).

[35] See, e.g., Florida v. J.L., 529 U.S. 266 (2000). See generally 4 LaFave, *supra* note 19.

[36] Boyd v. United States, 116 U.S. 616, 635 (1886).

[37] See, e.g., Terry, 392 U.S. at 35–39 (Douglas, J., dissenting).

II. *Arizona v. Johnson*

On the night of April 19, 2002, members of Arizona's gang task force were on patrol in an unmarked vehicle west of Sugar Hill, a Tucson neighborhood associated with the Crips street gang. At around 9 p.m., the officers pulled over an automobile on a major thoroughfare after a license plate check revealed that the vehicle's registration was suspended for an insurance violation, a civil infraction under state law without criminal repercussions. One of the task force members, Police Officer Maria Trevizo, testified that there was no reason to believe that anyone in the vehicle was involved in criminal activity. No crimes had been reported nearby, and the agents had no idea where the car had been or where it was going.[38] Trevizo also claimed that the vehicle had not been targeted or stopped with the purpose of investigating gang activity. She and her colleagues, Detectives Jack Machado and Dave Gittings, exited their unmarked police cruiser and approached the stopped vehicle, which contained three people—the driver, one passenger in the front seat, and another in the back seat. The occupants were told to keep their hands visible, and when asked whether there were any weapons in the vehicle, they all responded "no." Machado then told the driver to get out of the car—ostensibly to get his driver's license and information about vehicle registration and insurance—while Gittings focused on the front-seat passenger who remained in the car throughout the process.

For her part, Trevizo concentrated on the back-seat passenger, a young black man named Lemon Johnson. Supposedly, Johnson had stared at the law enforcement agents while they approached the car, which Trevizo deemed unusual. She also noted Johnson's all-blue clothing—an indicator of possible gang membership—as well as a radio scanner in his jacket. Nonetheless, the officer said she had no reason to believe that Johnson was involved in criminal activity and described him as cooperative in response to her questions. Although he did not have identification, Johnson provided his correct name and date of birth and even admitted serving time for burglary.

---

[38] See State v. Johnson, 170 P.3d 667, 668–69 (Ariz. App. 2007); Joint Appendix at 26, 30, Arizona v. Johnson, 129 S. Ct. 781 (2009) (No. 07-1122) (testimony of Officer Trevizo).

Johnson also mentioned that he was from Eloy, Arizona, a place Trevizo recognized as the home of a Crips-affiliated gang.

Believing that Johnson could be a gangster, Trevizo asked him to exit the vehicle so that she could talk to the young man away from the other occupants and "gather intelligence about the gang he might be in."[39] The officer acknowledged that her goal was unrelated to the justification for the traffic stop, that Johnson could have refused to get out of the vehicle, and that she did not intend to detain him. After he exited the vehicle in an ordinary manner, without sudden or furtive movements, Trevizo directed Johnson to turn around and proceeded to pat him down. The officer had "not observe[d] anything that appeared to be criminal" at that time—Trevizo even claimed that Johnson could have refused to turn around and put his arms up to be frisked—but she still believed that Johnson might be armed based on "the totality of what happened that evening."[40] During the patdown, Trevizo found a gun near Johnson's waist and a subsequent search uncovered marijuana.

The trial court denied Johnson's suppression motion, and a jury found him guilty of unlawful possession of a weapon and possession of marijuana, netting a presumptive eight-year term of imprisonment. By a divided vote, the Arizona Court of Appeals reversed, holding that the patdown of Johnson violated the Fourth Amendment and thus required the suppression of evidence derived from the search. Pursuant to the U.S. Supreme Court's stop and frisk doctrine, first articulated in *Terry v. Ohio,* law enforcement may briefly detain an individual for investigatory purposes (i.e., a stop) if it has reasonable suspicion that he is committing or has committed a crime. If law enforcement then has a reasonable suspicion that the detainee is armed and dangerous, it may conduct a limited search of his outer clothing for weapons (i.e., a patdown or frisk). But according to a majority of the Arizona court, the former suspicion that crime is afoot serves as a necessary predicate for the latter search: "An officer may not . . . conduct a pat-down search during a consensual encounter if the officer lacks reasonable suspicion that criminal activity is occurring, even if the officer has reason to believe

---

[39] Johnson, 170 P.3d at 669; Joint Appendix, *supra* note 38, at 19.

[40] Johnson, 170 P.3d at 669; Joint Appendix, *supra* note 38, at 19–20.

a suspect may be armed and dangerous."[41] The court reached this conclusion based on, inter alia, its reading of the original opinions in *Terry*.[42]

In this case, the constitutional issue boiled down to whether Johnson was seized immediately prior to being frisked or instead had been engaged in a consensual encounter. If he was not seized at that point, the appellate court reasoned, Officer Trevizo had no right to frisk Johnson. In a decision earlier that year, the U.S. Supreme Court had ruled that an automobile passenger is seized for Fourth Amendment purposes during a traffic stop.[43] The opinion gave no indication as to when the seizure ended, however, and the Arizona court was unable to locate a relevant precedent. But "common sense suggests that at some point during the encounter the passengers in the vehicle must be free to leave—their fate is not entirely tied to that of the driver."[44] An innocent passenger cannot be taken into custody or otherwise forced to convoy because his driver was arrested during a traffic stop. Given the facts and circumstances in this case, the appellate court determined that Johnson's initial seizure, incident to the stop of the driver, evolved into a separate consensual encounter where the officer was engaged in an unrelated investigation about potential gang affiliation. And without reasonable suspicion that Johnson was involved in criminal activity, Trevizo could not frisk the young man even if she had reason to believe he was armed and dangerous.

After the Arizona Supreme Court denied review, the U.S. Supreme Court granted certiorari; and on January 26, 2009, it reversed the lower court ruling in a relatively short, unanimous opinion. Writing for the Court, Justice Ruth Bader Ginsburg began by recapping *Terry*'s implications for street encounters: Law enforcement may stop an individual when it has a reasonable suspicion that he is involved in criminal activity. To proceed to a frisk, however, law enforcement must have a reasonable suspicion that the detainee is armed and dangerous.[45] Applying this doctrine to traffic stops,

---

[41] Johnson, 170 P.3d at 670 (citing In re Ilono H., 113 P.3d 696, 690 (Ariz. App. 2005)).

[42] See *id.* at 670–71.

[43] See Brendlin v. California, 551 U.S. 249, 262 (2007).

[44] Johnson, 170 P.3d at 671.

[45] See Arizona v. Johnson, 129 S. Ct. 781, 784 (2009).

> the first *Terry* condition—a lawful investigatory stop—is met whenever it is lawful for police to detain an automobile and its occupants pending inquiry into a vehicular violation. The police need not have, in addition, cause to believe any occupant of the vehicle is involved in criminal activity. To justify a patdown of the driver or a passenger during a traffic stop, however, just as in the case of a pedestrian reasonably suspected of criminal activity, the police must harbor reasonable suspicion that the person subjected to the frisk is armed and dangerous.[46]

Justice Ginsburg attempted to rationalize the doctrinal link between pedestrian and vehicular stops, as well as the differences, based on several propositions and a trio of precedents. To begin with, the Court had previously noted that traffic stops bear a resemblance to the brief detentions sanctioned by *Terry*, at least in terms of their duration and atmosphere. Prior cases also emphasized that traffic stops are "especially fraught with danger to police officers," a risk that is minimized when "officers routinely exercise unquestioned command of the situation."[47] After making these points, Justice Ginsburg offered three applications of the *Terry* doctrine to traffic stops. Law enforcement has the automatic power to order a driver out of his vehicle during a traffic stop without any suspicion that crime is afoot, and an officer may frisk the driver if there is a reasonable suspicion he might be armed and dangerous. Secondly, police may roust other occupants from their seats during a traffic stop, even though a passenger is innocent of the traffic violation and not suspected of any criminal activity. Finally, a passenger, like the driver, is considered seized from the moment the car comes to a halt on the side of the road until the end of the traffic stop. Justice Ginsburg then tied together the three applications of *Terry*: During routine traffic stops, an officer may pat down any passengers if he reasonably believes they may be armed and dangerous.

The *Johnson* opinion also offered a few parting shots about the notion of consent. The Arizona appellate court's portrayal of Officer Trevizo's dealings with Johnson as consensual was factually inaccurate and, to some extent, legally irrelevant. At trial, the officer all

---

[46] *Id.*

[47] *Id.* (quoting Maryland v. Wilson, 519 U.S. 408, 414 (1997)).

but conceded that she was not seeking Johnson's consent that night. Indeed, Justice Ginsburg wondered why the prosecutor had even tried to depict the encounter as consensual. This was "an 'unrealistic' characterization of the Trevizo-Johnson interaction," Ginsburg noted. "[B]eyond genuine debate, the point at which Johnson could have felt free to leave had not yet occurred."[48] As a matter of law, drivers and passengers remain seized throughout a traffic stop, which normally ends when a police officer says they are free to leave. Moreover, it was immaterial that Trevizo decided to conduct a separate investigation into Johnson's possible gang affiliation. So long as it did not measurably prolong the stop, "[a]n officer's inquiries into matters unrelated to the justification for the traffic stop . . . do not convert the encounter into something other than a lawful seizure."[49] Trevizo had done nothing wrong, the opinion concluded, as the officer need not allow Johnson to exit the car and leave the scene without making sure that a "dangerous person" was not behind her.[50]

Certainly, Justice Ginsburg (and the dissenting judge below) had good reason to reject the notion that any dealings between Officer Trevizo and defendant Johnson were consensual—at least if the word implies a voluntary interaction where an individual's will to refuse was not overborne by law enforcement. Here, the traffic stop was conducted by three agents who exited an unmarked vehicle wearing external tactical vests embossed with "Police" and "Street Gang Task Force" in large letters.[51] The occupants were first told to keep their hands visible. Then, one agent ordered the driver out of the car while the other agents trained their attention on the passengers, with Johnson being questioned about, among other things, whether he had spent time in prison. Officer Trevizo then asked Johnson to exit the car and immediately frisked him. Some of these details indicate that this was no ordinary traffic stop, such as the agents' tactical uniforms; other aspects are more banal but undermine the notion of consent, like the fact that the encounter unfolded rapidly and Trevizo never told Johnson that he could refuse to

---

[48] *Id.* at 787–88 (internal quotation omitted).

[49] *Id.* at 788.

[50] *Id.*

[51] See Joint Appendix, *supra* note 38, at 13–14.

comply. Under these circumstances, it is almost laughable to argue that the defendant could have said "no" to the officer's requests.[52] Johnson's cooperation is best described as submission to authority, or acquiescence to the inevitable, rather than voluntary consent.[53]

But if anyone is to blame for the lower court's "unrealistic" finding of consent, it is the Supreme Court justices themselves. They are the authors of the Fourth Amendment's problematic "consent doctrine," which claims to evaluate voluntariness under the totality of the circumstances,[54] yet in practice means utter deference to law enforcement.[55] For example, an individual need not be told of his right to refuse an officer's requests or that he is free to go after a traffic stop is complete.[56] Moreover, police deception does not necessarily vitiate consent.[57] Nor does it matter that consent to search someone's property was provided by another person who only *appeared* to have the authority to do so.[58] An individual's consent has even been judged voluntary despite the fact that it was obtained at police gunpoint.[59] In view of such decisions, leading scholars have surmised that the issue of voluntary consent does not depend on whether a suspect's will was actually overborne. Instead, it is a normative assessment of the governmental need to search versus concern about coercive police tactics—where law enforcement almost always prevails.[60] One might imagine that the Supreme Court would have found the Trevizo-Johnson interaction to be consensual if that were the only way the officer's search could be deemed lawful. But at least the seminal

---

[52] See, e.g., Arnold H. Loewy, Cops, Cars, and Citizens: Fixing the Broken Balance, 76 St. John's L. Rev. 535, 554 (2002).

[53] See Johnson, 170 P.3d at 675 (Espinosa, J., dissenting).

[54] See Schneckloth v. Bustamonte, 412 U.S. 218, 226–27 (1973).

[55] See, e.g., Janice Nadler, No Need to Shout: Bus Sweeps and the Psychology of Coercion, 2002 Sup. Ct. Rev. 153; Marcy Strauss, Reconstructing Consent, 92 J. Crim. L. & Criminology 211 (2002).

[56] See Schneckloth, 412 U.S. at 227; Ohio v. Robinette, 519 U.S. 33, 35 (1996); United States v. Drayton, 536 U.S. 194 (2002).

[57] See, e.g., Joshua Dressler & Alan C. Michaels, Understanding Criminal Procedure: Investigation 267–68 (4th ed. 2006); 4 LaFave, *supra* note 19, at § 8.2(m)–(n).

[58] See Illinois v. Rodriguez, 497 U.S. 177 (1990).

[59] See, e.g., United States v. Barnett, 989 F.2d 546, 555–56 (1st Cir. 1993); Strauss, *supra* note 55, at 226.

[60] See, e.g., Dressler & Michaels, *supra* note 57, at 266.

case on consent searches, the 1973 decision in *Schneckloth v. Busta-monte,* was relatively forthright about its real purpose and effect. In the words of the always pragmatic (but sometimes conceptually challenged) Justice Potter Stewart, consent searches "may be the only means of obtaining important and reliable evidence."[61]

In contrast, the doctrinal origin of the present case, *Terry v. Ohio,* did not allude to the subsequent deviations that would take place in its name. This is not to say that *Terry* wasn't controversial from the start; to the contrary, it was (and still is) a source of scholarly argument.[62] What is beyond debate, however, is that the *Terry* opinion itself cannot be read as empowering law enforcement to order a driver from his vehicle during a routine traffic stop, and it certainly did not license the automatic rousting of innocent passengers. Nor did *Terry* authorize the police conduct in *Johnson,* where law enforcement frisked a passenger without any belief that he was involved in criminal activity or even accountable for a civil violation. Similarly, it is a stretch to claim that the "suspicious" circumstances in this case—Lemon Johnson staring out the car window, the color of his clothes, his home town, etc.—would meet the *Terry* Court's description of the requisite level of proof. What is more, *Terry* seemed quite clear that the fact of a detention does not permit investigations wholly unrelated to the justification for the stop, let alone that an ancillary inquiry could serve as the occasion to frisk an otherwise innocent individual. To understand how this all became possible, we must turn back to the doctrine's source.

III. *Terry v. Ohio*

Chief Justice Earl Warren's majority opinion in *Terry v. Ohio* was motivated by admirable goals, including the pursuit of a remedy for the abusive policing of minority communities detailed in major

---

[61] Schneckloth, 412 U.S. at 227.

[62] See, e.g., Wayne R. LaFave, Street Encounters and the Constitution: *Terry, Sibron, Peters,* and Beyond, 67 Mich. L. Rev. 39, 39 n.4 (1968). See also Symposium on the 30th Anniversary of *Terry v. Ohio,* 72 St. John's L. Rev. 721 (1998); Scott E. Sundby, A Return to Fourth Amendment Basics: Undoing the Mischief of *Camara* and *Terry,* 72 Minn. L. Rev. 383 (1988).

commission reports.[63] The Court sought to bring within the fold of constitutional law the otherwise unregulated contacts between police and citizen.[64] When law enforcement accosts an individual on the street, inhibits his freedom to walk away, and thoroughly explores the outer surface of his clothing, he has been subjected to a Fourth Amendment intrusion. A seizure occurs not only upon formal arrest but whenever an officer, "by means of physical force or show of authority, has in some way restrained the liberty of a citizen."[65] Moreover, the Court found it impossible to argue that "a careful exploration of the outer surfaces of a person's clothing all over his or her body in an attempt to find weapons is not a 'search.'"[66] This is not a trifling interference but instead "a serious intrusion upon the sanctity of the person, which may inflict great indignity and arouse strong resentment."[67] The frisk represents a sharp infringement "upon cherished personal security, and it must surely be an annoying, frightening, and perhaps humiliating experience."[68] Given that the street detention amounted to a seizure and the pat-down constituted a search, a stop and frisk might seem to require judicial preclearance, or at least probable cause.[69]

But according to the *Terry* Court, the police conduct at issue here, "necessarily swift action predicated upon the on-the-spot observations on the beat," could not be governed by the warrant process.[70] And because the Warrant Clause of the Fourth Amendment is inapplicable, Chief Justice Warren proclaimed that probable cause is not a prerequisite. Instead, this police technique would be subject to

[63] See President's Comm'n on Law Enforcement & Admin. of Justice, Task Force Report: The Police (1967); Nat'l Advisory Comm'n on Civil Disorders, Report of the National Advisory Commission on Civil Disorders (1968). See also Gregory H. Williams, The Supreme Court and Broken Promises: The Gradual but Continual Erosion of *Terry v. Ohio*, 34 How. L.J. 567, 571–72 (1991). For an excellent review of the Court discussions leading to *Terry*, see John Q. Barrett, Deciding the Stop and Frisk Cases: A Look Inside the Supreme Court's Conference, 72 St. John's L. Rev. 749 (1998).

[64] See Terry, 392 U.S. at 28–31.

[65] *Id.* at 19 n.16.

[66] *Id.* at 16.

[67] *Id.* at 17.

[68] *Id.* at 25.

[69] See, e.g., Katz v. United States, 389 U.S. 347, 356–57 (1967).

[70] Terry, 392 U.S. at 20.

"the Fourth Amendment's general proscription against unreasonable searches and seizures."[71] Relying upon a case decided a year earlier, the *Terry* Court evaluated the reasonableness of the stop and frisk by balancing the government interests at stake—crime prevention and detection, and officer safety—against the individual's interest in freedom of movement and bodily autonomy.[72] The balance the Court ultimately struck would allow an officer to conduct a brief detention based on a reasonable suspicion that "criminal activity may be afoot" and then a patdown if he has a reasonable suspicion that a suspect is "armed and presently dangerous."[73]

There were, and still are, many reasons to be dissatisfied with *Terry*. At the time, dissenting Justice Douglas thought it was a "mystery" how a search and seizure could be lawful without probable cause of criminal activity.[74] A neutral magistrate could not issue a warrant in such circumstances, given the constitutional standard of proof—but after the Court's decision, "the police have greater authority to make a 'seizure' and conduct a 'search' than a judge has to authorize such action."[75] Probable cause is not only spelled out in the text of the Fourth Amendment and engrained in America's constitutional history, but it "rings a bell of certainty that is not sounded by phrases such as 'reasonable suspicion.'"[76] Douglas saw *Terry* as a "long step down the totalitarian path" brought about by the "hydraulic pressures" of crime and justice, creating the type of "new regime" that could be legitimate only after popular deliberation and constitutional amendment.[77] Likewise, Professor Anthony

---

[71] *Id.*

[72] See Camara v. Municipal Court, 387 U.S. 523 (1967).

[73] Terry, 392 U.S. at 30–31. The *Terry* Court itself did not use the words "reasonable suspicion," although it was used in Justice Douglas's *Terry* dissent, *id.* at 37 (Douglas, J., dissenting); as well as in a companion case to *Terry*, Sibron v. New York, 392 U.S. 40, 49, 60 (1968). Later cases would make clear that this was the term for the level of suspicion required for a *Terry* stop and frisk. See, e.g., Dressler & Michaels, *supra* note 57, at 285 n. 29.

[74] See Terry, 392 U.S. at 35 (Douglas, J., dissenting).

[75] *Id.* at 36.

[76] *Id.* at 37.

[77] *Id.* at 38–39.

Amsterdam cautioned against a graduated approach, which "converts the Fourth Amendment into one immense Rorschach blot."[78] *Terry* created a third category of street encounter between arrests based on probable cause and simple conversation that requires no justification. "But why only three categories?," Amsterdam rhetorically asked. "Why not six, or a dozen, or an even hundred?"[79] The Court's sliding scale approach to the Fourth Amendment would only provide "more slide than scale," with the intended distinctions of the graduated model dissolving in the practical realities of street enforcement and trial adjudication.

But the *Terry* opinion did not foresee these problems, with its language attempting to cabin the new doctrine. As mentioned, the Court sought to expand constitutional protection by applying the Fourth Amendment to stops and frisks, and a primary impetus was the "wholesale harassment" of minorities, especially African Americans. The abuses had become a leading source of conflict between law enforcement and minority communities, "as more police departments adopt 'aggressive patrol' in which officers are encouraged routinely to stop and question persons on the street who are unknown to them, who are suspicious, or whose purpose for being abroad is not readily evident."[80] For this reason, *Terry* acknowledged that "the degree of community resentment aroused by particular practices is clearly relevant to an assessment of the quality of the intrusion upon reasonable expectations of personal security caused by those practices."[81] The majority opinion also recognized that stops and frisks were serious invasions of liberty. Patdowns in particular inflicted a great indignity, "performed in public while a citizen stands helpless, perhaps facing a wall with his hands raised," with the officer fingering the individual's entire body— "arms and armpits, waistline and back, the groin and area about the testicles, and the entire surface of the legs down to the feet."[82]

---

[78] Anthony G. Amsterdam, Perspectives on the Fourth Amendment, 58 Minn. L. Rev. 349, 393 (1974). See also *id.* at 374.

[79] *Id.* at 376.

[80] Terry, 392 U.S. at 15 n.11 (quoting the President's Comm'n, *supra* note 63, at 183).

[81] *Id.* at 17 n.14.

[82] *Id.* at 17, 17 n.13 (quoting L.L. Priar & T.F. Martin, Searching and Disarming Criminals, 45 J. Crim. L. Criminology & Police Sci. 481 (1954)).

Police should not undertake these procedures lightly, the Court admonished, and the judiciary must condemn such activity if it is overbearing or harassing, or lacks a sufficient evidentiary basis. Chief Justice Warren made plain that there were predicates and limits to the stop and frisk process. *Terry* mandated two separate inquiries: "whether the officer's action was justified at its inception, and whether it was reasonably related in scope to the circumstances which justified the interference in the first place."[83] Specifically, the preliminary question asked if there was adequate reason to believe that criminal activity was afoot and a particular individual was involved. If so, the second issue came into play—whether there was reason to believe that the suspect was presently armed and dangerous. Between these stages, an officer could identify himself as a policeman and ask reasonable questions. A subsequent patdown would be permissible only if "nothing in the initial stages of the encounter serves to dispel his reasonable fear for his own or others' safety."[84] The frisk was thereby predicated on a lawful stop based on reasonable suspicion of criminal activity.

The facts in *Terry* illustrated the dual inquiry: A police officer witnessed two men walking back and forth in front of a store, "pausing to stare in the same store window roughly 24 times" and conferencing on a street corner after each roundtrip. The pair ultimately met with a third man, whom they followed and then rejoined a few blocks away. The officer believed that they were "casing a job," that is, checking out the store in preparation for an armed robbery. He stopped the three men and asked them questions; only after they "mumbled something" in response did the officer frisk the trio and uncover firearms.[85] The suspicion of crime thus preceded the frisk, the legal implications of which Justice John Marshall Harlan made "perfectly clear" in his concurrence: The authority to conduct a frisk "depends upon the reasonableness of a forcible stop to investigate a suspected crime."[86] Harlan noted that "[a]ny person, including a policeman, is at liberty to avoid a person he considers dangerous." During a voluntary conversation with law enforcement, a citizen

[83] *Id.* at 20.

[84] *Id.* at 30.

[85] *Id.* at 7.

[86] *Id.* at 33 (Harlan, J., concurring).

"certainly need not submit to a frisk for the questioner's protection." Any power to search does not originate from an officer's "right to disarm, to frisk for his own protection," but instead from his belief that criminal activity was afoot and his prerogative to prevent and investigate serious crime.[87]

Although stops and frisks required neither a warrant nor probable cause, *Terry* stated that "the notions which underlie both the warrant procedure and the requirement of probable cause remain fully relevant in this context."[88] Citing its core cases on probable cause and even using the language of these opinions, the Court held that an agent "must be able to point to specific and articulable facts, which taken together with rational inferences from those facts, reasonably warrant [the] intrusion."[89] The benchmark was a sensibly cautious individual—what "a reasonably prudent man in the circumstances" would have believed based on the objective facts, without reference to a given officer's unparticularized suspicions or hunches.[90] The requirement of specificity was nothing less than "the central teaching of this Court's Fourth Amendment jurisprudence."[91] By its words, then, *Terry* did not portray the standard of proof as insubstantial.

The conceptual connection between reasonable suspicion and probable cause was critical, grounding the *Terry* standard in a constitutional philosophy that "common rumor or report, suspicion, or even 'strong reason to suspect'" could not support a search and seizure.[92] The Supreme Court has never attempted to quantify probable cause, other than to say it is less than the amount of evidence necessary to convict at trial.[93] But the justices opined that "the resolution of doubtful or marginal cases [of probable cause] should be largely determined by the preference to be accorded to warrants," where any inferences can be "drawn by a neutral and detached magistrate instead of being judged by the officer engaged in the

---

[87] *Id.* at 32–33.

[88] *Id.* at 20 (majority opinion).

[89] *Id.* at 21 (citing, inter alia, Beck v. Ohio, 379 U.S. 89 (1964), and Brinegar v. United States, 338 U.S. 160 (1949)).

[90] *Id.* at 21–22, 27.

[91] *Id.* at 22 n.18.

[92] Henry v. United States, 361 U.S. 98, 101 (1959).

[93] See Brinegar, 338 U.S. at 175.

often competitive enterprise of ferreting out crime."[94] At perhaps the "high water" mark for probable cause determinations, the Court held that the smell of opium coming from a closed hotel room did not justify a warrantless search and seizure.[95] Although the opinions often appeared fact-bound, they occasionally provided rules for proof determinations under the Fourth Amendment—laying out a test to evaluate information supplied by informants,[96] for instance, and rejecting bald assertions about an individual's character or his mere propinquity to particular people or places.[97]

Against this background, one might wonder how the ostensibly reasonable and limited decision in *Terry* could be the precursor of cases like *Arizona v. Johnson*. Other than Justice Douglas's dissent, the opinions in *Terry* seemed oblivious to the potential consequences, that constant pressure to water down individual rights might lead the Court to adopt new deviations, which, over time, would remove any limitations outlined in the original decision. Once judges disregard the motto of *obsta principiis*—"resist the beginnings"—it becomes harder with each step to return to the constitutional principle that had been spurned at the outset.[98] To be clear, the expansion of law enforcement's power to stop and frisk was only one aspect of a more general, "continuing evisceration of Fourth Amendment protections,"[99] with the Supreme Court adopting new exceptions to the warrant requirement, allowing the admission of evidence despite its being illegally obtained, concocting procedural barriers to judicial review, and holding that a variety of privacy invasions were of no constitutional moment.[100] When dissenting justices would draw

[94] United States v. Ventresca, 380 U.S. 102, 109 (1965); Johnson v. United States, 333 U.S. 10, 14 (1948).

[95] Henry, 361 U.S. at 101; Johnson, 333 U.S. at 12–14.

[96] See generally Spinelli v. United States, 393 U.S. 410 (1969); Aguilar v. Texas, 378 U.S. 108 (1964).

[97] See Ybarra v. Illinois, 444 U.S. 85, 91 (1979); Sibron v. New York, 392 U.S. 40, 63 (1969); Spinelli, 393 U.S. at 414.

[98] See, e.g., Boyd v. United States, 116 U.S. 616, 635 (1886). See also Wayne R. LaFave, The Forgotten Motto of Obsta Principiis in Fourth Amendment Jurisprudence, 28 Ariz. L. Rev. 291 (1986).

[99] United States v. Martinez-Fuerte, 428 U.S. 543, 567 (1976) (Brennan, J., dissenting). See also Andresen v. Maryland, 427 U.S. 463, 485 n.1 (1976) (Brennan, J., dissenting).

[100] See, e.g., United States v. Leon, 468 U.S. 897 (1984) (establishing "good faith" exception to the exclusionary rule); Stone v. Powell, 428 U.S. 465 (1976) (concluding that Fourth Amendment violations are not cognizable on federal habeas corpus

attention to each deviation, their colleagues in the majority would reject any concerns as alarmist given the narrowness of their decision. But when a later case would take a further step, the dissenters were relegated to criticizing the Court for violating its promise.[101] Even where it was breaking from established doctrine, however, a majority opinion might repackage prior precedents as being more consistent with the new approach. Such was the case with the Fourth Amendment's standards of proof.

IV. Diluted Suspicion

In 1983, the Supreme Court abandoned the prevailing test for informant information, and with it, any hard rules that had been developed on probable cause.[102] That case, *Illinois v. Gates*, opted instead for the multifactor, all-things-considered "totality of the circumstances" test. In so doing, the Court argued that probable cause is "a fluid concept" that could not be "reduced to a neat set of legal rules."[103] The *Gates* majority said its approach was consonant with prior cases, boldly claiming that it was simply "reaffirm[ing]" the totality of the circumstances test that had "traditionally" been used in evaluations of probable cause. The dissenters rejected this revisionist history, as well as the Court's new standard, which provided no structure for probable cause inquiries and invited intrusions based on unreliable information, ultimately permitting an alleged

---

review); South Dakota v. Opperman, 428 U.S. 364 (1976) (upholding warrantless inventory searches). See also Erik Luna, The *Katz* Jury, 41 U.C. Davis L. Rev. 839, 840–45 (2008) (discussing Katz v. United States, 389 U.S. 347 (1967), and its progeny).

[101] See, e.g., United States v. Villamonte-Marquez, 462 U.S. 579, 610 (1983) (Brennan, J., dissenting):

> In dissent in *Martinez-Fuerte*, I expressed my fear that the Court's decision was part of a "continuing evisceration of Fourth Amendment protection against unreasonable searches and seizures." The majority chided me for my rhetoric and my "unwarranted concern," pointing out that its holding was expressly and narrowly limited: "Our holding today, approving routine stops for brief questioning . . . is confined to permanent checkpoints." Today the Court breaks that promise.

[102] Illinois v. Gates, 462 U.S. 213 (1983).

[103] *Id.* at 232.

"totality" to exceed "the sum of its circumstances."[104] Even concurring Justice Byron White recognized that *Gates* "may foretell an evisceration of the probable cause standard."[105]

As it turns out, Justice White, his dissenting colleagues, and numerous cynical scholars were right: For all intents and purposes, the totality of the circumstances standard has transformed probable cause into no standard at all. As suggested by empirical studies and subsequent case law, the judiciary rarely impedes police investigations by denying or second guessing their searches and seizures.[106] The Court's most recent precedents permit a type of guilt by association, where probable cause that someone within a group committed a crime means that all can be searched.[107] None of this should have been a surprise with the recrudescence of the totality of the circumstances test, which has meant judicial deference in the context of consent searches and had only sown confusion in the area of custodial interrogation.[108]

The Court had adopted the totality of the circumstances test for reasonable suspicion before applying it to probable cause, and it was inevitable that the test would have an even greater impact on stops and frisks. Many of the post-*Terry* cases had downplayed the requisite amount of proof while amplifying the gap between probable cause and reasonable suspicion. A stop and frisk needed only "some minimal level of objective justification," the Court noted, which "is considerably less than proof of wrongdoing by a preponderance of the evidence" and "obviously less demanding" than probable cause.[109] Moreover, reasonable suspicion can be established

---

[104] *Id.* at 286–91 (Brennan, J., dissenting); *id.* at 295 n.8 (Stevens, J., dissenting).

[105] *Id.* at 272 (White, J., concurring).

[106] See, e.g., Laurence A. Benner & Charles T. Samarkos, Preliminary Findings from the San Diego Search Warrant Project, 36 Cal. W. L. Rev. 221 (2000); George R. Nock, The Point of the Fourth Amendment and the Myth of Magisterial Discretion, 23 Conn. L. Rev. 1, 7 n.25 (1990) (discussing ACLU study in Washington state).

[107] See Maryland v. Pringle, 540 U.S. 366 (2003); Wyoming v. Houghton, 526 U.S. 295 (1999). See, e.g., Tracey Maclin, The *Pringle* Case's New Notion of Probable Cause: An Assault on *Di Re* and the Fourth Amendment, 2004 Cato Sup. Ct. Rev. 395 (2004).

[108] See *supra* notes 54–61 and accompany text (discussing consent doctrine); Yale Kamisar, *Gates,* "Probable Cause," "Good Faith," and Beyond, 69 Iowa L. Rev. 551, 570–71 (1984) (discussing pre-*Miranda* standard for custodial interrogation).

[109] United States v. Sokolow, 490 U.S. 1, 7–8 (1989) (quoting INS v. Delgado, 466 U.S. 210, 217 (1984)); United States v. Cortez, 449 U.S. 411, 417 (1981)).

by "information that is less reliable than that required to show probable cause."[110] Previously, police needed to provide some showing as to how an informant got his information, why it should be believed, or at least some details that officers independently verified. Now an anonymous tip that someone will depart for a particular place at a particular time offers reasonable suspicion to detain, despite the fact that many of the tipster's details are demonstrably erroneous.[111] Reasonable suspicion can even be provided by a series of innocuous facts, collectively amounting to lawful activity subject to innocent explanation, so long as law enforcement could infer criminal activity was afoot. It can be suspicious, for example, when a driver does not look over at a patrol car, based on that officer's "experience" that "most persons look over" and give him "a friendly wave."[112]

With this low threshold, entire categories of information might not only be relevant, but effectively dispositive by simple invocation of law enforcement. In 1979, the Court had held that being in a high-crime area, specifically, "a neighborhood frequented by drug users," was not itself a reason to suspect an individual of criminal activity.[113] Since then, however, some lower courts have found reasonable suspicion by pointing to otherwise harmless conduct—twice crossing the street, for instance, or sitting in a parked vehicle—because it occurred in an allegedly high-crime neighborhood.[114] In 2000, the Supreme Court condoned this approach in *Illinois v. Wardlow*, where it found that an individual's "unprovoked flight upon noticing the police" in a high-crime area provided sufficient justification to conduct a *Terry* stop and frisk.[115] In a partial dissent, Justice John Paul Stevens recognized that there are innocent reasons why someone might leave when law enforcement arrives at the scene.[116] Minorities,

[110] Cortez, 449 U.S. at 417–18 (1981). See also United States v. Brignoni-Ponce, 422 U.S. 873, 885 n.10 (1975).

[111] See, e.g., Alabama v. White, 496 U.S. 325, 353 (1990) (Stevens, J., dissenting).

[112] See, e.g., United States v. Arvizu, 534 U.S. 266, 270 (2002).

[113] Brown v. Texas, 443 U.S. 47, 52 (1979).

[114] See Margaret Raymond, Down on the Corner, Out in the Street: Considering the Character of the Neighborhood in Evaluating Reasonable Suspicion, 60 Ohio St. L.J. 99, 115–19 (1999) (discussing cases).

[115] See Illinois v. Wardlow, 528 U.S. 119, 125 (2000).

[116] See *id.* at 128–29 (Stevens, J., concurring and dissenting in part).

in particular, may have good reason to avoid encounters with police officers they perceive as aggressive, adversarial, and dangerous.[117] More generally, key concepts like "high-crime area" and "unprovoked flight" have never been defined by the Supreme Court, and some lower courts have been willing to give credence to less persuasive notions (e.g., "a slow run" or "a walk that accelerates").[118] In practice, the mere incantation of such terms at a suppression hearing may justify a stop.[119]

By comparison, the Supreme Court's jurisprudence on frisks is relatively thin. In a 1974 case, *Adams v. Williams,* an officer patrolling a "high-crime area" at around 2 a.m. was told by a known informant that someone sitting in a nearby car was carrying drugs and had a firearm at his waist. When the officer approached the individual and asked him to open the car door, the man rolled down the window instead—at which point, the officer reached into the vehicle and removed a gun from the man's waistband.[120] Given the tip, time of day and location, and the suspect's failure to open his car door, the *Adams* Court concluded that the officer justifiably believed that crime was afoot and had "ample reason to fear for his safety."[121] In dissent, Justice Douglas emphasized that state law permitted individuals to possess concealed weapons and that the only basis for arrest in this case was a tip about illegal drugs. "Can it be said that a man in possession of narcotics will not have a permit for his gun?," Douglas rhetorically asked.[122]

Subsequent cases would confirm Douglas's misgivings about presumptions in *Terry* analysis. In *Minnesota v. Dickerson,* two officers

[117] See *id.* at 132–34. See also Lenese C. Herbert, Can't You See What I Am Saying? Making Expressive Conduct a Crime in High Crime Areas, 9 Geo. J. on Poverty L. & Pol'y 135 (2002).

[118] See, e.g., State v. Harbison, 141 N.M. 392 (2007); Wilson v. United States, 802 A.2d 367 (D.C. App. 2002).

[119] See Andrew Guthrie Ferguson & Damien Bernache, The "High-Crime Area" Question: Requiring Verifiable and Quantifiable Evidence for Fourth Amendment Reasonable Suspicion Analysis, 57 Am. U. L. Rev. 1587 (2008). See also David A. Harris, Factors for Reasonable Suspicion: When Black and Poor Means Stopped and Frisked, 69 Ind. L.J. 659, 677–78 (1994); Herbert, *supra* note 117; Raymond, *supra* note 114.

[120] Adams v. Williams, 407 U.S. 143, 144–45 (1972).

[121] *Id.* at 147–48.

[122] *Id.* at 149–50 (Douglas, J., dissenting).

observed a person leaving a notorious "crack house," and when he spotted the patrol car, the individual turned and walked away in an apparent attempt to avoid contact with law enforcement. The officers stopped the man and frisked him, which uncovered a lump of crack cocaine but no weapons.[123] The Supreme Court did not question that there was reasonable suspicion in this case, and in fact, it made no mention of the purported grounds for the frisk: an officer's claim that other weapons had been seized from people at that location and his experience that drug traffickers often possess weapons.[124] Rather, the *Dickerson* opinion focused on the discovery of the drugs, which would have been perfectly permissible if the incriminating character of the item was immediately evident from an ordinary *Terry* frisk.[125]

The unmentioned basis for the patdown in *Dickerson* is hard to square with the Court's earlier decision in *Ybarra v. Illinois,* where it held that police could not conduct a "generalized cursory search for weapons" during a drug bust but instead must have an individualized reasonable suspicion that the person frisked is armed and dangerous.[126] Nor does the *Dickerson* patdown fit with the more recent decision in *J.L. v. Florida.* In that case, the Court found no reasonable suspicion for a police frisk based on an anonymous tip that a young black male, wearing a plaid shirt and standing at a bus stop, was armed. More generally, it refused to adopt a categorical "firearm exception."[127] Nonetheless, lower court decisions have created virtual per se rules permitting frisks when law enforcement is investigating particular classes of crime.[128] This may make eminent sense in a few offense categories—homicide, forcible rape, or the type of robbery suspected in *Terry*—which almost by definition

---

[123] See Minnesota v. Dickerson, 508 U.S. 366, 368–69 (1993).

[124] See State v. Dickerson, 469 N.W.2d 462, 464 (Minn. 1991).

[125] See Dickerson, 508 U.S. at 378–79 (holding that "*Terry* entitled [the officer] to place his hands on respondent's jacket" but "the incriminating character of the object was not immediately apparent to him" and required a further search not authorized by *Terry*).

[126] Ybarra, 444 U.S. at 92–96.

[127] See Florida v. J.L., 529 U.S. 266, 269–74 (2000).

[128] See 4 LaFave, Search and Seizure, *supra* note 19, at § 9.6(a); David A. Harris, Frisking Every Suspect: The Withering of *Terry*, 28 U.C. Davis L. Rev. 1, 22–32 (1994).

involve weapons and violence. But some cases have accepted automatic frisk rules for crimes without any obvious connection to armed belligerence, including burglary, car theft, fraud, gambling, and prostitution.[129] No empirical evidence is offered for such rules. Instead, courts simply assert a proposition, like burglary is "a crime normally and reasonably expected to involve a weapon."[130]

The most utilized instance of automatic suspicion to frisk is in the area of drug enforcement, where lower court cases have said, inter alia: "weapons and violence are frequently associated with drug transactions"; "drug dealers and weapons go hand in hand"; and "firearms are as much 'tools of the trade' as are most commonly recognized articles of drug paraphernalia."[131] The association between drugs, guns, and violence is the subject of ongoing empirical debate, and the actual likelihood that an individual involved in a drug transaction is armed and dangerous is unknown and likely unknowable.[132] In reality, though, the probabilistic question is almost beside the point when drug enforcement is at issue—judges generally defer to police. As argued elsewhere, acquiescence by the courts to the so-called "War on Drugs" has resulted in a de facto drug

---

[129] See, e.g., United States v. Bullock, 510 F.3d 342 (D.C. Cir. 2007) (citing cases on, inter alia, burglary, drug dealing, car theft, and fraud); United States v. Hanlon, 401 F.3d 926, 929–30 (8th Cir. 2005) ("when officers encounter suspected car thieves, they also may reasonably suspect the individuals might possess weapons"); United States v. Johnson, 364 F.3d 1185, 1195 (10th Cir. 2004) (prostitution among crimes "typically associated with some sort of weapon"); State v. James, 795 So.2d 1146, 1150 (La. 2000) ("the frequent association of narcotics trafficking with firearms justified the officer's brief, self-protective frisk"); People v. Tsang, 173 A.D.2d 173, 173 (N.Y. App. Div. 1991) ("guns usually accompany illegal gambling house operations").

[130] United States v. Barnett, 505 F.3d 637, 640 (7th Cir. 2007). This particular conclusion seems at odds with a Supreme Court opinion in another area of Fourth Amendment jurisprudence: the police use of deadly force. See Tennessee v. Garner, 471 U.S. 1, 21–22 (1985) (noting that "the available statistics demonstrate that burglaries only rarely involve physical violence").

[131] United States v. Bustos-Torres, 396 F.3d 935, 943 (8th Cir. 2005); United States v. Trullo, 809 F.2d 108, 114 (1st Cir. 1987); State v. Richardson, 456 N.W.2d 830, 836 (Wis. 1990).

[132] For instance, one comparative study suggested that higher levels of drug *enforcement* explain higher levels of violence. See, e.g., Jeffrey A. Miron, Violence, Guns, and Drugs: A Cross-Country Analysis, 44 J. L. & Econ. 615 (2001). See also, e.g., Bernard E. Harcourt, Judge Richard Posner on Civil Liberties: Pragmatic Authoritarian Libertarian, 74 U. Chi. L. Rev. 1723, 32–33 (2007) (critiquing judicial use of hit-rates in Fourth Amendment analysis).

exception to the Constitution.[133] Dissenting justices have criticized the judiciary for becoming "a loyal foot soldier" in the drug war, adopting "constitutionally forbidden shortcuts" in service of prohibition.[134]

In particular, the Fourth Amendment has been rendered *hors de combat*, as epitomized by the judiciary's tacit approval of the "drug courier profile." Among others, Professor David Cole offered a devastating critique of the profile—a set of traits and behaviors supposedly associated with individuals trafficking in drugs—noting how, over time, law enforcement used opposing characteristics or cited the entire universe of alternatives (e.g., too nervous, too calm, one of the first to deplane, one of the last to deplane, deplaned in the middle, etc.).[135] By the 1990s, however, the drug courier profile had been effectively endorsed by the Supreme Court's jurisprudence.[136] Other profiles, like gang membership—which include broad criteria like wearing particular colors, having tattoos, and frequenting a gang-related area—would be unsurprising extensions for *Terry* analysis.[137] The elasticity of these sketches, as well as the aforementioned notion of high-crime areas, has permitted a different, far more troubling form of profiling: the use of race or ethnicity in determining those individuals to be investigated or otherwise placed under suspicion. This phenomenon, known as "racial profiling," seemed to

[133] See Erik Luna, Drug Exceptionalism, 47 Vill. L. Rev. 753 (2002).

[134] California v. Acevedo, 500 U.S. 565, 601 (1991) (Stevens, J., dissenting); Harmelin v. Michigan, 501 U.S. 957, 1024 (1991) (White, J., dissenting). See also Employment Div. Dep't of Human Res. v. Smith, 494 U.S. 872, 908 (1990) (Blackmun, J., dissenting) (suggesting that Court's free exercise decision was "a product of overreaction to the serious problems the country's drug crisis has generated"); Nat'l Treasury Employees Union v. Von Raab, 489 U.S. 656, 680–81 (1989) (Scalia, J., dissenting) (arguing that drug testing regime approved by Court was "a kind of immolation of privacy and human dignity in symbolic opposition to drug use").

[135] David Cole, No Equal Justice: Race and Class in the American Criminal Justice System 47–48 (1999).

[136] See United States v. Sokolow, 490 U.S. 1 (1989); United States v. Sharpe, 470 U.S. 675 (1985); Florida v. Rodriguez, 469 U.S. 1 (1984); Florida v. Royer, 460 U.S. 491 (1983); United States v. Mendenhall, 446 U.S. 544 (1980).

[137] See, e.g., Suzin Kim, Gangs and Law Enforcement: The Necessity of Limiting the Use of Gang Profiles, 5 B.U. Pub. Int. L.J. 265, 270–71 (1996) (detailing specific gang profiles). Cf. State v. Jones, 835 P.2d 863, 866 (N.M. App. 1992) (noting that "an individual's membership in a gang is a factor which may properly be considered . . . in determining whether a stop and frisk is proper").

receive the imprimatur of the Supreme Court in border patrol cases from the mid-1970s, where it held that "Mexican appearance" was relevant for immigration enforcement.[138] In turn, several lower court cases have found race to be an acceptable factor in ordinary stop-and-frisk analysis.[139] Racial stereotyping under *Terry* is rarely overt, however, and instead it typically occurs under the pretext of a traffic stop pursuant to all-encompassing vehicular codes.

V. *Terry* Behind the Wheel

Some of the Supreme Court's pre-*Terry* decisions had upheld warrantless automobile searches and seizures—the earliest of which, ironically enough, involved a different type of drug crime, bootlegging. In *Carroll v. United States*, the Court recognized that it may not be possible to obtain a warrant "because the vehicle can be quickly moved out of the locality or jurisdiction in which the warrant must be sought."[140] But that did not justify a search and seizure in the absence of probable cause of criminal activity:

> It would be intolerable and unreasonable if a prohibition agent were authorized to stop every automobile on the chance of finding liquor, and thus subject all persons lawfully using the highways to the inconvenience and indignity of such a search. . . . [T]hose lawfully within the country, entitled to use the public highways, have a right to free passage without interruption or search unless there is known to a competent official, authorized to search, probable cause for believing that their vehicles are carrying contraband or illegal merchandise.[141]

Subsequent decisions reiterated that automobile searches and seizures required probable cause of criminal activity.[142] In fact, the

---

[138] See United States v. Brignoni-Ponce, 422 U.S. 873, 886–87 (1975); United States v. Martinez-Fuerte, 428 U.S. 543, 563 n.17 (1976).

[139] See, e.g., United States v. Weaver, 966 F.2d 391, 394 n.2 (8th Cir. 1992) (noting as factor in detaining defendant "that he was a roughly dressed young black male"); United States v. Malone, 886 F.2d 1162, 1164 (9th Cir. 1989) (noting that suspicion was based on fact that, inter alia, defendant was "a young, black male").

[140] Carroll v. United States, 267 U.S. 132, 153 (1924).

[141] *Id.* at 153–54.

[142] See, e.g., Chambers v. Maroney, 399 U.S. 42, 50–51 (1970); Dyke v. Taylor Implement Mfg. Co., 391 U.S. 216, 221–22 (1968); Brinegar v. United States, 338 U.S. 160, 164 (1949).

Court affirmed this principle in the first post-*Terry* border patrol case, *Almeida-Sanchez v. United States*: "[T]he *Carroll* doctrine does not declare a field day for the police in searching automobiles. Automobile or no automobile, there must be probable cause for the search."[143] In 1975, however, the Supreme Court's decision in *United States v. Brignoni-Ponce* held that law enforcement could stop a vehicle based on a reasonable suspicion that it contained illegal aliens. After describing the public interest in preventing illegal immigration and the limited intrusion by border patrol agents, the Court expressly relied upon *Terry* and its progeny to justify a brief automobile stop. "These cases together establish that in appropriate circumstances the Fourth Amendment allows a properly limited 'search' or 'seizure' on facts that do not constitute probable cause to arrest or to search for contraband or evidence of crime."[144] But the Court claimed that the decision was narrow, as it had rejected random border patrol stops and held that probable cause was required for anything extending beyond a brief detention to ask questions about suspicious circumstances.

Justice Douglas, however, saw *Brignoni-Ponce* as exemplifying the persistent deterioration of Fourth Amendment protection foreseen in his *Terry* dissent. The stop and frisk doctrine had now been extended from violent crime to drug and immigration offenses, and from street stops to seizures of moving vehicles. *Terry* had "come to be viewed as a legal construct for the regulation of a general investigatory police power," which was "warmly embraced by law enforcement forces and vigorously employed in the cause of crime detection."[145] Though the reasonable suspicion standard may capture evidence of crime, "the nature of the test permits the police to interfere as well with a multitude of law-abiding citizens, whose only transgression may be a nonconformist appearance or attitude."[146] If the erosion of the Fourth Amendment was to be limited, it would come from the Court's vigorous review of the doctrine's subsequent

---

[143] Almeida-Sanchez v. United States, 413 U.S. 266, 269 (1973). See also United States v. Ortiz, 422 U.S. 891 (1975).

[144] United States v. Brignoni-Ponce, 422 U.S. 873, 881 (1975).

[145] *Id.* at 889 (Douglas, J., concurring in the judgment).

[146] *Id.*

applications rather than the "qualifying language of today's opinion."[147] But "I am not optimistic," Douglas remarked, given case developments since *Terry*.[148]

Once again, his doubts were well-founded. The border patrol cases at least involved searches and seizures premised on suspicion of crime, the smuggling of illegal aliens. But ensuing decisions would dispense altogether with the justification of criminal law enforcement. In 1979, the Court held unconstitutional random suspicionless car stops, purportedly to check for a driver's license and vehicle registration.[149] The opinion in *Delaware v. Prouse* included strong language about the liberty interest in "a basic, pervasive, and often necessary mode of transportation," with many drivers finding "a greater sense of security and privacy in traveling in an automobile than they do in exposing themselves" as pedestrians.[150] Just as citizens are not deprived of Fourth Amendment protection by moving out of their homes and onto public sidewalks, "nor are they shorn of those interests when they step from the sidewalks into their automobiles."[151] Along the way, *Prouse* had made clear that the *Terry* framework applied to police detentions for civil traffic violations. This might be perfectly sensible and consistent with prior decisions; by denominating traffic stops as seizures for purposes of the Fourth Amendment, they would be subject to constitutional protection. The question, however, is what this would mean in terms of permissible police powers during ordinary traffic stops lacking suspicion that crime was afoot.

The first troubling indicator had been provided a little more than a year earlier in a relatively short per curiam summary disposition (i.e., without the benefit of full briefing and oral argument).[152] In that case, *Pennsylvania v. Mimms*, law enforcement pulled over an automobile with an expired license plate. The driver was ordered out of the car without suspecting that anyone was involved in criminal activity and posed a threat to police safety. Instead, the officer simply

---

[147] *Id.* at 890.

[148] *Id.*

[149] See Delaware v. Prouse, 440 U.S. 648 (1979).

[150] *Id.* at 662.

[151] *Id.* at 663.

[152] Pennsylvania v. Mimms, 434 U.S. 106 (1977) (per curiam).

claimed that it was his practice to remove all drivers from their vehicles whenever he makes a traffic stop. Outside of the car, the officer saw a large bulge in the driver's jacket, and a subsequent frisk uncovered a revolver. In analyzing the case, the Supreme Court drew upon the balancing approach in *Terry* and yet refused to distinguish stops for traffic violations from those premised on criminal activity. It described the interest in officer safety as "both legitimate and weighty," citing a study supposedly showing that nearly a third of all police shootings happened when officers approached individuals seated in vehicles.[153] In contrast, the intrusion upon individual liberty was depicted as *de minimis,* with a driver suffering a "petty indignity" by having to exit his stopped vehicle. "What is at most a mere inconvenience cannot prevail when balanced against legitimate concerns for officer safety," the *Mimms* Court concluded.[154]

In dissent, Justice Marshall argued that this new police power during traffic stops went well beyond any reasonable reading of *Terry.* The stop and frisk in that case had been related in scope to the circumstances justifying the officer's suspicion in the first place, namely, facts suggesting that an armed robbery was in the works. Here, however, the officer had no suspicion of crime and no reason to believe that the driver was armed, only routine information that would justify the issuance of a citation for an expired license plate. "There is simply no relation at all between the circumstance and the order to step out of the car," Marshall wrote.[155] Justice Stevens went even further in his dissent, arguing that the *Mimms* Court had upheld a new class of seizure, the rousting of drivers, which required no suspicion at all. The factual premise for this categorical rule—officer safety necessitates the power to order a driver out of his vehicle—was based on the mischaracterization of a single, non-randomized study of 110 police shootings.[156] The data offered little

---

[153] *Id.* at 110.

[154] *Id.* at 111.

[155] *Id.* at 114.

[156] See *id.* at 117–19 (discussing Allen P. Bristow, Police Officer Shootings—A Tactical Evaluation, 54 J. Crim. L. Criminology & Police Sci. 93 (1963)). Of the 110 shootings studied, 35 involved suspects in automobiles in a wide range of circumstances, such as shootings from *moving* vehicles. A dozen of the cases identified the suspect as seated behind the wheel of a car, while nine others occurred outside of the car while the officer was talking to the suspect. See also *infra* note 176 (discussing inapplicability of this study in *Michigan v. Long*).

information about the risk associated with traffic stops and provided no support for the idea that ordering a suspect out of the car increases officer safety. The existing evidence, particularly in light of the infinite factual variety of cases, could not justify the majority's per se rule. Nor could it be said that a driver always had a minimal interest in remaining in the car. For example, "a person in poor health may object to standing in the cold or rain," while "another who left home in haste to drive children or spouse to school or to the train may not be fully dressed."[157] The millions of traffic stops each year are "not fungible," Stevens argued, and to dispense with individualized suspicion is tantamount to abandoning judicial review.

In the end, Justice Stevens predicted that some drivers would be ordered out of their seats because of the color of their skin. Furthermore, the logic of *Mimms* necessarily covered passengers, who would be rousted from cars without having committed any offense, not even a trivial traffic violation. And if the concern truly is officer safety, "rather than a desire to permit pretextual searches," the Court's new rule would legitimate automatic frisks for weapons of those ordered out of their vehicles.[158] Without more, simply forcing people to stand on the road would have no protective value if, unbeknownst to law enforcement, an individual is actually armed and dangerous. To be sure, none of these corollaries had been specifically approved by the Supreme Court, and a few had been rejected or at least reserved in a majority opinion. For instance, one of the border patrol cases had noted that, "upon a proper showing," the judiciary would be empowered to prevent abusive stops based on race.[159] Of course, the real test would not be an earlier opinion's minimization of its impact, but what the Court did in future decisions.

Two decades later, the Supreme Court addressed a critical issue concerning pretextual and potentially race-based policing—whether an officer's actual intentions were relevant in assessing the constitutionality of a vehicle stop. In the 1996 case, *Whren v. United States*, plainclothes vice agents were patrolling a "high drug area" in an unmarked car when they saw a truck containing two young black

---

[157] Mimms, 434 U.S. at 120–21.

[158] *Id.* at 123.

[159] Martinez-Fuerte, 428 U.S. at 566 n.19.

men.[160] The officers ostensibly stopped the truck for minor, highly subjective traffic violations: turning without "an appropriate signal," driving away from a stop sign "at a speed greater than is reasonable and prudent," and failing to "give full time and attention to the operation of the vehicle."[161] When the officers approached the truck, they saw what appeared to be bags of crack cocaine and arrested the two men. In upholding the subsequent convictions, a unanimous Supreme Court declined to inquire into the officers' motivations for the traffic stop. It was irrelevant that moving and equipment violations offered a ready-made pretext for arbitrary or discriminatory policing. As a matter of fact, modern traffic codes are so broad in coverage—touching upon virtually every detail about vehicles and their operation, and often employing ambiguous language—that it is almost impossible for drivers to comply fully.[162] Worse yet, in this case it was not only unusual but also against department policy for plainclothes officers in an unmarked vehicle to make an ordinary traffic stop. Nonetheless, the Court rejected a limiting principle for minor code violations or a standard of reasonable officer behavior under the circumstances. And unlike the balancing approach in *Terry* and its progeny, *Whren* declined to weigh the diminished state interest in having vice agents enforce the vehicle code against the greater anxiety caused to motorists from stops by undercover police.

In combination, the Court's refusal to inquire into an officer's motivations and its indifference to the all-encompassing nature of modern traffic codes effectively means that law enforcement can stop any car at any time without a reason—or for reasons that are less likely to be "inarticulable than unspeakable,"[163] like the driver's

---

[160] Whren v. United States, 517 U.S. 806, 808 (1996).

[161] *Id.* at 810 (citing and quoting D.C. Traffic Code).

[162] See, e.g., David A. Harris, "Driving While Black" and All Other Traffic Offenses: The Supreme Court and Pretextual Traffic Stops, 87 J. Crim. L. & Criminology 544, 558 (1997). See also Maryland v. Wilson, 519 U.S. 408, 423 (1997) (Kennedy, J., dissenting) ("The practical effect of our holding in *Whren*, of course, is to allow the police to stop vehicles in almost countless circumstances."); Cady v. Dombrowski, 413 U.S. 433, 441 (1973) ("Because of the extensive regulation of motor vehicles and traffic ... the extent of police-citizen contact involving automobiles will be substantially greater than police-citizen contact in a home or office.").

[163] Florida v. Bostick, 501 U.S. 429, 442 n.1 (1991) (Marshall, J., dissenting).

race or ethnicity. The *Whren* Court did acknowledge that selective enforcement based on considerations such as race would be unconstitutional, but the basis for such a claim would be the Equal Protection Clause rather than the Fourth Amendment. As it turns out, however, this was less of a sop than a cruel joke given the standard for proving selective prosecution under equal protection jurisprudence. A month before *Whren,* the Supreme Court held that in order to obtain government discovery on the treatment of individuals of different races, a defendant must show that similarly situated individuals of a different race received disparate treatment—which is, of course, the precise information that the defendant seeks to discover.[164]

Aside from the troubling issue of race-based policing, subsequent cases have demonstrated the upshot of allowing minor traffic violations to be an unquestioned predicate for police action. In the 2005 case, *Illinois v. Caballes,* a state trooper pulled over a vehicle for driving 71 miles per hour in an area where the posted speed limit was 65 miles an hour. The officer asked the driver for the usual information—his license, vehicle registration, and proof of insurance. While the officer was still writing the speeding ticket, another state trooper arrived on the scene and walked his drug-detecting dog around the car. When the dog alerted at the car's trunk, the officers opened the trunk and found marijuana.[165] In a brief opinion, the Supreme Court found no Fourth Amendment violation. Although a traffic stop to issue a citation can become unlawful if it unreasonably prolongs the detention, the duration of the stop was justified by the traffic violation and concomitant inquiries. That a drug investigation was occurring simultaneously was of no significance.[166]

In dissent, Justice David Souter argued that the police intrusion must be confined to the initial rationale for the detention, noting that the *Terry* Court had been careful to keep a stop from "automatically becoming a foot in the door for all investigatory purposes."[167] To make sure that the *Terry* doctrine does not devolve into "an open

---

[164] See United States v. Armstrong, 517 U.S. 456, 465 (1996).

[165] See Illinois v. Caballes, 543 U.S. 405, 406 (2005); *id.* at 417–18 (Ginsburg, J., dissenting).

[166] See *id.* at 407–10.

[167] *Id.* at 415 (Souter, J., dissenting).

sesame for general searches," the rule had been that police may not "take advantage of a suspect's immobility to search for evidence unrelated to the reason for the detention."[168] Justice Ginsburg agreed in her dissent, noting that the scope restriction in *Terry* concerned not just the duration of any detention but also "the manner in which the seizure is conducted."[169] Existing doctrine could in no way justify the expansion of an ordinary traffic stop into a drug investigation. Lacking any apparent limitation, the *Caballes* decision would sanction the indiscriminate use of drug sniffs and similar techniques during traffic stops.[170] The *Terry* doctrine was thus converted into an all-purpose investigatory tool. A traffic stop for a civil infraction could be the predicate to investigate drug crime or, for that matter, *any* crime.

VI. Beyond Drivers

The cases discussed so far have involved seizures of pedestrians or drivers and searches of their persons. The question is whether—and how far—the doctrine might expand beyond the frisk of someone suspected of a crime or traffic violation. In its 1983 decision in *Michigan v. Long*, the Supreme Court extended *Terry* to allow "frisks" of an automobile.[171] Police officers patrolling a rural area around midnight saw a speeding, erratically moving vehicle that eventually swerved into a shallow ditch. The officers stopped to investigate and were met by the driver at the rear of his car. When they asked for the vehicle registration, the officers followed the man toward the open car door and observed a closed hunting knife on the floorboard. One officer stopped and frisked the driver, keeping the man under control at the rear of the car, while the other officer picked up the knife and shined his flashlight into the vehicle, purportedly to search for other weapons. He observed "something leather" under the armrest, knelt into the vehicle, lifted the armrest, and saw a pouch containing a small plastic bag of marijuana.

The *Long* Court upheld the search, arguing that "*Terry* need not be read as restricting the preventative search to the person of the

[168] *Id.*

[169] *Id.* at 420.

[170] See *id.* at 417 (Souter, J., dissenting); *id.* at 422 (Ginsburg, J., dissenting).

[171] See Michigan v. Long, 463 U.S. 1032 (1983).

detained suspect."[172] Relying upon *Mimms* and *Adams*, as well as decisions on searches incident to arrest, the majority opinion described traffic stops as exceptionally dangerous for police officers, including the threat that an *unarmed* person may have access to weapons. A driver might break away from police control at the rear of the vehicle, for example, and retrieve a gun or knife from his car. Besides, at some point a driver may be allowed to reenter his vehicle, the *Long* Court surmised, and might then have access to a weapon, making him "no less dangerous simply because he is not arrested."[173] For this reason, if officers suspect that the driver is "potentially dangerous," they may search the passenger compartment to uncover weapons.

In dissent, Justice Brennan argued that the *Long* Court was "simply continuing the process of distorting *Terry* beyond recognition and forcing it into service as an unlikely weapon against the Fourth Amendment's fundamental requirement that searches and seizures be based on probable cause."[174] *Terry* itself was explicit that a frisk must be *a carefully limited search of the outer clothing* of a detainee who is reasonably believed to be *armed and presently dangerous*. As such, the Supreme Court's extension to a broad search of an unarmed man's automobile "can only be described as disingenuous."[175] After all, the searches in *Mimms* and *Adams* were limited to the driver's person, not his car. The other precedents relied upon in *Long* involved searches incident to arrests, which the Court's previous cases had been careful to distinguish from the limited patdown of a suspect pursuant to *Terry*. Now, however, reasonable suspicion that a detainee was dangerous would permit the precise type of search that required a full custodial arrest based on probable cause.

This was not the only perverse aspect of *Long*, as argued by both Justice Brennan and prominent legal scholars. The majority had said that officers need not adopt alternative means to protect their safety. So although law enforcement could minimize any danger by moving the driver away from his car—which was the justification for rousting a driver in *Mimms*—an officer need not take protective measures

---

[172] Long, 463 U.S. at 1047.

[173] *Id.* at 1050.

[174] *Id.* at 1054 (Brennan, J., dissenting).

[175] *Id.* at 1056.

but instead may use the unmitigated risk to broaden his authority to search without probable cause. What is more, the suspicion of danger in *Long* was itself suspect. As Professor Wayne LaFave noted, the unremarkable discovery of a hunting knife in a car in rural Michigan "sheds little if any light on the questions of whether there is another weapon in the car or whether [the driver] was at all likely to make use of any weapon."[176] In this case, it takes an imagination to believe that an apparently intoxicated driver, removed from his car and whatever objects it may contain, is presently dangerous. It also seems implausible that an officer would allow a driver he believes to be dangerous to reenter his car during an ongoing stop, or that someone who has been told he is free to leave would then go grab a weapon from his vehicle to assault the officer. But by presenting hypothetical dangers to officer safety—as well as crediting circumstances that were not particularly suspicious and offering no limitations on the factual predicates—the Supreme Court had effectively created a new automatic *Terry* search rule.

In the automobile context, once *Terry* stops and frisks moved beyond the offending driver, who can be ordered from his seat under *Mimms* and his car searched pursuant to *Long*, the only question that remained was the permissible police action toward passengers. In 1997, the Supreme Court considered whether the *Mimms* rule applies to any occupant of a vehicle.[177] In that case, *Maryland v. Wilson*, a state trooper activated his lights and sirens when he saw a car driving

---

[176] *Long* also cited the study of officer shootings relied upon in *Mimms* and *Adams*. See Long, 463 U.S. at 1048 n.13 (citing Bristow, *supra* note 156):

> But a closer examination of that study reveals that it does not give credence to the *Long* analysis. The study reports that of police officers shot in connection with vehicle stops, about half were shot by persons seated in or concealed in a car, about a third by persons standing outside the car talking to the police, and the rest by persons then exiting the car or fleeing the scene. Quite clearly, a power to search the car is neither adequate nor necessary to protect the police in any of those situations. No mention is made in the study of any instance in which a person outside the car returned to the vehicle and then shot the officer, and thus it is quite understandable why the author does not propose that police be allowed to search cars, but rather that they maintain better "vehicle occupant control while issuing traffic tickets, interrogating, or [performing] other routine police business."

4 LaFave, Search and Seizure, *supra* note 19, at § 9.6(a).

[177] See Maryland v. Wilson, 519 U.S. 408 (1997).

over the speed limit and with no regular license tag. The car failed to pull over for a mile and a half, and along the way two passengers repeatedly ducked below sight level and then reemerged. During the subsequent stop, the trooper noticed that the front-seat passenger was sweating profusely and appeared extremely nervous. While the driver was sitting in the car looking for vehicle documents, the trooper ordered the nervous passenger out of the car and a quantity of crack cocaine fell to the ground as he exited.

In all likelihood, the now-flaccid standard for reasonable suspicion would have justified ordering the passenger out of the car based on a belief that crime was afoot. But that issue was not properly before the Court.[178] Instead, the *Wilson* majority crafted a per se rule permitting law enforcement to order passengers from a stopped car. Employing a reasonableness balancing test, the majority concluded that the same interest in officer safety credited in *Mimms* was implicated here, citing the nearly 6,000 officer assaults and 11 officer deaths that occurred during traffic pursuits and stops. The Court admitted that a presumptively innocent passenger may have a stronger case for personal liberty than the driver, who is at least suspected of committing a vehicular offense. The threat of violence, however, "stems not from the ordinary reaction of a motorist stopped for a speeding violation, but from the fact that evidence of a more serious crime might be uncovered during the stop."[179] With this understanding of the relevant risk, the *Wilson* Court reasoned that a passenger may have the same motivation to use violence as his driver, namely, to avoid apprehension for criminal activity. Given the weighty interest in officer safety and the minimal intrusion on liberty, passengers may be ordered out of the vehicle pending completion of the traffic stop.

Justice Stevens's prediction in *Mimms* had thus come to fruition. As Stevens now noted in his *Wilson* dissent, passengers can be rousted from their seats during traffic stops "without even a scintilla of evidence of potential risk to the police officer," thereby allowing "routine and arbitrary seizures of obviously innocent citizens."[180] The Court's rule received no support from the cited statistics, which

---

[178] See *id.* at 416 n.1 (Stevens, J., dissenting).

[179] *Id.* at 414.

[180] *Id.* at 416 (Stevens, J., dissenting).

did not reveal how many cases involved passengers, let alone whether the incidents occurred while passengers were in their seats or whether the attacks could have been prevented by ordering the passengers from the car. The majority's claim about officer safety was no more plausible than the hypothesis that ordering passengers out of a vehicle *increases* the risk of danger. Using available data and generous assumptions, the new rule might provide some possible advantage to Maryland police in only one out of every 20,000 traffic stops of cars with passengers.[181] This minimal benefit was far outweighed by the aggregate invasions upon "countless citizens who cherish individual liberty and are offended, embarrassed, and sometimes provoked by arbitrary official commands."[182] These passengers were no more lawfully seized than if they were stuck in a traffic jam caused by state highway construction. Their misfortune of being seated in a vehicle whose driver has committed a minor traffic violation did not justify a suspicionless seizure, forcing the blameless to expose themselves to the elements and the gaze of onlookers.[183]

The *Wilson* majority did acknowledge the undifferentiated nature of the statistics on officer assaults, saying it was "regrettable that the empirical data on a subject such as this are sparse."[184] A subsequent study found that male police officers were not at greater risk of homicide than all other males of similar age, a finding that the authors saw as "contradict[ing] the assumption in *Terry* and its progeny that police face greater risk than the general population."[185] Most likely, however, the statistics in the Court's opinions served as mere window dressing for legal conclusions, including bright-line rules allowing police to order drivers and passengers from vehicles. Still, *Wilson* left several legal questions unanswered,[186] for instance, whether law enforcement may forcibly detain a passenger

---

[181] See *id.* at 416–18.

[182] *Id.* at 419.

[183] See *id.* at 420–21.

[184] *Id.* at 413 n.2 (majority opinion).

[185] Illya D.Lichtenberg et al., *Terry* and Beyond: Testing the Underlying Assumptions of Reasonable Suspicion, 17 Touro L. Rev. 439, 459 (2001).

[186] See, e.g., Wilson, 519 U.S. at 415 n.3 (majority opinion). See also *id.* at 423 (Kennedy, J., dissenting) (noting that the Court did not have before it the issue of whether police can order passengers to remain in the vehicle "for a reasonable time while the police conduct their business").

for the entire duration of the traffic stop, and whether a passenger may be subjected to a *Terry* frisk without suspicion of criminal activity. Two years later, in *Knowles v. Iowa*, a unanimous Court reached the perfectly unobjectionable (and obvious) conclusion that a search incident to arrest must, in fact, be preceded by an actual arrest rather than the mere possibility of an arrest.[187] In dictum, the *Knowles* opinion mentioned what police might lawfully do during a routine traffic stop, including "a 'patdown' of a driver and any passengers upon suspicion that they may be armed and danger-ous."[188] But the passage was unclear whether such frisks must be based on the *Terry* predicate of a justifiable belief that crime was afoot.

Dictum or not, however, and regardless of any ambiguity, this language was now available for a subsequent decision to latch on to. All that was needed was one last case to "complet[e] the picture," as Justice Ginsburg would later say.[189] The Court's 2007 decision in *Brendlin v. California* considered whether a passenger, like the driver, was seized during a traffic stop.[190] In that case, the state had conceded that law enforcement lacked reasonable suspicion to conduct the stop, during which one of the officers recognized the passenger as "one of the Brendlin brothers."[191] After returning to the cruiser, the officer called for backup, confirmed that the passenger had an outstanding arrest warrant, ordered the man from the car at gun-point, and then arrested him. The lower court concluded that the passenger had not been seized, relying on, among other things, the Court's language in *Wilson* that there is no reason to detain passen-gers who are presumptively innocent and only impeded "as a practi-cal matter" in an ordinary traffic stop.[192] The Supreme Court unani-mously disagreed, describing the post-*Terry* definitional evolution of seizures for Fourth Amendment purposes and posing the relevant issue as "whether a reasonable person in [the passenger's] position

---

[187] See Knowles v. Iowa, 525 U.S. 113 (1998).

[188] *Id.* at 118.

[189] Johnson, 129 S. Ct. at 787.

[190] See Brendlin v. California, 127 S. Ct. 2400 (2007).

[191] *Id.* at 2404.

[192] People v. Brendlin, 136 P.3d 845, 853 (Cal. 2006) (quoting Wilson, 519 U.S. at 413–14).

when the car stopped would have believed himself free to 'terminate the encounter' between the police and himself.''[193]

In this case, no reasonable passenger would have believed that he could leave without police permission, or "come and go freely from the physical focal point of an investigation into faulty behavior or wrongdoing.''[194] Even when the stop is for a mere traffic violation, a passenger would reasonably expect to undergo some scrutiny. Here, the passenger had signaled his submission to authority by staying inside the car, and to hold that he was not seized for Fourth Amendment purposes would only invite random car stops by officers, who could use evidence of crime found during the detention against passengers. As in *Knowles,* the Court's decision in *Brendlin* seems obviously correct. The passenger is physically stopped along with the driver, and only an amazingly brave (or Pollyannaish) passenger would think that he could get out of the car, wave goodbye to everyone at the scene, and walk away. The problem is not *Brendlin*'s conclusion but how it fits with the stop and frisk cases that preceded it, as described above and illustrated this past term.

VII. *Johnson,* Again

Let's now return to the 2009 passenger frisk case, *Arizona v. Johnson.* As detailed earlier, the reasonable suspicion test has become so vacuous—and so minimized in comparison to the higher standard of probable cause, which itself was gutted by *Gates*—that little more than a hunch is required. Under the totality of the circumstances, mundane details, lawful in themselves and consistent with innocent explanations, can now rationalize a stop and frisk. In *Johnson,* Officer Trevizo found it suspicious that Lemon Johnson had watched from the back seat as agents approached the vehicle. In all fairness, though, his gaze was both innocuous and totally understandable. He was not witnessing an ordinary stop by a single traffic officer in a conspicuous police cruiser. Rather, Johnson and his colleagues had been pulled over by an unmarked white Cadillac containing multiple agents wearing tactical vests. Indeed, it might have been deemed

---

[193] Brendlin, 127 S. Ct. at 2406 (quoting Bostick, 501 U.S. 429 at 436).
[194] *Id.* at 2407.

abnormal if a vehicle occupant had failed to look at the agents, as was the case in *United States v. Arvizu*.[195]

In addition, Officer Trevizo found suspicious a scanner in Johnson's jacket, but she had no idea whether the device was on or not and admitted that there was nothing illegal about it. "I know there's plenty of people that like to listen to scanners," Trevizo testified, "and I have an uncle who listens to a scanner all the time." She just thought it was unusual for Johnson to be possessing one. Equally revealing was her use of the gang member profile, demonstrating how this instrument, like the drug courier profile, provides cover for police hunches. Trevizo testified about seven indicia of gang affiliation, but only one applied to Lemon Johnson—his blue attire—which the officer associated with the Crips street gang. Yet even this lone criterion was of dubious value, given that the driver was wearing *red*, the color of the Crips' arch-enemy, the Bloods street gang.[196]

The foregoing analysis also described how reasonable suspicion can be based on categories of information. Law enforcement may be justified in believing that an individual is armed and dangerous because of his location in a "high-crime area" or because the crime at issue is burglary, drug dealing, car theft, and so on—all without definition or meaningful parameters for these supposedly lawless zones, and despite the lack of a logical or empirical connection between the crime and violence or weapons. The facts in *Johnson* actually take the categories a step further. During the traffic stop, law enforcement did not suspect that burglary was afoot; rather, Johnson simply admitted that he had been incarcerated for burglary in the past. What is more, Johnson had not been found in the neighborhood Officer Trevizo described as "a gang-related area." Instead, he was stopped east of that neighborhood—an area where "the boundaries are not clearly defined," Trevizo admitted—while Johnson's car was traveling north on a major roadway used by thousands of vehicles each day.[197] The officer even relied upon the fact that Johnson hailed from a city with a known gang, thus making residency a potential point of suspicion against some 12,000 inhabitants of Eloy, Arizona.

---

[195] See *supra* note 112 and accompanying text (discussing *Arvizu*).

[196] See Johnson, 170 P.3d at 669.

[197] See Joint Appendix, *supra* note 38, at 10, 18, 30, 32.

In reality, most Americans are unlikely to be stopped and frisked without good reason. The same cannot be said for others, particularly minority citizens.[198] After *Johnson,* reasonable suspicion that someone is armed and dangerous can arise when, inter alia: an individual stares at officers or, conversely, does not look at them at all; the person is wearing blue, the shade of the Crips, even if he is with someone wearing red à la the Bloods; he is found in a purportedly high-crime or gang-related area, or simply driving on a major thoroughfare somewhere near it; the crime under suspicion is one that might conceivably involve weapons or ordinary tools, like burglary, although a past connection to this type of offense will suffice; the individual possesses a police scanner or, presumably, any number of other devices, regardless of whether it happens to be in use at the time; and the person came from a place that has a gang, which includes almost every sizeable city in America.

Using today's limp standard for reasonable suspicion, there may be no limit to the commonplace details that can be given a suspicious gloss under the totality of the circumstances. Moreover, the predicate for the frisk, a *Terry* stop, does not require much at all. On the road, police need not suspect that crime is afoot; a civil traffic offense, no matter how trifling, will do. As a practical matter, law enforcement need only follow an automobile for a short distance in order to find some reason to pull the car over. In *Johnson,* the violation was insurance related; *Whren* involved highly subjective infractions like driving faster than "reasonable and prudent"; other cases may entail a burnt-out bulb for a vehicle's rear tags or failure to use a turn signal as required. Law enforcement's true motivation for a traffic stop is immaterial, so long as an officer can cite some traffic violation.

The pretextual nature of the stop can even be blatant, as demonstrated in both *Johnson* and *Whren.* The cases involved specialized agents in unmarked vehicles assigned to investigate, respectively, gang activity and drug crime. In *Johnson,* the main focus of Officer Trevizo and her colleagues was gathering gang intelligence and

---

[198] See, e.g., Hon. Harold Baer Jr., Got a Bad Feeling? Is That Enough? The Irrationality of Police Hunches, 4 J.L. Econ. & Pol'y 91 (2007); Civil Rights Bureau, Office of the Att'y Gen. of the State of N.Y., The New York City Police Department's "Stop and Frisk" Practices: A Report to the People of the State of New York From The Office Of The Attorney General (Dec. 1999).

combating gang crime,[199] not serving as traffic cops and ticketing errant drivers. The plainclothes vice agents in *Whren* were actually breaking department rules by performing an ordinary traffic stop. In either case, it is hard to believe that the detentions were motivated by a desire to stamp out minor vehicle infractions. Police officers may evince the real motivation for the stop by their words and actions, pursuing an investigation that has nothing to do with the traffic violation. Officer Trevizo testified that during the stop she was trying "to gather intelligence about the gang [Johnson] might be in," including "how big the gang is, what the areas are, maybe what kind of crimes they're involved in [and] who the leaders are."[200] But again, an officer's actual reasons for the traffic stop are irrelevant, and conducting an investigation wholly unrelated to the stop is of no constitutional moment.

In the course of the stop, law enforcement may roust both the driver and any passengers out of the vehicle. Although based on officer safety, the categorical rules of *Mimms* and *Wilson* do not require any inkling that the occupants might be dangerous. Pursuant to *Long*, officers can search the passenger compartment of a vehicle without a belief that an unarmed detainee outside of the car is presently dangerous. Law enforcement need not minimize the risk of danger at all; in fact, officers may create the potential danger, and thus a justification for a frisk that was otherwise absent, by ordering an occupant out of his vehicle. And as the *Johnson* opinion makes clear, an individual need not be suspected of any criminal activity or even a civil infraction in order to be frisked. In other words, *Johnson* stands for the proposition that an individual who had done nothing wrong and may have been completely cooperative can be searched without any suspicion that crime is afoot, based on innocuous facts like the color of his clothes and the place he calls home. If any evidence is found during the patdown, courts will not second-guess the general, omnipresent fear for law enforcement safety and will be hesitant to question an officer's hodgepodge of details that allegedly triggered the search, as was true after *Johnson* was remanded back to the lower courts.[201]

---

[199] See Joint Appendix, *supra* note 38, at 8, 19.

[200] *Id.* at 19–20.

[201] See State v. Johnson, 207 P.3d 804, 807–09 (Ariz. App. 2009) (holding that Officer Trevizo had reasonable suspicion that Johnson was armed and dangerous).

The Supreme Court's authorization to frisk in the absence of crime may be surprising to some, even the legally trained, but it would be no news for those who live in minority neighborhoods, especially young black and Hispanic men in urban America. Consider the following interview with an officer in the Los Angeles County Sheriff's Department:

> [Deputy Jeffrey] Coates spent one day giving me what might be called a master class in the art of the pretext stop—pulling over blacks and Hispanics, hoping to come up with dope, or guns, or information. "There's a law against almost everything as it relates to a vehicle," Coates said. Coates knows the law, and uses it. For example, Coates spotted a type of car, a Monte Carlo, which is known to be favored by gangsters, moving along in traffic. He pulled in behind the car and studied it for a moment. "No mud flaps," Coates said, turning on his lights. They pulled the car over, and asked the three teen-agers, shaven-headed Hispanics, to step outside. They patted them down and looked through the vehicle. The teenagers freely admitted to being members of the South Los gang. "Now the reason we stopped you was that you have no mud flaps on your rear tires," Coates said. "But the real reason we stopped you is because we saw that you're rolling out of your area. Why don't you turn it around and go home." I asked Coates if it's his policy to remove every male from any car he stops, no matter what the cause for the stop. "Yes. Officer safety." Would you do that in a different part of the county? "I wouldn't do it in Santa Clarita,"[202] he said, pausing—realizing, perhaps, what that sounded like. "I mean, it all depends."[203]

Stories like this should be disconcerting to anyone who cares about the limitations on arbitrary power enshrined in the Fourth Amendment. It is not that this deputy stopped and frisked a naive school girl or an elderly war veteran; he pulled over three tough-looking, young men. The same might be said of Officer Trevizo's actions. Johnson may well be a gang member, and Trevizo was certainly correct that he was armed. The true measure of a constitutional right, however, is not the security it provides the majority and

---

[202] Santa Clarita is a mostly white, affluent city in Los Angeles County.

[203] Jeffrey Goldberg, The Color of Suspicion, N.Y. Times Mag., June 20, 1999, at 64.

people of impeccable character, but its application to the minorities, those of lower socio-economic classes, and the men and women whose lifestyles some may find distasteful. Moreover, a search and seizure is not legitimated by the evidence it turns up. "[T]here is nothing new in the realization that the Constitution sometimes insulates the criminality of a few in order to protect the privacy of us all."[204] The concept of individualized suspicion of wrongdoing is one of the key differences between a liberal constitutional democracy and a police state. Unless their words and deeds are strongly indicative of criminal activity, people should have the freedom to be left alone. This liberty comes by constitutional right, not at the discretion of any official.

As suggested in this article's introduction, the point here is not to condemn law enforcement for seeking greater powers, and none of the foregoing should be taken as impugning the integrity of Officer Trevizo or any other agent. Today's police have an enormously difficult job, preventing, detecting, and helping to prosecute many crimes of unquestionable gravity. The actions of Trevizo and her colleagues may be routine, and the result the Supreme Court reached in *Johnson* was supported by amicus curiae briefs filed by the federal government, more than three dozen states, and a litany of organizations representing law enforcement and state and local government. They embody the "powerful hydraulic pressures" placed on the Court to "give the police the upper hand,"[205] and that pressure is even greater today than it was when Justice Douglas uttered those words.

In light of prior decisions, *Johnson* is far from a watershed decision breaking from established doctrine. On the contrary, it was a slight deviation from the cases immediately before it, each of which was a slight deviation from the preceding decisions. Oppressive practices often begin this way, or so the Court warned more than a century ago.[206] The *Terry* decision might be lauded for bringing stops and frisks within the fold of the Fourth Amendment, or it may be criticized as permitting "the obnoxious thing in its mildest and least

---

[204] Arizona v. Hicks, 480 U.S. 321, 329 (1987).

[205] Terry, 392 U.S. at 39 (Douglas, J., dissenting).

[206] Boyd v. United States, 116 U.S. 616, 635 (1886).

repulsive form,"[207] a search and seizure without a warrant or probable cause. What is clear, however, is that the stop and frisk doctrine that exists today cannot be supported by *Terry* itself. While Chief Justice Warren's opinion drew upon the language of prior probable cause cases, requiring that law enforcement point to specific and articulable facts, not unparticularized suspicion, today's officers can rattle off generalities about locations of high-criminality and profiles of wrongdoers.

Although *Terry* required that any stop and frisk must be related in scope to the suspected criminal activity that justified the intrusion in the first place, police can now use the opportunity a detention provides to conduct investigations wholly unrelated to its initial suspicion. *Terry*'s predicate for a stop—individualized suspicion of crime—is not required on the road. A minor traffic violation is sufficient to stop a driver and his passengers, all of whom can be rousted from the vehicle as a matter of course. After *Johnson*, a passenger who is suspected of absolutely nothing, not even a civil violation, may be frisked because law enforcement perceives him to be dangerous. The conclusion can find no support in the majority opinion in *Terry* and is inconsistent with the concurrence by Justice Harlan, who argued that an individual does not have to submit to a patdown for the officer's wellbeing.[208] But that is exactly what happened to Lemon Johnson. In hindsight, however, the most ironic aspect of *Terry* is its original ambition: A decision that was prompted by "aggressive patrols" and "wholesale harassment" of minority communities has instead spawned a doctrine that effectively licenses the practice.

In itself, *Johnson* may have some disturbing consequences. The next step for the new crimeless frisk rule could be its application beyond vehicle stops, when officers pat down people on the streets not due to an individualized suspicion of criminal conduct but because they look "dangerous," the kind of police activity that the Supreme Court has found unconstitutional in its vagrancy and loitering decisions.[209] Maybe the Court will find such an extension unreasonable, not unlike this past term's decision in *Gant*, with the justices

---

[207] *Id.*

[208] Terry, 392 U.S. at 33 (Harlan, J., concurring).

[209] See Papachristou v. City of Jacksonville, 405 U.S. 156 (1972). See also City of Chicago v. Morales, 572 U.S. 41 (1999).

trying to tether a doctrine that had traveled far from its theoretical mooring. But given the development of stop and frisk law, I am not particularly optimistic. When *Terry* was decided, only Justice Douglas foresaw the potential mischief. Later, he was joined by Justices Brennan and Marshall, who had voted in favor of a limited exception to the warrant and probable cause requirements but then recognized the pressures that were leading to the evisceration of the Fourth Amendment. At various times Justices Ginsburg, Kennedy, Souter, and Stevens have dissented from further extensions of law enforcement's power to stop and frisk. The initial critics are long gone, and those who remain on the Court seem to have made their peace with a *Terry* doctrine radically transformed over the years, as evidenced by the unanimous decision in *Johnson.* When the next case comes, there may be no one left to dissent.

(Un)Reasonableness and the Roberts Court: The Fourth Amendment in Flux

Michael Edmund O'Neill*

The Fourth Amendment famously provides that:

> The right of the people to be secure in their persons, houses, papers, and effects, against unreasonable searches and seizures, shall not be violated, and no Warrants shall issue, but upon probable cause, supported by Oath or affirmation, and particularly describing the place to be searched, and the persons or things to be seized.

Although the Amendment's text appears straightforward, the legal community has long debated precisely what that text means. The first clause outlines a right enjoyed by the people to be "secure" in their persons and private possessions against not all, but only "unreasonable" searches and seizures. The difficulty, however, lies in determining what constitutes a reasonable search or a reasonable seizure and what the remedy ought to be for a violation of the right to be free from them. When the Fourth Amendment was ratified, public police forces held no monopoly on criminal investigation. In many places, victims could initiate criminal prosecutions with privately retained counsel.[1] One of the chief means of securing the right against unreasonable searches and seizures lay in the ability of the aggrieved party to file a civil suit in tort. A jury of one's peers could then determine whether a particular search or seizure was reasonable.

The Fourth Amendment's second clause, the Warrant Clause, enabled a person executing a search or effecting a seizure to do so

*Associate Professor, George Mason University School of Law. I'd like to thank Anthony Peluso and Genevieve Schmitt for their invaluable research assistance and Frank Buckley and the Law and Economics Center at George Mason for its generous financial support.

[1] Michael Edmund O'Neill, Private Vengeance and the Public Good, U. Pa. J. Const. L. (forthcoming 2010).

with immunity—provided a magistrate issued a warrant based upon probable cause and supported by the individual's personal oath or affirmation. With a warrant in hand, the person executing the search or effecting the seizure could act without fear of civil or criminal liability. The drafters of the Warrant Clause's "particularity" requirement sought to prevent the odious practice of general warrants, which proliferated among the colonies prior to the Revolutionary War.[2]

With the advent of public police forces and the government's monopolization of criminal investigation and prosecution, the Supreme Court interpreted the Fourth Amendment to require a warrant.[3] A search or seizure not accompanied by a warrant was deemed per se unreasonable.[4] A principal disagreement among criminal and constitutional law scholars is whether, as an historical matter, the Fourth Amendment in fact requires a warrant for a search to be considered reasonable. Historical textualists and constitutional originalists tend to argue that the Supreme Court conflated the Amendment's two clauses in requiring warrants to be issued for a search or seizure to be reasonable.[5] Other scholars argue that the Fourth Amendment requires a warrant to safeguard individual liberty.[6]

Although it would seem that the Supreme Court has sided with progressives on the warrant kerfuffle by requiring warrants to accompany nearly all searches and seizures, after it adopted the so-called categorical warrant requirement, the Court recognized that circumstances in the field made it impossible for police to secure

---

[2] John M. Burkoff, A Flame of Fire: The Fourth Amendment in Perilous Times, 74 Miss. L.J. 631, 633–34 (2004).

[3] Weeks v. United States, 232 U.S. 383 (1914).

[4] Id.

[5] See, e.g., Telford Taylor, Two Studies in Constitutional Interpretation: Search, Seizure, and Surveillance and Fair Trial and Free Press (1969); Akhil Reed Amar, Fourth Amendment First Principles, 107 Harv. L. Rev. 757 (1994).

[6] Timothy Lynch, In Defense of the Exclusionary Rule, 23 Harv. Journ. Law & Pub. Pol. 711 (2000); Yale Kamisar, Does (Did) (Should) the Exclusionary Rule Rest on a "Principled Basis" Rather Than an "Empirical Proposition"? 16 Creighton L. Rev. 565–667 (1983); Randy Barnett, Resolving the Dilemma of the Exclusionary Rule: An Application of Restitutive Principles of Justice, 32 Emory L.J. 937 (1987).

warrants in all situations.[7] Thus, when confronted with specific factual predicates, the Court proceeded on a case-by-case basis to articulate exceptions to the warrant requirement. Of course, once the Court
establishes an exception, that exception will affect a whole category
of similarly situated cases. And given the nature of judicial interpretation, lower courts tend to expand such precedents. Some decry
those exceptions as obliterating essential Fourth Amendment privacy protections.[8] Others, however, view the Court's chipping away
at the warrant requirement as a return to originalist principles.[9]

A second battleground in Fourth Amendment jurisprudence
involves the status of the exclusionary rule. Where a constitutional
right exists, there must also exist a remedy when that right is violated. Suppression of ill-gotten evidence was one of a number of such
remedies courts historically used to address Fourth Amendment
violations. In fact, the Supreme Court did not mandate the exclusion
of evidence as a remedy for Fourth Amendment violations until
1914 in *Weeks v. United States*.[10] Even so, the Court required exclusion
only when federal officers committed the violation, leaving states
free to fashion their own remedies. According to the Court, however,
alternative remedies proved ineffectual in securing the right.[11] Not
until *Mapp v. Ohio* was decided in 1961, did a divided Court apply

---

[7] See, e.g., U.S. v. Leon, 468 U.S. 897 (1984) (recognizing "good faith" exception to
the exclusionary rule where police rely on warrant later held invalid); Illinois v.
Krull, 480 U.S. 340 (1987) (allowing "reasonable reliance" on a statute authorizing
warrantless searches later held unconstitutional); Arizona v. Evans, 514 U.S. 1 (1995)
(permitting reasonable reliance on a warrant containing errors committed by court
personnel); U.S. v. Watson, 423 U.S. 411 (1976) (permitting warrantless public arrests);
Terry v. Ohio, 392 U.S. 1 (1968) (permitting warrantless "pat down" searches); Michigan v. Long, 463 U.S. 1032 (1983) (permitting warrantless protective searches).

[8] See, e.g., Yale Kamisar, Police Interrogations and Confessions (1980) (discussing
the importance of the exclusionary rule).

[9] See, e.g., Akhil Reed Amar, Fourth Amendment First Principles, 107 Harv. L.
Rev. 757 (1994) (systematic critique of common justifications propounded for the
exclusionary rule); Christopher Slobogin, Why Liberals Should Chuck the Exclusionary Rule, 1999 Univ. Ill. L. Rev. 363 (1999) (arguing that the exclusionary rule is not
as useful as certain alternative remedies); L. Timothy Perrin, et al., If It's Broken, Fix
It: Moving Beyond the Exclusionary Rule—A New and Extensive Empirical Study
of the Exclusionary Rule and a Call for a Civil Administrative Remedy to Partially
Replace the Rule, 83 Iowa L. Rev. 669 (1998).

[10] Weeks, 232 U.S. 383 (1914).

[11] Mapp v. Ohio, 367 U.S. 643, 643–50 (1961).

the exclusionary rule to the states.[12] Since *Mapp*, commentators have vigorously debated the rule's efficacy and constitutional status. Some argue that the rule operates at too high a cost for the justice system, suppressing otherwise probative evidence because of relatively minor police missteps.[13] Others argue that the rule deters police misconduct—thereby protecting both the innocent and the guilty— and has proved to be the only truly effective remedy for Fourth Amendment infringements.[14]

In light of these fundamental jurisprudential disagreements, judicial confirmation hearings have inevitably included questions about the "categorical warrant requirement" and the exclusionary rule's constitutional status.[15] With the confirmation of Chief Justice John Roberts and Associate Justice Samuel Alito, the bar eagerly awaited evidence of whether the newly anointed Roberts Court would further erode the warrant requirement, seek to reaffirm it, or call into question the exclusionary rule's constitutional status. October Term 2008 allowed the Court to consider several important Fourth Amendment cases. While no single term is definitive, this past one permitted interesting insights as to where the Court might go in the future.

Part I of this essay discusses the concept of (un)reasonableness under the Fourth Amendment and explores the exclusionary rule's background. Part II examines the four and a half cases decided in October Term 2008 that address Fourth Amendment issues.[16] Part III looks at the justices' voting patterns and offers a few thoughts about where the Court might be heading. Finally, Part IV suggests that it might be opportune for the Congress to step into the fray to

[12] Mapp v. Ohio, 367 U.S. 643 (1961).

[13] See William J. Stuntz, The Political Constitution of Criminal Justice, 119 Harv. L. Rev. 780, 793 (2006) ("The government pays for criminal procedure rules in the coin of forgone arrests and convictions.").

[14] See Albert W. Alschuler, Studying the Exclusionary Rule: An Empirical Classic, 75 U. Chi. L. Rev. 1365, 1371 (2008) ("Although no hard data prove the exclusionary rule's success, evidence of its success is not difficult to find.").

[15] Hearing on the Judicial Nomination of Samuel A. Alito Jr. of New Jersey to be Associate Justice of the Supreme Court of the United States Before the S. Comm. on the Judiciary, 109th Cong. (2006) (testimony of Prof. Ronald Sullivan Jr., Yale Law School).

[16] "A half" because while the Court asked the parties in *Pearson v. Callahan* to brief the Fourth Amendment issue, the majority opinion ultimately avoided the issue altogether. Pearson v. Callahan, 129 S. Ct. 808 (2009).

consider providing greater privacy protections for individuals and better guidance for law enforcement officers.

I. (Un)Reasonableness, Exclusion, and Fourth Amendment Discontents

The Supreme Court has long held that "searches conducted outside the judicial process, without prior approval by judge or magistrate, are per se unreasonable under the Fourth Amendment."[17] This was certainly not always the case, as the country plugged along without a categorical warrant requirement from independence to ratification of the Bill of Rights to the *Weeks* case. And the Court didn't apply the exclusionary rule to the states until 1961 in *Mapp v. Ohio.*

Shortly after creating a categorical warrant requirement, the Court recognized that circumstances police officers confront in the field might make obtaining a warrant impractical, but also not per se unreasonable. As a result, the Court has recognized that the warrant requirement is "subject only to a few specifically established and well-delineated exceptions."[18] Unfortunately—or fortunately, depending upon one's perspective—that list of exceptions has continued to expand. Those exceptions consist of whole categories of cases in which the Court has determined that the officers' decision to conduct a search or effect a seizure without a warrant is nevertheless reasonable under the Fourth Amendment.

In criticizing the warrant requirement, Justice Antonin Scalia has explained that the Court's Fourth Amendment jurisprudence has "lurched back and forth between imposing a categorical warrant requirement and looking to reasonableness alone."[19] For Scalia, the Court's warrant requirement has become "so riddled with exceptions that it (is) basically unrecognizable."[20] Aside from the fact that requiring a warrant under all circumstances does not seem faithful to the Constitution's text, a difficulty with adhering to a categorical warrant requirement is that certain absurdities may result. Should

[17] Katz v. United States, 389 U.S. 347, 357 (1967).

[18] *Id.* at 357.

[19] California v. Acevedo, 500 U.S. 565, 582 (1991). For a discussion of this tension, see generally Stephen A. Saltzburg and Daniel J. Capra, American Criminal Procedure: Cases and Commentary 86 (Eighth Edition 2007).

[20] *Id.*

police officers, for example, be prevented from entering a home when in hot pursuit of a murder suspect? Numerous situations exist in which it would be burdensome for police officers to obtain a warrant, but few would consider the resulting search to be necessarily unreasonable.

Part of the reluctance to adhere to a categorical warrant requirement is related to the harshness of the remedy: the suppression of otherwise relevant, probative evidence. Evidence suppression gained prominence in part because alternative remedies were thought to be ineffective protections. For example, juries are disinclined to reward criminals with damages and police departments—especially those that measure success by arrests, not convictions—may find it distasteful to discipline police officers who successfully uncover evidence of criminal activity. In a world that eschews tort remedies or officer disciplinary proceedings for Fourth Amendment violations, the exclusion of tainted evidence may be the last remedy standing. Even so, courts may be hard-pressed to exclude otherwise relevant evidence of criminal activity when the police's errors are relatively harmless. Courts thus may face strong incentives to collude with prosecutors to undermine the exclusionary rule. If the Constitution demands exclusion of the ill-gotten evidence in light of a Fourth Amendment violation, however, may courts constitutionally set it aside? And if exclusion is only one possible remedy, might not the courts or Congress be free to implement alternative remedies? The issue is not whether the Fourth Amendment demands a remedy for a violation—for surely it does—but rather what that remedy ought to be.

II. October Term 2008 Fourth Amendment Cases

This section examines the term's cases, set out in the chronological order in which they were decided. Fourth Amendment cases are necessarily fact-dependent, so I have erred on the side of including a more robust depiction of the facts to illuminate better the Court's decisions.

A. Herring v. United States[21]

The Court has carved out numerous exceptions to the warrant requirement. In one of those exceptions, *United States v. Leon*, the

---

[21] Herring v. United States, 555 U.S. ____, 129 S. Ct. 695 (2009).

Court held the exclusionary rule does not apply if police acted "in objectively reasonable reliance" on an invalid warrant.[22] In *Massachusetts v. Sheppard,* the Court explained that the rule does not apply if the warrant was invalidated due to a judge's failure to make "clerical corrections" to it.[23] In *Arizona v. Evans,* the Court held that the exclusionary rule does not apply when *court employees* make clerical errors or keep erroneous computer records.[24] However, the *Evans* Court left unresolved "whether the evidence should be suppressed if *police personnel* were responsible for the error,"[25] which was the issue confronted by the court in *Herring.*

On November 17, 2003, the Dale County, Alabama, Circuit Clerk's Office issued an arrest warrant for petitioner because he did not appear for his court date. The clerk promptly sent the warrant to the Dale County Sheriff's Department (DCSD) for execution. Personnel at the DCSD logged the information regarding the warrant into its records system. On February 2, 2004, however, the clerk's office recalled the arrest warrant and the DCSD removed the recalled warrant from the department's physical files and returned it to the clerk's office. Unfortunately, a "breakdown" occurred "someplace within the Sheriff's Department" and the DCSD neglected to update its computer files to reflect that the court had recalled petitioner's arrest warrant. Consequently, the computer file incorrectly listed an outstanding warrant for petitioner's arrest.[26]

On July 7, 2004, petitioner arrived at the Coffee County Sheriff's Department (CCSD) to retrieve personal possessions from his impounded vehicle. A CCSD deputy asked the warrant clerk to check if petitioner was the subject of any outstanding warrants. The clerk discovered the DCSD had a warrant for petitioner and requested a faxed copy of the actual warrant. When the DCSD clerk checked the file, she could not locate a physical copy of the warrant and subsequently called the circuit court clerk's office, which informed her that the warrant had been recalled. Meanwhile, disinclined to let the grass grow under their feet, DCSD officers stopped,

---

[22] United States v. Leon, 468 U.S. 897, 922 (1984).

[23] Massachusetts v. Sheppard, 468 U.S. 981, 991 (1984).

[24] Arizona v. Evans, 514 U.S. 1, 16 (1995).

[25] *Id.* at 16 n.5 (emphasis added).

[26] Herring, 129 S. Ct. 695, 698.

arrested, and performed a patdown of the petitioner, discovering methamphetamine on petitioner's person and a handgun and ammunition in petitioner's truck. The DCSD clerk at that point informed the officers at the scene of the mistake.

At the inevitable suppression hearing, the magistrate found that the arresting officers "acted in good faith" in stopping and arresting the petitioner based on the warrant clerks' representations as to the existence of an active outstanding felony warrant. The district court adopted the magistrate's recommendation and determined that *Arizona v. Evans* should be extended to cover situations where erroneous computer records kept by law enforcement personnel lead to arrests, so long as there is a "mechanism to ensure [the recordkeeping's] system accuracy over time" and, additionally, there is no evidence suggesting that "the system routinely leads to false arrests."[27] The district court found that the mistake in this case was quickly discovered and, likewise, corrected within a span of around 10 to 15 minutes. The quick correction supported the court's finding that there was "no credible evidence of routine problems with disposing of recalled warrants," and that the recordkeeping systems of the two clerks' offices "were, and are, reliable."[28]

The Eleventh Circuit Court of Appeals concluded that while the search violated petitioner's Fourth Amendment rights, "any minimal deterrence" that could possibly result from the exclusionary rule did "not outweigh the heavy cost of excluding otherwise admissible and highly probative evidence."[29]

Herring thus presented the issue of whether the good-faith exception to the exclusionary rule applies when a police officer relies on a mistake committed by fellow law enforcement agents. The Court accepted the parties' assumption that a Fourth Amendment violation occurred and focused on whether the exclusionary rule should apply.[30] Consequently, instead of deciding whether the search and subsequent seizure were reasonable, the Court examined whether

---

[27] Brief for the United States at 4–5, Herring v. United States, 129 S. Ct. 695 (2009) (No. 07-513) (internal quotations and citation omitted), 2008 WL 194291.

[28] *Id.* at 6 (internal quotations and citation omitted).

[29] *Id.* at 7 (citing United States v. Herring, 492 F.3d 1212, 1217 (11th Cir. 2007)).

[30] Herring, 129 S. Ct. at 699.

it was reasonable to suppress the evidence. If the Constitution mandates exclusion for a Fourth Amendment violation, however, should this even be an issue? Writing for the Court, Chief Justice Roberts explained that:

> When a probable-cause determination was based on reasonable but mistaken assumptions, the person subjected to a search or seizure has not necessarily been the victim of a constitutional violation.[31]

While this summary sounds straightforward, it points to some of the complications surrounding the Fourth Amendment. Namely, if the search was not covered by a warrant or an acknowledged exception to the warrant requirement, isn't it necessarily a constitutional violation?

If the Court accepts the assertion that a constitutional violation has occurred, then determining reasonableness does not depend on whether the search was unreasonable but rather whether it is reasonable to suppress the seized evidence. The Chief Justice noted that:

> The very phrase "probable cause" confirms that the Fourth Amendment does not demand all possible precision . . . whether the error can be traced to a mistake by a state actor or some other source may bear on the analysis.[32]

In effect, the warrant must be based upon probable cause, but probable cause is not absolute. If the probable cause standard is not itself precise, then a technically defective warrant reasonably relied upon may not provide grounds for suppression.

Roberts's opinion for the Court highlighted the disagreement between those who consider reasonableness to be the Fourth Amendment's touchstone and those who demand a warrant prior to any search or seizure. If the Constitution requires a warrant, then it should not matter whether the search was otherwise "reasonable." The steady flow of exceptions to the categorical warrant requirement, however, reaffirms the centrality of "reasonableness" to the Fourth Amendment determination.

[31] *Id.*
[32] *Id.*

Here, where the constitutional violation is assumed, the Court explained that the rule is "designed to safeguard Fourth Amendment rights generally through its deterrent effect"—a pragmatic consideration, seemingly not of constitutional dimension.[33] And to act as a deterrent, the officers must know they are about to engage in wrongdoing. Thus, the court of appeals' conclusion that the DCSD's error was negligent but not reckless or deliberate, is "crucial to [the Court's] holding that this error is not enough by itself to require 'the extreme sanction of exclusion'"—presumably because suppression could not deter what was a simple error on the part of the police.[34]

Interestingly, while the Court accepted that the error was unreasonable and therefore a violation—because it was neither an intentional nor a reckless mistake—the Court explained that it should not necessarily trigger the exclusionary rule.[35] The Court has "repeatedly rejected the argument that exclusion is a necessary consequence of a Fourth Amendment violation."[36] The "exclusionary rule is not an individual right and applies only where it 'result[s] in appreciable deterrence.'"[37] Moreover, the Court clarified that the remedy's deterrence benefits should outweigh the costs of, principally, "letting guilty and possibly dangerous defendants go free—something that 'offends basic concepts of the criminal justice system.'"[38]

In this case, the Court found the conduct "not so objectively culpable as to require exclusion."[39] As in *Leon*, "the marginal or nonexistent benefits produced by suppressing evidence obtained in objectively reasonable reliance on a subsequently invalidated search warrant cannot justify the substantial costs of exclusion."[40] Where the police are shown to have engaged in reckless maintenance of its warrant system or deliberately made false entries to allow future false arrests, application of the exclusionary rule is certainly justified

[33] *Id.* (quoting United States v. Calandra, 414 U.S. 338, 348 (1974)).

[34] *Id.* (quoting United States v. Leon, 468 U.S. 897, 916 (1984)).

[35] *Id.* (stating that exclusion "has always been our last resort, not our first impulse" (citing Hudson v. Michigan, 547 U.S. 586, 591 (2006))).

[36] *Id.* (citing Leon, 468 U.S. at 909; Arizona v. Evans, 514 U.S. 1, 13–14 (1995); Pa. Bd. of Prob. & Parole v. Scott, 524 U.S. 357, 363 (1998))).

[37] *Id.* (quoting Leon, 468 U.S. at 909).

[38] *Id.* at 700–01 (quoting Leon, 468 U.S. at 908).

[39] *Id.*

[40] *Id.* (quoting Leon, 468 U.S. at 922).

if such misconduct caused a Fourth Amendment violation.[41] The Court emphasized that this "analysis of deterrence and culpability" is objective—in other words, a court should not attempt to discern the officer's intentions, but rather "'whether a reasonably well trained officer would have known that the search was illegal' in light of 'all the circumstances.'"[42] In refusing to apply the exclusionary rule, the Court embraced the view that it is not constitutionally mandated. Indeed, the Court emphasized that the exclusionary rule is a "last resort" rather than a "necessary consequence of a Fourth Amendment violation."[43]

In light of the Court's "repeated holdings that the deterrent effect of suppression must be substantial and outweigh any harm to the justice system, [the Court] conclude[d] that when police mistakes are the result of negligence such as that described [in this case], rather than systemic error or reckless disregard of constitutional requirements, any marginal deterrence" is not justified and the exclusionary rule does not apply.[44]

The majority focused on the objective reasonableness of individual officers relying upon otherwise seemingly accurate information in executing warrants. By declining suppression in instances of what many might perceive as an "honest mistake," the majority effectively concluded that this is not the type of unreasonable action from which citizens need protection.[45] In other words, the Court has decided that the exclusionary rule will not deter an officer from making mistakes where he is unaware of a colleague's error and has no reason to suspect an error was made. But limits exist: the Court expressly held that that this new exception will not apply to systemic errors. Instead, the Court found it inherently unreasonable for an officer to rely on information from a warrant database the officer knows or has reason to know does not provide consistently accurate information.[46]

---

[41] *Id.* at 703.

[42] *Id.* (quoting Leon, 468 at 922 n.23).

[43] *Id.* at 700 (internal quotation and citation omitted).

[44] *Id.* at 704 (internal citation omitted).

[45] *Id.* at 702.

[46] *Id.* at 704.

Justice Ruth Bader Ginsburg was not impressed. Her dissent noted that the Court's decision would undermine "the need for a forceful exclusionary rule and the gravity of recordkeeping errors in law enforcement."[47] To Justice Ginsburg, "the 'most serious impact' of the Court's holding will be on innocent persons 'wrongfully arrested based on erroneous information [carelessly maintained] in a computer data base.' "[48] Her dissent explained that deterrence is not the only purpose of the exclusionary rule: "It 'enabl[es] the judiciary to avoid the taint of partnership in official lawlessness,' and it 'assur[es] the people—all potential victims of unlawful government conduct—that the government would not profit from its lawless behavior, thus minimizing the risk of seriously undermining popular trust in government.' "[49]

In addition to arguing that the rule is constitutionally mandated, Justice Ginsburg also offered a pragmatic argument and disputed the majority's conclusion that the rule would be of minimal deterrent value in cases such as these.[50] She analogized the exclusionary rule's function to a premise of tort law that liability for negligence "creates an incentive to act with greater care."[51] "The Sheriff's Department is in a position to remedy the situation and might well do so if the exclusionary rule is there to remove the incentive to do otherwise."[52] Ginsburg stated that the need for exclusionary rule is significant because "'the offense to the dignity of the citizen who is arrested, handcuffed, and searched on a public street simply because some bureaucrat has failed to maintain an accurate computer database' is evocative of the use of general warrants that so outraged the authors of our Bill of Rights."[53] She continued, explaining that "first, by restricting suppression to bookkeeping errors that are deliberate or reckless, the majority leaves Herring, and others like him, with no remedy for violations of their constitutional rights."[54] Because the

---

[47] *Id.* at 706 (Ginsburg, J., dissenting).

[48] *Id.* at 705 (quoting Arizona v. Evans, 514 U.S. 1, 22 (1995) (Stevens, J., dissenting)).

[49] *Id.* (quoting United States v. Calandra, 414 U.S. 338, 357 (1974) (Brennan, J., dissenting)).

[50] *Id.* at 708.

[51] *Id.* (internal quotation and citation omitted).

[52] *Id.* (citing Evans, 514 U.S. at 21) (internal quotations omitted).

[53] *Id.* at 709 (quoting Evans, 514 U.S. at 23 (Stevens, J., dissenting)).

[54] *Id.*

arresting officer would be protected by qualified immunity, the police department itself is not liable for its employees' negligent acts.[55] Further, it may be impossible to identify which police employee committed the error, so the formula is simple according to the dissenters: "Negligent recordkeeping errors by law enforcement threaten individual liberty, are susceptible to deterrence by the exclusionary rule, and cannot be remedied effectively through other means."[56]

The dissent underscored a significant rift in the Court's Fourth Amendment jurisprudence. The majority undertook a fact-based analysis of whether the constables' blunder was objectively reasonable and considered the exclusionary rule simply to be a useful remedy for Fourth Amendment violations, not something mandated by the Constitution itself. Ginsburg, however, seemed unconcerned with any kind of "reasonableness" analysis, objective or otherwise. Instead, she maintained that it is per se unreasonable ever to rely on a warrant that turned out to be invalid based on any police error. For her, because the exclusionary rule is part and parcel of the Fourth Amendment, suppression is an automatic consequence of the illegal search or seizure.

B. Pearson v. Callahan[57]

Much like the dog that did not bark in the well-known Sherlock Holmes story,[58] *Pearson v. Callahan* turns out to be the fascinating Fourth Amendment case that was not. Undercover police officers and confidential informants have consistently presented certain challenges to courts. While their use has become essential to law enforcement, how can a categorical warrant requirement be squared with plainclothes officers or informants warrantlessly entering homes or collecting evidence at the behest of the police? Do we waive our privacy interests when we don't know that the person with whom we're associating is actually a government proxy? If consent to enter

[55] See Harlow v. Fitzgerald, 457 U.S. 800 (1982); Monell v. Dep't of Soc. Servs., 436 U.S. 658 (1978).

[56] Herring, 129 S. Ct. at 709–10 (Ginsberg, J., dissenting) (internal quotations omitted).

[57] Pearson v. Callahan, 555 U.S. ___, 129 S. Ct. 808 (2009).

[58] Arthur Conan Doyle, Silver Blaze, in 1 Sherlock Holmes: The Complete Novels and Stories 455, 475 (1986).

a premises is given to a confidential informant, does that enable the government to enter as well?

In *Pearson*, Brian Bartholomew, a police informant for a narcotics task force, informed officers that respondent Afton Callahan had arranged to sell him methamphetamine. Later that evening, Bartholomew arrived at Callahan's residence carrying a marked $100 bill and wearing a wire. He had agreed upon a signal he would give police after completing the purchase. Callahan sold him a gram of methamphetamine, Bartholomew gave the arrest signal, and the officers entered the trailer. The officers seized methamphetamine and drug paraphernalia during the course of a protective sweep.

After the Utah Court of Appeals vacated Callahan's drug convictions, he brought suit under 42 U.S.C. §1983 against the officers who had conducted the warrantless search of his house.[59] The Tenth Circuit ruled that petitioners were not entitled to summary judgment on qualified immunity grounds, holding that Callahan had adduced sufficient facts to establish a Fourth Amendment violation.[60]

Although this case was primarily one involving qualified immunity, the Supreme Court requested the parties to brief "[w]hether the Fourth Amendment is violated when police officers enter a home after a confidential informant has been admitted inside to purchase drugs, the informant completes the purchase, and he then signals the purchase to the officers waiting outside."[61] In other words, was the officers' warrantless entry reasonable? Despite the Court's interest in the Fourth Amendment issue, and that issue's probable impact on whether the officers merited qualified immunity, the unanimous opinion, penned by Justice Alito, did not address it. The Court offered no explanation as to why it left the issue unresolved; perhaps consideration of privacy interests, and whether they could reasonably be waived merely by agreeing to the entry of the confidential informant, proved a difficult issue for a majority to coalesce around.

This case *could* have been significant in that it might have decided whether it was reasonable for the officers to enter a home without a warrant based on a confidential informant's entry into the premises.

---

[59] Pearson, 129 S. Ct. at 814.

[60] *Id.* at 814–15.

[61] Brief for Petitioners at i, Pearson v. Callahan, 129 S. Ct. 808 (2009) (No. 07-751), 2008 WL 2367229.

Petitioners did argue that the agents' entry did not violate the Fourth Amendment because Callahan had already lost his privacy expectation when he allowed the informant into his home.[62] After all, if an undercover officer can enter the home without a warrant, why not a confidential informant acting in concert with the police? For better or worse, this "consent once removed" scenario would have opened a new vista for warrantless searches.

C. Arizona v. Johnson[63]

The Court has traditionally deferred to officers' discretion at the scene of traffic stops. Although the Court's stated rationale has always been one of "officer safety," courts have permitted warrantless searches of automobiles even where the driver did not pose a threat to the arresting officers. In *Arizona v. Johnson*, the Court had the opportunity to assess the propriety of searching passengers not otherwise being arrested.

Three officers affiliated with an Arizona gang task force were patrolling a Tucson neighborhood allegedly frequented by the notorious Crips street gang. After discovering that a passing vehicle's registration had been suspended, the officers stopped the car. Officer Maria Trevizo noticed that respondent Lemon Johnson, the back seat passenger, exhibited "unusual behavior."[64] While Detective Machado asked the vehicle's driver to exit the vehicle, Officer Trevizo questioned Johnson, learning he was from Eloy, Arizona—a town with a Crips affiliated gang—and that he had recently served prison time for burglary. Officer Trevizo also noticed that Johnson carried a police scanner and dressed in colors signifying Crips membership.

Officer Trevizo asked Johnson to exit the vehicle; when he did, the officer asked him to turn around so she could pat him down. She testified that she performed the patdown "because [she] had a lot of information that would lead [her] to believe he might have a weapon on him," but that "[she] did not have probable cause at that point to believe that he was involved in criminal activity."[65]

---

[62] *Id.* at 20.

[63] Arizona v. Johnson, 555 U.S. ____, 129 S. Ct. 781 (2009).

[64] Brief for Petitioner at 3, Arizona v. Johnson, 129 S. Ct. 781 (2009) (No. 07-1222), 2008 WL 4080367.

[65] *Id.* (internal quotation marks and citations omitted).

The officer patted down Johnson's clothing and felt the butt of a handgun in the waist of his pants. At this point respondent began "to struggle," so the officer handcuffed him so that he could not reach his gun.

Officer Trevizo testified that a totality of circumstances, not any one specific factor, initially led her to believe respondent was armed and potentially dangerous. Johnson, without challenging the reasonableness of the officer's beliefs, instead argued he had consented to talk with the officer, but had not consented to the patdown. The trial court denied Johnson's motion to suppress, concluding that the officers had a reasonable basis to fear for their safety and that the traffic stop permitted the officers to perform a limited patdown. The Arizona Court of Appeals reversed respondent's convictions, holding that the "officer may not conduct a *Terry* frisk of the passenger without reasonable cause to believe 'criminal activity may be afoot' "[66]

Thus, the Supreme Court considered whether the officer could conduct a warrantless patdown of the passenger without any reasonable suspicion that the passenger had committed a criminal offense. In *Terry v. Ohio*, the Court had ruled that the police could conduct a limited patdown of a pedestrian believed to be armed and dangerous.[67] The level of suspicion necessary to justify a patdown need not rise to the level of probable cause, but could not be based upon the officer's mere hunch. Although the police may order the driver out of the vehicle during a routine traffic stop, to justify a patdown of the driver or a passenger during the stop, the police must harbor a reasonable suspicion that the person is armed and dangerous.

Indeed, the Supreme Court has long recognized that traffic stops are inherently dangerous for police officers.[68] In *Maryland v. Wilson*, the Court stressed that "[t]he risk of harm to both the police and the occupants [of a stopped vehicle] is minimized if the officers routinely exercise unquestioned command of the situation."[69] The Court has thus applied the *Terry* stop-and-frisk rationale to traffic stops and has held that "once a motor vehicle has been lawfully

---

[66] *Id.* (quoting Terry v. Ohio, 392 U.S. 1, 30 (1968)).

[67] Terry v. Ohio, 392 U.S. 1, 30 (1968).

[68] Johnson, 129 S. Ct. at 786.

[69] Maryland v. Wilson, 519 U.S. 408, 414 (1997).

detained for a traffic violation, the police officers may order the driver to get out of the vehicle without violating the Fourth Amendment."[70] The *Wilson* Court found that the same rationale supporting searches of drivers applies to passengers as well.[71]

Following these precedents, the Court reasoned that the government's "legitimate and weighty interest in officer safety outweighs the *de minimis* additional intrusion of requiring a driver, already lawfully stopped, to exit the vehicle."[72] Further, the Court found that "a driver, once outside the stopped vehicle, may be patted down for weapons if the officer reasonably concludes that the driver 'might be armed and presently dangerous.'"[73]

Applying *Wilson*, the Court determined that the officers lawfully detained the passenger, Johnson, because of the traffic stop.[74] "[A] traffic stop of a car communicates to a reasonable passenger that he or she is not free to terminate the encounter with the police and move about at will."[75] Nothing in this case would have conveyed to respondent "that, prior to the frisk, the traffic stop had ended or that he was otherwise free 'to depart without police permission.'"[76] Thus, the officer was not required by the Fourth Amendment to give defendant an opportunity to depart "without first ensuring that, in so doing, she was not permitting a dangerous person to get behind her."[77] The Court had little trouble upholding respondent's stop and frisk.

While the reasoning in this case can be construed as an extension of existing precedent, one is left to question whether the factual predicate is truly sufficient to justify the search of a passenger. Officer safety is understandably a reasonable concern at any traffic stop—and passengers doubtless present every bit of much a safety risk as the driver. But do those scenarios need a bright line that is never

---

[70] Pennsylvania v. Mimms, 434 U.S. 106, 111 n.6 (1977).

[71] Wilson, 519 U.S. at 413 (applying the *Mimms* rule to passengers because a passenger's motivation to use violence during the stop "is every bit as great as that of the driver.").

[72] Johnson, 129 S. Ct. at 786.

[73] *Id.* (quoting Mimms, 434 U.S. at 112).

[74] *Id.*

[75] *Id.*

[76] *Id.* (internal quotation and citation omitted).

[77] *Id.*

particularly bright, or is all this best left to the discretion of the trial court after weighing the relevant facts?

D. Arizona v. Gant[78]

If you're handcuffed and locked up in the back of a squad car that cannot be opened from the inside, do you present a sufficiently serious threat to police officers such that they can search your secured vehicle without a warrant? I suspect most people who are not judges would say, "No." Within the judiciary, however, the answer has proven to be a bit more complicated. In *Arizona v. Gant,* Tucson police officers responded to an anonymous tip concerning narcotics activity at a residence. Rodney Gant greeted the officers at the front door, identified himself, and informed them that the homeowner would return later that day. After they left the residence, the officers ran Gant's name through a records database and discovered that he had an outstanding warrant for failure to appear on a driving-with-a-suspended-license charge.

Later that same day, the officers returned to the residence and found a man and a woman sitting in a parked car in front of the residence. The officers obtained the woman's consent to search the vehicle and uncovered a crack pipe. The officers arrested the woman, as well as the man, upon learning he had given them a false name, handcuffed them both, and secured them in separate squad cars.

Shortly thereafter, officers recognized Gant when he drove his car into the residence's driveway. Gant parked and exited his car; the officers immediately handcuffed and arrested him for driving on a suspended license. Because the other man and woman were already secured in the only two squad cars at the scene, the officers radioed for backup. When another squad car arrived at the scene, the officers secured Gant in the third vehicle.

At this point, five officers were on scene and all three subjects, including Gant, were secured in separate squad cars that were incapable of being opened from the inside. Once Gant was locked in the squad car, the officers searched his vehicle and uncovered a handgun "somewhere within the interior compartment" and a plastic baggie containing cocaine in the pocket of a jacket lying on the

---

[78] Arizona v. Gant, 556 U.S. ____, 129 S. Ct. 1710 (2009).

backseat.[79] During the search, one of the officers supervised Gant and remained in the immediate area of the squad car in which he was secured. Absent supernatural powers, it was unlikely Gant could present much of a threat to anyone.

The trial court ruled that the search of Gant's car was incident to his arrest because he was a recent occupant of the vehicle, the officers arrested him only "seconds" after he exited the vehicle, and the officers searched the car "immediately" after securing Gant in the squad car.[80] Sounds perfectly reasonable. The state court of appeals reversed in a split decision, however, ruling that the search of the passenger compartment was not incidental to the arrest because the underlying justifications for such a search—officer safety and evidence preservation—were no longer present after Gant was secured. The Arizona Supreme Court affirmed, agreeing that the search violated the Fourth Amendment and ruling that it was not incident to the arrest because neither officer safety nor evidence destruction was at issue. The court further concluded that because the record revealed no unsecured civilians in the area and at least four officers present, the officers "had no reason to believe that anyone at the scene could have gained access to Gant's vehicle or that the officers' safety was at risk."[81]

The U.S. Supreme Court granted certiorari to consider whether, given the circumstances, the Fourth Amendment required the officers to obtain a warrant prior to the vehicle's search. In a surprising decision—surprising because the Court has traditionally granted officers wide latitude to search vehicles at an arrest scene—the Court held that the police may search the passenger compartment of a vehicle incident to a recent occupant's arrest only where it is reasonable to believe that the arrestee might access the vehicle at the time of the search.[82] Justice John Paul Stevens wrote for a majority that included Justices Antonin Scalia, David Souter, Clarence Thomas, and Ruth Bader Ginsburg—a line-up not often seen.

---

[79] Brief for Respondent at 4, Arizona v. Gant, 129 S. Ct. 1710 (2009) (No. 07-542), 2008 WL 2817675, at *4.

[80] Brief for Petitioner at 7, Arizona v. Gant, 129 S. Ct. 1710 (2009) (No. 07-542), 2008 WL 2066112.

[81] *Id.*

[82] Gant, 129 S. Ct. at 1719.

A search incident to a lawful arrest that encompasses the "arrest-ee's person and the area 'within his immediate control'" has stood as a long-standing exception to the warrant requirement. In other words, the police may search any area where the suspect could realistically "gain possession of a weapon or destructible evidence"[83] without first obtaining a warrant. Interests in officer safety and evidence preservation typically justify this exception.[84] Over time, the search incident to arrest has been extended, such as in *New York v. Belton,* in which the Court held that where an officer lawfully arrests an occupant of the car, he may, "as a contemporaneous incident of that arrest, search the passenger compartment of the automobile" and any containers therein.[85] The *Gant* Court explained, however, that when it is not possible for the arrestee to access the area the officers want to search, then the rule does not apply.[86]

While this makes perfect sense—no one expects someone hand-cuffed and locked in a police car to be able to escape easily and threaten officers or destroy evidence—since *Belton,* a number of courts have read the decision broadly. For example, in *Thornton v. United States,* the Court "treat[ed] the ability to search a vehicle incident to the arrest of a recent occupant as a police entitlement rather than as an exception justified by the twin rationales of *Chi-mel.*"[87] "Under this construction of *Belton,* a vehicle search would be authorized incident to every arrest of a recent occupant notwith-standing that in most cases the vehicle's passenger compartment will not be within the arrestee's reach at the time of the search."[88] To the *Gant* majority, such a reading would untether the rule from the underlying safety and evidentiary justifications of the *Chimel* exception—"a result clearly incompatible with [the Court's] state-ment in *Belton* that it 'in no way alters the fundamental principles established in the *Chimel* case regarding the basic scope of searches

---

[83] *Id.* at 1716 (quoting Chimel v. California, 395 U.S. 752, 763 (1969)).

[84] *Id.*

[85] New York v. Belton, 453 U.S. 454, 460 (1981).

[86] Gant, 129 S. Ct. at 1717.

[87] Thornton v. United States, 541 U.S. 615, 624 (2004) (O'Connor, J., concurring in part).

[88] Gant, 129 S. Ct. at 1719.

incident to lawful custodial arrests.'''[89] Hence, the *Gant* Court rejected this understanding of *Belton* and held "that the *Chimel* rationale authorizes police to search a vehicle incident to a recent occupant's arrest only when the arrestee is unsecured and within reaching distance of the passenger compartment at the time of the search."[90]

Granted, in this case, the five officers outnumbered the three suspects already secured in separate patrol cars at the time of the search, but, why should it, the state argued, be unreasonable to search a vehicle—which already has a somewhat lessened expectation of privacy—attendant to the arrest? The Court flatly rejected the state's expansive reading of *Belton*. The Court focused less on the reasonableness of the search and more on the individual's privacy expectation, noting that the state seriously undervalued the privacy interests at stake for a motorist in his vehicle. A rule that gives police the unbridled power "to search not just the passenger compartment but every purse, briefcase, or other container within that space . . . when there is no basis for believing evidence of [an] offense might be found in the vehicle, creates a serious and recurring threat to the privacy of countless individuals."[91]

Despite the state's touting of its proposed reading as a "bright line" rule, the Court found that broad interpretations of *Belton* have "generated a great deal of uncertainty" with respect to the timing of the arrest, the arrestee's proximity to the vehicle, and the reasonableness of a search commencing after an arrestee has been removed from the scene.[92] Instead, the Court explained that a broad reading of *Belton* was unnecessary to protect officer safety or address evidentiary concerns.[93] Rather than focusing on whether the officers' actions in this case were unreasonable, the Court found that "construing *Belton* broadly to allow vehicle searches incident to any arrest would serve no purpose except to provide police entitlement, and it is anathema to the Fourth Amendment to permit a warrantless search on that basis."[94]

[89] *Id.*
[90] *Id.*
[91] *Id.*
[92] *Id.* at 1720–21.
[93] *Id.* at 1721.
[94] *Id.*

The Court further rejected the claim that *stare decisis* required adherence to a broad reading of *Belton*, noting that "the experience of the 28 years since [the Court] decided *Belton* has shown that the generalization underpinning the broad reading of that decision is unfounded," especially since it became clear that articles within passenger compartments were rarely within reach or a safety concern.[95] In many respects, the Court simply reflected what most people already know: If you're secured in the back of a police car, surrounded by officers, it's unlikely you can grab anything left back in your vehicle.

In one respect, the majority inserted an actual "reasonableness" analysis to searches incident to arrest at a vehicular stop. Presumably, officers can now search a vehicle incident to arrest only if the arrestee can "reasonably" access the automobile during the search (almost impossible to satisfy where the arrestee is secured, for example, in a squad car), or the officer himself "reasonably" believes that evidence of the arresting offense may be found in the vehicle (a limitation designed to keep officers "honest").

In his concurrence, Justice Scalia noted that "since the historical scope of officers' authority to search vehicles incident to arrest is uncertain, traditional standards of reasonableness govern. It is abundantly clear that those standards do not justify . . . that arresting officers may always search an arrestee's vehicle in order to protect themselves from hidden weapons."[96] Scalia would have preferred to overrule *Belton* and *Thornton*, but was forced to side with the majority to avoid what he viewed as the greater evil of continuing with the broad interpretation of *Belton* that allowed searches incident to any arrest of a vehicle occupant.[97] He would rather have a rule making vehicle searches incident to arrest "reasonable" only where the officer has a reasonable belief that evidence of the arresting offense, or another offense for which the officer has probable cause, will be discovered within the vehicle. Scalia appeared unconcerned about upholding a categorical warrant requirement, but instead examined whether a search performed under these circumstances was reasonable.[98]

[95] *Id.* at 1722–23.
[96] Gant, 129 S. Ct. at 1724 (Scalia, J., concurring).
[97] *Id.*
[98] *Id.*

In dissent, Justice Stephen Breyer wrote that the majority was upending *Belton* "and those who wish [the] Court to change a well-established legal precedent—where, as here, there has been consider-able reliance on the legal rule in question—bear a heavy burden."[99] In his view, this burden had not been met.

Justice Samuel Alito similarly dissented, largely because "[a]lthough the Court refuses to acknowledge that it is overruling *Belton* and *Thornton*, there can be no doubt that it does so."[100] He explained that "the [*Belton*] Court unequivocally stated its holding that "when a policeman has made a lawful custodial arrest of the occupant of an automobile, he may, as a contemporaneous incident of that arrest, search the passenger compartment of that automobile."[101] The majority, Alito wrote, "curiously suggests that *Belton* may reasonably be read as adopting a holding that is narrower than the one explicitly set out" and that "this 'bright-line rule' has now been interred."[102] Because the respondent had not asked the Court to overrule *Belton*, much less *Chimel*, and because his argument rested entirely on a faulty interpretation of *Belton*, Justice Alito would have upheld the search.[103]

E. Safford Unified School Dist. No. 1 v. Redding[104]

Safford v. Redding served a twofold purpose: first, it enabled the Supreme Court to consider the appropriate scope of searching a student for drugs; and second, it allowed Justice Ginsburg to press the importance of having some semblance of gender balance on the Court. The respondent, Savana Redding, was a middle-school student who was strip-searched by school authorities. The lively oral argument prompted Justice Ginsburg to comment: "[The other Court members] have never been a 13-year-old girl. . . . It's a very sensitive age for a girl. I didn't think that my colleagues, some of them, quite understood."[105]

---

[99] *Id.* at 1726 (Breyer, J., dissenting).

[100] *Id.* at 1727 (Alito, J., dissenting).

[101] *Id.* (quoting New York v. Belton, 453 U.S. 454, 460 (1981)).

[102] *Id.*

[103] *Id.*

[104] Safford Unified Sch. Dist. No. 1 v. Redding, 557 U.S. ____, 129 S. Ct. 2633 (2009).

[105] Joan Biskupic, Ginsburg: Court Needs Another Woman, USA Today, May 5, 2009, at A1.

Safford Middle School had experienced a serious drug problem among its students, which prompted the administration to adopt a "zero tolerance" policy prohibiting the nonmedical possession of drugs on campus. One afternoon, Assistant Principal Kerry Wilson received a call from the mother of a student, Jordan Romero, who informed Wilson that Jordan had gotten sick after taking pills he received from a classmate. Romero identified several students who had been distributing drugs, including Marissa Glines and Savana Redding. Romero subsequently approached Wilson, handed him a white pill—later identified as prescription Ibuprofen—that he claimed Glines had just given to him and informed him that a group of students planned to take the pills at lunch.

Wilson went to Glines's class and asked her to accompany him to the office. As the girl stood up, Wilson noticed a black planner sitting on the adjacent desk that turned out to contain several knives and lighters, a cigarette, and a black marker. After escorting Glines to his office, Wilson and an administrative assistant observed her remove a blue pill from her pockets, several white pills identical to the one Romero had given to Wilson, and a razor blade. Glines identified Redding as the person who gave her the pills and the planner.

Wilson then pulled Redding from class and confronted her with the black planner and the prescription pills. Redding admitted that the planner belonged to her, but denied owning the present contents or having distributed the pills.

Given the confirmed distribution of prescription pills in school that morning, the ostensibly reliable implication of Redding as the pill supplier, and Redding's admission that she owned the black planner, Wilson asked the administrative assistant, Helen Romero, to escort Redding to the nurse's office to be searched. Once in the nurse's office, Ms. Romero and the female nurse directed Redding to undress. The assistant also asked Redding to shake out her bra as well as the elastic band of her underwear. Although the entire search was performed without anyone physically touching Redding, she was forced to expose her genital area and breasts to the school officials. The search, however, failed to yield any additional contraband. Redding later described the school officials' viewing of her nearly naked body as "the most humiliating experience" of her life.[106]

<hr/>

[106] Brief for Respondent at 2–3, Safford Unified Sch. Dist. No. 1 v. Redding, 2009 WL 852123.

Redding sued the school district, as well as the school officials involved in the search, and included a claim under 43 U.S.C. § 1983 alleging that the search violated her Fourth Amendment rights. The district court determined that the school officials had not violated the Fourth Amendment as the search complied with the standard set forth in *New Jersey v. T.L.O.*, which permitted school authorities wide latitude to search students without first obtaining a warrant.[107] The district court explained that the search was reasonable under the circumstances because grounds existed for suspecting that Redding was in possession of drugs in violation of Safford policies. The Ninth Circuit Court of Appeals, rehearing the case en banc after a panel decision affirming the district court, reversed the district court's determination that there was no violation of Redding's constitutional rights and subsequently denied Wilson qualified immunity.

The Supreme Court granted certiorari to decide whether Redding's warrantless strip search violated the Fourth Amendment and whether the officials enjoyed qualified immunity.[108] The Court held that because the school officials had no reason to suspect that the drugs presented a danger or that they were concealed in the student's underwear, the warrantless strip search was unreasonable.[109] The Court's opinion explained that *New Jersey v. T.L.O.* "recognized that the school setting 'requires some modification of the level of suspicion of illicit activity needed to justify a search,' and held that for searches by school officials 'a careful balancing of governmental and private interests, suggests that the public interest is best served by a Fourth Amendment standard of reasonableness that stops short of probable cause.'"[110] In other words, the Fourth Amendment is all about reasonableness and its values can be satisfied without a categorical warrant requirement. Under the resulting reasonable suspicion standard, a school search "will be permissible in its scope when the measures adopted are reasonably related to the objectives of the search and not excessively intrusive in light of the age and

---

[107] See New Jersey v. T.L.O., 469 U.S. 325 (1985).

[108] While not germane to our discussion, the Court also considered whether "qualified immunity applies to public school officials in a damages lawsuit under 43 U.S.C. section 1983 for conducting a strip search of a student suspected of possessing and distributing a prescription drug on campus."

[109] *Id.* at 2644.

[110] *Id.* at 2639 (quoting T.L.O., 469 U.S. at 340–41).

sex of the student and the nature of the infraction"[111] Echoing *T.L.O.*, the Court explained that although the required knowledge component for probable cause must rise to the level of "fair probability" or "substantial chance," a lesser standard applies to school evidence searches.[112] This required knowledge component for reasonable suspicion can "readily be described as a *moderate chance* of finding evidence of wrongdoing."[113]

According to the Court, Wilson was justified in searching Redding's backpack and outer clothing because sufficient evidence existed to tie Redding to the pill distribution. "If a student is reasonably suspected of giving out contraband pills," Justice Souter wrote for the Court, "she is reasonably suspected of carrying them on her person and in the carryall that has become an item of student uniform in most places today. If [petitioner's] reasonable suspicion of pill distribution were not understood to support searches of outer clothes and backpack, it would not justify any search worth making."[114] As a consequence, Wilson's search of Redding's backpack "in her presence and in the relative privacy of Wilson's office, was not excessively intrusive, any more than [Helen] Romero's subsequent search of her outer clothing."[115]

The reasonableness of the *strip* search, however, took on a new dimension. Because Redding had to expose her breasts and pelvic area to school officials, Souter explained that "both subjective and reasonable societal expectations of personal privacy support the treatment of such a search as categorically distinct, requiring distinct elements of justification on the part of school authorities for going beyond a search of outer clothing and belongings."[116] Redding's subjective expectation of privacy against such a strip search "is inherent in her account of it as embarrassing, frightening, and humiliating."[117] Although the subjective view of the search as degrading does not outlaw the search, it does implicate the rule that "the

---

[111] *Id.* (quoting T.L.O., 469 U.S. at 342).

[112] *Id.* (citing Illinois v. Gates, 462 U.S. 213, 238, 244 n.13 (1983)).

[113] *Id.* (emphasis added).

[114] *Id.*

[115] *Id.*

[116] *Id.*

[117] *Id.*

search as actually conducted [be] reasonably related in scope to the circumstances which justified the interference in the first place"— in other words, the search must be reasonable.[118]

Here, Wilson did not have sufficient suspicion to merit forcing the privacy intrusion to the extent that was done; the facts simply failed to suggest, according to Souter, that Redding had concealed pills in her underwear. Indeed, a search "that extensive calls for suspicion that it will pay off."[119] Wilson knew the pills were common pain relievers, must have known of their nature and limited threat, and had no reason suspect a large volume was being distributed. Possession of nondangerous school contraband does not suggest stashes in intimate places, and there was no evidence of such a practice at the school.[120] Furthermore, neither of the student informants suggested that Redding was hiding drugs in her underwear. "[T]he combination of these deficiencies was fatal to finding the search reasonable."[121] With this decision, the Court intended to make the following clear:

> The *T.L.O.* concern to limit a school search to reasonable scope requires the support of reasonable suspicion of danger or of resort to underwear for hiding evidence of wrongdoing before a search can reasonably make the quantum leap from outer clothes and backpacks to exposure of intimate parts. The meaning of such a search, and the degradation its subject may reasonably feel, place a search that intrusive in a category of its own demanding its own specific suspicions.[122]

Thus, the Court used a reasonableness test for determining the legality of a school search.

This reasonableness determination is necessarily fact-dependent. To no great surprise, the more intrusive the search's scope (even in the school setting) the higher the showing of reasonable suspicion required. What this holding also suggests is that what might not be reasonable for a thirteen-year-old girl might be reasonable for a

---

[118] *Id.* at 2642 (quoting New Jersey v. T.L.O., 469 U.S. 325, 341 (1985)).

[119] *Id.* at 2642.

[120] *Id.*

[121] *Id.* at 2643.

[122] *Id.*

seventeen-year-old boy. In balancing the reasonableness of a student's expectation of privacy, the Court explained that the search must be "reasonably related in scope" to the circumstances that initially justified the interference. The Court also seemed to create a substantial hurdle for making a showing of reasonable suspicion when it comes to the "categorically extreme intrusiveness of a search down to the body of an adolescent" by school officials.[123] Even so, if the drugs had been heroin instead of common prescription anti-inflammatories, the strip search might have been deemed reasonable.

While Justice Stevens joined as to Parts I–III of the Court's opinion, he would not have afforded the officials qualified immunity.[124] Similarly, Justice Ginsburg agreed that the search was unreasonable, but like Stevens, balked at allowing the school officials to hide behind the shield of qualified immunity. According to Ginsburg, the determination was simple: "Any reasonable search for the pills would have ended when inspection of Redding's backpack and jacket pockets yielded nothing."[125] But is that a reasonable assumption? If you suspect the student to have pills, wouldn't the underwear be an eminently reasonable place to search? Ginsburg's more salient concern was that "[a]t no point did he attempt to call her parent."[126] Under the circumstances, she did not find the search a reasonable exercise of the school officials' authority.

Alone in dissent, Justice Thomas found the search reasonable given existing legal precedents and the unique relationship between students and school officials. He explained that "[s]chool officials retain broad authority to protect students and preserve 'order and a proper educational environment' under the Fourth Amendment."[127] "Seeking to reconcile the Fourth Amendment with this unique public school setting, the Court in *T.L.O.* held that a school search is 'reasonable' if it is 'justified at its inception' and 'reasonably related in scope to the circumstances which justified the interference in the first

---

[123] *Id.* at 2642.

[124] *Id.* at 2644 (Stevens, J., concurring in part and dissenting in part).

[125] *Id.* at 2645 (Ginsberg, J., concurring in part and dissenting in part).

[126] *Id.*

[127] *Id.* at 2647 (quoting New Jersey v. T.L.O., 469 U.S. 325, 339 (1985)).

place.'"128 For Justice Thomas, "[t]he search under review easily meets this standard."129

Thomas asserted, "[E]ach of these additional requirements [(i.e., of weighing the dangerousness of the drugs or reasonable suspicion of hidden drugs in the underwear)] is an unjustifiable departure from bedrock Fourth Amendment law in the school setting, where this Court has heretofore read the Fourth Amendment to grant considerable leeway to school officials. Because the school officials searched in a location where the pills could have been hidden, the search was reasonable in scope under *T.L.O.*"130 According to Thomas, pills could certainly be secreted in one's underwear, as had been done by others before, and so he further opined that the Court had placed school officials in an "impossible spot" by questioning whether the possession of nondangerous drug causes a severe enough threat to warrant investigation.131 He questioned the majority's simplification that the search might be warranted if the violation involved a street drug:

> In effect, then, the majority has replaced a school rule that draws no distinction among drugs with a new one that does. As a result, a full search of a student's person for prohibited drugs will be permitted only if the Court agrees that the drug in question was sufficiently dangerous. Such a test is unworkable and unsound.132 ... Judges are not qualified to second-guess the best manner for maintaining quiet and order in the school environment.... [I]t is a mistake for judges to assume the responsibility for deciding which school rules are important enough to allow for invasive searches and which rules are not.133

Moreover, according to Thomas, the high rate of prescription drug abuse justifies school officials in punishing the unauthorized possession of prescription drugs as severely as street drugs.134 He asserted,

---

128 *Id.* (quoting T.L.O., 469 U.S. at 341–42).
129 *Id.*
130 *Id.* at 2649.
131 *Id.* at 2650–51.
132 *Id.*
133 *Id.* at 2651–52.
134 *Id.* at 2653.

"It is therefore irrelevant whether officials suspected Redding of possessing prescription-strength Ibuprofen . . . or some harder street drug. Safford prohibited its possession on school property. Reasonable suspicion that Redding was in possession of drugs in violation of these policies, therefore, justified a search extending to any area where small pills could be concealed."[135]

Justice Thomas then sought to graft a common-law doctrine into the reasonableness equation: "The Court's interference in these matters . . . illustrates why the most constitutionally sound approach to the question of applying the Fourth Amendment in local public schools would in fact be the complete restoration of the common-law doctrine of *in loco parentis*."[136] If this common-law doctrine were applied to this case, the search of Redding would stand, as parents' authority is "not subject to the limits of the Fourth Amendment."[137] Restoring this doctrine "would not, however, leave public schools entirely free to impose any rule they choose," since parents and local government can quite capably challenge "overly harsh school rules or the enforcement of sensible rules in insensible ways."[138] He concluded that "in the end, the task of implementing and amending public school policies is beyond this Court's function," since "parents, teachers, school administrators, local politicians, and state officials are all better suited than judges to determine the appropriate limits on searches conducted by school officials."[139]

III. Reinforcing Reasonableness: Voting Patterns of the Justices

While it is unfair, if not impossible, to attempt to predict trends for a single term or how the justices may vote in the future, the Fourth Amendment cases decided in October Term 2008 do provide several interesting insights.

---

[135] *Id.* at 2655.

[136] *Id.*

[137] *Id.* at 2656 (internal quotation and citation omitted).

[138] *Id.*

[139] *Id.*

Case[140]	Majority Opinion	Concurring Opinion	Dissenting Opinion	Search/Seizure Upheld
Herring v. United States	Roberts,* Scalia, Kennedy, Thomas, Alito	N/A	Ginsburg,* Stevens, Souter, Breyer	Yes
*Pearson v. Callahan***	Alito* (unanimous)	N/A	N/A	**
Arizona v. Johnson	Ginsburg* (unanimous)	N/A	N/A	Yes
Arizona v. Gant	Stevens,* Scalia, Souter, Thomas, Ginsburg	Scalia*	Breyer,* Alito,* Roberts, Kennedy, Breyer (in part)	No
Safford Unified School Dist. No. 1 v. Redding	Souter,* Roberts, Scalia, Kennedy, Breyer, Alito, Stevens (in part), Ginsburg (in part)	Stevens,* Ginsburg*	Thomas* (concurring in the judgment in part)	No

*Author.   **Did not address the Fourth Amendment issue.

The Roberts Court seems aptly named, as the Chief Justice found himself in the majority in all but one of these cases. In fact, he assigned himself the opinion in the only case in which he found himself in the majority that sharply split the Court. *Herring* proved to be the sole opinion directly taking on the exclusionary rule's constitutional status. In that opinion, the Court declined to apply the exclusionary rule when police personnel erred in the technical aspects of record keeping and that error led to an invalid arrest or seizure. The Chief Justice not only sided with the rule of "reasonable error," but also suggested that the Constitution does not mandate exclusion as a remedy for all Fourth Amendment violations—a proposition upon which much might be built.

[140] I took this useful concept from Daniel Troy and Rebecca Wood's contribution to this same journal last year. See, Daniel E. Troy & Rebecca K. Wood, *Federal Preemption at the Supreme Court, 2007–2008* Cato Sup. Ct. Rev. 257 (2008).

Roberts's adherence to reasonableness as the Fourth Amendment's touchstone is underscored by his position joining the unanimous *Johnson* decision, where the Court expanded the application of a *Terry* "stop and frisk" to not just the driver of a lawfully stopped vehicle, but to passengers as well. Interestingly, however, the Chief Justice chose not to join the *Gant* majority, which focused on the reasonableness of the individual circumstances to determine whether a vehicle should be subject to a warrantless search anytime the occupants are arrested. Instead, Roberts deferred to *stare decisis* and the creation of a "bright-line rule" over a "reasonableness" analysis in individual cases. Perhaps the biggest surprise to anyone seeking to pigeonhole the Chief Justice as a critic of the Fourth Amendment privacy right would be in his majority vote in *Redding*, where the Court used the language of "reasonableness" to strike down the search. Even there, however, the Chief Justice demonstrated a preference for giving police officers and school officials the benefit of the doubt before subjecting the school officials to civil liability.

Justice Stevens, much as he has done in the past, championed the position that any search or seizure resulting from reliance upon a defective warrant is per se unreasonable and that suppression is an automatic consequence of a violation—regardless of how objectively reasonable the reliance may have been.[141] He demonstrated his apparent belief that exclusion is constitutionally mandated for all Fourth Amendment violations. The only detour this term that Stevens may have taken was in the unanimous *Johnson* decision. Although it might be possible to chalk this detour up to his reliance on precedent, it remains an example of a case in which Justice Stevens rejects the categorical warrant requirement in favor of a reasonableness approach. Similarly, Stevens used a reasonableness determination to strike down the search in his *Gant* opinion, which arguably bucked precedent by requiring either a showing that the arrestee could reasonably reach the vehicle during the search or that the officer reasonably believes evidence may be uncovered that otherwise might be compromised. Stevens not only joined the *Redding*

---

[141] See Christopher E. Smith, Michael A. McCall, Madhavi M. McCall, The Roberts Court and Criminal Justice at the Dawn of the 2008 Term, 3 Charleston L. Rev. 265, 267 (2009).

majority to rein in *T.L.O.*, but wrote separately to express his distaste with extending qualified immunity to the school officials. Justice Stevens wavered somewhat on whether a categorical warrant requirement should exist—based largely on precedent—but firmly supported the exclusionary rule as a necessary component of the Fourth Amendment.

By contrast, Justice Scalia dismissed both a categorical warrant requirement and automatic application of the exclusionary rule, instead favoring a case-by-case determination of reasonableness. Thus, he rejected using exclusion as a remedy in *Herring* and made much of the reasonableness of the officials' actions in *Johnson, Gant,* and *Redding*. Scalia is the only justice appearing in the majority in each of the Fourth Amendment cases. Notably, however, in his concurring opinion in *Gant*, he explained that he would have preferred a rule making vehicle searches reasonable only where the officer has a reasonable belief that evidence of the arresting offense, or another offense for which he has probable cause, will be discovered within the vehicle.[142]

Consistent with his preference for requiring a legitimate showing of objective reasonableness before upholding searches or seizures, Justice Scalia twice voted to uphold warrantless searches and twice voted to strike such searches down. Despite his interest in a rule of reasonableness, which necessarily entails particular attention to the case's specific facts, Scalia showed little trouble dispensing with the trial courts' factual determinations in *Gant* and *Redding*. While it could be argued that the trial courts relied upon interpretations of precedent the Supreme Court ultimately modified, it remains interesting to see an unwillingness to defer to lower courts' reasonableness determinations. Ordinarily, one might suspect that Scalia would both defer to the trial court's determination on reasonableness *and* say that while exclusion might be a preferred remedy on practical grounds, it is hardly compelled by the Constitution.

Justice Kennedy voted to uphold each of the searches except for that in *Redding*. Although Kennedy did not write in any of these cases, his voting pattern mirrored that of the Chief Justice. Whether that tells us anything about what Justice Kennedy is likely to do in

---

[142] Arizona v. Gant, 129 S. Ct. 1710, 1724 (2009).

the future is questionable, but he does seem to agree that exclusion is not constitutionally mandated.

The only search Justice Souter voted to uphold was that in Justice Ginsburg's unanimous *Johnson* opinion. With the exception of the qualified immunity opinion he penned in *Redding*, Souter's votes were identical to Justice Stevens. As with Stevens, Souter appeared to accept the proposition that once a Fourth Amendment violation is found, any evidence uncovered must be suppressed. Justice Souter, of course, has since resigned from the Supreme Court, so it will be interesting to see whether newly confirmed Justice Sonia Sotomayor follows in his Fourth Amendment footsteps.[143]

---

[143] Although it is difficult to determine how *Justice* Sotomayor will differ from *Judge* Sotomayor—in no small part because she will no longer be bound by Second Circuit precedent and only bound by Supreme Court precedent to the extent that she is willing to abide by *stare decisis*—three of her prior cases contain marked similarities to those decided this term. In United States v. Falso, 544 F.3d 110 (2d Cir. 2008), FBI agents, after searching the defendant's home, arrested him for possession of child pornography. The warrant application stated that the defendant "either gained access or attempted to gain access" to a child porn website under investigation and also revealed that the defendant had once pleaded guilty to misdemeanor charges of sexually abusing a seven-year-old girl. *Id.* at 114. Sotomayor's opinion held that while these facts failed to establish probable cause, this constitutional violation did not require the evidence's suppression because the officers acted in good faith. *Id.* at 128. Although this decision may be viewed as adhering to *Leon*'s "good faith" exception, it does seem to indicate a belief that suppression need not automatically follow a Fourth Amendment violation. Judge Sotomayor also had the opportunity to consider the reasonableness of the strip search of adolescents. In N.G. & N.G. ex rel. S.C. v. Connecticut, Sotomayor dissented from an opinion upholding a series of strip searches of "troubled adolescent girls" in juvenile detention centers. 382 F.3d 225, 228 (2d Cir. 2004) (Sotomayor, J., concurring in part and dissenting in part). Although Sotomayor agreed that certain strip searches were lawful, she would have held that due to the "the severely intrusive nature of strip searches," they should not be allowed "in the absence of individualized suspicion, of adolescents who have never been charged with a crime." *Id.* Portending *Redding*, she explained that an "individualized suspicion" rule was more consistent with Second Circuit precedent than the majority's rule. *Id.* Finally, in United States v. Santa, Judge Sotomayor analyzed the effect of a clerical error on the validity of an arrest. There, after an arrest warrant had been issued for the defendant and duly logged into a statewide computer database, the issuing court recalled the warrant, but the computer database was not updated to reflect that fact. 180 F.3d 20, 22–23 (2d Cir. 1999). When the police arrested Anthony Santa, wrongly believing that an outstanding warrant for him existed, they searched him and found drugs. *Id.* at 24. Sotomayor, writing for the majority, ruled that the evidence should not be suppressed because of *Leon* and *Arizona v. Evans*. *Id.* at 30. While this case does not address the issue dealt with in *Herring*, namely, whether police department employees' clerical errors could be reasonably relied upon, it does

Justice Thomas, who found himself in the majority in all but the *Safford* case, voted to uphold the searches on reasonableness grounds. In *Gant*, however, he seemed to agree with the Court's determination that it was not reasonable to conduct a search based upon fears of officer safety or destruction of evidence if the suspect is secured in a police cruiser. Thomas seems firmly attached to a reasonableness analysis for Fourth Amendment violations, which illuminates his dissent in *Redding*, where he wrote that a school search is permissible so long as it is objectively reasonable to believe that the area searched was capable of concealing the particular contraband.

Justice Ginsburg found herself most closely allied with Justice Stevens. Indeed, she wrote the *Herring* dissent, joined by Stevens, in which she argued that any search or seizure resulting from reliance upon a warrant that is invalid due to a police error is per se unreasonable and evidence suppression is an automatic consequence, regardless of how objectively reasonable the reliance. That position now appears to command no more than four solid votes. Similarly, Ginsburg joined Stevens's concurrence in *Redding*, agreeing that the school officials ought not to receive qualified immunity. Although Justice Ginsburg seemed to adhere to precedent in upholding the search in *Johnson*, she also appeared to believe firmly that exclusion is a remedy required by the Fourth Amendment to protect individual liberty.

Justice Breyer found himself twice in dissent, once where he would have suppressed the seized evidence and once where he would have let it in. Breyer did author a dissent in *Gant*, the thrust of which was that it ought to be difficult to overrule a well-established precedent—a precedent that he may or may not have agreed with, but that was precedent nonetheless.

Justice Alito's voting pattern was identical to that of the Chief Justice, who also joined Alito's dissent in *Gant*. Thus, Justice Alito voted to uphold the searches in each of the cases except for *Redding*. Although Alito sided with the reasonableness analysis generally, he broke with the majority in *Gant* and argued in dissent—echoing Breyer—that the Court was effectively overruling both *Belton* and

---

show a willingness to rely upon *Evans* and to acknowledge that minor clerical errors need not invalidate a warrant.

Thorton v. United States even though not asked to do so by the respondent. Justice Alito demonstrated a particular reverence for precedent but did not appear wedded to the exclusion of evidence as an automatic remedy for Fourth Amendment violations.

Although it is unfair to try to decipher a justice's jurisprudence from only a small sample of cases, it is fair to say that none of the justices supports a categorical warrant requirement (or at least each is willing to tolerate certain exceptions) and each believes that reasonableness must factor into the determination of when an exception to the warrant requirement will be considered. It is also fair to say that Justices Stevens, Souter, Ginsburg, and Breyer find the exclusionary rule to be "an essential auxiliary" to the Fourth Amendment and consider the two "inseparable,"[144] while the other members of the Court—indeed a narrow majority—view the rule as simply a remedy, the force of which must also be considered by determining "reasonableness." One suspects those members of the Court would agree that a Fourth Amendment violation requires a remedy—one that deters potential future misconduct, recompenses the individual whose rights have been violated, and preserves the constitutional right—but that the remedy need not exclusively be suppression. Each of the opinions is shaded by respect for precedent, with several members of the Court being somewhat more willing to defer to the decisions of officials in the field.

Two of the more significant trends that seem to be emerging from the Roberts Court are first, a continued drift away from a categorical warrant requirement and towards case-by-case reasonableness determinations, and second, a renewed understanding that exclusion may not be constitutionally compelled. While reasonableness has long been a component of determining whether a Fourth Amendment violation has occurred, the unmooring of the exclusionary rule is a more recent trend. Depending upon upcoming vacancies, the Court could easily be on the brink of declaring the exclusionary rule to be "just another remedy." With the list of exceptions to the warrant requirement continuing to grow, more deference is likely to be accorded trial judges who have the opportunity to scrutinize the facts in a way no appellate court could hope to.

---

[144] Herring, 129 S. Ct. at 707 (Ginsburg, J., dissenting, joined by Stevens, Souter, and Breyer, JJ.).

The Court may ultimately move closer to the following two-step type inquiry: first, was the search or seizure reasonable (with no consideration given to the possible effect of the remedy)? If so, then no Fourth Amendment violation has occurred and no remedy is needed. If, however, the search or seizure was unreasonable, the Court would move to the second step and determine what the appropriate remedy ought to be—exclusion, a tort remedy, discipline of the infringing officers, or some combination thereof. While the presence of a warrant might create a rebuttable presumption of reasonableness, even a search accompanied by a warrant would be subject to attack, like now, on the grounds of reasonableness, insufficiency of probable cause, failure to fulfill the particularity requirement, or any of the other common attacks on the validity of an issued warrant. The Court seems to have inched ever-closer to this sort of two-step determination and may well be willing to consider alternative remedies in the future.

IV. A Role for Congress?

Courts, as institutions, operate best in resolving concrete disputes between identifiable parties and crafting remedies to correct inequities. Courts are on less secure ground, given their institutional limitations, when forced to establish rules that will have broad, prospective application. The categorical warrant requirement, which was then followed by a plethora of exceptions, is an example of the difficulty courts face in trying to create "policy." Courts do perhaps better, under such circumstances, when they proclaim fundamental principles that reflect deeply held beliefs, such as in *Brown v. Board of Education*, where the Court announced that "separate" was anything but "equal."[145] Even so, courts tread on difficult ground when their decisions go far beyond the specific factual circumstances of a particular case. For example, courts do not have the luxury of bringing in experts to advise them or receiving information from wide-ranging interests potentially affected by their decisions. Instead, the information courts receive is necessarily limited and presented in the context of adversarial proceedings—so even amicus briefs (common only before the Supreme Court) may have limited value.

---

[145] 347 U.S. 483 (1954).

Often left out of the debate is Congress, which enjoys the precise institutional characteristics needed for drafting policy that will enjoy far-ranging prospective application. Congress can hold hearings and request testimony from numerous witnesses to understand better the implications of its legislative actions. Legislation is also considerably easier to modify than Supreme Court precedent; so if a legislative pronouncement proves unworkable or deficient in some way, Congress is in a superior position to modify it. Moreover, Congress, not unlike the courts, must also consider and interpret the Constitution in fulfilling its legislative obligations. Although the Court may be the final arbiter of the Constitution and may have the authority "to say what the law is,"[146] that does not mean Congress has no role to play. For example, Congress could choose to promulgate rules for federal officials to protect individual privacy or provide for administrative disciplinary procedures when federal agents intentionally violate the Fourth Amendment.

Congress has, in fact, long protected constitutional liberties through legislation. Congress has even contributed to defining the meaning of certain constitutional rights. To define the Sixth Amendment's guarantee of a "speedy and public trial," for example, Congress enacted the Speedy Trial Act, which provides meaning to the right by statutorily defining periods of exclusion for determining what constitutes a speedy trial.[147] Congress's efforts to define the scope of the Sixth Amendment right demonstrates an interesting interplay between the Supreme Court—which in cases like *Barker v. Wingo*[148] outlined the right's contours—and Congress—which statutorily defined specific events that would go into the calculation of pre-trial time. This interplay could serve as a model for Congress to use the Court's constitutional pronouncements as a floor for defining officers' "reasonableness," ensuring privacy protections, providing officers guidance, and crafting additional remedies to be used in conjunction with exclusion as a means of securing Fourth Amendment values.

---

[146] Marbury v. Madison, 5 U.S. (1 Cranch) 137, 177 (1803).

[147] Speedy Trial Act of 1974, Pub. L. No. 93-619, 88 Stat. 2076 (codified as amended in scattered sections of 18 U.S.C.).

[148] 407 U.S. 514 (1972).

Congress might do well in creating a categorical warrant requirement with specifically delineated exceptions. Congress might also be able to provide clearer guidance to officers than the courts have. In the past, for example, Congress has sought to extend the *Leon* "good faith exception" to other circumstances. Without commenting on its substance, a piece of legislation introduced in 1995, sought to codify the good faith exception by removing the exclusion remedy in cases in which police officers had acted in good faith in relying on an otherwise defective warrant.[149] While this effort met with failure, given, at least in part, questions as to whether Congress could constitutionally do so, more recent Court pronouncements suggest that Congress may have greater leeway to act. Certainly, Congress could always choose to create a categorical warrant requirement and demand that federal officers always obtain a warrant prior to conducting a search or effecting a seizure. Such a requirement would obviously bolster individual privacy protections.

Similarly, Congress could reinvigorate efforts to supplement the exclusionary rule as a remedy for Fourth Amendment violations. Senator Orrin Hatch, for example, has previously offered legislation that would replace the exclusionary rule with a tort remedy.[150] Although the Hatch proposal has been criticized for eliminating the exclusionary rule altogether and creating stringent limits on tort recovery awards, civil remedies and other proposals (e.g., administrative disciplinary actions for violators or sentencing adjustments for those convicted) could be used in conjunction with evidence suppression. Providing the courts with a broader palate of choices would offer courts a variety of remedies from which to select an appropriate response to a Fourth Amendment violation. Courts might then be in a better position to secure the privacy interests of the individual and to ensure that the public's interest in appropriate law enforcement is upheld. If anything, the *Herring* decision, which casts further doubt on the exclusionary rule's constitutional status, and its heavy reliance upon using objective "reasonableness" standards to determine whether a violation has even occurred, provides Congress with considerable room in which it may legislate.

---

[149] Exclusionary Rule Reform Act of 1995, H.R. 666, 104th Cong. (1995).
[150] 21st Century Justice Act of 1999, S. 899, 106th Cong. VII(B) (1999).

Conclusion

While a single term doth not a coherent jurisprudence make, October Term 2008 proved an interesting one for the Fourth Amendment. The Court continues to struggle with what constitutes an unreasonable search or seizure. The justices have come to recognize that broadening police power in a specific category of cases—such as those searches occurring on the roadside—have serious implications for Fourth Amendment privacy interests generally. At the same time, a slim majority on the Court seems willing to recognize that the exclusionary rule is not constitutionally mandated and may function as a machete where, in fact, a scalpel is needed. Given the highly fact-dependent nature of these cases, one can't help but wonder whether at some point in the future the Supreme Court will leave even more of these determinations to the trial courts.

With the Court's willingness to sideline the categorical warrant requirement in favor of an expanded list of exceptions and ever-greater reliance on reasonableness as the Fourth Amendment's touchstone, it would prove interesting if Congress decided to step into the fray to buttress privacy interests or to provide officers with clearer guidance or to legislate remedies in addition to exclusion. Crafting appropriate remedies for Fourth Amendment violations presents a considerable, but hardly insurmountable, challenge.

One difficulty with the casuistic approach is that the reasonableness determination, by the time it reaches the courts, is framed in the context in which the police have seized inculpatory evidence. Judges and juries may be reluctant to exclude otherwise relevant evidence of criminal activity. When the possibility of an overturned conviction is weighed against police mistake—or even official misconduct—courts are hard pressed to preserve an ephemeral privacy interest when clear evidence of criminal conduct exists. This situation has always created difficulties for the suppression of evidence and makes it hard to imagine that tort remedies, without more, would serve as a sufficient protector of the Fourth Amendment right. Regardless, with the recent change in the Supreme Court's membership, many of these old battles may be fought anew.

Using Its Sixth Sense: The Roberts Court Revamps the Rights of the Accused

*Mark Chenoweth**

The Sixth Amendment loomed large during the Supreme Court's 2008 October Term.[1] Fittingly, the justices heard six oral arguments touching on nearly every aspect of that amendment.[2] This outsized fraction of cases indicates the recent tumult in criminal procedure law.[3] In particular, the latter-stage Rehnquist Court decisions in

---

* Senior Fellow in Legal Studies, Pacific Research Institute. The author would like to thank Laura Scully Chenoweth for her encouragement, keen editorial eye, and invaluable assistance on this project.

[1] "In all criminal prosecutions, the accused shall enjoy the right to a speedy and public trial, by an impartial jury of the state and district wherein the crime shall have been committed, which district shall have been previously ascertained by law, and to be informed of the nature and cause of the accusation; to be confronted with the witnesses against him; to have compulsory process for obtaining witnesses in his favor, and to have the assistance of counsel for his defense." U.S. Const. amend. VI.

[2] The four argued Sixth Amendment cases from the term not discussed herein are Vermont v. Brillon, 556 U.S. ___, 129 S. Ct. 1283 (2009) (Ginsburg, J., 7-2 decision holding that delays created by defense counsel do not count against speedy trial deadlines); Knowles v. Mirzayance, 556 U.S. ___, 129 S. Ct. 1411 (2009) (Thomas, J., 9-0 decision holding that abandoning a not guilty by reason of insanity claim that was not likely to succeed does not rise to the level of ineffective assistance of counsel); Kansas v. Ventris, 556 U.S. ___, 129 S. Ct. 1841 (2009) (Scalia, J., 7-2 decision overturning a prophylactic rule that would prohibit the use of evidence obtained in violation of the right to counsel even for impeaching a defendant's perjurious testimony); and Montejo v. Louisiana, 556 U.S. ___, 129 S. Ct. 2079 (2009) (Scalia, J., 5-4 decision breaking on "traditional" lines that repealed Michigan v. Jackson, 475 U.S. 625 (1986), which forbade police from initiating any interrogation of a defendant in custody who has invoked the right to counsel).

[3] The Court decided nine Sixth Amendment cases overall out of 83 cases this term, over 10 percent of the entire docket. The three cases decided without oral argument were Moore v. United States, 552 U.S. ___, 129 S. Ct. 4 (2008) (per curiam) (holding that district courts enjoy discretion on crack/powder sentencing disparity issue); Spears v. United States, 552 U.S. ___, 129 S. Ct. 840 (2008) (per curiam) (holding that judges may depart downward for policy reasons alone on crack/powder disparity sentencing issue); Nelson v. United States, 555 U.S. ___, 129 S. Ct. 890 (2009) (per curiam) (holding that the *Rita* presumption is for appellate courts to apply to district

Apprendi v. New Jersey and *Crawford v. Washington* raised numerous questions that the Court had not answered fully by the time Chief Justice John Roberts and Justice Samuel Alito replaced Chief Justice William Rehnquist and Justice Sandra Day O'Connor.[4] Among the six argued cases, the Roberts Court heard two especially significant ones, which afforded it an early opportunity to clarify lingering issues in Sixth Amendment law and put its own stamp on constitutional criminal procedure jurisprudence. Considered separately, *Oregon v. Ice* and *Melendez-Diaz v. Massachusetts* are momentous cases, because each of them reshapes a major line of Rehnquist-era (albeit not Rehnquist-endorsed) precedent.[5] Perhaps more importantly, however, these two cases taken together signify that the Roberts Court will continue the Rehnquist Court's renovation of the Sixth Amendment along originalist lines.

This pair of major cases explored the parameters of two separate Sixth Amendment protections afforded to criminal defendants: the right to a jury trial in the sentencing context, and the right to confront adverse witnesses. More specifically, *Oregon v. Ice* posed the question whether a post-*Apprendi* sentencing judge may find facts apart from the jury verdict to decide whether the defendant will serve consecutive or concurrent sentences. *Melendez-Diaz v. Massachusetts* asked if, given *Crawford*, it infringes a defendant's right to confront his accusers for the prosecution to enter lab test data into evidence via affidavit rather than via a lab technician's live testimony.

This article will first examine the Court's reasoning in *Ice* and *Melendez-Diaz*, and it will then address the implications of those decisions for the *Apprendi* and *Crawford* lines of precedent, respectively. In so doing, it will consider what questions remain open following this term's decisions, surmise where the jurisprudence regarding each of these major precedents may evolve, and discuss how Justice David Souter's retirement could affect that evolution.

---

court sentences within guidelines ranges, not a presumption for district courts to apply to guidelines sentences).

[4] Apprendi v. New Jersey, 530 U.S. 466 (2000); Crawford v. Washington, 541 U.S. 36 (2004).

[5] Oregon v. Ice, 555 U.S. ____, 129 S. Ct. 711 (2009); Melendez-Diaz v. Massachusetts, 557 U.S. ____, 129 S. Ct. 2527 (2009).

The article will conclude by explaining how these cases exemplify the trend of originalist renovation.

I. Slipping on *Ice*: The *Apprendi* March Slows Down

A. Apprendi *Jurisprudence before* Ice

Justice Ruth Bader Ginsburg's opinion for a narrowly divided court in *Oregon v. Ice* must be understood against the backdrop of the previous decade's dramatic developments in the Court's Sixth Amendment sentencing law jurisprudence. Led by an unusual coalition of justices, the Rehnquist Court staged a radical renovation of the right to a jury trial in its later years. The odd alliance joined that Court's three most consistently liberal jurists—Justices John Paul Stevens, David Souter, and Ruth Bader Ginsburg—with its two most thoroughgoing conservatives, Justices Antonin Scalia and Clarence Thomas.

Beginning with the *Apprendi* decision in 2000, the Court broke from its prior approval of sentencing regimes that rely upon post-verdict judicial fact-finding.[6] By a 5-4 margin, the Court held that the prosecution must both charge in the indictment and prove to the jury beyond a reasonable doubt every fact that contributes to the length of a defendant's sentence in order to uphold the accused's right to a trial by jury. As a result, judges may no longer enhance a defendant's sentence based on facts found by the judge during the sentencing phase, except for the fact of a prior conviction, which, after all, another jury already determined.[7] Although *Apprendi* did not put an end to the controversial practice of judges basing sentencing decisions on acquitted conduct,[8] it did curtail the previous prosecutorial practice of holding back facts or charges that might not be

---

[6] Cf. McMillan v. Pennsylvania, 477 U.S. 79 (1986); Mistretta v. United States, 488 U.S. 361 (1989) (upholding the federal sentencing guidelines).

[7] See Almendarez-Torres v. United States, 523 U.S. 224 (1998). Members of the Court have noted that even that exception no longer enjoys support from the majority of the justices. See Shepard v. United States, 544 U.S. 13, 26 (2005) (Thomas, J.) (concurring in part and concurring in the judgment); see also Jones v. United States, 526 U.S. 227, 249 (1999) (noting that prior convictions had to have satisfied "fair notice, reasonable doubt, and jury trial guarantees").

[8] Cf. United States v. Watts, 519 U.S. 148 (1997) (holding that acquittal of offense does not bar consideration of the acquitted conduct for sentencing enhancement purposes).

proved beyond a reasonable doubt to the jury in order to present them to the judge as factors meriting an enhanced sentence.[9]

The Court followed *Apprendi* two years later with *Ring v. Arizona*, deciding that a jury—not a judge—had to decide whether aggravating factors outweighed mitigating factors in rendering a death sentence.[10] Although *Ring* was a 7-2 decision, the five-justice *Apprendi* majority added Justice Anthony Kennedy explicitly on *stare decisis* grounds and Justice Stephen Breyer on sui generis Eighth Amendment grounds.[11] The very same day, in *Harris v. United States*, the Court seemed to depart from *Apprendi*'s logic.[12] Even though a jury must decide facts that increase a defendant's maximum sentence, the *Harris* majority held that a judge could permissibly find the facts necessary for increasing a defendant's mandatory minimum sentence (based, in that case, on having brandished a weapon). Four of the five *Apprendi* justices hung together in dissent, but Justice Scalia crossed over to join the *Harris* majority without comment. *Harris* involved the same potential for prosecutors holding back facts not provable to the jury—brandishing is a crime with its own elements—in order to present them to the judge post-verdict and raise a defendant's minimum sentence. The Court reasoned, however, that no Sixth Amendment violation had occurred, because the higher mandatory minimum fell within the available sentence for the guilty verdict returned by the jury.

In the waning days of the 2003–04 term, *Apprendi* struck yet again. In *Blakely v. Washington*, the Court held that Washington state's sentencing guidelines regime was an unconstitutional violation of the jury trial right described in *Apprendi*, because it permitted the sentencing judge to find additional facts justifying an enhanced sentence.[13] Because Washington's system closely resembled the federal sentencing guidelines, the *Blakely* decision generated immediate

---

[9] Cf. Jones, 526 U.S. at 252 (construing the federal carjacking statute to contain offense elements rather than sentencing factors in order to avoid deciding whether a jury must find facts at issue rather than a judge). See also Stephen P. Halbrook, Redefining a "Crime" as a Sentencing Factor to Circumvent the Right to Jury Trial: *Harris v. United States*, 2001–2002 Cato Sup. Ct. Rev. 187 (2002).

[10] Ring v. Arizona, 536 U.S. 584 (2002).

[11] *Id.* at 613 (Kennedy, J., concurring); *id.* at 614 (Breyer, J., concurring in the judgment).

[12] Harris v. United States, 536 U.S. 545 (2002).

[13] Blakely v. Washington, 542 U.S. 296 (2004).

confusion and uncertainty in federal sentencing. To deal with the *Blakely* aftermath, the Court set two cases for oral argument on the first day of October Term 2004. Come January 2005, when *Booker v. United States* and *Fanfan v. United States* were decided, the *Apprendi* five held together once again, and the Court decided that the federal sentencing guidelines as constructed also violated the Sixth Amendment's jury trial guarantee.[14]

The victors, however, did not get the spoils. Justice Ginsburg deserted the *Apprendi* five to join in crafting a remedy favored by the *Booker / Fanfan* dissenters.[15] Whereas the remainder of the *Apprendi* five would have required juries to find the necessary facts for enhanced sentences under the mandatory guidelines (following existing practice in states like Kansas),[16] the *Booker* dissenters plus Justice Ginsburg excised just that portion of the statute making the federal sentencing guidelines mandatory.[17] This way federal trial judges could still look to the guidelines as instructive or persuasive authority, but they were not impermissibly bound to find facts or issue enhanced sentences. The *Booker* remedy majority reasoned that such a result did less violence to the statute and came closer to preserving what Congress had intended.[18]

The *Apprendi* line of cases stood at this juncture when Chief Justice Roberts and Justice Alito replaced Chief Justice Rehnquist and Justice O'Connor. In a nearly unbroken chain of 5-4 decisions, generally pitting the three most liberal and two most conservative justices against the middle four, the Court had steadily reinforced its holding in *Apprendi* and extended the application of *Apprendi*'s rule to strike down several sentencing regimes—including New Jersey's, Arizona's, and Washington's, as well as the federal sentencing guidelines.[19]

---

[14] United States v. Booker and United States v. Fanfan, 543 U.S. 220 (2005).

[15] *Id.* at 244 (Breyer, J.) (remedy decision).

[16] *Id.* at 243–44 (Stevens, J.) (constitutional decision). See also Blakely, 542 U.S. 296, 309–10, 124 S. Ct. 2531, 2541–42 (2004) (citing Act of May 29, 2002, ch. 170, 2002 Kan. Sess. Laws 1018–23 (codified at Kan. Stat. Ann. § 21-4716(b) (Cum. Supp.))).

[17] *Id.* at 245 (Breyer, J.) (remedy decision).

[18] *Id.* at 246–49.

[19] Eight cases over an eight-year period beginning with the *Apprendi* precursor case of *Almendarez-Torres* and ending with *Shepard* were decided by 5-4 margins (or 5-3 in *Shepard*, because Chief Justice Rehnquist did not participate). That includes every *Apprendi* case during that time except for *Ring. Jones, Apprendi, Blakely, Booker,* and *Shepard* featured the same five-justice majority of Stevens, Scalia, Souter, Thomas, and Ginsburg. *Almendarez-Torres* featured the same line-up, except Justice Thomas

The pro-*Apprendi* trend showed no signs of abating in the newly reconstituted court's first full term together in 2006–07. For example, the constitutionality of California's sentencing guidelines regime came under review in *California v. Cunningham*.[20] The *Apprendi* five became six with the addition of Chief Justice Roberts, and the Court held that California's three-tiered sentencing system, where judge-found facts can move defendants into higher sentencing tiers, violated the right to trial by jury. Later in the term, in *Rita v. United States*, a nearly unanimous Court held that federal courts of appeals could apply a presumption of reasonableness to trial-court sentences falling within the guidelines range.[21] Finally, in a pair of 7-2 decisions from December 2007—*Gall v. United States* and *Kimbrough v. United States*—the Court held that two lower courts had erred in overturning sentences below the guidelines range, because judges may depart downward from the now merely advisory federal sentencing guidelines.[22] The reasonableness of sentencing decisions, said the Supreme Court, must be reviewed under an abuse of discretion standard.

B. *The Majority's Reasoning in* Oregon v. Ice

With this flood of decisions as a backdrop, *Oregon v. Ice* posed the question whether a judge may find post-verdict facts to justify ordering a defendant to serve consecutive rather than concurrent sentences, or whether, given *Apprendi*, a jury must make that decision. Unlike most states, Oregon's state legislature had established concurrent sentences as the default, specifying that consecutive sentences may be given only if the judge finds that the defendant's offenses were not part of the same "continuous and uninterrupted course of conduct," or that the offenses indicated a "willingness to commit more than one criminal offense," or that they caused or

---

switched sides (later confessing his error in his *Apprendi* concurrence). The *Booker* remedy was also nearly identical, with only Justice Ginsburg switching sides. Finally, *Harris* was also nearly identical to *Apprendi*, with only Justice Scalia switching sides (strangely without writing an opinion in the case). Justice O'Connor led the fight against the *Apprendi* five, authoring the lead dissent in *Apprendi*, *Ring*, *Blakely*, and *Shepard*—conceding in the last of these, "It is a battle I have lost." Shepard v. United States, 544 U.S. 13, 37 (2005) (O'Connor, J., dissenting).

[20] Cunningham v. California, 549 U.S. 270 (2007).

[21] Rita v. United States, 551 U.S. 338 (2007).

[22] Gall v. United States, 552 U.S. 38 (2007); Kimbrough v. United States, 552 U.S. 85 (2007).

risked causing the victim "greater or qualitatively different loss, injury or harm . . . ."[23]

Apartment superintendent Thomas Ice twice entered the unit of his 11-year-old female victim and sexually assaulted her. The jury convicted him on two counts of first-degree burglary (entering with the intent to commit a crime), two counts of first-degree sexual assault for touching the victim's vagina, and two additional counts of first-degree sexual assault for touching the victim's breasts. The judge deemed the two burglaries separate incidents and imposed those sentences consecutively. The court further deemed that the sexual assaults both exhibited the requisite willingness to commit multiple offenses and caused qualitatively different harm. The court imposed the vaginal sexual assault sentences consecutive to the burglary sentences but exercised discretion to impose the breast sexual assault sentences concurrent to the rest (effectively earning no additional time for the latter). Based on the judge's predicate findings, Ice received a total sentence of 28 years, 4 months (340 months), rather than the fully concurrent default sentence of 7 years, 6 months (90 months).[24]

In approving the practice of basing consecutive sentences on judge-found facts, the Supreme Court relies primarily on prevailing historical practice under the common law and the sovereign authority of states over administration of their own criminal justice systems. The Court first asks whether the judge-found facts at issue in the case were the kind of facts that the framers of the Bill of Rights would have understood to be within the jury's domain.[25] After a brief consideration of English and early American common-law tradition, the Court concludes that juries have not historically found facts pertaining to the decision to impose consecutive sentences. Because juries played no such role historically—and the decision itself was not a common-law jury function—the *Ice* Court reasons that Oregon's scheme poses no threat to the traditional jury role as a bulwark between the accused and the state that the Sixth Amendment sought to protect.[26] Furthermore, since historical practice must

---

[23] Or. Rev. Stat. § 137.123(2); § 137.123(5)(a); § 137.123(5)(b).

[24] Ice, 129 S. Ct. at 715–16.

[25] *Id.* at 717.

[26] *Id.*

inform the scope of constitutional rights, the right to trial by jury will not automatically "attach[] to every contemporary state-law 'entitlement' to predicate findings" that constrains judicial sentencing discretion.[27]

Turning then to the prerogatives of sovereign states, the Court notes that state legislatures have long determined the kind of regime states would employ in administering multiple sentences.[28] The Court refers to an amicus brief filed by several of Oregon's sister states and voices concern that a contrary ruling could imperil a broad swath of sentencing practices.[29] For example, judge-found facts can govern decisions regarding supervised release, drug rehabilitation, community service, and the amount of fines or restitution imposed. To avoid prejudicing a jury during the guilt phase of trial, a bifurcated trial might be required with the facts forming the basis for a consecutive sentence being considered at a later stage of the proceedings. Before infringing state power by imposing such requirements, the Court indicates that it would need to see a "genuine affront to *Apprendi*'s instruction."[30]

Just such federalism concerns permeated many of Justice O'Connor's dissents in the *Apprendi* line of cases, yet she never received a single vote from either Justice Ginsburg or Justice Stevens. For example, they did not evince concern with the effects of striking down the sentencing guidelines in *Blakely*. That fact raises some question whether the newfound concern for state prerogatives they voice in *Ice* is decidedly secondary. Perhaps they would argue that a real "affront to *Apprendi*'s instruction" existed in the prior cases.[31] Alternatively, perhaps Justice Ginsburg inserted the federalism language to accommodate Justices Kennedy and Breyer—other justices in the majority who did join the earlier O'Connor dissents.[32]

[27] *Id.* at 718.

[28] *Id.* at 718–19.

[29] *Id.* at 719.

[30] *Id.*

[31] *Id.*

[32] See Apprendi, 530 U.S. at 523 (2000) (O'Connor, J., joined by Rehnquist, C.J., and Kennedy and Breyer, JJ., dissenting); Blakely v. Washington, 542 U.S. at 314 (2004) (O'Connor, J., joined by Breyer, J., dissenting, and by Rehnquist, C.J., and Kennedy, J., dissenting in part); and Shepard v. United States, 544 U.S. at 29 (2005) (O'Connor, J., joined by Kennedy and Breyer, JJ., dissenting).

In the course of discussing the twin pillars of historical practice and state sovereignty that support its decision, the *Ice* Court repeatedly distinguishes the consecutive sentence context at issue in *Ice* from the enhanced sentencing context at issue in most other *Apprendi* cases. The opinion's opening paragraph notes, "[T]he Court has not extended the *Apprendi* and *Blakely* line of decisions beyond the offense-specific context."[33] Then, amid its discussion of prior applications of *Apprendi*, the Court once again observes: "All of these [prior] decisions involved sentencing for a discrete crime, not—as here—for multiple offenses different in character or committed at different times."[34] The *Ice* majority makes this point too often and too deliberately to disregard it, yet distinguishing *Ice* on the basis that it involved sentencing for more than one discrete crime hardly seems promising.

The dissent characterizes this discreteness distinction as a "strange exception," and it simply does not withstand much scrutiny.[35] For example, it does not seem like a consistent principle for *Apprendi*'s application to death penalty cases to turn on whether the capital defendant committed a discrete crime or multiple offenses. If this were the rule of *Ice*, then a death sentence for a discrete crime, such as the armed robbery/felony murder at issue in *Ring v. Arizona*, would require a jury to find aggravating factors even as a death sentence for a serial killer who committed multiple offenses over a lengthy period of time could have aggravating factors determined by a judge. A rule based on whether a defendant committed a discrete crime would not necessarily help even in the consecutive-versus-concurrent sentence context. Consider a judge needing to impose sentence upon a federal defendant who has been convicted and sentenced already on the same facts for a state-level offense (or

---

[33] Ice, 129 S. Ct. at 714. See also *id.* at 717 (putting the same point a bit confusingly: "These twin considerations—historical practice and respect for state sovereignty—counsel against extending *Apprendi*'s rule to the imposition of sentences for discrete crimes."). Perhaps the use of the plural "crimes" here is meant to connote a difference from the status quo, but this is at best a very awkward phrasing—and it could be just a misstatement. The *Apprendi* rule already extends to sentencing for a discrete crime, so it would be clearer to say: ". . . counsel against extending *Apprendi*'s rule *beyond* the imposition of sentences for discrete crimes" or ". . . to the imposition of sentences for *multiple* crimes."

[34] *Id.* at 717.

[35] *Id.* at 720 (Scalia, J., dissenting).

vice versa). On the one hand, a judge might think *Apprendi* still requires a jury to determine facts relevant to a consecutive sentence because the defendant committed a discrete crime. On the other hand, a judge might well think that *Ice* empowers the judge to decide those facts because the circumstances implicate the unique consecutive-versus-concurrent sentence context—and because the judge could construe a second trial under a separate sovereign authority to be an offense "different in character" from the one for which the defendant already received the other sentence.

A rule turning on discreteness would not even safeguard judicial discretion over traditional sentencing decisions—another apparent motivating factor in *Ice*. The majority expresses concern that extending *Apprendi* to the facts of *Ice* would lead to jury intrusion into other decisions typically within a judge's purview, such as the terms of supervised release or community service. Among other things, the majority worries that such intrusion could be unworkable and that it would infringe state sovereignty unnecessarily. But a discreteness rule would not prevent the extension of *Apprendi* to such decisions whenever a defendant has committed a discrete crime. So, while the *Ice* majority makes a valid and accurate distinction between the crime at issue in *Ice* and the discrete crimes committed in prior *Apprendi* cases, it is not a distinction that provides a workable rule or exception to *Apprendi* going forward.

Finally, the majority opinion also mentions the tempering nature of Oregon's judicial fact-finding favorably. By making concurrent sentences the rule absent particular judicial findings, the Oregon state legislature flipped the common law's presumption (or at least its prevailing practice) of rendering consecutive sentences.[36] The *Ice* majority argues that it "makes scant sense" to forbid making concurrent sentences the rule (and consecutive sentences the exception), when all agree that consecutive sentences could permissibly

---

[36] The dissent expresses concern that the judge's deciding consecutive sentences in place of the jury changes the burden of proof from reasonable doubt to preponderance of the evidence. However, disallowing the Oregon regime would switch the burden of proof from the prosecution (arguing that certain facts favor the imposition of consecutive sentences despite the background presumption of concurrent sentences) to the defendant (arguing that certain facts favor the imposition of concurrent sentences despite the background presumption of consecutive sentences). Shifting the burden of proof to the defendant poses a greater problem than reducing the prosecution's burden of proof from reasonable doubt to preponderance.

be the rule with judicial findings leading to concurrent sentences in exceptional cases.[37] Likewise, the Court said it "bears emphasis" that Oregon's regime tempered judicial discretion to impose consecutive sentences, noting that limited judicial discretion promotes proportionate sentencing and reduces disparity in sentencing between similarly situated defendants.[38] The Court seems to imply that defendants fare better under a system like Oregon's than they do in most other states. Even if that is true, it is not clear what constitutional significance the tempered nature of Oregon's regime has. There is no rule of lenity in constitutional interpretation. Perhaps the Court means that the regime's favoring defendants provides another factor suggesting that the jury function as a bulwark against the state is not compromised in this instance. Still, as Justice Scalia points out in his dissent, if Oregon's regime truly favors defendants, then why did the National Association of Criminal Defense Lawyers file an amicus brief opposing that regime in this case?

C. *Why the Dissent's Defense of* Apprendi *Falls Short*

Justice Scalia took issue with the departure of Justices Ginsburg and Stevens from the *Apprendi* fold and penned a forceful dissent rebuking the majority's *Ice* capade. Joined by Chief Justice Roberts and Justices Souter and Thomas, Justice Scalia avers that the rule of *Apprendi* cannot properly be interpreted to support the majority's position in *Oregon v. Ice.*[39] Furthermore, contrary to Justice Ginsburg's reckoning, the dissent argues that the common law history of fact-finding about consecutive sentences is irrelevant, that the majority's state sovereignty arguments were rejected in previous *Apprendi* cases, and that the discreteness point is a formalistic distinction without a difference.[40]

Initially, the dissent contends that the decision in *Ice* does not follow from *Apprendi*, and that it is no different from subsequent cases like *Ring*, which held that post-verdict facts increasing punishment—specifically aggravating circumstances in a death penalty case—have to be found by the jury.[41] It points out that consecutive

[37] Ice, 129 S. Ct. at 713.

[38] *Id.* at 719.

[39] *Id.* at 720 (Scalia, J., dissenting).

[40] *Id.* at 721.

[41] *Id.* at 720.

sentences have long been understood as a greater punishment and that Oregon's regime permits judges to find facts that commit defendants to consecutive sentences longer than what the jury's verdict alone would permit.[42] For the dissent then, *Ice* is an easy case because when the judge's separate factual findings are essential to the punishment imposed, the Sixth Amendment insists that the jury determine the facts instead: "If the doubling or tripling of a defendant's jail time through fact-dependent consecutive sentencing does not meet this description, nothing does."[43] As explicated above, however, the majority freely acknowledges that its ruling in *Ice* readjusts the rule of *Apprendi* somewhat. It does not refute the dissent's contention and in fact barely mentions the *Ring* case. For the dissent then to contend that the majority has redefined *Apprendi* merely states the obvious and does not address the altered rule's workability.

In fact though, had the majority wanted to distinguish *Ice* from cases like *Ring* under the existing *Apprendi* rule, it could have made a decent case. While it is true that the sentencing judges mulled statutory factors in both *Ice* and *Ring*, the tenor of fact-finding differs tremendously. Whereas the judge in *Ring* considered aggravating and mitigating factors not at issue in the guilt phase, the judge in *Ice* sought to figure out whether the guilty verdicts themselves covered any overlapping conduct (where consecutive sentences might entail excess punishment) or whether they covered distinct crimes (meriting consecutive sentences). In considering the statutory factors, the Oregon judge's sentencing role is not so much to increase punishment as it is to regulate the imposition of consecutive sentences to filter out the effects of any charge-stacking, be it intentional or inadvertent. A judge who is a repeat player in the criminal justice system stands a far better chance of fulfilling that role effectively than a one-off jury.[44]

---

[42] *Id.* at 720–21.

[43] *Id.* at 723.

[44] The dissent suggests that it is always okay for the judge to decide these things as long as the judge is decreasing punishment, but the Court would surely balk (for Eighth Amendment reasons if nothing else) at a background rule that set the death penalty as the default sentence for some crime but let the judge reduce that to life imprisonment or something less based on certain factual findings. Flipping the background rule to make consecutive sentences the default, as the dissent would have Oregon do, subtly changes the judge's role and would not be acceptable in a case like *Ring*.

Ice also differs from the sentencing enhancement cases in that the *Ice* jury controls the maximum sentence that may be imposed. The judge has no power to impose a total sentence beyond the sum of the maximum sentence for each of the jury's guilty verdicts, and that upper bound remains the same whether the judge decides with full discretion based on unstated reasons or according to legislatively prescribed factors. Finally, some of the *Ice* judge's fact-finding resembles that approved in *Almendarez-Torres* more closely than it does that disapproved in *Apprendi.*[45] The judge's main finding, which sufficed to impose the two burglary sentences consecutively, determined that the two burglaries represented "separate incidents" that did not arise from a continuous course of conduct.[46] That inquiry is almost identical to the recidivism inquiry regarding prior convictions the Court approved in *Almendarez-Torres*, except that it calls for the judge to look at the instant verdict as opposed to the verdict in a previously adjudicated matter. Had the majority sought to avoid directly confronting *Apprendi* in this fashion, the dissent's arguing that *Ice* does not follow from *Apprendi* would then have made more sense.

The dissent next dispenses with the majority's historical analysis, deeming the common-law practice "entirely irrelevant," because it "had no bearing upon whether the jury must find the fact where a law conditions the higher sentence upon the fact. The jury's role *is* diminished when the length of a sentence is made to depend upon a fact removed from its determination."[47] The dismissive treatment of historical consecutive sentencing practices seems odd coming from an ardent originalist like Justice Scalia. More importantly, the equation of the historical argument here with that in *Apprendi* elides

[45] At a minimum, the *Almendarez-Torres* precedent should encompass the fact of a defendant's incarceration, bail, or probation status during the commission of another crime. The Oregon statute at issue here states that sentences must run consecutively when a defendant is sentenced for a crime committed while defendant was incarcerated. A similar Tennessee statute requires sentencing terms to run consecutively if a defendant commits a crime while released on bail, see Tenn. Code Ann. § 40-20-111(b) (2006), or while on probation, see Tenn. Code Ann. § 40-35-115(b)(6) (2006). These statutes permit the judge to determine the fact of whether or not a defendant was incarcerated, released on bail, or on probation, but the dissent's rule in *Ice* would forbid even that.

[46] Ice, 129 S. Ct. at 715.

[47] *Id.* at 721 (Scalia, J., dissenting) (citing Apprendi, 530 U.S. at 482–83).

an important distinction. In the enhanced sentencing context, it is true that judicial fact-finding removes facts from the jury and diminishes its role. However, when legislatures condition consecutive sentences on certain judge-found facts, they are not diminishing the jury's role. Because juries apparently never had a role in deciding consecutive sentences, legislatures are not removing those facts from the jury's consideration. At most, legislatures are refusing to enhance the role of the jury beyond historical norms.

Because judge-determined consecutive sentences do not circumvent any traditional jury function, it is hard to see how they can possibly implicate the Sixth Amendment's right to a jury trial (at least on an original understanding of what that entailed). Although judicial fact-finding for consecutive sentences may well violate the *Apprendi* rule, it does so only because the bright-line rule that case established would forbid as unconstitutional a variety of judicial fact-finding that is not in fact defective—and hence the *Ice* case is really an artifact of the *Apprendi* rule's being stated too broadly. Besides which, the *Apprendi* rule does not protect the jury's role. Although the *Apprendi* five (and the *Ice* dissenters) voice concern for lost jury prerogatives, *Apprendi* invites discretionary judicial sentencing as its solution. Under a return to that regime, the jury would have no more of a role than it did pre-*Apprendi* (or has under *Ice*).[48]

The dissent likewise rejects the majority's state sovereignty analysis primarily because prior dissents made similar arguments unsuccessfully. For example, Justice Scalia notes that the fear of bifurcated trials did not preclude the outcomes in *Apprendi* and *Blakely*.[49] He neglects to note, however, that just such a concern may well have influenced the *Booker* remedy that Justice Ginsburg joined. Of course the failure of state sovereignty arguments to carry the day earlier does not mean those arguments necessarily lacked any merit; other considerations supervened. Where a Sixth Amendment interpretation based on history dictates a different outcome in the consecutive sentencing context, the majority properly touts the virtue of respecting state sovereignty.

---

[48] See Ron Allen and Ethan Hastert, From *Winship* to *Apprendi* to *Booker*: Constitutional Command or Constitutional Blunder?, 58 Stan. L. Rev. 195, 200 (2005).

[49] *Ice*, 129 S. Ct. at 720 (Scalia, J., dissenting).

Finally, the dissent derides the majority's discreteness distinction as unduly formalistic (and as a "distinction without a difference"), because it applies *Apprendi* to the length of the sentence for each of a defendant's individual crimes but not to the total length of a defendant's jail term.[50] While the *Ice* decision does produce that formalistic result, the line *Apprendi* draws generates formalistic results too. For example, Justice Scalia and the dissenters would accept judicial fact-finding whenever it reduces a sentence found by the jury. So, in *Ice*, they would be perfectly fine with a background rule that mandates consecutive sentences unless the judge finds facts justifying a concurrent sentence. But in terms of results, that regime does not differ from Oregon's facially opposite rule (that mandates concurrent sentences unless the judge finds facts justifying a consecutive sentence). By insisting on one of these background rules over the other, the dissenters uphold no less formalistic a distinction than the *Ice* majority.

Moreover, all sides agree that a judge acting alone may impose a consecutive sentence without any additional overt fact-finding, but the dissenters would prohibit the legislature from specifying facts to consider explicitly before imposing such a sentence.[51] That kind of forced concealment of judicial reasoning seems not only formalistic, but also antagonistic to the rule of law ideal of transparency. Put to a choice between two formalistic rules, the *Ice* majority's brand of formalism leaves traditional jury calls to the jury, leaves traditional judicial calls to the judges, and leaves state legislatures free to set the rules. Under the dissenters' brand of formalism, by contrast, "[n]o constitutional values are served . . . while its constitutional costs in statutes struck down . . . are real."[52]

D. Harris *Redux or New Line Drawing? Will* Ice *Matter?*

Oregon v. Ice is the first case since *Harris v. United States* where the Supreme Court has declined an invitation to apply *Apprendi*.[53] At first blush, *Ice* might strike some observers as *Harris* redux—a failure of the Court to apply *Apprendi* in circumstances calling for

---

[50] *Id.* at 721 (Scalia, J., dissenting).

[51] *Id.*

[52] Jones v. United States, 526 U.S. 227, 267 (1999) (Kennedy, J., dissenting).

[53] Harris v. United States, 536 U.S. 545 (2002).

it due to the inexplicable defection of one or two of the *Apprendi* five.[54] Certainly the *Ice* dissenters regard it that way, much as the dissenting justices in *Harris* viewed that case as an aberration. Nothing indicates that Justices Ginsburg and Stevens have had a change of heart about *Apprendi*, however, and the defection of two justices— including the author of *Apprendi* himself—suggests that something more than idiosyncrasy is at work.[55] Ginsburg and Stevens have voted identically in every *Apprendi* case save the *Booker* remedy, and until this case they had voted in favor of applying *Apprendi* every single time.[56] If they do merely regard the consecutive-versus-concurrent sentence context as exceptional in some unique respect, then *Ice* could turn out to be inconsequential. Like *Harris*, it could then be followed by a succession of cases further extending *Apprendi*. If they instead believe that applying *Apprendi* to cover *Ice* would extend the rule to an entire category of cases they cannot accept, then *Ice* may well mark a new line that reconfigures the ambit of the *Apprendi* precedent going forward. Given the tenor of the arguments put forth in Justice Ginsburg's opinion, the latter result seems more likely.

Apart from the unconvincing effort to distinguish *Ice* from the other *Apprendi* cases on discreteness grounds, the majority does not appear to view the case as an outlier. Nor does the majority attempt to argue that *Apprendi* does not apply on its own terms to the facts of *Ice*. It does not, for example, suggest that a consecutive sentence represents no increase in punishment over a concurrent sentence. Nor does the *Ice* majority contain a vote merely concurring in the judgment—like Justice Breyer's in *Harris*—which rendered that opinion a plurality and called into question the logic it used to distinguish *Harris* from *Apprendi*. Nor does it make the "decent case" outlined above for distinguishing *Ice* from *Ring*.

Instead, precisely because a straightforward reading of the rule would seem to apply, the *Ice* majority evinces a wider concern with pushing the rule's logic too far. The Court declares that inserting the *Apprendi* rule into decisions about supervised release and the

---

[54] See Halbrook, *supra* note 10.

[55] *Cunningham*'s 6-3 vote to extend *Apprendi* became a 5-4 vote against extending *Apprendi* in *Ice* as a result of two switched votes.

[56] For example, Justices Ginsburg and Stevens voted together in the following 12 cases: *Almendarez-Torres, Jones, Apprendi, Ring, Harris, Blakely, Booker, Shepard, Cunningham, Rita, Gall,* and *Kimbrough*.

like "surely would cut the rule loose from its moorings."[57] It then echoes Justice Kennedy's prior criticism of a "wooden, unyielding insistence on expanding the *Apprendi* doctrine far beyond its necessary boundaries."[58] The Court concludes self-consciously that it is seeking a "principled rationale" that would confine the rule's application to those "cases 'within the central sphere of [the *Apprendi* cases'] concern.'"[59] Hence, apparently once Justices Ginsburg and Stevens discovered that a contrary result in *Ice* would extend *Apprendi*'s reach beyond their comfort, they reasoned back from that realization to find a more defensible specification of the rule. If so, then the *Ice* majority has drawn a line that marks a stopping point for the *Apprendi* precedent in a way that *Harris* did not. In thus retreating from applying the *Apprendi* rule to a novel context, Ginsburg and Stevens crossed over to form a new majority that now speaks the language of reining in—though not necessarily turning back—*Apprendi*. In other words, they have put *Apprendi* on ice.

Justices Ginsburg and Stevens encountered a line-drawing problem in applying the *Apprendi* rule to the facts of *Ice* because the circumstances of that case revealed that the originally specified rule could infringe upon well-established judicial fact-finding responsibilities. In the ongoing tug-of-war over what belongs in the jury's province and what belongs in the judge's, the *Apprendi* five generally have construed the right to a jury trial to require reserving more decisions to jurors. The *Apprendi* dissenters, on the other hand, have shown themselves willing to leave a great deal of decisionmaking to the judge and legislature. As *Apprendi*'s domain widens, it threatens to encroach on sentencing choices that typically have been left to judicial discretion and ones that are far removed from the original problem that motivated *Apprendi* itself. That issue finally came to a head in *Ice*.

That is, *Apprendi* redressed a problem that had grown up around sentencing guideline regimes, namely that legislatures and prosecutors were redefining elements of a crime—properly tried by juries—

---

[57] Ice, 129 S. Ct. at 719 (quoting Cunningham v. California, 549 U.S. 270, 295 (2007) (Kennedy, J., dissenting)).

[58] *Id.* (quoting Cunningham, 549 U.S. at 295 (Kennedy, J., dissenting) (internal quotation marks omitted)).

[59] *Id.*

as sentencing factors for judges to consider. Removing such basic fact-finding from juries violated the accused's Sixth Amendment right to a jury trial. But that same problem does not manifest itself in *Ice*.[60] Unlike those cases where an element of the crime gets framed as a factor for the judge to consider in enhancing a defendant's sentence, requiring predicate judicial findings to order consecutive sentences does not enable the prosecution to circumvent the jury in any way. A guilty verdict on each separate offense already authorizes the full sentence imposed for each crime, and consecutive sentences probably accord with a lay jury's expectations in any event. Extending *Apprendi* to cover the facts of *Ice*, however, threatened to create an unprecedented right to jury sentencing—something from which Justice Ginsburg had already retreated in joining the *Booker* remedy.[61] To solve the line-drawing dilemma in the end, Ginsburg's majority opinion had to rewrite the *Apprendi* rule to restrict its domain from entering traditional judicial fact-finding territory.

E. What's in Store for Apprendi in the Ice Age?

At the close of his dissent in *Ice*, Justice Scalia asserts, "Today's opinion muddies the waters, and gives cause to doubt whether the Court is willing to stand by *Apprendi*'s interpretation of the Sixth Amendment's jury-trial guarantee."[62] If *Ice* indeed marks a redrawing of the *Apprendi* boundary, the question still remains just how broadly limiting on *Apprendi* the *Ice* precedent will prove. That question itself has three parts. First, is *Apprendi* itself now in jeopardy of being overruled? Second, are any other previous cases in the *Apprendi* line now in such jeopardy? Third and finally, are any future extensions of *Apprendi* now less likely? *Cunningham* showed Chief Justice Roberts to be an *Apprendi* acolyte whereas Chief Justice Rehnquist was a critic. Therefore—notwithstanding Justice Souter's retirement—there are still five votes for *Apprendi* among the current

---

[60] Oregon v. Ice, 170 P.3d 1049 (2007) (holding that no jury trial violation exists under the state constitutional guarantee, because the facts informing the concurrent/consecutive decision do not require adjudging the elements of any crime).

[61] A jury trial has never meant that a jury decides every issue in the case. Judges, for example, have always made evidentiary rulings during the trial and charged the jury with its instructions for deliberation. Once the jury has found a defendant guilty as charged, judges also traditionally have enjoyed some measure of discretion in determining the appropriate sentence.

[62] Ice, 129 S. Ct. at 723 (Scalia, J., dissenting).

justices and *Apprendi* itself should remain secure. Furthermore, Justices Ginsburg and Stevens give no indication of rethinking their core commitment to *Apprendi* itself. Instead, they expressed qualms about extending *Apprendi* further. So, despite Justice Scalia's concern for muddied waters, the rule in *Apprendi* does not appear to be in further jeopardy.

The same cannot be said for other cases in the *Apprendi* line. However, the two cases most likely to be overruled—*Harris* and *Almendarez-Torres*—would each represent extensions, not limitations, of *Apprendi*. *Harris,* the 2002 mandatory minimum case, is the single precedent that seems most at risk of being revisited. Justice Breyer concurred in the judgment only, so *Harris* was a plurality decision to begin with. The problem with *Harris* has become even more acute in a post-*Booker* world of restored judicial discretion because any prisoner sentenced at the bottom of the mandatory minimum (like Harris himself, who was raised from a five to a seven-year minimum) can argue more convincingly than ever that he would have received a lower sentence but for the mandatory minimum. Moreover, a judge's post-verdict factual findings can now raise the defendant's mandatory minimum to greater than before due to intervening statutory changes. The fact that a judge's findings are the sole determinant of a defendant's sentence being increased starkly from, say, 10 to 30 years, may ultimately persuade the Court to reconsider exempting mandatory minimum sentences from the *Apprendi* rule.[63]

The fact that only two justices—Kennedy and Breyer—supported the outcome in both *Harris* and *Ice* further suggests the *Harris* precedent's vulnerability. Although Justice Alito could represent a third *Harris* supporter, at most one-third of the sitting Court supports both decisions. Nothing suggests the *Ice* majority is fragile, so any instability between the two decisions most likely will be resolved against maintaining *Harris.* Justices Stevens, Thomas, and Ginsburg (along with the departed Souter) dissented in *Harris,* so two more justices would suffice to overturn *Harris* and apply the *Apprendi* rule

---

[63] See, e.g., 18 U.S.C. § 924(c)(1)(B)(ii) (creating a mandatory minimum sentence of 30 years for possessing a firearm "equipped with a firearm silencer or firearm muffler" in furtherance of a federal crime of violence or drug trafficking crime).

to mandatory minimums.[64] Chief Justice Roberts's pro-*Apprendi* vote in *Cunningham* already promised that his might be the fifth vote to vindicate the *Harris* dissenters (assuming that his vote in *Harris* would have mirrored his position on *Apprendi*, as did every justice's save Scalia).[65] By virtue of his joining the *Ice* dissent, the Chief Justice's support for an extension of *Apprendi* to the mandatory minimum context seems even more likely.

The overturning of the 1998 *Almendarez-Torres* case is possible as well, though it seems somewhat less likely than it did before this term. Several commentators, including Cato's own Tim Lynch in a previous volume of this publication, have noted that a majority of the Court no longer supports the *Almendarez-Torres* exception to *Apprendi*, which permits a judge to find the fact of a prior conviction.[66] Justice Thomas has expressed regret in joining the *Almendarez-Torres* majority, so the assumption had been that his vote combined with the four dissenters in that case—Justices Stevens, Scalia, Souter, and Ginsburg—would flip the result.[67] Indeed, those five justices comprised the majority in *Shepard*, which limited the materials upon which a judge may rely in determining the fact of a prior conviction. The outcome in *Ice* and the departure of Justice Souter could mean that *Almendarez-Torres* is somewhat less imperiled now. At least it is not immediately apparent why the rule of *Apprendi* would forbid judges from finding the fact of a prior conviction now that *Ice* permits them to find facts to justify consecutive sentences. The Oregon statute, for example, requires judicial fact-finding that bears a striking resemblance to the fact-finding in which judges would engage to find a prior conviction—whether actions were part of the same course of conduct and whether the offense indicated a willingness to commit more than one crime.

---

[64] Overturning *Harris* would probably also result in overturning McMillan v. Pennsylvania, 477 U.S. 79 (1986), upon which *Harris* largely relied.

[65] Justice Scalia's earlier vote in *Harris* is all the more inexplicable in light of his dissent in *Ice*, in which he criticizes Justices Ginsburg and Stevens for inconsistency. Oddly, his vote in *Harris* also came after he had joined Justice Thomas's *Apprendi* concurrence, which presaged the application of the *Apprendi* rule to mandatory minimum sentences.

[66] See Timothy Lynch, One Cheer for *United States v. Booker*, 2004–2005 Cato Sup. Ct. Rev. 232 n.97 (2005) (citing Shepard v. United States, 544 U.S. 13, 26–28 (2005) (Thomas, J., concurring in part and concurring in the judgment)).

[67] Apprendi, 530 U.S. at 520 (Thomas, J., concurring).

Justice Souter's retirement could matter for both of these cases. Justice Sonia Sotomayor's district court experience could push her to guard the discretion of sentencing judges.[68] Conversely, as she has been notably hostile to mandatory minimums, she may support applying the *Apprendi* rule in that context and force the factors leading to the enhanced sentence to be tried to the jury—a possibility strengthened by the Second Circuit's robust extension of *Apprendi* in drug cases. Even if Justice Sotomayor would not support application of *Apprendi* across the board, which remains to be seen, her documented antipathy to mandatory minimums could mean that she would join an effort to reverse *Harris*.[69] Regarding Sotomayor's potential attitude toward *Almendarez-Torres*, she has interpreted its exception to *Apprendi* broadly[70] and has upheld its continuing validity against challenge—which could indicate less of a proclivity on her part to overrule *Almendarez-Torres* than Justice Souter had.[71]

In terms of future extensions of the *Apprendi* rule, a closer look at the logic underlying the four possible vote pairings in *Harris* and *Ice* reveals the implicit rule endorsed by each pairing and may suggest where the Court would come out on extending *Apprendi*. First, Justices Kennedy and Breyer (and perhaps Alito would have) extended *Apprendi* to neither *Harris* nor *Ice*, which suggests that they believe judges should enjoy discretion in determining punishment and would presumably oppose further *Apprendi* extensions generally. Justices Souter and Thomas (and possibly Chief Justice Roberts would have) extended *Apprendi* to both *Harris* and *Ice* because they appear to believe that both mandatory minimums and concurrent

---

[68] Justice Sotomayor is the first Supreme Court justice to have served as a federal district court judge in almost half a century, since Justice Charles Whittaker took senior status in 1962.

[69] See United States v. Estrada, 428 F.3d 387, 390 (2d Cir. 2005) (Sotomayor, J.) (noting that *Harris* "deprives the judge of sentencing discretion").

[70] See United States v. Santiago, 268 F.3d 151, 156 (2d Cir. 2001) (Sotomayor, J.) ("In short, we read *Apprendi* as leaving to the judge, consistent with due process, the task of finding not only the mere fact of previous convictions but other related issues as well. Judges frequently must make factual determinations for sentencing, so it is hardly anomalous to require that they also determine the 'who, what, when, and where' of a prior conviction.").

[71] See Estrada, 428 F.3d at 391 (noting that we are "bound by the Supreme Court's rulings in *Almendarez-Torres* and *Harris*").

sentences represent increases in punishment, and that any such increase has to be a jury decision.

Justices Ginsburg and Stevens extended *Apprendi* to *Harris* but not to *Ice*. They appear to believe that the facts to be decided in the mandatory minimum context resemble facts that have traditionally been a jury function to decide—because they are effectively elements of a greater crime that must be charged subject to the constitutional requirements of indictment, jury trial, and proof beyond a reasonable doubt—but that juries have not traditionally considered facts that would determine imposition of a concurrent or consecutive sentence. They may tend to favor further extensions of *Apprendi* that neither bestow unprecedented fact-finding duties on jurors nor remove traditional fact-finding duties from judges. Finally, Justice Scalia extended *Apprendi* to *Ice* but not to *Harris* because he appears to believe that imposing a consecutive sentence represents an increase in punishment, whereas increasing a defendant's mandatory minimum sentence does not (at least where the new minimum was always within the available sentence). He may support extending *Apprendi* wherever he perceives an increase in the statutory *maximum* punishment faced by a defendant.[72]

Putting together the implicit rules above, the circumstances under which the new *Apprendi* five (with the Chief Justice in place of Justice Souter) would coalesce become clear. Future extensions of *Apprendi* will most likely occur if the particular fact-finding at issue implicates an increase in the defendant's maximum punishment *and* extending *Apprendi* will not remove traditional judicial fact-finding responsibilities. While dicta in *Ice* call into doubt the permissibility of judge-found facts in the discrete crime context, the distinction offered between defendants who have committed discrete crimes and those who have committed multiple offenses seems unlikely to make a difference. In contrast, the majority's statement in *Ice* that "[t]rial judges often find facts about the nature of the offense or the character of the defendant in determining, for example, the length of supervised release" seems destined for further dispute.[73] The *Ice* dissenters

---

[72] Justice Scalia was the silent swing vote in *Harris*, as he did not author an opinion, making it a bit difficult to discern exactly what separates *Harris* from *Ice* in his view.

[73] Ice, 129 S. Ct. at 719. To the extent that Justices Ginsburg and Stevens embraced an originalist jurisprudence in *Ice* out of any-port-in-a-storm expedience, the new rule ultimately may not suffice to protect some judicial determinations that they would wish to preserve for sheer policy reasons.

are likely to argue that the Sixth Amendment permits trial judges to find facts only when they are reducing a defendant's punishment, whereas the *Ice* majority may uphold as constitutional the prerogative of judges to make some factual findings that lengthen sentences, if the type of fact-finding has a sufficiently strong historical pedigree.

These predictions presume that the Court will hear additional cases with *Apprendi* implications. In dissenting from the summary reversal in *Spears v. United States* this term, however, Chief Justice Roberts, joined by Justice Alito, signaled reluctance to consider further cases in this line in the near future:

> *Apprendi, Booker, Rita, Gall,* and *Kimbrough* have given the lower courts a good deal to digest over a relatively short period. We should give them some time to address the nuances of these precedents before adding new ones. As has been said, a plant cannot grow if you constantly yank it out of the ground to see if the roots are healthy.[74]

If this sentiment means that Roberts and Alito will not provide certiorari votes for *Apprendi* cases, then this line of precedent may be frozen in place for the time being.

F. A Liberal Originalist Result

Aside from the ruling itself, several other aspects of *Ice* merit brief attention. As has been true all along with *Apprendi* cases, the justices' votes did not break along predictable ideological lines, but here their votes also lined up oddly given past breakdowns in these cases. Even though the *Apprendi* coalition ruptured—along with its formalist/pragmatist split—the Court still produced a clean, non-ideological division (with no concurrences) that fractured both the conservative and liberal wings. Justices Kennedy and Alito joined Justices Ginsburg, Stevens, and Breyer in a predominantly liberal majority, just as Justice Souter joined Chief Justice Roberts, Justice Scalia, and Justice Thomas in a predominantly conservative dissent.

Thus Chief Justice Roberts and Justice Alito found themselves on opposite sides of an *Apprendi* case once again. While the Chief Justice has replaced his predecessor's staunch anti-*Apprendi* presence with a supporting voice, Justice Alito has replicated Justice O'Connor's

---

[74] Spears v. United States, 129 S. Ct. 840, 846 (2008) (Roberts, C.J., dissenting).

longstanding skepticism towards this line of precedent. *Ice* is also the fourth *Apprendi* case in a row (following *Rita, Gall,* and *Kimbrough*) where Justices Ginsburg and Stevens have joined Justices Kennedy and Breyer in the majority. That may just be an odd coincidence rather than a trend, however, because the previous three lopsided cases also found Justice Scalia in the majority.

Ironically, given who dissented, the reasoning and result in *Oregon v. Ice* continue to renovate Sixth Amendment jurisprudence along originalist lines. Although faithful application of the *Apprendi* rule probably would have led to a different result in *Ice,* the historical lack of jury involvement in consecutive sentencing suggests that the Sixth Amendment Framers would not have envisioned the right to a jury trial to include jury input on this matter. Justice Scalia's dissent deems the common-law practice irrelevant to modern statutes that condition higher sentences upon judicial fact-finding. But since the jury traditionally did not have a role in determining the appropriateness of concurrent or consecutive sentences, the jury's role is not diminished under Oregon's scheme; nothing is taken away from the jury that belonged to it at the time of the Framing. That seems like logic that originalists ought to accept readily, but Justice Scalia and his fellow dissenters will have none of it. Even so, the future evolution of *Apprendi* jurisprudence, now more than ever, appears bound up tightly with the kinds of post-verdict judicial fact-finding that have the strongest traditional foundation.

II. *Crawford* with a Vengeance: Expanding the Right to Confront Witnesses

A. *From* Crawford v. Washington *to* Melendez-Diaz v. Massachusetts

Like *Apprendi,* the 2004 *Crawford v. Washington* case portended a sea change in Sixth Amendment jurisprudence that also left many unsettled questions.[75] With *Crawford,* the Rehnquist Court discarded a longstanding (and seemingly settled) interpretive approach to the Confrontation Clause, first articulated in *Ohio v. Roberts,*[76] which balanced the right to confront witnesses against the reliability of the proffered evidence. The Court eschewed applying the *Roberts*

---

[75] Crawford v. Washington, 541 U.S. 36 (2004).

[76] Ohio v. Roberts, 448 U.S. 56 (1980).

precedent because that case's approach ignored the Confrontation Clause's original meaning as a "procedural, rather than a substantive, guarantee" of the reliability of evidence.[77] The less stringent prior approach allowed hearsay evidence to be admitted if it either fell within a "firmly rooted hearsay exception" or else bore "particularized guarantees of trustworthiness."[78] The *Crawford* Court instead held that the Confrontation Clause operates as a "categorical constitutional guarante[e]" that always precludes judges from admitting testimonial evidence by unavailable witnesses unless a previous opportunity for cross-examination existed.[79] The *Crawford* majority canvassed the long history of English and American common law and provided a Cook's tour of the origin of the right to confront one's accusers, as well as its status at the time of the Sixth Amendment's ratification. The Court gleaned two constitutional principles from its historical review. First, it deemed that the Confrontation Clause is chiefly "concerned with testimonial hearsay."[80] Second, it determined that "the Framers would not have allowed admission of testimonial statements of a witness who did not appear at trial unless he was unavailable to testify, and the defendant had had a prior opportunity for cross-examination."[81] Based on these principles, the Court held, "Where testimonial statements are at issue, the only indicium of reliability sufficient to satisfy constitutional demands is the one the Constitution actually prescribes: confrontation."[82]

The *Crawford* Court did not offer a comprehensive definition of "testimonial statements," and subsequent cases have not shed much, if any, further light on the meaning of the term. In *Davis v. Washington*, the Court unanimously held that admitting the transcript of a 911 call involving a domestic disturbance did not violate the Confrontation Clause because the statements made to the dispatcher were not testimonial.[83] In the companion case of *Hammon v. Indiana*, however, the Court ruled 8-1 that admitting a victim's statement to

---

[77] Crawford, 541 U.S. at 61.

[78] Roberts, 448 U.S. at 66.

[79] Crawford, 541 U.S. at 67.

[80] *Id.* at 53.

[81] *Id.* at 54.

[82] *Id.* at 68–69.

[83] Davis v. Washington and Hammon v. Indiana, 547 U.S. 813 (2006).

police in the immediate aftermath of an otherwise similar domestic disturbance did violate the Confrontation Clause.[84] Like the formal statement given to police by the victim in *Crawford*, the Court reasoned that the victim in *Hammon* provided her statement to police under circumstances suggesting that the information would be used in a court case. Hence, by the time the Court agreed to hear *Melendez-Diaz v. Massachusetts*, it had already passed on a few opportunities in lopsided rulings to clarify the meaning of the term "testimonial statement." *Melendez-Diaz* raised the precise issue of whether a particular kind of statement—a sworn affidavit by a crime lab technician—constitutes a testimonial statement, so it seemingly afforded the Court the perfect occasion to define the term in the context of a closer question.[85] The Court's decision did not live up to those expectations, instead offering the rationale that the statement at issue fell squarely within the class of testimonial statements described in *Crawford*.[86] But by holding that *Crawford*'s rule applies even to lab tests done on drug evidence, the *Melendez-Diaz* decision confirmed *Crawford*'s revolutionary import as another complete originalist renovation of a Sixth Amendment right. Indeed, one defense attorney characterized the ruling as "the biggest case for the defense since *Miranda*."[87]

B. The Melendez-Diaz *Majority's Reasoning*

Police officers arrested Luis Melendez-Diaz following a surveillance operation in a Kmart parking lot that began in response to an informant's tip regarding a store employee's suspicious behavior. Officers observed the employee leave the store during his shift, get into a car with Melendez-Diaz and another man, drive away briefly, and then get dropped off back at the store. An officer who detained and searched the employee discovered four clear plastic bags on the employee's person containing a white substance that appeared to be cocaine. Officers then arrested the employee and the two occupants of the car and drove all three men back to the police station together. A search of the police cruiser following the trip turned up

---

[84] *Id.*

[85] Melendez-Diaz v. Massachusetts, 557 U.S. ___, 129 S. Ct. 2527 (2009).

[86] *Id.* at 2532.

[87] Tom Jackman, Lab Analyst Decision Complicates Prosecutions, Washington Post, July 15, 2009, at A1.

a hidden plastic bag containing smaller plastic bags also filled with a white powdery substance. Police sent all of the bags to a state laboratory for chemical analysis. When prosecutors sought to introduce certificates of analysis from the laboratory reporting the weight and identity of the substance in the plastic bags at Melendez-Diaz's trial for cocaine distribution and trafficking, he objected on the ground that *Crawford*'s interpretation of the Confrontation Clause required in-court testimony by the lab analysts. The trial court overruled that objection and admitted the certificates. The jury found Melendez-Diaz guilty, and he appealed. The intermediate appellate court in Massachusetts denied the claim, and the highest court there declined review.

The question framed for the U.S. Supreme Court asked whether the trial court should have construed the certificates of analysis as "testimonial" affidavits under *Crawford*, and, if so, whether admitting the certificates into evidence violated Melendez-Diaz's Sixth Amendment right to confront the witnesses against him.[88] The majority not only answers yes to both of these questions, but it treats the answers as manifestly obvious rather than borderline calls, downplaying the significance of the case and calling the decision a "rather straightforward application of our holding in *Crawford*."[89] True to its word, the majority reaches its conclusion in a mere five paragraphs—the same amount of space it devotes to laying out the facts in the case. The remainder of the opinion refutes arguments advanced by the dissent and respondent. For the longest-held case of the term[90]—it was argued on November 10, 2008, and not decided until June 25, 2009—the brevity of the majority's affirmative argument is surprising, particularly in a 5-4 decision where the fifth justice based his vote on a different and narrower rationale, discussed in further detail in the next section.

[88] Melendez-Diaz, 129 S. Ct. at 2530.

[89] *Id.* at 2533. The Court also said the decision "involves little more than the application of our holding in *Crawford.*" *Id.* at 2542.

[90] The *Citizens United* campaign finance case, which was initially argued on March 24 and set for re-argument on September 9, 2009, could surpass it. Citizens United v. Federal Election Commission, 2008 U.S. Dist. WL 2788753 (D.D.C. July 18, 2008), appellate jurisdiction noted, 129 S. Ct. 594 (2008), reargument scheduled, 2009 WL 1841614 (U.S. June 29, 2009) (No. 08-205).

The Court provides a rationale as simple as it is brief: (1) *Crawford* held affidavits to be testimonial statements; (2) the certificates of analysis at issue are the functional equivalent of affidavits; and hence (3) the analysts who swore the affidavits are witnesses whom Melendez-Diaz has the right to confront under the Confrontation Clause (absent a showing of unavailability and a prior opportunity for cross-examination). Following *Crawford*'s originalist methodology, the Court initially relies on Noah Webster's 1828 definition of a witness as one who "bear[s] testimony" to read the term "witnesses" in the Confrontation Clause to cover all testimonial statements.[91] The Court then asserts that *Crawford*'s description of the class of testimonial statements "mention[ed] affidavits twice."[92] The Court deems the analysts' certificates to be affidavits because they meet the definition of sworn declarations in proof of some fact. They are also testimonial because they were "made under circumstances which would lead an objective witness reasonably to believe that the statement would be available for use at a later trial."[93] Finally, the face of the certificates themselves specified their evidentiary purpose, so the analysts must have been aware that their certificates would be used in criminal trials.[94]

Although Justice Scalia's majority opinion thus rests heavily on the assumption that *Crawford* already settled the question of whether affidavits are testimonial statements, *Crawford* did no such thing. In mentioning affidavits twice, the *Crawford* Court merely collected— *without endorsing*—various possible formulations of the class of testimonial statements. It quoted one definition proposed in Crawford's own brief, another proposed in the amicus brief filed by the National Association of Criminal Defense Lawyers, and some language put forth by Justice Thomas in his concurrence in *White v. Illinois*.[95] At the conclusion of the opinion, the *Crawford* Court explicitly left open the question of the meaning of testimonial, leaving "for another day

---

[91] Melendez-Diaz, 129 S. Ct. at 2531 (citing Crawford v. Washington, 541 U.S. 36, 51 (2004)).

[92] *Id.* at 2532.

[93] *Id.* at 2531 (quoting Crawford, 541 U.S. at 51–52).

[94] *Id.* at 2532.

[95] Crawford, 541 U.S. at 51–52 (citing White v. Illinois, 502 U. S. 346, 365 (1992) (Thomas, J., concurring in part and concurring in judgment).

any effort to spell out a comprehensive definition."[96] It offered only the limited holding that the term "testimonial" applies at least "to prior testimony at a preliminary hearing, before a grand jury, or at a former trial; and to police interrogations."[97] That reduced list notably excluded affidavits. So to now characterize *Crawford* as having determined that affidavits are testimonial is not accurate. None of which means that affidavits are *not* testimonial, but the majority's failure to grapple fully with the question renders a key justification for its holding in *Melendez-Diaz* incomplete.

C. Hammon's *Renewed Relevance: Why Justice Thomas's Concurrence Matters*

Justice Thomas provides the *Melendez-Diaz* majority its fifth vote, but he also writes a separate concurrence reiterating his own distinct perspective on the Confrontation Clause, which he has espoused consistently since his first term on the Court.[98] In his view, the clause does not extend to all testimonial statements, as the rest of the majority would have it. Instead, the clause extends only to formal testimonial statements "such as affidavits, depositions, prior testimony, or confessions"[99] (as well as any other testimonial statements contrived to avoid the demands of confrontation), because those were the kinds of statements that the Framers had in mind when instantiating the common-law right of confrontation. Because certificates of analysis meet the more stringent test of formal testimonial statements (because they are effectively sworn affidavits), Thomas shares the majority's view that admitting them violated Melendez-Diaz's right to confront the witnesses against him.

As his lone dissenting vote in *Hammon v. Indiana* indicates, however, Justice Thomas's view will not always generate the same outcome as Justice Scalia's for the *Melendez-Diaz* majority.[100] Given the

[96] Crawford, 541 U.S. at 68.

[97] *Id.*

[98] See White v. Illinois, 502 U.S. 346, 365 (1992) (Thomas, J., concurring in part and concurring in judgment).

[99] Melendez-Diaz, 129 S. Ct. at 2543 (Thomas, J., concurring) (quoting his own concurrence in White, 502 U.S. at 365).

[100] Given all the criticism Justice Thomas receives when a lone vote of his comes against, say, an abused prisoner, it should be noted that this lone vote came in defense of a victim of domestic violence. Whereas the other eight justices would exclude Amy Hammon's informal statements to police investigating a domestic disturbance report—statements that helped convict her attacker—Justice Thomas's more limited rule would have admitted her statements into evidence. The Court noted the possibil-

narrowness of that 5-4 majority, what may have appeared to be an idiosyncratic view holding little future practical import in *Hammon*, now becomes crucial for determining the course of Confrontation Clause jurisprudence. Nor is *Hammon* the only case where Justice Thomas's perspective makes a difference. For example, *White v. Illinois*, which dealt with a child victim whose statements to an investigating police officer were admitted as spontaneous declarations, would be affected. Although the Court in that case did not consider whether the statements had to be excluded even if the witness was unavailable, the *Crawford* rule would clearly exclude the statements as testimonial. *White* thus belies Justice Scalia's assertion that the *Crawford* test "is an empirically accurate explanation of the results our cases have reached."[101] Justice Thomas's narrower rule, however, would not find a Sixth Amendment problem with admitting the child's informal statements to police because, like the statements in *Hammon*, they did not rise to the necessary level of formality.

To fully understand Thomas's position, his overlooked opinion concurring in the judgment in *Davis v. Washington*, but dissenting from the outcome in *Hammon*, merits renewed attention. In that partial dissent, Justice Thomas asserted that the *Hammon* Court should not have interpreted *Crawford* to treat informal statements made to police as testimonial statements, because such statements did not rise to the level of formality required for being deemed testimonial.[102] Because the *Crawford* Court construed the term "witnesses" to include those who "bear testimony" based on Noah Webster's definition, Thomas reasoned that the Court must further accept Webster's definition of testimony as a "solemn declaration or affirmation made for the purpose of establishing or proving some fact."[103]

---

ity of equitable forfeiture of the confrontation right on remand if the state could prove that Mr. Hammon secured Mrs. Hammon's absence from the courtroom. Davis v. Washington, 547 U.S. 813, 833 (2006). But the Court later circumscribed the forfeiture doctrine. Giles v. California, 554 U.S. ___, 128 S. Ct. 2678 (2008) (holding that forfeiture exception applies only if the defendant acts with the specific intention to make the witness unavailable *to testify*).

[101] Crawford, 541 U.S. at 59 n.9.

[102] Because the *Davis* and *Hammon* cases were heard together, the case cites here are to *Davis*. However, I will refer to *Hammon* in the text of the article for reasons of clarity.

[103] Davis, 547 U.S. at 836 (Thomas, J., concurring in judgment in part and dissenting in part) (quoting 1 N. Webster, An American Dictionary of the English Language (1828) (internal quotation marks omitted)).

Doing so limits the class of testimonial statements to those made with a certain degree of solemnity, which Thomas argued was lacking with regard to the victim's original statement to the police. In addition to Webster's definition, Thomas based his interpretation of the original meaning of the Confrontation Clause on his belief that the Framers of the Sixth Amendment meant to protect criminal defendants from the abuses of the Marian bail and committal statutes, not from all testimonial hearsay:

> The history surrounding the right to confrontation supports the conclusion that it was developed to target particular practices that occurred under the English bail and committal statutes passed during the reign of Queen Mary, namely, the "civil-law mode of criminal procedure, and particularly its use of *ex parte* examinations as evidence against the accused."[104]

On this view, admitting informal statements when there's no evidence of prosecutorial efforts to evade confrontation would not violate the Sixth Amendment. The *Crawford* Court expressed concern that prosecutors could evade the strictures of the Confrontation Clause if its scope were limited to formalized testimonial statements, but Justice Thomas argued in his *Hammon* dissent that courts could admit "evidence offered by the prosecution in good faith" and legitimately invoke the Confrontation Clause to prohibit any prosecutorial attempts to "circumvent[] the literal right of confrontation."[105]

The *Hammon* majority held that admitting a victim's statements given when the police responded to a domestic disturbance report violated the Confrontation Clause. Justice Thomas accepted—as did the parties—that Amy Hammon's affidavit could not be admitted into evidence unless she were unavailable to testify at trial and the defendant had a prior opportunity to cross-examine her. Applying his solemnity criteria, however, Thomas argued that Mrs. Hammon's informal police statement, given when they initially responded to the domestic violence incident, could be admitted because it did not rise to the formal testimonial level. The police questioning was not a "formalized dialogue," and bore no marks of a Marian examination

---

[104] *Id.* at 835 (quoting Crawford, 541 U.S. at 43, 50).

[105] Davis, 547 U.S. at 838 (Thomas, J.) (concurring in judgment in part and dissenting in part).

because "the statements were neither Mirandized nor custodial, nor accompanied by any similar indicia of formality."[106] By excluding the statement as evidence against Mr. Hammon, Thomas argued that the Court "extend[ed] the Confrontation Clause far beyond the abuses it was intended to prevent."[107] All of this matters not for *Melendez-Diaz* itself, which majority Justice Thomas joined, but it could alter the outcome in future cases because it indicates that only four justices adhere to a construction of *Crawford* as broad as that offered in Justice Scalia's *Melendez-Diaz* majority opinion. Future litigants would thus be well advised to take Justice Thomas's position into consideration.

D. Justice Kennedy's Dissent and Three Versions of Originalism

Justice Kennedy, who voted with the *Crawford* majority, sharply dissented in *Melendez-Diaz*, joined by the Chief Justice and Justices Breyer and Alito. Although pragmatist in its tenor, Kennedy's lengthy and detailed dissent follows an originalist methodology in attempting to debunk the majority's reasoning. About half of his critiques comprise pragmatic concerns with the effects the Court's decision will produce, but the other half of his points attack the majority's argument on originalist grounds. Kennedy himself admits that the numerous practical considerations he mentions "would be of no moment if the Constitution did, in fact, require the Court to rule as it does."[108] Contrary to Justice Scalia's reckoning, the dissent argues that the Sixth Amendment does not focus on "testimonial" evidence, that the rule of *Melendez-Diaz* ignores the purpose of the Confrontation Clause, and that the historical record is too meager (and conflicted) to support the majority's speculation that the Sixth Amendment would exclude lab analysts' affidavits absent their in-person testimony or the defendant's waiver of his right "to be confronted with the witnesses against him."[109] Despite the originalist objections lodged and pragmatic concerns detailed in Justice Kennedy's forceful dissent, the *Melendez-Diaz* majority's *result* may be right, even though its *rule* may be overly broad.

[106] *Id.* at 840.

[107] *Id.*

[108] Melendez-Diaz v. Massachusetts, 129 S. Ct. 2527, 2550 (2009) (Kennedy, J., dissenting).

[109] U.S. Const. amend. VI.

Justice Kennedy chiefly argues along originalist lines that the word "testimonial" does not appear in the Sixth Amendment. Whereas Justices Scalia and Thomas extrapolate from a near contemporaneous definition of "witness" to find a right to confront certain kinds of testimony, Justice Kennedy contends that "[t]he Clause does not refer to kinds of statements . . . . The text, instead, refers to kinds of persons, namely, to 'witnesses against' the defendant."[110] Hence, he would confine the Confrontation Clause to witnesses with personal knowledge of the defendant's guilt or innocence. The statements at issue in the *Crawford* and *Davis* cases came from just this kind of conventional witness. Kennedy argues that *Melendez-Diaz* significantly expands the *Crawford* holding and upbraids the majority for "assum[ing], with little analysis, that *Crawford* and *Davis* extended the Clause to any person who makes a 'testimonial' statement."[111] In fact, earlier cases did not hold and could not have held that *every* testimonial statement that lacks corresponding in-person testimony must be excluded, because the issue was not presented in them.

Justice Kennedy provides three reasons to treat conventional witnesses differently from the kind of witness represented by the lab analysts. First, he notes that conventional witnesses have to recall events they may have seen but once and may have misperceived. Lab analysts, in contrast, simply record the result of a test and do not have to rely on their memory.[112] Second, he argues that a lab analyst is not a witness "against" the defendant, because an analyst does not "observe[] . . . the crime, . . . know the defendant's identity, . . . [or] have personal knowledge of an aspect of the defendant's guilt."[113] Finally, Justice Kennedy points out that conventional witnesses give answers in response to official interrogation, whereas lab tests follow "scientific protocols . . . [that] are not dependent upon or controlled by interrogation of any sort."[114] The majority objects that the analyst certificates were prepared some time after the tests themselves, that witnesses testify either for or against a defendant and so cannot be neutral, that some lab analysts falsify

---

[110] Melendez-Diaz, 129 S. Ct. at 2550 (Kennedy, J., dissenting).

[111] *Id.* at 2552.

[112] *Id.* at 2551–52.

[113] *Id.* at 2552.

[114] *Id.*

tests, and that officials sometimes try to influence lab results.[115] But whether or not each of the differences Kennedy posits withstands scrutiny, he identifies a difference in kind between eyewitnesses and other kinds of witnesses (e.g., character witnesses, expert witnesses).[116]

Perhaps the best way to see Justice Kennedy's point is to consider the Constitution's Treason Clause: "No person shall be convicted of Treason unless on the Testimony of two Witnesses to the same overt Act, or on Confession in open Court."[117] A few things jump out from reading this clause in the context of Sixth Amendment analysis. First, the Framers could use the word "Testimony" when they meant testimony—no extrapolation required. Second, the term "Witnesses" is used here to refer to personal knowledge gleaned through direct observation of a particular act by the accused, consistent with the way that Kennedy defines the term. Third, a lab analyst's testimony would not suffice as one of the two witnesses referred to in this clause because an analyst does not witness human action. Finally, the Framers could insist on certain kinds of testimony taking place "in open Court" when they explicitly meant that. Whether that phrase applies just to the (traitor's own) confession or also to the testimony of the two witnesses, no similar requirement exists in the Sixth Amendment. These points call into question the *Melendez-Diaz* rule's broad formulation that anyone who makes a testimonial statement is a witness—unless the word "witnesses" has different meanings in Article III and the Sixth Amendment. But because the Sixth Amendment was ratified soon after the main articles, it seems proper to assume that its words have the same meaning as those used in the main document. If so, then the Treason Clause lends credence to Justice Kennedy's definition of "witnesses."

---

[115] *Id.* at 2536 (majority opinion).

[116] The use of the term "witnesses" in the Compulsory Process Clause raises questions similar to those discussed below regarding the Treason Clause. It would not be reasonable to limit a defendant's right to compulsory process to just those witnesses who have given testimonial statements to the police. This fact calls into question a definition of "witnesses" extrapolated to mean testimonial statements and further reinforces Justice Kennedy's point that the term refers to kinds of people, not kinds of statements.

[117] U.S. Const. art. III, § 3.

To further buttress his interpretation, Justice Kennedy argues that the majority's rule ignores the Confrontation Clause's purpose. In his view, confrontation impresses the gravity of the testimony on the witness and prevents one-sided or high-pressure questioning—and it provides an opportunity for recantation. Because a lab analyst does not have personal knowledge and may not even remember conducting a particular test, Kennedy asserts that analysts will be unlikely to retract. Worse yet, he argues, where "the defendant does not even dispute the accuracy of the analyst's work, confrontation adds nothing."[118] The majority persuasively counters that lab analysts may be less likely to fudge results if they have to testify about them, but that may be more a fortuitous result of the majority's interpretation than part of the Confrontation Clause's original purpose. And it is an open question whether the gain in test reliability would be offset by guilty defendants going free due to innocent problems with the availability of analysts to testify.

Next, Justice Kennedy makes an historical argument, analogizing the lab analyst with the role of the Framing-Era functionary known as a copyist. Copyists made copies for use at trial of records that could not be removed from state archives, and they frequently swore affidavits attesting to the accuracy of the item copied. When early American courts allowed copyists' affidavits in criminal trials, which they did regularly, they admitted out-of-court statements, prepared for prosecutorial purposes, for the truth of the matter asserted—precisely what the Court rules illegitimate in *Melendez-Diaz*. To the extent any history supports one reading of the Confrontation Clause over another when it comes to lab analysts, Kennedy suggests that the example of copyists supports his account.[119] The majority dismisses the copyist as a person with "narrowly circumscribed"[120] authority, but that hardly explains how the role of modern lab analysts' affidavits differs from that of copyists' affidavits in criminal trials for Sixth Amendment purposes—particularly as regards those analysts whose results require little interpretation.

Justices Scalia, Thomas, and Kennedy strive to determine the original meaning of the Confrontation Clause, more specifically the word

---

[118] Melendez-Diaz, 129 S. Ct. at 2549 (Kennedy, J., dissenting).

[119] *Id.* at 2553 (Kennedy, J., dissenting).

[120] *Id.* at 2539 (majority opinion).

"witnesses," but arrive at differing conclusions. Scalia's version of originalism in *Melendez-Diaz* is bolder than the others. In his determination to get it right and avoid confusion, however, he downplays contrary historical evidence, serious practical concerns, and the amount of existing authority his rule will overrun. Thomas's variety of originalism sticks closer to the historical record. While he does not hesitate to overturn erroneous precedent where he feels that fidelity to original meaning requires it, he substantially limits the potential scope of such overrulings. He seeks the most established historical ground and extrapolates less readily while still setting forth a clear definition. Kennedy's brand of originalism is humbler. Where *stare decisis* and strong practical considerations weigh against departing too far from existing practice, he looks to vindicate original meaning more tentatively. Without a compelling basis for concluding that original meaning runs contrary to existing precedent, he will not abandon potentially flawed case law where doing so risks creating practical difficulties. Kennedy does not want to throw originalism overboard, but he does not want to go overboard with originalism either.

Although the majority no doubt intends to be pursuing the original meaning of the Confrontation Clause, it devises a hard and fast rule that may not actually comport with the Framers' meaning. The dissent overstates matters slightly in saying that "[t]he only authority on which the Court can rely is its own speculation on the meaning of the word 'testimonial,'" but the question remains whether the Confrontation Clause uses the term "witnesses" in a sense closer to Justice Scalia's, Justice Thomas's, or Justice Kennedy's.[121] The *Melendez-Diaz* Court's rule may well exceed the reasonable limit of what constitutional principle can be inferred from the text and supported by the limited historical record available here to determine original meaning.

E. What Impact Will Justice Souter's Departure and Briscoe v. Virginia *Have?*

The *Crawford* Court abandoned the *Roberts* precedent because it found that test to be *"inherently, and therefore permanently,* unpredictable."[122] Justice Thomas worried, in his *Hammon* dissent, that the

---

[121] *Id.* at 2555 (Kennedy, J., dissenting).

[122] Crawford v. Washington, 541 U.S. 36, 68 n.10 (2004).

Court had adopted "an equally unpredictable test, under which district courts are charged with divining the 'primary purpose' of police interrogations."[123] Now, in *Melendez-Diaz*, the dissent expresses concern that "a wooden application of the *Crawford* and *Davis* definition of 'testimonial,'" provides "no way to predict the future applications of today's holding. . . . There is nothing predictable here . . . other than the uncertainty and disruption that now must ensue."[124] The collective concern of a majority of the Court over the unpredictability of the *Crawford/Davis/Melendez-Diaz* line of precedent—and the unwillingness or inability of the Court thus far to articulate a comprehensive definition of testimonial statements—raises the question whether the Court has replaced *Roberts'* rule of order with *Crawford*'s ukase of chaos.

In addition to the mounting skepticism from a majority of justices, two other factors suggest that *Melendez-Diaz* may have a short shelf life. First, the Court granted certiorari in *Briscoe v. Virginia* less than a week after handing down *Melendez-Diaz*.[125] Second, Justice Souter stepped down from the Court, and he had voted with the majority in every case in the *Crawford* line. *Briscoe* presents the following question: "If a state allows a prosecutor to introduce a certificate of a forensic laboratory analysis, without presenting the testimony of the analyst who prepared the certificate, does the state avoid violating the Confrontation Clause of the Sixth Amendment by providing that the accused has a right to call the analyst as his own witness?"[126] The Court noted in *Melendez-Diaz* that it had "no occasion today to pass on the constitutionality of every variety of statute commonly given the notice-and-demand label. It suffices to say that what we have referred to as the simplest form [of] notice-and-demand statutes, is constitutional."[127] The simplest such statute, unlike Virginia's, merely (1) requires the state to notify the defendant of any plans to

---

[123] Davis v. Washington, 547 U.S. 813, 834 (2006) (Thomas, J., concurring in judgment in part and dissenting in part).

[124] Melendez-Diaz, 129 S. Ct. at 2547 (Kennedy, J., dissenting).

[125] Magruder v. Commonwealth, 657 S.E.2d 113 (Va. 2008), cert. granted sub nom., Briscoe v. Virginia, 2009 WL 1841615 (U.S. June 29, 2009) (No. 07-11191).

[126] Petition for a Writ of Certiorari at i, Briscoe v. Virginia, 07-11191 (U.S. May 29, 2008), 2008 WL 6485425, at *i.

[127] Melendez-Diaz, 129 S. Ct. at 2541 n.12 (internal quotation marks and citation omitted).

introduce an analyst's report into evidence and (2) provides the defendant time in which he must object to the report's admission sans analyst or else forfeit the right. If the Court approves Virginia's notice-and-demand regime, under which defendants have a confrontation right to call the analyst as a defense witness but cannot force the prosecution to introduce the analyst's live testimony as part of the prosecution's case-in-chief, then the apparent breadth of *Melendez-Diaz* will be reduced and practical concerns muted. More than one commentator has observed that it is somewhat unusual for the Court to reconsider a decision the very next term, but "there is little else to suggest" why the Court took on *Briscoe* so soon after deciding *Melendez-Diaz*.[128]

If the *Briscoe* Court reads the *Melendez-Diaz* decision as straightforwardly as the *Melendez-Diaz* Court reads the *Crawford* decision, however, then it will not uphold Virginia's statute. The *Melendez-Diaz* majority explicitly rejects Massachusetts's argument that the defendant's ability to subpoena lab analysts precluded any Confrontation Clause violation. "[T]hat power . . . is no substitute for the right of confrontation," because it "shifts the consequences of adverse-witness no-shows from the State to the accused."[129] Moreover, the Court reads the Confrontation Clause to "impose[] a burden on the prosecution to present its witnesses, not on the defendant to bring those adverse witnesses into court."[130] It bases this interpretation on a contrast in wording between the Confrontation Clause and the Compulsory Process Clause.[131] An accused enjoys a right under the latter "to have compulsory process for obtaining witnesses in his favor," but an accused has a right under the former "to be confronted with the witnesses against him."[132]

While not mandatory, it is reasonable for the Court to read the juxtaposed clauses to require no action on the part of a defendant to secure his confrontation right other than raising an objection. If *Briscoe* confirms that result, it would resurrect all of the practical

---

[128] Lyle Denniston, Analysis: Is Melendez-Diaz already endangered?, SCOTUSblog, June 29, 2009, http://www.scotusblog.com/wp/new-lab-report-case-granted/.

[129] Melendez-Diaz, 129 S. Ct. at 2540.

[130] *Id.*

[131] *Id.* at 2533–34.

[132] U.S. Const. amend. VI.

concerns voiced in Justice Kennedy's *Melendez-Diaz* dissent (e.g., enormous financial and logistical costs, guilty defendants going free due to analyst no-shows, defense counsel extracting large concessions in exchange for surrendering the confrontation right). Of course whether Kennedy's menagerie of misfortunes will actually befall a post-*Melendez-Diaz* criminal justice system remains to be seen. If the dire consequences predicted do not materialize during the ensuing months, their lack could even embolden the *Briscoe* Court to preserve the full scope of *Melendez-Diaz*.

Justice Sotomayor's vote probably represents the largest single variable in determining what the Court will decide in *Briscoe*. She did not reveal any definite views about the proper scope of the Confrontation Clause during her confirmation hearing when Senator Amy Klobuchar asked about *Melendez-Diaz*.[133] However, in a post-*Crawford* opinion Judge Sotomayor authored in the Second Circuit, *United States v. Saget,* she interpreted *Crawford* as "at least suggest[-ing] that the determinative factor in determining whether a declarant bears testimony is the declarant's awareness or expectation that his or her statements may later be used at a trial."[134] The *Saget* case, as Sotomayor recognized, did not require any exposition of *Crawford*'s efforts to define testimonial statements because its fact pattern fell squarely within an example of non-testimonial evidence cited approvingly by the *Crawford* Court.[135] Nevertheless, Judge Sotomayor predicted, "[T]he [Supreme] Court would use the reasonable expectation of the declarant as the anchor of a more concrete definition of testimony."[136] Such a broad and open-ended gloss on *Crawford*'s definition of testimonial statements—in dicta—suggests that

[133] Hearing on the Nomination of Judge Sonia Sotomayor to be an Associate Justice of the United States Supreme Court before the S. Comm. on the Judiciary, 111th Cong. (2009), available at 2009 WL 2039064.

[134] United States v. Saget, 377 F.3d 223, 228 (2d Cir. 2004); see also United States v. Vallee, 304 Fed. Appx. 916 (2d Cir. 2008) (summary order) (holding that the confrontation clause does not bar admission of testimony from an agent to whom defendant admitted killing an individual based on the forfeiture-by-wrongdoing doctrine).

[135] Saget, 377 F.3d at 229 (citing Bourjaily v. United States, 483 U.S. 171, 173–74 (1987)) (both *Bourjaily* and *Saget* dealt with statements made to confidential informants whose true allegiance was not known to the declarant).

[136] Id.

Justice Sotomayor would fully support *Melendez-Diaz*, despite commentators who argue that she has shown less deference to criminal defendants than did Justice Souter. Lab analysts obviously expect that their reports may be used at trial; therefore, a test for testimonial statements grounded in the declarant's expectation would not reduce the scope of *Melendez-Diaz* one iota.

Because the Court has not yet held what the definition of testimonial statements precisely entails, and because a majority of the Court did not endorse the rule of *Melendez-Diaz*, a newly ensconced Justice Sotomayor might not feel bound to honor the interpretation of *Crawford* outlined in *Melendez-Diaz* and *Saget*. Ironically, if she does instead hew to a more pragmatic and methodologically liberal jurisprudence, that would work to the detriment of criminal defendants—because the formalist alliance that has recently expanded criminal defendants' rights on originalist grounds would lose sway.

F. Does the Melendez-Diaz Decision Aid Daubert or Endanger It?

A lesser appreciated, but nonetheless noteworthy consequence of the Court's *Melendez-Diaz* decision comes in its dual impact on expert testimony. On the one hand, the ruling removes a major impediment to state legislatures' and state court rulemaking authorities' accepting the Court's *Daubert* decision.[137] On the other hand, language in the decision undermines the very basis on which the Court adopted the *Daubert* standard in the first place. First, on the pro-*Daubert* side, *Melendez-Diaz* helpfully requires lab analysts to testify more often. One major source of resistance to the expansion of *Daubert* in state courts—second only to plaintiffs' attorneys—has been prosecutors who fear its effects. Many district attorneys and state attorneys general with limited federal court exposure worry that *Daubert* will either divert scarce crime lab resources by requiring analysts to take time and money away from the lab to testify, or that standard forensic tests will not withstand *Daubert*-level scrutiny. In fact, *Daubert* has governed federal practice for 16 years with no apparent ill effects on criminal trials. Because lab analysts will now have to testify under

---

[137] Daubert v. Merrell Dow Pharmaceuticals, 509 U.S. 579 (1993) (holding that federal rules of evidence superseded the common law even with regard to expert testimony and requiring judges to ensure that expert testimony actually comes from scientific knowledge).

certain circumstances regardless, state legislatures may face less opposition from prosecutors in adopting the *Daubert* standard.

In addition, *Daubert* hearings may resolve some of the logistical problems posed by *Melendez-Diaz*. If a defendant wishes to challenge the basis for an analyst's findings or the reliability of an analyst's methods, a *Daubert* hearing would work nicely. The ability to schedule an analyst's appearance would be eased and the possibility of a no-show minimized. If a defendant waives a *Daubert* hearing, then the Confrontation Clause objection disappears. Further, a *Daubert* hearing would constitute a previous opportunity for cross-examination in the event that the analyst is not available for trial—if unavailability remains a criterion for expert witnesses. *Melendez-Diaz* may thus ultimately promote the universal adoption of the *Daubert* standard. That eventuality would, in turn, greatly enhance the quality and reliability of expert evidence.

On the negative side, Justice Scalia's *Crawford* and *Melendez-Diaz* opinions set up a false dichotomy between reliability secured through judicial determinations and reliability obtained via cross-examination. Just as a general reliability standard does not suffice for Confrontation Clause purposes, so too cross-examination does not necessarily suffice to establish reliability—even though criminal trials require it. The Supreme Court itself recognized this fact in the context of scientific evidence when the *Daubert* Court instructed federal trial judges to act as gatekeepers for expert testimony using several factors (e.g., error rate, peer review, use of reliable methodology).

The *Frye* test relies much more heavily on cross-examination to determine the truth and treats even serious defects in testimony as matters going to the weight of the evidence rather than its admissibility.[138] By abandoning the *Frye* test, the Court rejected the capacity for cross-examination alone to prevent juries from getting persuaded by junk science. By instead requiring trial judges to ascertain the reliability of expert testimony before it goes to the jury, the *Daubert* standard has performed admirably in keeping pseudoscience and

---

[138] Frye v. United States, 293 F. 1013 (D.C. Cir. 1923) (holding that expert testimony based on a scientific technique is admissible only if the technique is generally accepted in the relevant scientific community).

"quackspertise" out of the courtroom.[139] Regrettably, in many state courts where *Frye* governs, any charlatan with a sheepskin (or well-intentioned doctor unwilling to recognize the limits of his training) can still peddle unsubstantiated theories or otherwise unreliable "expert" testimony to an impressionable jury and facilitate unjust results.

Section III.C. of *Melendez-Diaz* goes to great lengths to spell out some deficiencies of forensic evidence used in criminal trials and to highlight concerns with the "honesty, proficiency, and methodology" of lab analysts.[140] It stands out as a rather remarkable detour given that not even a hint of forensic malfeasance is suggested in the underlying case. Likewise, *Crawford* casts aspersions on reliability—the touchstone of *Daubert*—as "an amorphous, if not entirely subjective, concept."[141] It criticizes reliability as a "vague" and "manipulable"[142] standard with "countless factors. . . . Whether a statement is deemed reliable depends heavily on which factors the judge considers and how much weight he accords each of them."[143] It even derides the *Roberts* test for "leav[ing] too much discretion in judicial hands"[144] and "allow[ing] a jury to hear evidence, untested by the adversary process, [and] based on a *mere* judicial determination of reliability," which, of course, is the kind of determination *Daubert* calls for.[145] Although the *Daubert* standard does not supplant the adversary process, it does de-emphasize the crucible of cross-examination in favor of excluding unreliable testimony via judicial determination.

Finally, *Crawford* nearly implied that *Daubert* could not apply to criminal cases: "The Constitution prescribes a procedure for determining the reliability of testimony in criminal trials, and we, no less than the state courts, lack authority to replace it with one of our own devising."[146] Hence, while the *Crawford* and *Melendez-Diaz*

---

[139] See David E. Bernstein, Quackspertise, The Wall Street Journal, Sept. 30, 2006, at A9.

[140] Melendez-Diaz, 129 S. Ct. at 2538.

[141] Crawford, 541 U.S. at 63.

[142] *Id.* at 68.

[143] *Id.* at 63.

[144] *Id.* at 67.

[145] *Id.* at 62 (emphasis added).

[146] *Id.* at 67.

Courts came down opposed to a reliability standard per se, as well as to judicial determinations of reliability, the *Daubert* Court came down foursquare in favor of reliability and judicial determinations. It seems odd that a judge-directed inquiry into the reliability of hearsay evidence would be less predictable and trustworthy than one into the reliability of a causation study or other scientific claim—often well outside the judge's areas of specialized training—via the assorted scientific means required by *Daubert*.

All of the *Melendez-Diaz* Court's discussion of forensic evidence is dicta, and the Court freely admits it "would reach the same conclusion if all analysts always possessed the scientific acumen of Mme. Curie and the veracity of Mother Theresa."[147] The Court indicates that this portion of the opinion intends merely to refute the dissent's claim that analysts' evidence is relatively more reliable and relatively less amenable to productive cross-examination. However, the Court's extensive critique of criminal forensic lab standards and practices inadvertently delivers an early Christmas present to criminal defense attorneys and plaintiffs' trial lawyers. They will now mine the dicta for critical verbiage to use against *Daubert*—which is a shame because none of the attacks on the *Roberts* test (and on reliability) were necessary to reject the *Roberts* test as invalid in the Confrontation Clause context. Yet if the Court truly harbors as much concern over the quality and reliability of forensic evidence as the *Melendez-Diaz* discussion suggests, the solution lies in more strictly enforcing *Daubert*'s application to criminal cases—*not* in impugning the judicial determination of testimony's reliability inherent in *Daubert*.

This misunderstanding regarding reliability may arise from confusion in the majority opinion regarding people and testimony identified by Justice Kennedy in his dissent. In the *Roberts* context reliability refers chiefly to credibility, but in the *Daubert* context it refers mainly to scientific soundness. The *Crawford* Court criticizes lower courts' determining reliability by attaching the same significance to opposite facts when applying factors from the *Roberts* test, but that phenomenon occurs more frequently when courts make credibility determinations than when they assess scientific validity. In other

---

[147] Melendez-Diaz, 129 S. Ct. at 2537 n.6.

words, when employing multifactor tests to determine *witness* reliability under *Roberts*, courts tend to produce inconsistent outcomes. But when using *Daubert*'s multi-factor test to determine *testimony* reliability, courts tend to produce consistent results.

This conflation of reliable witnesses and reliable testimony suggests that Justice Kennedy's distinction between conventional and unconventional (analyst-type) witnesses has merit. Lab analysts really are a different kind of witness in some important respect, and admitting their testimony generally requires a different kind of reliability assessment. But perhaps Justices Scalia and Kennedy are both right. Scalia is right that the accused has the right to be confronted with lab analysts, but Kennedy is right that unconventional witnesses are different in a way that justifies not allowing criminal defendants to confront them in the exact same manner as other witnesses. The Court should attend to the double-edged effect of the *Crawford* line of precedent and ensure that its next ruling in this area more clearly respects and preserves the Court's carefully wrought regime for ensuring the reliability of expert testimony, perhaps by holding that a *Daubert* hearing for criminal trials satisfies the Confrontation Clause.

G. Another Originalist Result

By discarding *Roberts* in favor of *Crawford*, the Rehnquist Court sparked the recognition of a much broader confrontation right. Because *Crawford* involved the formal testimony of a conventional witness (the victim) with firsthand knowledge of the defendant's guilt, the possibility remained that the Court would later confine *Crawford*'s absolute bar on admissibility to similar testimonial statements (i.e., formal statements of conventional witnesses with personal knowledge). Instead, the Roberts Court's originalist *Melendez-Diaz* decision dramatically expands the scope of a defendant's right to be confronted with adverse witnesses by construing the confrontation right to extend to crime lab analysts and their affidavits. Although the reasoning behind the broad *Melendez-Diaz* rule may prove a bridge too far, even a less ambitious originalism would have generated the same result in this case. The Court's grant of certiorari in *Briscoe* leaves the door slightly ajar, but at a minimum *Melendez-Diaz* confirms *Crawford*'s thorough renovation of the Confrontation Clause along originalist lines. How far *Melendez-Diaz* ultimately takes that renovation now awaits the decision in *Briscoe*.

The future development of *Crawford* jurisprudence thus depends on which version of originalism Justice Sotomayor endorses. If she sides with the *Melendez-Diaz* majority—as seems likely from her *Saget* opinion—then *Crawford*'s revolutionary impact on confrontation rights will endure. If instead she shares the *Melendez-Diaz* dissenters' caution regarding extrapolation from limited originalist foundations in this instance—as her generally pragmatic reputation might portend—then the Court may develop a more restrained and nuanced view of the proper limits of the confrontation right.

If the empirical results of the Court's new rule wreak havoc, a new majority—perhaps formed by Justice Sotomayor—might retreat to *Crawford* as interpreted by the *Melendez-Diaz* dissenters. Without returning to the repudiated *Roberts* approach, the Court could say that *Crawford* applies only to conventional witnesses (and that the Confrontation Clause does not extend to other kinds of witnesses). More realistically, if a future majority rejects the *Melendez-Diaz* rule in a case testing its outer limits, the narrower justification inherent in the Thomas viewpoint provides a fallback. Similarly, because Thomas largely avoids the need to define "testimonial statement," a new majority may resort to his position rather than hash out a comprehensive definition. Ever since *Crawford* left open the definition question, each case in this line has raised it. Now four cases later the Court has still not supplied an answer, and it is not clear why the Court has been so loath to provide one. The question remains whether "unconventional" witnesses must always be treated exactly the same as "conventional" ones.

III. Liberal Originalism in *Ice* and *Melendez-Diaz*

Considering *Ice* and *Melendez-Diaz* together, some interesting voting patterns emerge. Justices Scalia and Thomas find themselves back in good standing with an originalist majority once again in *Melendez-Diaz*. As in *Ice,* however, a majority of the Court's five most conservative members fell on the opposite side of an originalist opinion. Hence, the Court's more liberal members perpetuated the originalist trend in Sixth Amendment jurisprudence this term, especially Justice Ginsburg. *Ice* and *Melendez-Diaz* also represent two examples from a large handful this term where one or two conservative justices (Alito in *Ice,* Scalia and Thomas in *Melendez-Diaz*) have crossed over to form a majority with three or four of the liberal justices, suggesting independent streaks in some of the court's more conservative justices.

Melendez-Diaz also marks perhaps the most prominent and momentous decision to date in which Justices Scalia and Thomas have cast their votes on the opposite side of Chief Justice Roberts and Justice Alito, so it will be interesting to watch their votes in *Briscoe* and other future Confrontation Clause cases. In sharp contrast, according to one prominent commentator, this term did not contain a single example of a liberal justice crossing over to form a majority with the more conservative justices.[148] Moreover, Chief Justice Roberts is the only member of his Court to dissent in both *Ice* and *Melendez-Diaz*, casting him in the same role his mentor Chief Justice Rehnquist played in *Apprendi* and *Crawford* (although, as noted in the earlier discussion of *Ice*, Roberts joined the *Cunningham* majority and a dissent in *Ice* may actually reflect support for *Apprendi*).

While *Ice* did not reproduce the formalist/pragmatist split that has drawn so much attention in other recent Jury Trial Clause cases, the five-justice *Apprendi* coalition that fractured in *Ice* re-formed in *Melendez-Diaz*. This development may mean that the split first revealed in Jury Trial Clause cases will carry over to Confrontation Clause cases as well. In fact, it lurked beneath the surface all along. The larger margins of decision in the previous three Confrontation Clause cases obscured the existence of a formalist/pragmatist undercurrent in them. However, in retrospect, the *Apprendi* five held together in *Crawford, Davis,* and *Giles,* with the small exceptions of Justice Thomas's partial dissent in *Davis* and Justice Stevens's negative vote in *Giles.*

Ice and *Melendez-Diaz* promised to determine whether the Roberts Court would validate the dramatic shifts in Sixth Amendment jurisprudence made during the latter years of the Rehnquist Court—and they did. By permitting sentencing judges to make explicit findings to justify consecutive sentences, *Ice* enables states with default rules preferring concurrent sentences to keep them. By

---

[148] Tom Goldstein, Thoughts on this Term and the Next, SCOTUSblog, June 29, 2009, http://www.scotusblog.com/wp/thoughts-on-this-term-and-the-next/ ("There is no counter-example in which a member of the left joined the Court's four most conservative Justices to provide a majority.").

declaring that sworn lab results are testimonial statements, *Melendez-Diaz* forces prosecutors to prove forensic results with in-person lab analyst testimony any time that a defendant demands it. Standing alone *Melendez-Diaz* represents the most significant Sixth Amendment development for criminal defendants in many terms, and the other cases decided this term come nowhere close to offsetting its effects. If the Court promotes the right to confront state-retained forensics experts without denigrating the trial judge's role as a gatekeeper of reliable scientific evidence, then *Melendez-Diaz* will surely improve the quality of forensic evidence used in criminal trials.

Indeed, each of the outcomes in this term's Sixth Amendment cases accords with a sensible approach to criminal procedure that respects the rights of the accused without handcuffing prosecutors and judges. Together these decisions simultaneously make it less likely that a guilty criminal defendant will go free for procedural reasons *and* less likely that a criminal defendant will be wrongly convicted based on erroneous forensic evidence. Neither constitutional originalists nor civil libertarians—nor criminal defendants, for that matter—can gainsay that result.

Pleasant Grove City v. Summum: The Supreme Court Finds a Public Display of the Ten Commandments to Be Permissible Government Speech

Patrick M. Garry*

I. Introduction

In *Pleasant Grove City v. Summum*, the Supreme Court reversed a Tenth Circuit Court of Appeals decision to grant an obscure religious sect's request to display a permanent religious monument in a city park that contained other privately donated monuments, including a Ten Commandments monument.[1] In granting the request, the Tenth Circuit found that the city had engaged in viewpoint discrimination by refusing to include the proffered monument in its park.[2]

For the Supreme Court, this case presented several important issues and challenges. As Justice Samuel Alito wrote in his opinion for the Court: "No prior decision of this Court has addressed the application of the Free Speech Clause to a government entity's acceptance of privately donated, permanent monuments for installation in a public park."[3] If the Tenth Circuit ruling were upheld, municipal governments would lose practically all ability to shape and design their public spaces to reflect local tastes, values, and culture.

This case was also the first opportunity for the Supreme Court to address the relatively new government speech doctrine in a context that did not involve public funding. The Court's previous government speech decisions had involved publicly funded programs seeking to promote a specific governmental policy through private speakers, or

---

* Professor and Director, Hagemann Center for Empirical Legal Research, University of South Dakota School of Law.

[1] Pleasant Grove City v. Summum, 555 U.S. _____, 129 S. Ct. 1125 (2009).

[2] Summum v. Pleasant Grove City, 483 F.3d 1044 (10th Cir. 2007).

[3] Summum, 129 S. Ct. at 1131.

271

programs involving discretionary decisionmaking in the areas of arts-funding or state-owned broadcasting.[4]

By ruling that, for free speech purposes, public parks constitute traditional public forums irrespective of the particular means of communication sought (e.g., permanent monuments versus public gatherings or leaflet distributions), the Tenth Circuit undercut the city's authority to determine what monuments it could place in public parks. Municipalities would thus have an all-or-nothing choice: they had to prohibit all monuments or permit all monuments unconditionally. As a practical matter, this is not a choice. No government would be so careless as to open a public park to any monument knowing that it would have no subsequent ability to deny any other monument.

Finally, even though no Establishment Clause issue was involved in the litigation or ruled on by the Court, the case does present various Establishment Clause implications for future cases. Indeed, these implications may well turn out to have the most significant impact on *Summum*'s legacy.

After describing in Part II the factual and procedural background of the case, this article in Part III will examine the Supreme Court opinion in *Summum*. While the Court's decision rested solely on the government speech doctrine and the Free Speech Clause, Part IV analyzes the implicit Establishment Clause issues the decision did not resolve. This analysis will include a discussion of how the endorsement test might apply to similar factual settings. It will also examine in depth how the nonpreferentialism model of the Establishment Clause might be violated by a monument refusal of the kind that occurred in *Summum*.

II. Background

A. Facts of the Case

In 1971, the city of Pleasant Grove, Utah, accepted a Ten Commandments monument from the local Fraternal Order of Eagles to

---

[4] See Johanns v. Livestock Mktg. Ass'n, 544 U.S. 550, 553–57, 562, 564–67 (2005) (finding that a government-sponsored beef advertising campaign funded by a beef producers' tax was government speech, since the message of the ads was effectively controlled by the federal government, and not unconstitutionally compelled speech); Rust v. Sullivan, 500 U.S. 173, 177–78, 203 (1991) (allowing government promotion of pro-life policy through selective funding of family planning clinics); Nat'l Endowment of the Arts v. Finley, 524 U.S. 569, 572–73 (1998) (involving decency guidelines on public arts funding decisions); Ark. Educ. Television Comm'n v. Forbes, 523 U.S. 666, 669 (1998) (involving public broadcasting decisions on programming).

be displayed in Pioneer Park, a 2.5 acre public park containing some 15 permanent historical displays, most of which were donated by private individuals or groups. In 2003, Summum, a religious organization founded in 1975 and headquartered in Salt Lake City, requested permission to erect a monument of its Seven Aphorisms in Pioneer Park, to be similar in size and appearance to the Ten Commandments monument.[5] The mayor of Pleasant Grove denied that request, stating that all permanent displays in Pioneer Park had to either "directly relate to the history of Pleasant Grove or be donated by groups with longstanding ties to the Pleasant Grove community."[6] Even though Summum met neither of these requirements, it made a second request in 2005 to erect its monument in Pioneer Park. After this request was denied, Summum filed suit in Federal District Court, claiming that the city's refusal to accept the proposed Seven Aphorisms monument, while simultaneously displaying the privately donated Ten Commandments monument, amounted to viewpoint discrimination in violation of the Free Speech Clause of the First Amendment.[7]

B. The Tenth Circuit Decision

The Tenth Circuit Court of Appeals ruled in favor of Summum and ordered Pleasant Grove to display the Seven Aphorisms monument in Pioneer Park.[8] This holding rested on the finding that the Ten Commandments monument already on display in the park constituted the private speech of the Fraternal Order of Eagles rather than government speech.[9] This finding was important because government speech is generally immune from First Amendment mandates. The government, after all, can engage in its own expressive

---

[5] The Seven Aphorisms form the central beliefs of the Summum religion. According to Summum belief, the Seven Aphorisms were set out on the original tablets given to Moses by God on Mount Sinai. But Moses, believing the Israelites unprepared to receive the Aphorisms, revealed them to only a select group of people. He then destroyed the tablets on which the Aphorisms were inscribed and returned to Mount Sinai, where he acquired a second set of tablets containing the Ten Commandments. Brief for the Respondent at ¶ 1, Pleasant Grove City v. Summum, 129 S. Ct. 1125 (2009) (No. 07-665), 2008 WL 3851624, at *1–2.

[6] Summum, 483 F.3d at 1047 (internal quotation marks and citation omitted).

[7] *Id.*

[8] Summum, 483 F.3d at 1057.

[9] *Id.* at 1047.

conduct, free from any content-neutrality requirements.[10] Only after the speech at issue—the Ten Commandments monument—is found to be private speech can a court then engage in a forum analysis to see if the government can exclude the proposed speech—the Seven Aphorisms monument—from the forum.[11]

Finding that Pioneer Park was a traditional public forum with respect to every kind of speech activity, the Tenth Circuit found that all speech activities within the park, including the placement of permanent monuments, had to be treated with the same kind of content-neutral consideration.[12] The Tenth Circuit reached this decision, concluding that the monuments within the park were a traditional public forum themselves, because that forum (or expressive use) was located inside a city park—which the Supreme Court had previously characterized as a traditional public forum.[13] Because the city of Pleasant Grove had created a public forum for permanent monuments, any content-based decision on the installation of future permanent monuments was thus subject to strict scrutiny.[14] The court also concluded that the reasons underlying the city's refusal of the Seven Aphorisms monument—namely, that the monument had no local historical significance and that Summum had no longstanding ties to the city—amounted to viewpoint discrimination and could not survive a strict scrutiny review.[15]

In dissent, Judge Michael McConnell disagreed with the court's holding that the donated monuments within Pioneer Park constituted the private speech of their donors.[16] According to McConnell,

---

[10] See Bd. of Regents of Univ. of Wis. Sys. v. Southworth, 529 U.S. 217, 229 (2000) (stating that the government is free to "speak for itself"); Rust v. Sullivan, 500 U.S. 173, 194 (1991) (stating that government is free to select the views it wishes to express).

[11] See Cornelius v. NAACP Legal Def. & Educ. Fund, 473 U.S. 788, 797 (1985).

[12] Summum, 483 F.3d at 1050–52. In conducting its forum analysis, the Tenth Circuit considered both the government property at issue and the type of access sought, and in doing so found the permanent monuments in the park to be the relevant forum. Id. at 1050.

[13] See Perry Educ. Ass'n v. Perry Local Educators Ass'n, 460 U.S. 37, 45 (1983) (designating public streets and parks as traditional public forums). A traditional public forum is open to all speech activities. See Ark. Educ. Television Comm'n v. Forbes, 523 U.S. 666, 667 (1998).

[14] Summum, 483 F.3d at 1050.

[15] Id. at 1054.

[16] Summum v. Pleasant Grove City, 499 F.3d 1170, 1177 (10th Cir. 2007) (McConnell, J., dissenting) (dissenting from the Tenth Circuit's denial of the city's petition for a rehearing en banc).

the monuments were government speech, and so there was no need for any forum analysis because government speech is generally not subject to Free Speech Clause restrictions.[17] McConnell argued that once a city accepted a donated monument and displayed it on public land, the monument became government speech.[18] Thus, no forum was created because the city did not "invite private citizens to erect monuments of their own choosing in these parks."[19] In a separate dissent, Judge Carlos Lucero argued that Pioneer Park did not qualify as a traditional public forum for the purpose of displaying permanent monuments.[20]

III. The Supreme Court Opinion

The issue before the Supreme Court was whether the First Amendment's Free Speech Clause entitled a private group to insist that a municipality permit it to place a permanent monument in a city park in which other donated monuments had been previously erected.[21] In answering this question in the negative, the Court essentially agreed with Judge McConnell's dissent and held that the Pioneer Park display of permanent monuments constituted government speech, to which forum analysis does not apply to prohibit content-based decisions.[22]

The specific claim asserted by respondent Summum was that the city of Pleasant Grove had violated the Free Speech Clause by displaying the Ten Commandments monument but rejecting the proposed Seven Aphorisms monument, thereby engaging in an impermissible viewpoint discrimination between the two religious symbols.[23] In addressing this claim, the Supreme Court first examined the issue of

[17] *Id.* (stating that even though the monuments had been donated by private donors, the government had adopted the message of the monuments).

[18] *Id.* at 1175.

[19] *Id.*

[20] *Id.* at 1171, (Lucero, J., dissenting) (dissenting from the Tenth Circuit's denial of the City's petition for a rehearing en banc).

[21] Summum, 129 S. Ct. at 1129 (2009).

[22] *Id.*

[23] *Id.* at 1130. Viewpoint discrimination occurs when the government discriminates against the ideology of the message. See e.g., Boos v. Berry, 485 U.S. 312, 317 (1988). When such content-based regulation occurs, it is subject to strict scrutiny. Perry Educ. Ass'n v. Perry Local Educators Ass'n, 460 U.S. 37, 45–46 (1983). In recent years, the rule against viewpoint discrimination has been of great value to speakers of religious messages. See, e.g., Good News Club v. Milford Cent. Sch., 533 U.S. 98, 106–07 (2001).

whether the Ten Commandments monument constituted private or government speech. The question was whether, by previously permitting privately donated monuments to be erected in Pioneer Park, the city was engaging in its own expressive conduct or whether it was simply providing a forum for private speech. If the city was engaging in its own expressive conduct—thus rendering the Ten Commandments monument a form of government speech—then the Free Speech Clause had no application. As Justice Alito wrote for the Court: "The Free Speech Clause restricts government regulation of private speech; it does not regulate government speech."[24]

In analyzing this issue—whether a permanent monument constituted government or private speech—the Court did not engage in a merely formalistic inquiry. The fact that a monument was designed and donated by a private group did not thus, by itself, determine the issue. According to the Court, "A government entity may exercise the same freedom to express its views when it receives assistance from private sources for the purpose of delivering a government-controlled message."[25] Determining whether, through the display of privately donated permanent monuments, a government entity is speaking on its own behalf or is providing a forum for private speech was not a difficult one for the Court. There was no disagreement on this point.[26] As Justice Alito noted, permanent monuments displayed on public property have typically represented government speech and, indeed, "governments have long used monuments to speak to the public."[27] The opinion made no distinction between government-commissioned monuments and privately financed monuments that the government accepts and displays on public land. In either case, the monument becomes government speech once it is erected on public property.

After citing a number of famous monuments that have been privately financed and then donated for display on public property—

---

[24] Summum, 129 S. Ct. at 1131 (citing Johanns v. Livestock Mktg. Ass'n, 544 U.S. 550, 553 (2005); Columbia Broad. Sys., Inc. v. Democratic Nat'l Comm., 412 U.S. 94, 139 (1973) (Stewart, J., concurring)).

[25] Id. at 1131.

[26] Justice Alito wrote that there "may be situations in which it is difficult to tell whether a government entity is speaking on its own behalf or is providing a forum for private speech, but this case does not present such a situation." Id. at 1132.

[27] Id. at 1132–33 (discussing the historical use of monuments by an array of governmental entities).

the Statue of Liberty, the Marine Corps War Memorial (the Iwo Jima monument), and the Vietnam Veterans Memorial—Justice Alito concluded that the traditional practice has been one of "selective receptivity" by the accepting governmental entity, reflecting a specific government endorsement or expression of a particular message to be conveyed by the particular monument.[28] Pursuant to this traditional practice, government entities have been highly discriminating in their choices of which monuments to accept for public display.[29] This selectivity occurs because public parks, and the monuments within those parks, play an important role in defining a city's identity that is projected to the outside world. In *Summum*, this desire to project a particular image greatly influenced the city's choice of monuments: "The City has selected those monuments that it wants to display for the purpose of presenting the image of the City that it wishes to project to all who frequent the Park."[30]

The Court dismissed the argument that the Ten Commandments monument was not government speech. Although the city had not participated in designing the monument or composing its text, by adopting or embracing the monument, the city effectively made that message its own.[31] Indeed, after the monument has been adopted or embraced by a governmental entity, that entity possesses sole control over the expressive nature of the monument.[32] Despite not

[28] *Id.* at 1133 (stating that a "great many of the monuments that adorn the Nation's public parks were financed with private funds or donated by private parties").

[29] *Id.* (recognizing that all across the country, "municipalities generally exercise editorial control over donated monuments through prior submission requirements, design input, requested modifications, written criteria, and legislative approvals of specific content proposals" (internal quotation omitted)).

[30] *Id.* at 1134.

[31] *Id.* at 1135. In People for the Ethical Treatment of Animals, Inc. v. Gittens, the Court found government speech where the government worked with private sources to create a display of public art. 414 F.3d 23 (D.C. Cir. 2005). In *Gittens*, the city sponsored a temporary sidewalk sculpture display of 100 donkeys and 100 elephants, entitled "Party Animals." *Id.* at 25. The court found that the displayed sculptures were government speech, because the city officials had retained the right to approve designs and reject any entries they considered inappropriate. *Id.* at 29–30.

[32] The Court rejected respondent's claim that the city had to go through a formal legislative-type process of adopting a particular message to be conveyed by the privately donated monument. 129 S. Ct. at 1134 (stating that requiring such statements of formal adoption "would be a pointless exercise that the Constitution does not mandate").

having any involvement in the original design of the donated monuments, the government's editorial control over them is ongoing and continual, extending over generations.

Justice Alito disagreed that a monument can convey only one "message"—namely, that intended by the original donor of that monument—and hence that only the donor could control the message of the monument. Once the monument has been adopted and displayed on public property, the message conveyed by that monument can change over time.[33] As an example of how messages conveyed by monuments may change over time, Justice Alito cited the history of the Vietnam Veterans Memorial in Washington, D.C. and found that, particularly with respect to war memorials, "people reinterpret the meaning of these memorials as historical interpretations and the society around them changes."[34]

Although he concluded that the Ten Commandments monument in Pioneer Park constituted government speech, Justice Alito nonetheless conducted a sort of public forum analysis—if only to show that the public forum doctrine didn't apply here. According to the Tenth Circuit, the installation of permanent monuments in a public park was similar to the delivery of speeches or the holding of demonstrations in such parks, and thus subject to all the requirements pertaining to governmental regulation of speech in a traditional public forum.

As Justice Alito explained, however, the public forum doctrine has been applied only "in situations in which government-owned property or a government program was capable of accommodating a large number of public speakers without defeating the essential function of the land or the program."[35] Unlike the situation with

---

[33] Summum, 129 S. Ct. at 1136 ("By accepting a privately donated monument and placing it on city property, a city engages in expressive conduct, but the intended and perceived significance of that conduct may not coincide with the thinking of the monument's donor or creator."). Moreover, by recognizing that the meaning given by a city to a donated monument may differ from the meaning intended by the donor, Justice Alito gave some Establishment Clause breathing room to cities that accept a monument from a private group that espouses strong religious meanings regarding its donated monument.

[34] Id. (internal quotation marks and citation omitted).

[35] Id. at 1137 (stating that a public park "can accommodate many speakers and, over time, many parades and demonstrations"). For this rule, the Court cited Cornelius v. NAACP Legal Def. & Educ. Fund, where the federal campaign program at issue permitted hundreds of groups to solicit donations from federal employees. 473 U.S. 788, 804–05 (1985). The Court also cited Rosenberger v. Rector & Visitors of the Univ. of Va., where a public university's student activity fund provided money for many

individual speakers and literature distributors, public parks can accommodate only a limited number of permanent monuments; whereas temporary speech may last only hours or perhaps days, permanent speech—such as a monument—most likely lasts for the life of the forum. The Court stated that, "it is hard to imagine how a public park could be opened up for the installation of permanent monuments by every person or group wishing to engage in that form of expression."[36] Moreover, any finding that the placement of permanent monuments in public parks constituted a public forum would inevitably lead to a closing of that forum, because if government entities had to maintain viewpoint neutrality in their selection of donated monuments, they would either have to "brace themselves for an influx of clutter or face the pressure to remove longstanding and cherished monuments."[37]

In *Summum*, the Court unanimously agreed that the donated monuments displayed in Pioneer Park constituted government speech. Even Justice John Paul Stevens, a critic of the Court's previous government speech decisions, had no objections on this issue.[38] In previous cases, the Court had articulated two factors that needed to be present for the government speech doctrine to apply: the government had to control the message[39] and there had to be political accountability regarding the speech.[40] For this accountability to exist, there must be

campus activities, and *Widmar v. Vincent,* where a public university's buildings provided meeting space for hundreds of student groups. Rosenberger, 515 U.S. 819, 825 (1995); Widmar, 454 U.S. 263, 274–75 (1981).

[36] Summum, 129 S. Ct. at 1137.

[37] *Id.* at 1138 (internal quotation marks and citation omitted) ("The obvious truth of the matter is that if public parks were considered to be traditional public forums for the purpose of erecting privately donated monuments, most parks would have little choice but to refuse all such donations."). The Tenth Circuit, on the other hand, by holding that a city's display of privately donated monuments in a public park creates a public forum for such monuments, effectively ruled that the acceptance of a single donated monument at any time wiped away a city's ability to control its permanent landmarks. Summum v. Pleasant Grove City, 483 F.3d 1044, 1050–52 (10th Cir. 2007).

[38] See Summum, 129 S. Ct. at 1139 (Stevens, J., concurring) ("To date, our decisions relying on the recently minted government speech doctrine to uphold government action have been few and, in my view, of doubtful merit.").

[39] See Johanns v. Livestock Mktg. Ass'n, 544 U.S. 550, 560, 562 (2005) (finding that government speech can occur even when the text is composed by private persons).

[40] See Bd. of Regents of Univ. of Wis. Sys. v. Southworth, 529 U.S. 217, 235 (2000) ("When the government speaks, for instance to promote its own policies or to advance a particular idea, it is, in the end, accountable to the electorate and the political

transparency regarding the source of the speech—that is, citizens must be aware that the government is the entity responsible for the speech.

The political accountability factor has previously been the source of much criticism surrounding the government speech doctrine. For instance, as Justice David Souter stated in his *Johanns* dissent, few Americans would be aware that the government was actually sponsoring advertisements that carried the tagline "Funded by America's Beef Processors."[41] Donated monuments on display in public parks have no such accountability problem, however, because their sponsor's identity is completely obvious and transparent. As a result, none of the justices in *Summum* found a political accountability problem in connection with the monuments displayed in Pioneer Park.[42]

Aside from the political accountability factor, the object of some previous criticism concerning the government speech doctrine involved the risk of government control of, or interference with, the private speech market.[43] But, as Justice Stevens recognized in his concurrence in *Summum*, there is little risk that governmental displays of donated monuments on public lands will eliminate or crowd out other private speech on those lands.[44] Indeed, because Pioneer Park is so large and the permanent monuments occupy such a relatively small amount of space, there is ample opportunity for other speech activities in the park. Even with the presence of the Ten Commandments monument and without a monument of its own, Summum still retained the opportunity to disseminate its message in the park through such traditional public forum speech activities as organized gatherings and literature distribution.

---

process for its advocacy. If the citizenry objects, newly elected officials later could espouse some different or contrary position.").

[41] Johanns, 544 U.S. at 577 (Souter, J., dissenting) (referring to ads that stated: "Beef. It's What's For Dinner").

[42] See Summum, 129 S. Ct. at 1139 (Stevens, J., concurring) (stating that the city would not "be able to avoid political accountability for the views that it endorses or expresses through" its monuments).

[43] The decision in *Rust v. Sullivan*, for instance, sparked "sharply critical academic commentary." Robert Post, Subsidized Speech, 106 Yale L.J. 151, 168 (1996). See Rust v. Sullivan, 500 U.S. 173, 177–80 (1991) (upholding a law limiting federal funding to those family planning clinics where medical personnel agreed not to discuss the abortion option with their patients).

[44] See Summum, 129 S. Ct. at 1139 (Stevens, J., concurring) ("[O]ur decision in this case excuses no retaliation for, or coercion of, private speech.").

IV. Establishment Clause Implications

A. *Concerns Raised by the Concurring Opinions*

The only issue argued by the parties before the Court in *Summum* involved the First Amendment's Free Speech Clause and whether it required the city to place the Seven Aphorisms monument in Pioneer Park. The plaintiffs made no claims based on the Establishment Clause.[45] Consequently, the Court did not address possible Establishment Clause violations. The Court did recognize, however, that the Establishment Clause could have some bearing on similar types of factual settings. For instance, even though Justice Alito found that the Free Speech Clause has no application to government speech, he acknowledged that "government speech must comport with the Establishment Clause."[46]

Curiously, in reviewing a history of public monuments for the purpose of determining whether the Pioneer Park monuments constituted government speech, the Court cited only secular monuments. The Court stated that such monuments "commonly play an important role in defining the identity that a city projects to its own residents and to the outside world."[47] This finding was, of course, important for the purpose of concluding that such monuments constitute government speech.

But what if the image or identity that a city wishes to convey relates to a particular religious faith or denomination? Even though the government speech doctrine permits a city to express a message, identity, or image to the public, the Establishment Clause may well act to carve out an exception to that rule: namely, that the city cannot convey a message constituting an endorsement of religion.

Although no Establishment Clause claim was before the Court here, Justice Antonin Scalia recognized in his concurrence that the issue had been lurking in the shadows since the case's onset.[48] Justice

---

[45] This may have been because of a belief that the Court's decision in Van Orden v. Perry, 545 U.S. 677 (2005), had foreclosed any such claims.

[46] Summum, 129 S. Ct. at 1132.

[47] *Id.* at 1134 (stating that such monuments "are meant to convey and have the effect of conveying a government message").

[48] See 129 S. Ct. at 1139 (Scalia, J., concurring) ("It is also obvious that from the start, the case has been litigated in the shadow of the First Amendment's Establishment Clause: the city wary of associating itself too closely with the Ten Commandments monument displayed in the park, lest that be deemed a breach in the so-called wall of separation between church and state; respondent exploiting that hesitation to argue

Souter's concurring opinion similarly recognized that even though "Establishment Clause issues have been neither raised nor briefed before us, there is no doubt that this case and its government speech claim has been litigated by the parties with one eye on the Establishment Clause."[49]

According to Scalia, any *Summum*-related Establishment Clause issue had already been settled in *Van Orden v. Perry*, where the Court dismissed a challenge to a Ten Commandments monument displayed on the Texas State Capitol grounds that was virtually identical to the monument displayed in Pioneer Park.[50] But the issue in *Van Orden* was whether the mere display of a particular Ten Commandments monument violated the Establishment Clause. *Summum*, on the other hand, implicated a slightly different issue: whether by displaying such a monument it then had to display monuments offered by other religious groups. An argument could be made that the Establishment Clause forbids any governmental preference for one religious sect over another, and that such favoritism was evident in Pleasant Grove's refusal to display the Seven Aphorisms while continuing to display the Ten Commandments.

A related Establishment Clause issue involves the distinction between temporary monuments or displays and permanent ones.[51]

---

that the monument is not government speech because the city has not sufficiently adopted its message." (internal quotation marks and citation omitted)).

[49] *Id.* at 1141 (Souter, J., concurring).

[50] 545 U.S. 677 (2005). But this ruling also rested on the plurality's finding that the Ten Commandments "have an undeniable historical meaning," and thus a secular meaning, in addition to their "religious significance." *Id.* at 678, 690. Of course, one way to avoid any Establishment Clause issues with publicly displayed monuments such as the Ten Commandments is for courts to find that such monuments carry secular messages or meanings, and to focus only on those meanings and messages rather than on any religious meaning or message. This was the approach offered by Justice Scalia during oral arguments in *Summum*. He argued that a city could erect a Ten Commandments monument not for the purpose of endorsing any religious message but just for the purpose of conveying a more limited message that the Ten Commandments is "worthy of respect." Transcript of Oral Argument at 55–56, Pleasant Grove City v. Summum, 129 S. Ct. 1125 (2009) (No. 07-665) (statement of Scalia, J.), 2008 WL 4892845, at *55–56.

[51] Several circuits have previously distinguished between temporary and permanent speech in connection with determining traditional public forums. See Kaplan v. City of Burlington, 891 F.2d 1024 (2d Cir. 1989); Lubavitch Chabad House, Inc. v. City of Chicago, 917 F.2d 341 (7th Cir. 1990). But the Tenth Circuit failed to make such a distinction between temporary and permanent speech here.

In *Summum*, the fact that the Ten Commandments monument was a permanent one played a significant role in the Court's ruling that it was government speech—and hence immune from any Free Speech Clause restrictions. But the nature of the Ten Commandments display in *Summum*, as well as the Court's treatment of it, stands in contrast to the Court's treatment of the Ten Commandments display in *Van Orden*'s companion case, *McCreary County v. ACLU*.[52]

In *McCreary County*, the Court's ruling of unconstitutionality hinged on a finding that the purpose behind the display was religious rather than secular, even though the county had altered and modified its displays on two different occasions so as to give them an increasingly secular image.[53] The display's ultimate version, entitled "The Foundations of American Law and Government," contained nine framed documents of equal size, including the Declaration of Independence, the Bill of Rights, the Mayflower Compact, the lyrics of the Star Spangled Banner, and the Ten Commandments—all of which were accompanied by an educational statement about the documents' "historical and legal significance."[54] But the Court ruled that the county's attempts to expand and modify the displays merely demonstrated an initial and continuing religious purpose.[55] The Court also ruled that a "reasonable observer" would in fact reach certain specific understandings regarding the county's intent to endorse the Commandments' religious message.[56] According to the Court, a reasonable observer would read into all the documents contained in the display a religious theme highlighting and supporting that of the Ten Commandments.[57]

A comparison of *Summum* and *McCreary County* raises the question of whether the Establishment Clause might apply differently to permanent displays of religious messages than to temporary ones.[58]

---

[52] 545 U.S. 844 (2005) (finding that a framed poster of the Ten Commandments hanging in a county courthouse hallway violated the Establishment Clause).

[53] *Id.* at 869–72.

[54] *Id.* at 856–57.

[55] *Id.* at 871–74.

[56] *Id.* at 868–69.

[57] *Id.* at 871–74.

[58] The Court seemed to recognize this distinction when it suggested that religious displays, at particular times of the year—for example, a menorah—were temporary displays, which public parks can much more easily accommodate then they can permanent monuments. Pleasant Grove City v. Summum, 129 S. Ct. 1125, 1138 (2009).

That question in turn raises the issues of when a Ten Commandments display becomes permanent and what makes a display sufficiently secular in nature rather than impermissibly religious.

In his *Summum* concurrence, Justice Souter seemed to anticipate these questions when he stated that "[t]he interaction between the "government speech doctrine" and Establishment Clause principles has not, however, begun to be worked out."[59] There was no dispute among the justices that municipalities could use monuments such as those displayed in Pioneer Park to convey a particular communal image or identity to the outside world. If the communal image was to be a religious one, however, expressed through permanent monuments reflecting particular religious sects or beliefs, then there seems to be a rather obvious Establishment Clause problem because "the government's adoption of the tenets expressed or symbolized" in the monuments might rise to the level of an establishment of religion.[60] Such a preference for a particular religion would very likely violate the Establishment Clause prohibition "against preferring some religious speakers over others."[61]

Justice Souter warned that the government speech doctrine, as articulated in *Summum*, could possibly be used to circumvent the Establishment Clause's prohibition of government discrimination among religious sects or groups. He warned that the government should not be allowed to exercise such sectarian preferences simply by engaging in government speech. As Justice Souter stated, "It is simply unclear how the relatively new category of government speech will relate to the more traditional categories of Establishment Clause analysis, and this case is not an occasion to speculate."[62] Of course, it is precisely this speculation that will likely lead to further litigation over the relationship between the government speech doctrine and the Establishment Clause.

---

[59] Summum, 129 S. Ct. at 1141 (Souter, J., concurring).

[60] *Id.*

[61] *Id.* at 1142 (Souter, J., concurring) (citing Wallace v. Jaffree, 472 U.S. 38, 113 (1985) (Rehnquist, J., dissenting) ("The Clause was also designed to stop the Federal Government from asserting a preference for one religious denomination or sect over others.")).

[62] *Id.* at 1142.

B. *The Endorsement Test and a City's Refusal to Display Competing Religious Monuments*

While the government speech doctrine may protect the city against a First Amendment challenge regarding its refusal to display a particular monument offered by a particular religious group, it may not necessarily prevent Establishment Clause liability. According to *Van Orden*, the Establishment Clause does not prohibit a government entity from displaying a permanent Ten Commandments monument, especially given the Commandments' historical and cultural importance.[63] The issue left unanswered in *Summum*, however, is whether the Establishment Clause might apply differently if a government entity that is already displaying a Ten Commandments monument subsequently refuses to display a monument reflecting the beliefs of another religion. Such a refusal might be judged under the endorsement test to convey to the reasonable observer a message of establishment of the religion (or religions) associated with the Ten Commandments.[64]

In 1984, Justice Sandra Day O'Connor offered the endorsement test as a means of resolving Establishment Clause issues relating to religious expression on public property.[65] Courts have since then frequently used this test for analyzing the constitutionality of displays similar—for legal purposes—to the ones at issue in *Summum*.[66] Under the test, the government unconstitutionally endorses a religion whenever it conveys the message that this religion or its religious beliefs are favored by the state.[67] In *County of Allegheny v. ACLU*, for example, the Court decided that the display of a crèche violated the Establishment Clause, but that the display of a menorah

[63] Van Orden v. Perry, 545 U.S. 677, 691-92 (2005).

[64] The distinction between *Van Orden* and *Summum*, in terms of possible Establishment Clause implications, can also be seen in terms of the differing "injured parties" in each case. In *Van Orden*, the party was the observer of the Ten Commandments who was offended by its display; in *Summum*, it was the religious believer (the Summum) who was denied equal treatment.

[65] Lynch v. Donnelly, 465 U.S. 668 (1984).

[66] See Alberto B. Lopez, *Equal Access and the Public Forum: Pinette's Imbalance of Free Speech and Establishment*, 55 Baylor L. Rev. 167, 195 (2003) (stating that since County of Allegheny, which confirmed the endorsement test as the Court's preferred method of analysis, the Court has continued its reliance on the endorsement test for Establishment Clause cases).

[67] County of Allegheny v. ACLU, 492 U.S. 573, 593 (1989).

next to a Christmas tree did not.[68] The Court held that the crèche, located on the steps of a county courthouse, was prominent enough to constitute an endorsement of Christianity.[69] The tree and menorah display were acceptable, on the other hand, insofar as together they did not give the impression that the state was endorsing any one religion.[70] Any religious message conveyed by the menorah was sufficiently diluted by the presence of the tree.

The endorsement test is grounded upon the premise that the Establishment Clause prohibits the government from conveying ideas that divide the community into outsiders (the minority) and insiders (the majority).[71] In *Lynch*, Justice O'Connor wrote that "[e]ndorsement sends a message to nonadherents that they are outsiders, not full members of the political community, and an accompanying message to adherents that they are insiders, favored members of the political community."[72] Under this interpretation, the endorsement test strives to become a vehicle for ensuring an equality of treatment between all religions—a kind of religious equal protection clause.[73]

In his *Summum* concurrence, Justice Souter suggested that the endorsement test should be used to evaluate the relationship between the government speech doctrine and the Establishment Clause.[74] This suggestion seems somewhat suspect or perhaps outdated, however, especially after the Court declined to employ the endorsement test in either *Van Orden* or *McCreary County*. Moreover, because the test calls for judges to speculate about the impressions that unknown viewers may have received from various religious

[68] *Id.* at 578–79.

[69] *Id.* at 598–602.

[70] *Id.* at 620–21. The Court concluded that, as to the crèche, "[n]o viewer could reasonably think that it occupied this location without the support and approval of the government." *Id.* at 599–600. The tree and menorah, on the other hand, did not present a "sufficiently likely" probability that observers would see them as endorsing a particular religion. *Id.* at 620.

[71] Lynch v. Donnelly, 465 U.S. 668, 692 (1984) (O'Connor, J., concurring).

[72] *Id.* at 688. To Justice O'Connor, the endorsement test functioned to prevent government from "making a citizen's religious affiliation a criterion for full membership in the political community." *Id.* at 690.

[73] Edward B. Foley, Political Liberalism and Establishment Clause Jurisprudence, 43 Case W. Res. L. Rev. 963, 972 (1993).

[74] Summum, 129 S. Ct. at 1142 (Souter, J., concurring).

speech or symbols, it is incapable of achieving certainty.[75] One judge has written that the endorsement test requires "scrutiny more commonly associated with interior decorators than with the judiciary."[76] In *County of Allegheny*, this meant that the Court had to examine "whether the city has included Santas, talking wishing wells, reindeer, or other secular symbols" to draw attention away from the religious message conveyed by the crèche display.[77]

If, per Justice Souter, the endorsement test is to be used to determine Establishment Clause violations, then the key issue is what the reasonable observer perceives from the relevant government action. That is, if a government entity refuses to accept one religious display while continuing to display another, then that denial alone could convey a message of endorsement, even when the previous display did not convey such a message. So even though Pleasant Grove's acceptance of the Ten Commandments monument in 1971 may have passed constitutional muster, the refusal to display the Summum monument may make the Ten Commandments' continuing display an Establishment Clause violation.[78]

---

[75] Steven D. Smith, Symbols, Perceptions, and Doctrinal Illusions: Establishment Neutrality and the "No Endorsement" Test, 86 Mich. L. Rev. 266, 301 (1987).

[76] Am. Jewish Cong. v. City of Chicago, 827 F.2d 120, 129 (7th Cir. 1987) (Easterbrook, J., dissenting).

[77] County of Allegheny v. ACLU, 492 U.S. 573, 674 (1989).

[78] In *Freethought Soc'y v. Chester County*, the Third Circuit Court of Appeals dealt with an array of factual issues relating to whether a "reasonable observer" would view a Ten Commandments display as a governmental endorsement of religion. 334 F.3d 247, 251, 270 (3d Cir. 2003). The subject of the lawsuit was a plaque of the Ten Commandments that had been erected in the county courthouse in 1920, and that a group of atheists, agnostics, and other "freethinkers" demanded be taken down in 2001. *Id.* at 255. In subsequent litigation seeking to force the county to remove the plaque, the plaintiff stated that although she had been aware of the plaque since 1960 she did not find it offensive until she became an atheist in 1996. *Id.* at 254. Replying to the plaintiffs' claim that the plaque represented an affirmative governmental endorsement of religion, the county argued that the plaque's long history detracted from any conclusion that the county was endorsing religion. *Id.* To decide the issue, the court investigated not only the initial purpose behind the plaque's erection, but also the reasons for why the county refused to remove the plaque when so demanded—as well as whether a reasonable observer would know of the plaque's long history and whether the age of the plaque was visually apparent. *Id.* at 262. This inquiry then devolved into one of whether a viewer would be aware of the entire context in which the plaque was erected. *Id.* at 264.

C. Constitutional History and the Tradition of Nonpreferentialism

One paradigm that may relate directly to the factual setting of *Summum,* as well as to the interaction between the government speech doctrine and the Establishment Clause, is nonpreferentialism. American constitutional history lends much support to the nonpreferential model. As this history demonstrates, the ratifying generation believed that religion should play a prominent part in society and that government should acknowledge and support this role.

To Americans of the constitutional period, religion was an indispensable ingredient to self-government. According to the Framers, only through the guidance of religion would people develop the civic virtue necessary for self-government.[79] Late-eighteenth-century Americans generally agreed that "republican government required a virtuous citizenry, and a virtuous citizenry required morality, with religious observance the only sound ground for morality."[80] They "saw clearly that religion would be a great aid in maintaining civil government on a high plane" and hence would be "a great moral asset to the nation."[81] The prevailing view during the constitutional period was expressed by a 1788 New Hampshire pamphleteer: "Civil governments can't well be supported without the assistance of religion."[82]

As the Founders believed, religion "fostered republicanism and was therefore central to the life of the new nation."[83] George Washington, for instance, was committed to the notion of religion being an incubator for the kind of civic virtue needed to serve as a foundation for democratic government.[84] In his Farewell Address to the nation at the end of his presidency, he warned that "reason and

[79] See Joseph Viteritti, Choosing Equality: School Choice, the Constitution, and Civil Society (1999).

[80] J. William Frost, Pennsylvania Institutes Religious Liberty, in All Imaginable Liberty: The Religious Liberty Clauses of the First Amendment 45 (Francis Graham Lee ed., 1995).

[81] Anson Phelps Stokes, Church and State in the United States 515 (1950).

[82] The Complete Anti-Federalist 4:242 (Herbert J. Storing ed., 1981).

[83] Richard Vetterli & Gary C. Bryner, Religion, Public Virtue, and the Founding of the American Republic, in Toward a More Perfect Union: Six Essays on the Constitution 91–92 (Neil L. York ed., 1988).

[84] *Id.* at 127.

experience both forbid us to expect that national morality can prevail in exclusion of religious principle."[85]

During this time, there was overwhelming agreement that government could provide special assistance to religion, so long as such assistance was given without any preference among sects.[86] Catholics in Maryland, for instance, opposed any state established religion, yet supported state aid to religion if conferred without discrimination.[87] As Thomas Cooley argued, the Establishment Clause prohibited only "discrimination in favor of or against any one Religious denomination or sect."[88]

The nonpreferentialist tradition was firmly embraced by the post-ratification generation.[89] This tradition reflected the belief that the religion clauses were designed to foster a spirit of accommodation between religion and the state, as long as no single church was officially established and governmental encouragement did not deny any citizen freedom of religious expression.[90] James Madison repeatedly stressed that government could accommodate or facilitate religious exercise, so long as it did so in a nonpreferential manner.[91]

More broadly, the early adherence to nonpreferentialism hinged on the belief that the Exercise Clause is superior to the Establishment Clause.[92] This superiority meant that government should not be

[85] A Compilation of the Messages and Papers of the Presidents 212 (James D. Richardson ed., 1897).

[86] Patrick W. Carey, American Catholics and the First Amendment, in All Imaginable Liberty 115 (Francis Graham Lee ed., 1995). Even in Virginia, with the established Anglican Church, the growing sentiment in the late eighteenth century was that, while government could indeed give aid to religion, there should be equal treatment in such aid. See Rodney Smith, Public Prayer and the Constitution 45 (1987).

[87] Mary Virginia Geiger, Daniel Carroll: A Framer of the Constitution 83–84 (1943).

[88] Thomas M. Cooley, A Treatise on the Constitutional Limitations 583 (1883). The Reverend Jaspar Adams, cousin of John Quincy Adams, wrote in 1833 that the term "establishment of religion" meant "the preference and establishment given by law to one sect of Christians over every other." Daniel Dreisbach, Real Threat and Mere Shadow: Religious Liberty and the First Amendment 70 (1987).

[89] James McClellan, Joseph Story and the American Constitution 134 (1971).

[90] *Id.*

[91] Rodney K. Smith, Public Prayer and the Constitution 56 (1987). What Madison opposed was government promotion of religion in a manner that would compel individuals to worship contrary to their conscience. *Id.* at 82.

[92] James Madison agreed with Justice Story's articulation of the intent of the Framers: that the right of free exercise was the preeminent right protected by the First Amendment. *Id.* at 111.

hindered in accommodating individuals in their efforts to exercise their religious beliefs in public.[93] Daniel Webster, for one, believed that government could not only permit, but *promote* religious exercise in the public square.[94] Indeed, the ratifying generation was almost universally opposed to the kind of strict separation of church and state that twentieth-century separationists would later espouse because those in the eighteenth century believed such separation would hinder the free exercise of religion.[95]

D. Government Speech and the Threat to Nonpreferentialism

Nonpreferentialism, which strives to be even simpler and more accommodating of government interactions with religion than does the endorsement test, is generally favored by those who support public displays of religious symbols like Ten Commandments monuments. Strangely enough, the result in *Summum* may actually violate nonpreferentialism despite the Court's sanction of the continuing display of the Ten Commandments monument—even though the Ten Commandments may represent the freely chosen beliefs or values of the Pleasant Grove community. This is because, under nonpreferentialism, Pleasant Grove may have violated the Establishment Clause by giving preference to the Ten Commandments monument and discriminating against a monument expressing the beliefs of a different religious sect.

Under the nonpreferential model, the Establishment Clause does not forbid the government from conferring special recognition or benefits on religion in general, as long as the recognition or benefits are given without preference to any religious sect or denomination. Accordingly, the Establishment Clause should apply only when government singles out one or more sects for special benefits or burdens, or when governmental accommodation of one religion begins to

[93] *Id.* at 84. See also Mark DeWolfe Howe, The Garden and the Wilderness 31 (1965).

[94] See 6 Works of Daniel Webster 176, cited by Carl Zollman, Religious Liberty in American Law, 17 Mich. L. Rev. 355, 370 (1919).

[95] *Id.* at 108. See also Joseph Story, 2 Commentaries on the Constitution of the United States 593–97 (1851). According to Story, the Establishment Clause merely helped to effectuate the inalienable right of free exercise by preventing any particular sect from being established, at the national level. *Id.* For the seminal treatment of the First Amendment's religion clauses and myths surrounding the separation concept during the Founding Era and beyond, see Philip Hamburger, Separation of Church and State (2002).

infringe on some other individual's or group's religious exercise rights. A nonpreferential approach tries to understand and accommodate the special needs of religious exercise and expression, based on a recognition of the uniqueness of religion in general.[96] The Establishment Clause issue under this approach is not whether religion in general is better off because of some government recognition or support, but whether the government has singled out one or more religious sects for preferential treatment or burden. In then-Justice William Rehnquist's words: "governmental assistance which does not have the effect of 'inducing' religious belief, but instead merely 'accommodates' or implements an independent religious choice does not . . . violate the Establishment Clause."[97]

The nonpreferentialism model is favored by many who wish to narrow the reach of the Establishment Clause and thus give greater freedom to representative government to acknowledge and support religion in general.[98] Those who advocate nonpreferentialism believe that democratic society should be free to express its religious values and identity, and that the Establishment Clause should not be interpreted to prohibit such expression by mandating that religion be confined to some strictly private sphere. Nonpreferentialism thus reflects an interpretation of the Establishment Clause that permits a greater public role for religion in civil society.

Nonpreferentialism supports the freedom of public expression of religious symbols and messages, such as the public display of the Ten Commandments. But even though nonpreferentialists would support a display of the Ten Commandments in a public park, as occurred in *Summum*, they might find something troubling about the Court's decision—something that could actually undermine the nonpreferentialist position. The troubling aspect is that the Court essentially sanctioned the governmental display of a monument to one religious belief while simultaneously denying the display of a monument reflecting the beliefs of another.

In short, nonpreferentialists favor a vibrant presence of religion in society. To facilitate this, government must be able to acknowledge

---

[96] For a discussion of the nonpreferentialism model, see Patrick M. Garry, Wrestling With God: The Courts' Tortuous Treatment of Religion 147–65 (2005).

[97] Thomas v. Review Bd., 450 U.S. 707, 727 (1981) (Rehnquist, J., dissenting).

[98] See Garry, *supra* note 96, at 147–65.

and support religion to some degree, given the pervasive role that government plays in civil society. But the only way to achieve such a governmental recognition of religion is to require that government treat all religious denominations the same. The *Summum* Court arguably used the government speech doctrine to sanction treating different religions differently. And if the government is allowed to engage in such religious discrimination when it comes to monuments, it could cause a backlash against future governmental acknowledgment or support of religion in general.

E. Summum *and the Possible Conflict with Nonpreferentialism*

During the 1960s and 1970s, the Court crafted a broad view of the Establishment Clause.[99] This broad view extended the reach of the clause so as to invalidate many government programs that sought to accommodate the traditional religious practices of American society. It was during this time period that the Court began taking a more separationist view of the Establishment Clause—a view that seemed to cast constitutional doubt on the value of religion in American society. Under this view, the Establishment Clause was interpreted to mandate a wall of separation between government and religion. But eventually, this strict separationist reading of the Establishment Clause came under criticism for being unnecessarily hostile and antagonistic to religion.

Throughout the 1980s and 1990s, as jurists and scholars began searching for an Establishment Clause doctrine that would be more accommodating to longstanding religious practices and traditions, they made gains in crafting a more narrow doctrine.[100] These gains occurred in part because of the realization that religion played a special and historic role in society, and that it was not unconstitutional for the state to acknowledge and accommodate this special role.

Among the scholars who most contributed to this liberalization of the Establishment Clause were those who believed in nonpreferentialism.[101] The nonpreferentialists believed that, given the history of

[99] For a discussion of the recent constitutional history of the Establishment Clause, see Garry, *supra* note 96, at 44–54.

[100] See *id.* at 55–57, 69–73.

[101] See *id.* at 139–46. Justice Scalia has also endorsed nonpreferentialism. In *Board of Education of Kiryas Joel* v. *Grumet*, he stated that "I have always believed, and all my opinions are consistent with the view, that the Establishment Clause prohibits the favoring of one religion over others." 512 U.S. 687, 748 (1994) (Scalia, J., dissenting).

religion in American society, government could indeed give special accommodation and treatment to religion in general, so long as it never discriminated among religious sects. Therefore, to allow the government to discriminate in any way among sects is to risk losing the gains made in Establishment Clause doctrines that allowed the Court to move away from the historically dubious strict separationism of the 1960s and 1970s.

This risk, however, is one that is subtly raised in *Summum*. In its decision, the Court ended up sanctioning—indirectly—a government's preferential treatment of one set of religious beliefs over another. As I described in Part IV.A *supra*, although *Summum* involved the Free Speech Clause, the case does highlight a future Establishment Clause conflict—namely, a possible challenge to a city's refusal to display one religious symbol even though it is displaying a symbol representing another religious sect.[102] To reiterate, if the city is seen as giving preferential treatment based on religion, it would violate the most fundamental principle of Establishment Clause doctrine—and one on which virtually no First Amendment scholar disagrees.

V. Conclusion

The primary issue in *Summum* involved the government speech doctrine. The question was whether a permanent Ten Commandments monument constituted government speech. As it turned out, that issue proved relatively simple to the Court. There was no disagreement among the justices that the monument constituted government speech and that the city did not have to maintain content neutrality in the choice of the monuments it publicly displayed.

Aside from its unanimity on the doctrinal aspects of its holding, the Court also seemed in complete agreement regarding the practical

His dissent in *McCreary*, however, might indicate a belief that the First Amendment tolerates some preference toward monotheistic religions: the Ten Commandments "are assuredly a religious symbol, but they are not so closely associated with a single religious belief that their display can reasonably be understood as preferring one religious sect over another. The Ten Commandments are recognized by Judaism, Christianity, and Islam alike as divinely given." McCreary County v. ACLU, 545 U.S. 844, 909 (2005) (Scalia, J., joined by Rehnquist, C.J., and Thomas, J., dissenting).

[102] Of course, the resolution of this issue will depend on the resolution of the issue of when a monument, such as a Ten Commandments monument, qualifies as a religious monument, rather than as a secular one.

aspects of its decision. It recognized that if it held otherwise, government units would be incapable of designing their public spaces and the monuments in them once they accepted even one privately donated monument—and as a result would never allow any monument to be displayed in those spaces.

The issue that was not litigated or even addressed, however— but which is the more complex (and academically interesting) one— is the Establishment Clause issue. This issue arises not because the city was displaying a religious monument but because it refused to display the Seven Aphorisms while continuing to display the Ten Commandments. Several of the concurring justices articulated concern about Establishment Clause challenges that might arise in similar factual situations. In that future litigation, courts may have a much more difficult time resolving the Establishment Clause issues than the *Summum* Court did in resolving the free speech issues.

FCC v. Fox Television Stations, Inc.: Awaiting the Next Act

Robert Corn-Revere*

This term the U.S. Supreme Court considered the validity of the Federal Communications Commission's policies prohibiting broadcast indecency for the first time in 30 years.[1] In its only previous decision on the broadcast indecency restrictions, the Court in 1978 narrowly upheld an FCC reprimand issued to Pacifica Radio for its broadcast of the George Carlin monologue "Filthy Words," more popularly known as "the seven dirty words." The *Pacifica* decision also upheld the Commission's general definition of indecency.[2] In the intervening years, however, the FCC consciously followed a restrained enforcement policy.

Because *Fox* represented the Court's first review of the issue in three decades, the decision was widely anticipated. However, the case addressed only a specific application of the indecency policy—whether the FCC could legitimately enforce the law against so-called "fleeting expletives." Once again, the Court narrowly upheld the Commission's decision. The 5-4 decision in *Fox* reversed the holding of the U.S. Court of Appeals for the Second Circuit that the FCC acted arbitrarily and capriciously when it abandoned its longstanding policy.

The case presented the question of whether the FCC could sanction Fox television stations for airing brief, unscripted remarks during the 2002 and 2003 broadcasts of the *Billboard Music Awards*. When

---

* Robert Corn-Revere, a partner at Davis Wright Tremaine LLP in Washington, D.C., practices First Amendment and communications law, and is a Cato Institute adjunct scholar. He represents CBS in *FCC v. Fox Television Stations, Inc.; CBS Corporation v. FCC;* and *ABC Inc. v. FCC.* The views expressed in this article are solely those of the author.

[1] FCC v. Fox Television Stations, Inc., 556 U.S. ____, 129 S. Ct. 1800 (2009), reversing 489 F.3d 444 (2d Cir. 2007).

[2] FCC v. Pacifica Found., Inc., 438 U.S. 726 (1978).

accepting an award in 2002, Cher stated, "People have been telling me I'm on the way out every year, right? So fuck 'em." The following year, Nicole Richie, a presenter on the show, went off-script and said: "Have you ever tried to get cow shit out of a Prada purse? It's not so fucking simple."[3] The Second Circuit Court of Appeals examined not just the validity of the Commission's findings with respect to the Fox broadcasts, but also reviewed the agency's decision to eliminate its historic policy of treating such unplanned, spontaneous, and brief remarks as "not actionable" under its indecency rules. The circuit court ruled that the FCC failed to adequately explain its change in policy.

The Supreme Court reversed, however, with a slim majority holding that the Commission's explanation was sufficient. The fragmented decision generated six opinions. Justice Antonin Scalia wrote the opinion for the Court, joined by Chief Justice John Roberts and Justices Samuel Alito, Clarence Thomas and Anthony Kennedy, with Justices Thomas and Kennedy writing separate concurring opinions. Justice Stephen Breyer wrote a dissent joined by Justices David Souter, John Paul Stevens and Ruth Bader Ginsburg—the latter two of whom also wrote separate brief dissents.

The *Fox* decision focused solely on the narrow issue of whether the FCC's explanation for the policy change was adequate under the Administrative Procedure Act.[4] The majority concluded that agencies face no greater burden justifying their actions when changing existing policy than when setting policy in the first instance, and held that the FCC adequately explained why it would no longer forbear from enforcing broadcast indecency rules against fleeting expletives. Although an agency must show that good reasons support its change in policy under the APA, the Court held that this does not create an obligation to convince a reviewing court that the reasons are "better" than the rationale for the previous policy. Instead, it is necessary only to show that the new policy is permissible under the law, that there are good reasons for it, and "that the agency *believes* it to be better."[5]

---

[3] Fox Television Stations, Inc., 489 F.3d at 452.

[4] 5 U.S.C. § 551 et seq.; see *id.* § 706(2)(a).

[5] FCC v. Fox, 129 S. Ct. at 1811 (emphasis in original).

The Court rejected the idea that there should be heightened scrutiny of FCC actions "that implicate constitutional liberties." Additionally, noting that the APA authorizes courts to set aside agency action that is "unlawful," as well as action that is "arbitrary and capricious," the Court declined to do so in this case because the "lawfulness under the Constitution is a separate question to be addressed in a constitutional challenge."[6] Thus, although the parties extensively briefed and argued whether the new policy violates the First Amendment, the decision focused solely on whether the FCC's decision was arbitrary and capricious under the APA.

For that reason, the *Fox* decision is far from the end of the story, and is more like an intermission between acts. The case was decided not only by a close vote, but on a narrow rationale. The Court remanded the case to the Second Circuit for further proceedings on issues that were not resolved in the initial appeal, including whether the new FCC policy violates the First Amendment. In addition, two other cases challenging FCC indecency enforcement actions are currently pending in circuit courts.[7] Consequently, more momentous judicial review of the FCC's ban on broadcast indecency is yet to come.

The Statutory Prohibition of Indecent Broadcasting

The law governing broadcast indecency was written when radio was the only electronic mass medium and at a time when that industry was in its infancy. Originally enacted as part of Section 29 of the Radio Act of 1927,[8] and incorporated into the Communications Act of 1934,[9] the statutory prohibition was transferred to the U.S. Criminal Code in 1948. Section 1464 of the Criminal Code provides:

> Whoever utters any obscene, indecent, or profane language by means of radio communication shall be fined under this title or imprisoned not more than two years, or both.[10]

[6] *Id.* at 1812.

[7] See FCC v. CBS Corp., 129 S. Ct. 2176 (2009), granting cert., vacating, and remanding 535 F.3d 167 (3d Cir. 2008). The Third Circuit had reversed the FCC's imposition of a $550,000 fine for the 2004 Super Bowl broadcast in CBS. That case has been remanded to the Third Circuit and currently is subject to supplemental briefing. In ABC Inc. v. FCC, No. 08-0841 (2d Cir.), a challenge to an FCC fine for an episode of *NYPD Blue* is pending.

[8] Radio Act of 1927, § 29, 44 Stat. 1172–1173.

[9] Communications Act of 1934, §§ 312, 326, 501, 48 Stat. 1086, 1091 and 1100.

[10] 18 U.S.C. § 1464.

The law was adopted without any statutory definition of its key terms or clear indication of congressional intent.[11] The scant legislative history indicates "that 'obscenity' was the concern of those members of Congress who spoke" about the provision.[12] This is not surprising; the law was written at a time when the terms "obscene," "indecent," and "profane" were treated as essentially synonymous, long before the Supreme Court held that the First Amendment limited the government's ability to regulate in this area.[13]

Though Section 1464 is part of the Criminal Code, it is enforced primarily by the FCC, which construes the law's operative terms to establish what "utterances" fall within the statutory prohibition. The Communications Act gives the FCC authority both to determine whether Section 1464 has been violated and to impose penalties for such violations, ranging from civil sanctions called "forfeitures," to conditional or short-term renewal of licenses, to license revocation. Criminal sanctions also are potentially available.[14]

Developing the "Indecency" Standard

For years, the FCC treated transgressions of Section 1464 as obscenity cases to the extent it made any distinction at all among the

[11] See, e.g., 67 Cong. Rec. 12615 (1926) (remarks of Sen. Dill); *id.* at 5480 (remarks of Rep. White); 68 Cong. Rec. 2567 (1927) (remarks of Rep. Scott); Hearings on S. 1 and S. 1754 before the Senate Committee on Interstate Commerce, 69th Cong. 121 (1926); Hearings on H.R. 5589 before the House Committee on the Merchant Marine and Fisheries, 69th Cong. 26, 40 (1926). See also Hearings on H.R. 8825 before the House Committee on the Merchant Marine and Fisheries, 70th Cong. (1928).

[12] See United States v. Simpson, 561 F.2d 53, 57 (7th Cir. 1977) (citing legislative history of Radio Act of 1927).

[13] See, e.g., Swearingen v. United States, 161 U.S. 446, 450–451 (1896) (describing the words "obscene, lewd and lascivious" as describing "a single offense"). See generally Zechariah Chafee Jr., Free Speech in the United States 149–152 (2d ed. 1941) (equating laws regarding obscenity, indecency, profanity, and blasphemy); Edythe Wise, A Historical Perspective on the Protection of Children From Broadcast Indecency, 3 Vill. Sports & Ent. L.J. 15, 18 (1996) ("the concept of indecency has developed from an amorphous generalization poorly differentiated from obscenity").

[14] See 47 U.S.C. §§ 503(b)(1)(D), 312(a)(6), 312(b)(2). See also 47 U.S.C. § 501 (criminal penalties for "willful" violations of the Communications Act). See Tallman v. United States, 465 F.2d 282, 284 (7th Cir. 1972) (Section 1464 conviction upheld for CB radio user). But see United States v. Simpson, 561 F.2d 53 (7th Cir. 1977) (conviction for CB radio user reversed).

statutory terms.[15] As the law of obscenity evolved and courts increasingly recognized that the First Amendment cabined its reach, however, the Commission began to develop a separate meaning for the statutory term "indecency." In 1970, the FCC construed Section 1464's reference to "indecent" as material that "is (a) patently offensive by contemporary community standards; and (b) is utterly without redeeming social value." This definition was a variation on the then-applicable test for obscenity.[16]

The Commission revisited the issue following the Supreme Court's revision of the obscenity standard in *Miller v. California*,[17] using as its vehicle a complaint concerning a broadcast of George Carlin's "seven dirty words" monologue. Specifically, the FCC sought to "review the applicable legal principles and clarify the standards which will be utilized in considering the public's complaints about the broadcast of 'indecent' language."[18] Noting that "the term 'indecent' ha[d] never been authoritatively construed by the Courts in connection with Section 1464," the Commission "reformulate[ed] the concept" of indecent speech as:

> language that describes, in terms patently offensive as measured by contemporary community standards for the broadcast medium, sexual or excretory activities and organs, at times of day when there is a reasonable risk that children may be in the audience.[19]

Although the FCC's construction of Section 1464's regulation of "indecent" language was inspired by *Miller*, there are significant differences between that term and the Supreme Court's definition

---

[15] See, e.g., Ill. Citizens Comm. for Broad. v. FCC, 515 F.2d 397, 403–04 (D.C. Cir. 1974); Sonderling Broad., Corp., 41 FCC 2d 777, 782 n.14 (1975). See Wise, *supra* note 13 at 21 ("The Commission . . . did not focus on the distinction between obscenity and indecency in broadcasting until the 1970s.").

[16] Eastern Educational Radio (WUHY-FM), 24 F.C.C.2d 408, 412 (1970).

[17] 413 U.S. 15 (1973).

[18] A Citizen's Complaint Against Pacifica Found. Station WBAI(FM), New York, N.Y., 56 F.C.C.2d 94, 99 (1975) ("FCC Pacifica Order").

[19] *Id.* at 97–98.

of "obscene" speech that is not protected by the First Amendment.[20] The focus of indecency regulation is the impact of sexually oriented material on children, not on the "average person" in a community as in *Miller*.[21] Unlike the test for obscenity, the indecency standard does not require an examination of the work "as a whole," and does not ask whether the material appeals primarily to the prurient interest.[22] Indecency is not limited to patently offensive depictions of sex acts that are "specifically defined by law," and it is not a complete defense that the material has serious literary, artistic, political or scientific value.[23]

Rather than articulate a test with *Miller*'s level of specificity to keep Section 1464 within constitutional bounds, the Commission instead sought to avoid First Amendment problems by interpreting the term "indecent" narrowly and exercising its authority cautiously. As then-FCC Commissioner Glen O. Robinson explained, "the statute (18 U.S.C. § 1464) on its face expresses no limit on our power to forbid 'indecent' language over the air, [but] the First Amendment does not permit us to read the statute broadly."[24] The Commission therefore stressed that in order to "avoid the error of overbreadth" it was necessary "to make explicit whom we are protecting and from

---

[20] *Miller* established a three-part test for obscenity under the First Amendment that requires the government to prove that (1) the average person, applying contemporary community standards, would find that the work, taken as a whole, appeals primarily to the prurient interest; (2) the work depicts or describes, in a patently offensive way, sexual conduct specifically defined by the applicable state law, and (3) the work, taken as a whole, lacks serious literary, artistic, political, or scientific value." 413 U.S. at 24.

[21] FCC Pacifica Order, 56 F.C.C.2d at 98.

[22] The Commission consistently has rejected claims that it "is required [to] take into account the work as a whole." Implementation of Section 10 of the Cable Consumer Protection and Competition Act of 1992, 8 F.C.C.R. 998, 1004 (1993), aff'd, Alliance for Community Media v. FCC, 56 F.3d 105 (D.C. Cir. 1995), rev'd in part and aff'd in part sub nom. Denver Area Educ. Telecomms. Consortium v. FCC, 518 U.S. 717, 756 (1996).

[23] See Infinity Broad. Corp., 3 F.C.C.R. 930, 932 (1987), aff'd in part and rev'd in part on other grounds sub nom., Action for Children's Television v. FCC, 852 F.2d 1332 (D.C. Cir. 1988) ("ACT I") ("We must . . . reject an approach that would hold that if a work has merit, it is not per se indecent."). See *id.* at 937 n.36 ("[W]e would not permit merit to 'save' programming that is nonetheless patently offensive.").

[24] FCC Pacifica Order, 56 F.C.C.2d 94 103–104 (1975) (Concurring statement of Commissioners Robinson and Hooks).

what."[25] It reasoned that its updated indecency definition would not "stifle robust, free debate on any of the controversial issues confronting our society" and would not "force upon the general listening public debates and ideas which are 'only fit for children'" because "the number of words which fall within the definition of indecent is clearly limited."[26]

In that regard, in denying a petition to reconsider its Pacifica Order, the Commission explained that inadvertent, isolated or fleeting transmissions of "indecent" language would not violate Section 1464 because it would be inequitable to hold a licensee responsible for indecent language when "public events likely to produce offensive speech are covered live, and there is no opportunity for journalistic editing."[27] Recognizing the vital First Amendment issues at stake, the Commission cautiously enforced its narrow construction of the statute. It stressed that "in sensitive areas like this ... the Commission can act only in clear-cut, flagrant cases" and that "doubtful or close cases are clearly to be resolved in the licensee's favor."[28]

When it did take action pursuant to Section 1464, the FCC did not seek to impose punitive sanctions even in cases where there were repeated "indecent" utterances, and it sought to ensure unimpeded access to judicial review. Thus, the Commission did not impose any sanctions on Pacifica Radio for the "verbal shock treatment" of George Carlin's "seven dirty words" and merely placed the resulting order in the station's license file.[29] Similarly, the FCC levied a fine of only $100 for the broadcast of an interview with Grateful Dead guitarist Jerry Garcia in which "comments were frequently interspersed with the words 'f—k' and 's—t', used as adjectives, or

---

[25] *Id.* at 98.

[26] FCC Pacifica Order, 56 F.C.C.2d at 99–100. See also *id.* at 108–109 (concurring statement of Commissioners Robinson and Hooks) ("[T]he legal enforcement of manners is an activity of government with a breathtakingly narrow scope in a free society.").

[27] Petition for Reconsideration of a Citizen's Complaint Against Pacifica Foundation Station WBAI (FM), New York, N.Y., 59 F.C.C.2d 892, 893 n.1 (1976) (Pacifica Reconsideration Order).

[28] Eastern Educ. Radio, 24 F.C.C.2d 408, 414 (1970). See Wise, *supra* note 13 at 19 ("The path the Commission followed over the decades, with some detours, was toward narrowing the protected group and refining indecency's definition.").

[29] FCC Pacifica Order, 56 F.C.C.2d at 99.

simply as an introductory expletive."[30] The Commission imposed the fine only to ensure that the decision would be reviewable in court. Overall, the Commission did not seek to enforce a complete ban on broadcast indecency as the unambiguous language of the statute appeared to require.[31]

The FCC's Restrained Enforcement Policy

The FCC's enforcement of Section 1464 historically was governed by the overall philosophy of the Communications Act that the government should avoid involvement with licensees' editorial decisions. As a general matter, therefore, the Commission had made clear that program choice is "the responsibility of the licensee" and that "the charge that the broadcast programs are vulgar or presented without 'due regard for sensitivity, intelligence, and taste,' is not properly cognizable by this government agency, in light of the proscription against censorship." The FCC explained that "there can be no governmental arbiter of taste in the broadcast field."[32] Particularly with respect to specific programming decisions, the Commission gave substantial deference to the "editorial discretion of licensees."[33]

The Commission expressly relied on this restrained approach to Section 1464 when it defended its definition of "indecency" in court. One week before oral argument at the D.C. Circuit Court of Appeals in *Pacifica*, the FCC issued its reconsideration order, which the court described as "the most important ruling" in that proceeding, because "the Commission indirectly admitted it had gone too far in banning 'indecent' language from the airwaves."[34] The court took special note of the FCC's clarifications that "it would be inequitable to hold

---

[30] Eastern Educ. Radio, 24 F.C.C.2d at 414 ("We believe that a most crucial peg underlying all Commission action in the programming field is the vital consideration that the courts are there to review and reverse any action which runs afoul of the First Amendment.").

[31] FCC Pacifica Order, 56 F.C.C.2d at 98 (emphasis in original).

[32] In re: Petition by Oliver R. Grace, 22 F.C.C.2d 667, 668 (1970).

[33] Eastern Educ. Radio, 24 F.C.C.2d at 414; see also Pacifica Reconsideration Order, 59 F.C.C.2d 892 ("the real solution to this problem [is] the 'exercise of licensee judgment, responsibility, and sensitivity to the community's needs, interests and tastes' "); Banzhaf v. FCC, 405 F.2d 1082, 1095 (D.C. Cir. 1968) (FCC practice of according licensees broad discretion over programming, focusing on "overall performance and good faith rather than on specific errors" minimizes First Amendment tensions).

[34] Pacifica Found. v. FCC, 556 F.2d 9, 14–15 (D.C. Cir. 1977), rev'd, 438 U.S. 726 (1978).

a licensee responsible for indecent language broadcast during live coverage of a newsmaking event" and that it was preferable to "trust the licensee to exercise judgment, responsibility and sensitivity to the needs, interest, and tastes of the community."[35]

Nevertheless, the court of appeals rejected the FCC's construction of Section 1464, holding that despite the FCC's efforts to exercise restraint and construe the statute narrowly, the law remained overly broad and vague.[36] The court observed that the FCC's decision "would prohibit the broadcast of Shakespeare's *The Tempest* or *Two Gentlemen of Verona*" along with "certain passages of the Bible" and the "works of Auden, Becket, Lord Byron, Chaucer, Fielding, Greene, Hemingway, Joyce, Knowles, Lawrence, Orwell, Scott, Swift, and the Nixon tapes."[37] It stressed that "[t]o whatever extent ... the Commission errs in balancing its duties, it must be in favor of preserving the values of free expression and freedom from governmental interference in matters of taste."[38]

On appeal to the Supreme Court, the FCC faulted the D.C. Circuit for considering a "post-record parade of horribles" and stressed that its decision should be limited to the facts of the case.[39] Specifically, the FCC argued that its decision "must be read narrowly, limited to the language 'as broadcast' in the early afternoon." It emphasized "the deliberate repetition of these words" noting that the case involved "prerecorded language with the words repeated over and over [and] deliberately broadcast."[40] The Commission further asserted that its Pacifica Order "was not retreating from previous decisions recognizing the broad programming discretion broadcast licensees enjoy" and that it in fact addressed only "a limited number of patently offensive words."[41]

The Supreme Court Decision in *Pacifica*

The Supreme Court took the Commission at its word, and reversed the D.C. Circuit on a very limited basis. The Court characterized its

[35] *Id.* at 13.

[36] *Id.* at 17.

[37] *Id.* at 18.

[38] *Id.*

[39] Brief for the Federal Communications Commission, FCC v. Pacifica Found., No. 77–528 (March 3, 1978), 1978 WL 206838 at 44 (citation omitted).

[40] *Id.* at 25–26.

[41] *Id.* at 14.

5-4 decision as "an emphatically narrow holding."[42] As Justice Lewis Powell explained in his concurring opinion, the Court approved "only the Commission's holding that Carlin's monologue was indecent 'as broadcast' at two o'clock in the afternoon, and not the broad sweep of the Commission's opinion."[43] Acknowledging that restrictions on indecent expression in other media have been found unconstitutional, the Supreme Court in *Pacifica* identified two attributes of the broadcast medium that it said justified a limited exception to the First Amendment norm. First, it noted that "the broadcast media have established a uniquely pervasive presence in the lives of all Americans." Because of this, the Court said, "prior warnings cannot completely protect the listener or viewer from unexpected program content." Second, it described broadcasting as "uniquely accessible to children" and observed that "[o]ther forms of offensive expression may be withheld from the young without restricting the expression at its source."[44]

In line with the FCC's defense of Section 1464, the *Pacifica* Court approved only a narrow definition of the term "indecent." Justices Powell and Harry Blackmun, who supplied the crucial votes for *Pacifica*'s slim majority, noted "[t]he Commission's holding, and certainly the Court's holding today, does not speak to cases involving the isolated use of a potentially offensive word."[45] They stressed that the FCC does not have "unrestricted license to decide what speech, protected in other media, may be banned from the airwaves in order to protect unwilling adults from momentary exposure to it in their homes."[46] Critical to the Court's holding was the level of

---

[42] Pacifica, 438 U.S. at 742 ("our review is limited to the question whether the Commission has the authority to proscribe this particular broadcast" in a "specific factual context"), *id*. at 750 ("[i]t is appropriate. . .to emphasize the narrowness of our holding"). See also Sable Communications of Cal., Inc. v. FCC, 492 U.S. 115, 127 (1989) (*Pacifica* was "an emphatically narrow holding"); Bolger v. Youngs Drug Prods. Corp., 463 U.S. 60, 74 (1983) (emphasizing narrowness of *Pacifica*); Cruz v. Ferre, 755 F.2d 1415, 1421 (11th Cir. 1985) ("[r]ecent decisions of the Court have largely limited *Pacifica* to its facts").

[43] Pacifica, 438 U.S. at 755–56 (Powell, J., concurring).

[44] *Id*. at 748–749.

[45] *Id*. at 760–761 (Powell, J., joined by Blackmun, J., concurring).

[46] *Id*. See also *id*. at 772 (Brennan J., dissenting) ("I believe that the FCC is estopped from using either this decision or its own orders in this case . . . as a basis for imposing sanctions on any public radio broadcast other than one aired during the daytime or early evening and containing the relentless repetition, for longer than a brief interval, of [offensive language].").

restraint the FCC historically had shown in construing and enforcing Section 1464. In that regard, Justice Powell noted the incentive to self-censorship in what he described as a "relatively new and difficult area of law," but allowed the FCC some latitude because "the Commission may be expected to proceed cautiously, as it has in the past."[47] Powell expressed confidence that the Commission would recognize and reflect the danger of inhibiting the dissemination of protected expression "as it develops standards in this area."[48]

The FCC's Policy After *Pacifica*

After the Supreme Court upheld its authority to enforce Section 1464, the Commission continued—as it had promised—to show great restraint in its construction of the law. Its first opportunity to do so came just three weeks after the *Pacifica* decision, when it rejected a petition to deny the renewal of plaintiff WGBH-TV's broadcast license on indecency grounds. The activist group Morality in Media had challenged license renewal on grounds of alleged indecency, and submitted to the Commission "five and one-half pages of characterizations of programs and/or words and phases" it characterized as "offensive, vulgar and otherwise . . . harmful to children."[49] The Commission held, however, that "we cannot base the denial of a license renewal application upon the 'subjective determination' of a viewer, or group of viewers, as to what is or is not 'good' programming."[50]

With respect to the construction of Section 1464 as upheld by the Supreme Court, the Commission explained:

---

[47] *Id.* at 756, 760–61 (Powell, J., concurring).

[48] *Id.* at 760.

[49] WGBH Educ. Found., 69 F.C.C.2d 1250 (1978). The petition focused on (1) an unidentified installment of *Masterpiece Theater* that it described as "a story principally concerned with adultery expressing a philosophy that approved of adulterous relationships"; (2) a program called *The Thin Edge,* that allegedly "espoused a hedonistic attitude about guilt resulting from adultery and fornication"; (3) numerous episodes of *Monty Python's Flying Circus,* which it said "relies primarily on scatology, immodesty, vulgarity, nudity, profanity and sacrilege" for humor; (4) a program entitled *Rock Follies,* which it described "as 'vulgar' and as containing 'profanity' (i.e., 'The name of God (six times)'), 'obscenities' such as 'shit,' 'bullshit,' etc., and action indicating some sexually-oriented content in the program"; and (5) other programs that allegedly contained nudity and/or sexually-oriented material.

[50] *Id.* at 1251–52.

> We intend strictly to observe the narrowness of the *Pacifica* holding. In this regard, the Commission's opinion, as approved by the Court, relied in part on the repetitive occurrence of the "indecent" words in question. The opinion of the Court specifically stated that it was not ruling that "an occasional expletive ... would justify any sanction ... ." Further, Justice Powell's concurring opinion emphasized the fact that the language there in issue had been "repeated over and over as a sort of verbal shock treatment." He specifically distinguished "the verbal shock treatment [in *Pacifica*]" from "the isolated use of a potentially offensive word in the course of a radio broadcast."[51]

Consistent with this approach, the FCC in 1983 denied a license renewal challenge to Pacifica station WPFW based in part on indecency allegations, despite the fact that there were "a number of instances where language similar to that in [the George Carlin monologue] was broadcast."[52] The Commission concluded that the petitioner had "failed to make a *prima facie* case that WPFW has violated 18 U.S.C. 1464" because it had not shown that "indecent" programs were "more than 'isolated use in the course of' a three year license term."[53]

Over time, the Commission modified its approach to enforcement to apply beyond just Carlin's "seven dirty words" and to encompass what it called a "generic definition" of the statutory term "indecent." In three declaratory rulings issued in 1987, it set forth what it described as a "clarification" of its construction of Section 1464 to apply to "a broader range of material than the seven specific words at issue in *Pacifica*."[54] The FCC did not purport to alter the indecency

---

[51] *Id.* at 1254 (internal citations omitted).

[52] Pacifica Found., 95 F.C.C.2d 750, 760 (1983). The Commission noted complaints alleging that "a male announcer repeatedly used such words as 'motherfucker,' 'fuck' and similar indecent language" during one morning program, as well as like allegations involving two other morning shows. It also noted complaints that evening and late evening programs contained the same type of language. *Id.*

[53] *Id.* at 760–761.

[54] Pacifica Radio, 2 F.C.C.R. 2698, 2699 (1987), aff'd on recon., Infinity Broad. Corp. of Pa., 3 F.C.C.R. 930 (1987), aff'd in part, rev'd in part, ACT I, 852 F.2d 1332. See Regents of the Univ. of Cal., 2 F.C.C.R. 2703 (1987) (same subsequent history); Infinity Broad. of Pa., 2 F.C.C.R. 2705 (1987) (same subsequent history). See also New Indecency Enforcement Standards to be Applied to all Broadcast and Amateur Radio Licensees, 2 F.C.C.R. 2726 (1987) ("New Indecency Enforcement Standards").

standard it had previously articulated, and it reaffirmed that isolated or fleeting utterances would not be actionable. It stressed that "deliberate and repetitive use in a patently offensive manner is a requisite to a finding of indecency,"[55] and that indecency "must involve more than the isolated use of an offensive word."[56] The D.C. Circuit approved the FCC's adoption of a "generic" definition of indecency, but it did so based on the "expectation that Commission will continue to proceed cautiously." As then-Judge Ruth Bader Ginsburg explained, "the potential chilling effect of the FCC's generic definition . . . will be tempered by the Commission's restrained enforcement policy."[57]

In 2001, the Commission issued a policy statement to provide "interpretive guidance" to broadcasters regarding enforcement of the indecency rules.[58] The Indecency Policy Statement posited two fundamental determinations that must be made in any Section 1464 case: (1) whether the material depicts or describes sexual or excretory organs or activities, and (2) whether the material is "patently offensive" as measured by contemporary community standards for the broadcast medium.[59] To determine patent offensiveness, the FCC explained that it relies on three factors: (a) the explicitness or graphic nature of the depiction; (b) whether the material dwells on or repeats at length the depictions; and (c) whether the material appears to pander or is used to titillate or shock.[60] The FCC's analysis was based on a synthesis of various enforcement decisions issued over the years, and illustrative examples were set forth in the policy statement to provide guidance to broadcasters.

The FCC Changes Its "Fleeting Expletives" Policy

The FCC expressly abandoned its restrained enforcement policy toward fleeting expletives in March 2004, in a decision relating to

---

[55] Pacifica Radio, 2 F.C.C.R. at 2699.

[56] Infinity Broad. of Pa., 2 F.C.C.R. at 2705; Regents of the Univ. of Cal., 2 F.C.C.R. at 2703.

[57] ACT I, 852 F.2d at 1340 n.14.

[58] Industry Guidance on the Commission's Case Law Interpreting 18 U.S.C. § 1464 and Enforcement Policies Regarding Broadcast Indecency, 16 F.C.C.R. 7999, 8008–09 (2001) ("Indecency Policy Statement").

[59] Id. at 8002.

[60] Id. at 8002–03.

the January 2003 telecast of the *Golden Globe Awards*. U2's Bono had spontaneously declared that it was "fucking brilliant" that his band won a statuette. Complaints about the broadcast initially were dismissed by the FCC's Enforcement Bureau. Applying existing precedent, the Commission staff explained that "fleeting and isolated remarks of this nature do not" violate Section 1464, and that "the material aired . . . does not describe or depict sexual and excretory activities and organs" as required by the FCC's long-standing definition of indecent speech.[61]

After being subjected to significant pressure from Congress, however, the FCC reversed the Golden Globes Bureau Order.[62] In so doing, the FCC expressly held that its prior interpretations of Section 1464 suggesting "that isolated or fleeting broadcasts of the 'F-Word' . . . are not indecent or would not be acted upon" are "no longer good law."[63] The Commission also overruled similar cases cited in the Indecency Policy Statement and stated that licensees could no longer rely on "unpublished staff decisions" to the contrary.[64] The FCC explained that "[t]he fact that the use of [an indecent] word may have been unintentional is irrelevant."[65] It reinforced its new construction of Section 1464 by stressing that broadcasters failing to institute technological delays could be penalized if they inadvertently transmit "indecent" or "profane" material, regardless of

---

[61] Complaints Against Various Broadcast Licensees Regarding Their Airing of the "Golden Globe Awards" Program, 18 F.C.C.R. 19859, 19861–62 (Enf. Bur. 2003) ("Golden Globes Bureau Order"). The staff decision cited numerous previous cases in which the Commission had declined to take action to restrict fleeting expletives or had otherwise shown restraint. *Id.* at 19861 (citing Entercom Buffalo License LLC (WGR(AM)), 17 F.C.C.R. 11997 (Enf. Bur. 2002); L.M. Communications of S.C., Inc. (WYBB(FM)), 7 F.C.C.R. 1595 (Mass Med. Bur. 1992); Peter Branton, 6 F.C.C.R. 610 (1991); Indecency Policy Statement, 16 F.C.C.R. at 8008–09).

[62] See Complaints Against Various Broadcast Licensees Regarding Their Airing of the "Golden Globe Awards" Program, 19 F.C.C.R. 4975 (2004) ("Golden Globe Awards Decision").

[63] *Id.* at 4980 (overruling portions of prior holdings that "isolated use of expletives is not indecent" including Pacifica Radio, 2 F.C.C.R. at 2699; Infinity Broad. of Pa., 2 F.C.C.R. at 2705; and Regents of the Univ. of Cal., 2 F.C.C.R. at 2703).

[64] *Id.* at 4890 n.32 (overruling Lincoln Dellar, Renewal of License for Stations KPRL (AM) and KDDB (FM), 8 F.C.C.R. 2582, 2585 (Mass Media Bur. 1993) and L.M. Communications of S.C., Inc. (WYBB(FM)), 7 F.C.C.R. 1595 (Mass Med. Bur. 1992)).

[65] Golden Globe Awards Decision, 19 F.C.C.R. at 4979.

whether they had otherwise taken precautions to prevent such a thing from occurring.[66]

Although broadcasters sought reconsideration of the Golden Globes Bureau Order and the Commission's revised policy, the agency did not act on the petitions. Instead, the FCC issued an "omnibus" indecency order in February 2006 that expanded on the policy change first announced in the Golden Globe Awards Decision and addressed several dozen shows against which indecency complaints had been filed over a three-year period.[67] The so-called Omnibus Order proposed fines against six programs on various networks and also found four other shows to be indecent and profane but declined to impose fines because the programs aired before the 2004 Golden Globe Awards Decision. The four programs in this final category included the 2002 and 2003 *Billboard Music Awards* on Fox (on which, respectively, Cher and Nicole Richie uttered brief unscripted expletives during the live awards show), episodes of *NYPD Blue* on ABC (that included various iterations of the word "bullshit"), and a December 2004 edition of *The Early Show* on CBS (in which the interviewee in a news segment used the term "bullshitter").[68]

The FCC's action with respect to these four programs resulted in petitions for review in *Fox v. FCC*. The major broadcast networks and their affiliates filed petitions that were consolidated in the Second Circuit. After a brief mid-appeal remand in which the FCC reversed its decisions regarding *The Early Show* and *NYPD Blue*, the appellate proceeding continued with the Commission's decisions regarding the *Billboard Music Awards* still at issue.[69]

---

[66] *Id.* at 4981–82 (broadcasters can ensure "they are not subject to an enforcement action" by "adopt[ing] and successfully implement[ing] a delay/bleeping system for live broadcasts").

[67] Complaints Regarding Various Television Broadcasts Between February 2, 2002 and March 8, 2005, 21 F.C.C.R. 2664 (2006) ("Omnibus Order").

[68] *Id.* at 2690–2700.

[69] Complaints Regarding Various Television Broadcasts Between February 2, 2002 and March 8, 2005, FCC 06-166 (Nov. 6, 2006). In its remand order the FCC reaffirmed its findings against the 2002 and 2003 *Billboard Music Award* programs but reversed its indecency finding against *The Early Show*. It dismissed the complaints against *NYPD Blue* on procedural grounds.

The Second Circuit Reverses the FCC

In a 2-1 decision, the Second Circuit held that the FCC's decision to apply its broadcast indecency rules to "isolated" and "fleeting" expletives was arbitrary and capricious under the APA.[70] The circuit court did not limit its holding to the two episodes of the *Billboard Music Awards* on Fox, but invalidated the entire "fleeting expletives" policy, as first articulated in the Golden Globes Awards Decision. The court held that the policy was arbitrary and capricious because it departed from the FCC's longstanding policy of restraint and because the agency failed to articulate a reasoned basis for the change.

In addition to finding that the FCC had failed to adequately explain its change of policy, the court said that the FCC had an obligation to show that indecent speech is harmful in some way. The majority opinion noted that the FCC's order was "devoid of any evidence that suggests a fleeting expletive is harmful, let alone establish[ing] that this harm is serious enough to warrant government regulation. Such evidence would seem to be particularly relevant today when children likely hear this language far more often from other sources than they did in the 1970s when the Commission first began sanctioning indecent speech."[71]

Because the majority decided that the FCC's decision was arbitrary and capricious, it found it unnecessary to reach the constitutional issues raised by the networks. However, the court issued several pages of dicta that expressed "skepticism" that "the Commission can provide a reasoned explanation for its 'fleeting expletive' regime that would pass constitutional muster."[72] The court broadly "question[ed] whether the FCC's indecency test can survive First Amendment scrutiny," and sympathized with "the Networks' contention that the FCC's indecency test is undefined, indiscernible, inconsistent, and consequently, unconstitutionally vague."[73] It also stated that "the FCC's indecency test" raises "the separate constitutional question of whether it permits the FCC to sanction speech based on [the agency's] subjective view of the merit of that speech," and

---

[70] Fox Television Stations, Inc., 489 F.3d at 447.

[71] *Id.* at 461.

[72] *Id.* at 462.

[73] *Id.* at 463.

added, "we are hard pressed to imagine a regime that is more vague than one that relies entirely on consideration of the otherwise unspecified 'context' of a broadcast indecency."[74]

Judge Pierre Leval dissented on the ground that the FCC adequately explained its policy change, writing that the majority simply had a "difference of opinion" on the FCC's direction in altering course.[75] He characterized the reversal on "fleeting expletives" as a "small change . . . by the FCC in its [indecency] standards" that merely "diminished the significance of the fact that the . . . expletive was not repeated." The dissent found the change in position justified by the FCC's "sensible, although not necessarily compelling" explanation that "the 'F-Word' . . . inherently has a sexual connotation" and "is one of the most vulgar, graphic and explicit descriptions of sexual activity in the English language." This was sufficient, Leval argued, under the deferential standard of review afforded agencies and their right to make changes in policy. Judge Leval's dissent did not address the constitutional implications of the FCC's new policy.[76]

Supreme Court Reverses on Administrative Law Grounds

The Court's 5-4 decision in *Fox* focused solely on the narrow issue of whether the FCC's explanation for the policy change was adequate under the APA. As noted above, the Court did not address at length the lower court's discussion of the First Amendment, in which the Second Circuit was openly skeptical about the constitutionality of the Commission's new policy.[77] The majority opinion did acknowledge, however, that whether the policy is unconstitutional "will be determined soon enough, perhaps in this very case."[78] Accordingly, it remanded the case to the circuit court to consider whether the enforcement policy violates the First Amendment or is otherwise invalid.[79]

The narrow focus of the majority opinion tended to obscure the importance of the underlying constitutional challenge. In this

---

[74] *Id.* at 464.

[75] *Id.* at 473 (Leval, J., dissenting).

[76] *Id.* at 468–474.

[77] Fox Television Stations, Inc., 489 F.3d at 462.

[78] Fox, 129 S.Ct. at 1819.

[79] *Id.* at 1819.

respect, however, the combined opinions suggested that most justices may vote to reverse the FCC policy if the First Amendment issue returns to the Court. Among the five justices in the majority, Justices Thomas and Kennedy wrote that the answer might be different were the Court to review the policy on constitutional grounds. In particular, though he concurred on the APA issues, Justice Thomas wrote it may be time to reconsider the *Pacifica* and *Red Lion* cases that give the FCC greater leeway to regulate broadcast content.[80] Separately, Justice Kennedy stressed that his concurrence rested on a narrow, technical reading of the APA and did not take into account constitutional concerns.[81]

Justice Breyer's dissent noted the constitutional underpinnings of the Commission's formerly restrained enforcement policy and found the FCC's explanation for its policy change inadequate because it failed to address the underlying First Amendment issue. The result, he wrote, "is not simply *Hamlet* without the prince, but *Hamlet* with a prince who, in mid-play and without explanation, just disappears."[82] Justice Stevens, who wrote the *Pacifica* majority opinion in 1978, dissented separately and observed that "*Pacifica* was not so sweeping, and the Commission's changed view of its statutory mandate certainly would have been rejected if presented to the Court at the time."[83] Similarly, Justice Ginsburg wrote in dissent that "there is no way to hide the long shadow the First Amendment casts over what the Commission has done."[84]

Given the arguments previously presented in the case, and particularly in light of most justices' comments in *Fox*, the First Amendment implications of the FCC's new enforcement policy regarding "fleeting expletives" will be foremost in the Second Circuit's review on remand. Accordingly, the constitutional basis for the Commission's previous forbearance from enforcing the law against fleeting or unintentional broadcasts of indecent material should play a critical role as the case progresses.

---

[80] *Id.* at 1822 (Thomas, J., concurring).

[81] *Id.* at 1824 (Kennedy, J., concurring).

[82] *Id.* at 1834 (Breyer, J., dissenting).

[83] *Id.* at 1825 (Stevens, J., dissenting).

[84] *Id.* at 1828 (Ginsburg, J., dissenting).

The Next Stage

Much has changed in the three decades since the Supreme Court last considered the constitutionality of the indecency standard in *Pacifica*, making it difficult to conclude with any certainty that the Court would reaffirm its earlier holding if the issue is squarely presented. Contrary to the underlying premise of *Pacifica*, that broadcasting must be regulated more intensively because it is "uniquely pervasive,"[85] the FCC more recently has found that "the modern media marketplace is far different than just a decade ago" in that traditional media "have greatly evolved," and "new modes of media have transformed the landscape, providing more choice, greater flexibility, and more control than at any other time in history."[86] For that reason, the Second Circuit in *Fox* observed that "it is increasingly difficult to describe the broadcast media as uniquely pervasive and uniquely accessible to children, and at some point in the future, strict scrutiny may properly apply in the context of regulating broadcast television."[87]

Applying strict scrutiny would bring First Amendment review of broadcast content restrictions in line with the rule for all other media. The Supreme Court has invalidated efforts to restrict indecency in print,[88] on film,[89] in the mails,[90] in the public forum,[91] on cable television,[92] and on the internet.[93] Although the Court historically treated broadcasting differently because of technological reasons, it has also recognized that "the broadcast industry is dynamic in terms of technological change," that "solutions adequate a decade ago are not necessarily so now, and those acceptable today may well be outmoded ten years hence."[94]

---

[85] Pacifica, 438 U.S. at 748.

[86] 2002 Biennial Regulatory Review, 18 F.C.C.R. 13620, ¶¶ 86–87 (2003).

[87] Fox Television Stations, 489 F.3d at 465.

[88] Butler v. Michigan, 352 U.S. 380, 383 (1957). See also Hamling v. United States, 418 U.S. 87, 113–114 (1974) (statutory prohibition on "indecent" or "obscene" speech may be constitutionally enforced only against obscenity).

[89] United States v. 12 200-ft. Reels of Film, 413 U.S. 123, 130 n.7 (1973).

[90] Bolger, v. Youngs Drug Prods. Corp., 463 U.S. 60 (1983).

[91] Erznoznik v. City of Jacksonville, 422 U.S. 205 (1975).

[92] United States v. Playboy Entmt. Group, Inc., 529 U.S. 803 (2000).

[93] Reno v. ACLU, 521 U.S. 844 (1997).

[94] CBS v. DNC, 412 U.S. at 102.

In addition to technological changes, the law governing indecency has evolved significantly in the 30 years since *Pacifica*. The Supreme Court has confirmed that "indecent" speech is fully protected by the First Amendment and is not subject to diminished scrutiny as "low value" speech, as three justices who joined the *Pacifica* plurality opinion had suggested.[95] Instead, the Court has found that "[t]he history of the law of free expression is one of vindication in cases involving speech that many citizens find shabby, offensive, or even ugly," and that the government cannot assume that it has greater latitude to regulate because of its belief that "the speech is not very important."[96] Additionally, since *Pacifica* the Court has invalidated government-imposed indecency restrictions on cable television channels despite its finding that "[c]able television broadcasting, including access channel broadcasting, is as 'accessible to children' as over-the-air broadcasting, if not more so."[97]

With respect to online speech, the Court subjected the indecency standard to rigorous First Amendment review in *Reno v. ACLU*, and found it to be seriously deficient. Writing for a near-unanimous Court, Justice Stevens concluded that the indecency restrictions of the Communications Decency Act were invalid because of vagueness and overbreadth.[98] This finding is especially meaningful because the language of the CDA was virtually identical to the test the FCC uses to regulate broadcasting. Moreover, Stevens reaffirmed as a bedrock constitutional rule that the governmental interest in protecting children from harmful materials "does not justify an unnecessarily broad suppression of speech addressed to adults."[99] Justice Sandra Day O'Connor, joined by Chief Justice William Rehnquist, wrote an opinion concurring in part and dissenting in part on other grounds, but the Court unanimously held that the CDA provisions requiring

[95] Only Justices Stevens, William Rehnquist, and Chief Justice Warren Burger joined that part of the opinion asserting that indecent speech lies "at the periphery of First Amendment concern." Pacifica, 438 U.S. at 743.

[96] Playboy Entmt. Group, 529 U.S. at 826.

[97] Denver Area Educ. Telecomms. Consortium, 518 U.S. at 744. The Court upheld a provision that permitted cable operators to adopt editorial policies for leased access channels, but rejected government-imposed restrictions on indecent programs on leased and public access channels.

[98] Reno, 521 U.S. at 875.

[99] *Id.* at 870–874, 881–882.

the screening of "indecent" displays from minors "cannot pass muster."[100]

In *Fox*, Justice Thomas signaled his willingness to reconsider precedents, like *Pacifica*, that he wrote have resulted in a "deep intrusion into the First Amendment rights of broadcasters."[101] Noting that logical weakness of such cases "has been apparent for some time," he noted that, "[w]hatever the merits of *Pacifica* when it was issued[,] . . . it makes no sense now."[102] Thomas was the only justice to express such open skepticism of *Pacifica*'s continuing validity, although a solid majority of the Court raised constitutional doubts about the FCC's "fleeting expletives" policy.[103] In this regard, Justice Stevens wrote that he disagreed with Thomas "about the continued wisdom of *Pacifica*," but stressed that "the changes in technology and the availability of broadcast spectrum he identifies certainly counsel a restrained approach to indecency regulation, not the wildly expansive path the FCC has chosen."[104]

This suggests that further First Amendment review, either by the Second Circuit or by the Supreme Court, may result in a reexamination of *Pacifica*, but it need not do so. Instead, additional constitutional review may ask whether the restrained enforcement policy that exempted fleeting or inadvertent expletives from FCC enforcement actions is constitutionally required. Such a conclusion has already been reached with another Commission enforcement policy—the so-called "safe harbor" rule. Even though the language of Section 1464 imposes a categorical ban on the broadcast of indecent

---

[100] *Id.* at 886.

[101] Fox, 129 S. Ct. at 1820 (Thomas, J., concurring).

[102] *Id.* at 1821 (Thomas, J., concurring) (quoting Action for Children's Television v. FCC, 58 F.3d 654, 673 (D.C. Cir. 1995) (Edwards, C.J., dissenting)).

[103] *Id.* at 1819 (predicting whether the FCC's policy change violates the First Amendment "will be determined soon enough"). See also *id.* at 1824 (Kennedy, J., concurring) (reserving judgment on constitutional issues); *id.* at 1825 (Stevens, J., dissenting) (noting that "the Commission's changed view of its statutory mandate certainly would have been rejected if presented to the Court" in *Pacifica*); *id.* at 1828 (Ginsburg, J., dissenting) (noting that "there is no way to hide the long shadow the First Amendment casts over what the Commission has done"); *id.* at 1840 (Breyer, J., dissenting) (describing the FCC's policy change as a "constitutionally suspect interpretation of a statute").

[104] *Id.* at 1828 n.5 (Stevens, J., dissenting).

utterances, the Commission recognized in 1975 that the First Amendment would not permit it to prohibit all on-air indecency.[105] Consequently, the Commission limited the enforcement of the indecency rules to certain hours (eventually settling on the hours between 6 a.m. and 10 p.m.), presumably the time when children may be in the audience. Reviewing courts subsequently held that the Commission-made limitation on enforcement is compelled by the First Amendment.[106] Consistent with such prior restrictions on the FCC's enforcement authority, remand proceedings in *Fox* may address whether a "safe harbor" for the broadcast of inadvertent or ephemeral material should continue to exist alongside the time-channeling safe harbor.

Further proceedings are also likely to address whether the unscripted and unplanned expletives at issue constitute a "willful" violation of Section 1464, as both the Communications Act and the First Amendment require.[107] This question was argued in the original *Fox* appeal but was not decided either by the Second Circuit or by the Supreme Court. However, the issue was addressed by the Third Circuit in *CBS Corp. v. FCC*, and the court held that "the First Amendment precludes a strict liability regime for broadcast indecency." It explained that the Constitution requires the FCC to "prove scienter [guilty knowledge] when it seeks to hold a broadcaster liable for indecent material," and that it would not be sufficient for the Commission to show that a broadcaster was negligent in permitting indecent material to air. Rather, the government must prove recklessness as a "constitutional minimum."[108] Although the *CBS* decision was remanded for reconsideration in light of *Fox*, nothing in the

---

[105] FCC Pacifica Order, 56 F.C.C.2d 94, 103–04 (Concurring statement of Commissioners Robinson and Hooks) ("the First Amendment does not permit us to read the statute broadly [as a total ban]").

[106] See Action for Children's Television v. FCC, 932 F.2d 1504, 1509–10 (D.C. Cir. 1991) ("ACT II"); ACT I, 852 F.2d at 1342.

[107] The statutory authority for the FCC's civil indecency enforcement power is the forfeiture statute, 47 U.S.C. § 503(b), pursuant to which it can impose forfeitures only for "willful" or "repeated" violations of the Act, rules, or Commission orders. Specifically, Section 503(b)(1)(D) empowers the FCC to impose forfeitures for specific statutory provisions, including Section 1464. The First Amendment likewise requires scienter to avoid any unconstitutional chill on protected speech. See United States v. X-Citement Video, Inc., 513 U.S. 64, 71 (1994); Smith v. California, 361 U.S. 147 (1959).

[108] CBS Corp. v. FCC, 535 F.3d 167 (3d Cir. 2008), cert. granted, vacated, and remanded, 129 S. Ct. 2176 (2009).

Supreme Court's discussion of the APA provides any basis for reconsidering the resolution of this issue.[109] Accordingly, the question of scienter or "willfulness" provides an independent reason to set aside the Commission's decision that presumably will be considered on remand.

Conclusion

The widely anticipated holding in *FCC v. Fox* did not produce the constitutional confrontation some had hoped for. Nor did it vindicate the FCC's decision to enforce its indecency rules against inadvertent, accidental, or fleeting expletives. Instead, the Supreme Court decided only that the Commission's explanation for its policy change was adequate to avoid being considered arbitrary and capricious under the APA. The resulting remand proceeding will determine the extent to which the FCC's more restrictive policy is vulnerable under what Justice Ginsburg described as "the long shadow of the First Amendment."[110]

---

[109] A grant, vacate, and remand order (known as a "GVR") is not "a thinly-veiled direction to alter . . . course" but asks only "whether [the intervening decision] demands a different result." Gonzalez v. Justices of Mun. Court of Boston, 420 F.3d 5, 7–8 (1st Cir. 2005); Fontroy v. Owens, 23 F.3d 63, 66 (3d Cir. 1994).

[110] Fox, 129 S. Ct. at 1828 (Ginsburg, J., dissenting).

The *Caperton* Caper and the Kennedy Conundrum

Stephen M. Hoersting* and Bradley A. Smith**

Introduction

Caperton v. Massey Coal[1] typifies the old maxim that hard cases make bad law. In *Caperton*, the Supreme Court created a new, largely unworkable standard for judicial recusal, then elevated it to a matter of constitutional due process. But this is not all. *Caperton* has the potential to erode the Supreme Court's traditional protection for independent political speech in election campaigns dating back to at least *Buckley v. Valeo*,[2] and may one day threaten the Court's recent decision on free speech in judicial elections, *Republican Party of Minnesota v. White*.[3]

In this article, we argue that the events in *Caperton* are best handled under state recusal procedures, and that elevating them to matters of constitutional due process is both unnecessary and unwise. We will argue that the "probability of bias" standard adopted by the Supreme Court in *Caperton* is a marked departure from the Court's due process standard, and suggest that the standard—based as it is upon "debts of gratitude" to campaign speakers—will prove to be largely unworkable. We will then show how court holdings that independent expenditures cause bias in a judge are contrary to cases holding that independent expenditures do not cause corruption in candidates, and thus, if followed by the Court in future cases, will

---

* Vice President and Co-Founder, Center for Competitive Politics; former General Counsel, National Republican Senatorial Committee.

** Josiah H. Blackmore II/Shirley M. Nault Designated Professor of Law at Capital University Law School; Chairman and Co-Founder, Center for Competitive Politics; former Chairman, Federal Election Commission.

[1] Caperton v. A.T. Massey Coal Co., Inc., 129 S. Ct. 2252 (2009).

[2] 424 U.S. 1 (1976).

[3] 536 U.S. 765 (2002).

tend to threaten independent political speech. Lastly, we will examine the *Caperton* opinion itself and suggest that Justice Anthony Kennedy's opinion for the Court, with its emphasis on the "extraordinary" facts of the case, was an attempt to reverse a hard case without creating bad law. By referring to independent political expenditures as campaign "contributions" instead of "independent expenditures," Justice Kennedy's opinion attempts to address a case that, on its facts, seemed to shock the conscience—without damaging Kennedy's longstanding position in campaign finance cases that judicial elections are much like other elections, and that independent election expenditures enjoy the highest constitutional protection.[4]

Facts

Caperton v. Massey Coal has its roots in a complicated tale of political and corporate intrigue between two coal companies, Harman Mining Co., owned by Hugh Caperton, and A.T. Massey Coal Company. In 2002, a West Virginia jury returned a verdict against Massey Coal for "tortious interference with . . . contractual relations, fraudulent misrepresentation [and] fraudulent concealment," and assessed compensatory and punitive damages in the amount of more than $50 million for actions taken by Massey at the direction of its CEO, Don L. Blankenship.[5] Blankenship swore publicly that he would appeal. While awaiting the trial court's final disposition of several post-trial motions, Blankenship, owner of 250,000 shares (0.035 percent) of Massey stock, made independent expenditures[6] of approximately $3 million from his personal funds—not Massey funds—to oppose the reelection of incumbent Justice Warren McGraw to the West Virginia Supreme Court of Appeals.[7] McGraw's opponent,

---

[4] See Buckley, 424 U.S. 1 (1976); White, 536 U.S. 765 (2002).

[5] Brief of Petitioner at 5, Caperton v. A.T. Massey Coal Co., Inc., 129 S. Ct. 2252 (2009).

[6] We will describe Mr. Blankenship's independent speech and his contributions (or donations as the case may be) to "And for the Sake of the Kids" as "independent expenditures," though the record indicates that not all of the communications may have contained express words of election or defeat. See Buckley v. Valeo, 424 U.S. 1, 44 n.52 (1976) (per curiam). While the express advocacy distinction is of critical importance to campaign finance law, clarifying the distinction while describing the events in *Caperton* is less critical.

[7] Brief of Petitioner, *supra* note 5, at 7 ("Mr. Blankenship had donated $2,460,500 to And For The Sake Of The Kids" and "spent another $517,707 of his personal funds on independent expenditures"). West Virginia has no intermediate appellate courts, so appeals from a trial court judgment go directly to the state supreme court.

Brent Benjamin, won that election and later joined the 3-2 majority that threw out the verdict against Massey.

To read press accounts of the matter, one might think that Blankenship gave the money to Benjamin directly, and that the *Caperton* Court had thus struck a major blow against corrupt businessmen in favor of judicial impartiality.

Caperton was a "Supreme Court case with the feel of a best seller," proclaimed *USA Today*, stating that after Massey Coal was ordered to pay $50 million in a fraud lawsuit, Blankenship *"contributed* $3 million to help unseat incumbent Democratic Judge Warren McGraw in his race against a Republican, Charleston lawyer Brent Benjamin . . . "* and that "Benjamin cast a crucial vote to overturn the verdict that had favored Caperton."[8]

Other news articles depicted the facts in a similar light. *Slate* stated that, "While the appeal was still pending, Massey's CEO, Don Blankenship, spent $3 million of his own money to remove one state supreme-court justice and seat another—his *contributions* amounting to more than two thirds of all funds raised."[9] Numerous other press organizations, including the *Wall Street Journal, New York Times, Congressional Quarterly, National Law Journal,* and *The Atlantic Monthly,* also directly stated or strongly implied that Blankenship contributed $3 million directly to Benjamin's campaign.[10] Even the

---

[8] Joan Biskupic, Supreme Court Case With the Feel of a Best Seller, USA Today, February 16, 2009, available at http://www.usatoday.com/news/washington/2009-02-16-grisham-court_N.htm (emphasis added).

[9] Dahlia Lithwick, The Great Caperton Caper, Slate, June 8, 2009, available at http://slate.com/id/2220031/pagenum/all/#p2 (emphasis added).

[10] See Ashby Jones, Pregaming the Massey Coal Arguments: A Spotlight on the Lawyers, Wall Street Journal Law Blog, February 18, 2009, available at http://blogs.wsj.com/law/2009/02/18/pregaming-the-massey-coal-arguments-spotlighting-the-lawyers. (Saying the case "ask[ed] the Court to lay down a constitutional rule to define when a campaign donation is so big that the judge who received it must recuse."); Adam Liptak, Justices Tell Judges Not to Rule on Major Backers, N.Y. Times, June 9, 2009, at A1. ("[J]udges routinely accept contributions from lawyers and litigants who appear before them, and they seldom disqualify themselves for cases involving donors." The fact that Blankenship contributed merely $1,000 directly to Benjamin's campaign was mentioned only in passing thirteen paragraphs later.); Keith Perine, Conflict-of-Interest Decision Could Reverberate Among State Justices, CQ Politics Legal Beat Blog, June 8, 2009, available at http://blogs.cqpolitics.com/legal_beat/2009/06/high-court-rules-on-judicial-r.html. (Saying Blankenship "engineered massive financial contributions to Benjamin's election effort."); Tony Mauro, Supreme Court Issues Landmark Ruling on Judicial Recusal, The National Law Journal, June 8, 2009, available at http://www.law.com/jsp/nlj/PubArticleNLJ.

ABA Journal, which one might expect to be more attuned to the legal nuances between contributions given directly to Benjamin and expenditures made independently of Benjamin, stated repeatedly that Blankenship made contributions that were "accepted" by Benjamin.[11]

The press depiction of the *Caperton* facts is enough to horrify anyone who believes in impartial justice. It is also completely incorrect. Such easy facts as bribing a judicial candidate or sale of public office did not make up the record in *Caperton*. Caperton asserted, and the press regularly reported, that Brent Benjamin was "a previously unknown lawyer," perhaps in the hope that the Court would infer— or that the Court would worry the public would infer, much as John Grisham wrote in a novel loosely based on the case—that Blankenship plucked Benjamin from obscurity to run against Blankenship's nemesis, Justice McGraw, all for the price of voting for Massey when the time came.[12] In fact, Benjamin was a senior partner in one the state's largest law firms and had previously served as the treasurer of the West Virginia Republican Party. The race was also targeted by the U.S. Chamber of Commerce as one of the most important Supreme Court races of the year, all but assuring that a challenger would be well funded.[13] In any event, such subjective conjecture could not form the basis of the Court's holding in the case. If Blankenship handpicked Benjamin to run for a seat on the West Virginia Supreme Court of Appeals in exchange for an eventual vote in the case, *Caperton* would not have been before the U.S.

---

jsp?id = 1202431304207&Supreme_Court_issues_landmark_ruling_on_judicial_ recusal&slreturn = 1 (describing the money as an "outsized campaign donation"); Marc Ambinder, Out of a Grisham Novel: Supreme Court Invalidates Judicial Election, The Atlantic, June 8, 2009, available at http://politics.theatlantic.com/2009/06/ out_of_a_grisham_novel_supreme_court_invalidates_judicial_election.php (expressing skepticism by putting "independent" in quotation marks, and in the same sentence describing the $3 million as a "contribution").

[11] John Gibeaut, Caperton's Coal, ABA Journal, February 2009, available at http:// www.abajournal.com/magazine/capertons_coal/.

[12] Caperton failed to explain how "a previously unknown lawyer" could receive the endorsements of all but one of the major West Virginia daily newspapers to offer endorsements shortly before the election, as did Brent Benjamin. See also Brief of Respondent at 5, 54, Caperton v. A.T. Massey Coal Co., Inc., 129 S. Ct. 2252 (2009).

[13] Scott Wartman, Some Say Justice Race Most Important, The Herald-Dispatch, May 5, 2004, available at http://www.restorebalancewv.org/news/NewsCoverage/ Articles2004/HerDispatch_Race_05052004.htm.

Supreme Court because the law would have dealt with both men severely.[14]

In fact, Don Blankenship is a prominent West Virginia business-man with a long history of political activism. He frequently spends large sums of his own money on causes and issues important to him. His independent expenditures, Blankenship said, were not spent with the primary goal of supporting Brent Benjamin, a man with whom he had no personal connections. Rather, the independent expenditures were made to oppose the reelection of Justice McGraw, who Blankenship believed made decisions that harmed the state's economy, depressed wages, and supported trial lawyers over the working class.[15] Blankenship contributed only $1,000—the statutory maximum—to Benjamin's campaign.[16] That $1,000 contribution was the only money from Blankenship over which the Benjamin cam-paign had any control. Blankenship then gave about $2.5 million to And for the Sake of the Kids, a "527" nonprofit group that opposed McGraw's reelection.[17] Blankenship also directly spent about $500,000 on advertisements and literature opposing McGraw.[18] Thus, over 99.99 percent of the money Blankenship put towards the West Virginia Supreme Court election was spent without the consent, cooperation, or approval of Benjamin or his campaign. Blankenship's spending is known in campaign finance law as "independent expen-ditures," money for communications that advocate the election or defeat of a clearly identified candidate for office, but made entirely independently of the candidate, his party, or his agents.

It is unclear whether the independent expenditures were the cause of Benjamin's victory. Benjamin won by a reasonably comfortable seven-point margin. He had received the endorsements of every West Virginia newspaper except for one. Shortly before the election, his opponent gave a strange and widely publicized speech in which

---

[14] See generally W. Va. Code §§ 61-5A-1 (Bribery and Corrupt Practices Act), 61-5A-3 (making unlawful bribery in official and political matters), 61-5A-4 (unlawful rewarding of public servants for past behavior).

[15] Brief of Respondent, *supra* note 12, at 3.

[16] *Id.* at 4.

[17] "527s" are groups organized under §527(e) of the Internal Revenue Code for political purposes. Such groups often make independent expenditures supporting or opposing candidates or discussing candidates and political issues.

[18] Brief of Respondent, *supra* note 15, at 3–4.

he falsely claimed the West Virginia Supreme Court had approved gay marriage. These factors could have easily led to Benjamin's victory regardless of whether Blankenship had spent money on independent expenditures.

Beyond the mere fact of Blankenship's spending, nothing suggests that these independent expenditures obligated Justice Benjamin to rule in Massey's favor. Courts have recognized for years that independent expenditures, rather than help, can easily backfire, and carry the risk of "provid[ing] little assistance to the candidate's campaign" and perhaps even "prov[ing] counterproductive."[19] More specifically, during the 2004 election, "Benjamin welcomed the support of those who wanted a judge who 'would follow the law' but warned that 'if you want something in return, I'm not your candidate.'"[20] In the years between his election and *Caperton* reaching the West Virginia Supreme Court, Justice Benjamin ruled against Massey Coal in other cases "at both the merits stage, and the petition stage."[21] One decision where Justice Benjamin ruled against Massey Coal "left standing a $243 million judgment against Massey...."[22] That Justice Benjamin had previously upheld a $243 million judgment but overturned a $50 million judgment is entirely inconsistent with the assertion that Blankenship's independent expenditures caused Benjamin to make biased judgments in favor of Massey Coal.

In sum, the press portrayal of the facts in *Caperton* was and has continued to be one-sided and misleading. Blankenship did not pluck Benjamin from obscurity to serve as his handpicked opponent to McGraw. He did not contribute $3 million to Benjamin's campaign or coordinate his expenditures with the campaign to ensure Benjamin's victory. The money was spent independently, with no input, advice, or approval from Benjamin or his campaign committee. Despite the independent expenditures, Justice Benjamin, once elected, ruled against the Massey Coal company in a case with a verdict nearly five times as large as the sum at stake in *Caperton*.

---

[19] Buckley v. Valeo, 424 U.S. 1, 47 (1976).

[20] Brief of Respondent, *supra* note 15, at 5 (quoting JA319a).

[21] Brief of Respondent, *supra* note 15, at 5–6 ((citing McNeely v. Independence Coal Co., No. 04156 (W. Va. Feb. 9, 2005) and Brown v. Rawl Sales and Processing Co., No. 070889 (W. Va. Sept. 11, 2007)).

[22] Brief of Respondent, *supra* note 15, at 9.

Benjamin fell under none of the traditional standards requiring recusal. He made no public comments on the case or the principals involved. He had no pecuniary interest in the outcome. At no point in the proceedings did he exhibit bias. Nonetheless, the Court found that Benjamin's failure to recuse violated the Fourteenth Amendment's Due Process Clause.

Judicial Recusals

Given that Justice Benjamin did not act improperly under West Virginia's recusal canons, Caperton argued that Benjamin's failure to recuse violated the United States Constitution—particularly the Fourteenth Amendment's Due Process Clause. Caperton and various amici argued for a "probability of bias" standard on the idea that independent spending in a judicial campaign can be so "outsized" that it creates a "debt of gratitude" that must be repaid by the candidate once elected. It would have been better had the Supreme Court rejected this argument and left the matter of future recusal questions of this kind to state law.

Most matters "relating to judicial disqualification [do] not rise to a constitutional level."[23] The vast majority are handled by way of various recusal canons adopted by the several states. Federal case law teaches that the recusal standard "is an objective one, made from the perspective of a reasonable observer who is informed of all the surrounding facts and circumstances."[24] The ABA Model of Judicial Conduct provides that a "judge shall disqualify himself or herself in any proceeding in which the judge's impartiality might *reasonably* be questioned."[25] The standard, therefore, is largely in the eye of the beholder, and depends largely upon the life experience of the observer. "If the 'reasonable observer' must take into account State-to-State differences in deciding on which side of the sometimes line a particular item of support falls—whether or not it gave rise to a 'debt of gratitude' that, in turn, created a disqualifying 'probability of bias'—surely it makes more sense to leave recusal specifics to state policymakers, who are intimately familiar with state history

---

[23] FTC v. Cement Institute, 333 U.S. 683, 702 (1948).

[24] Microsoft Corp. v. United States, 530 U.S. 1301, 1302 (2000).

[25] ABA Model Code of Judicial Conduct Rule 2.11(A) (2007) (emphasis added).

and practice, as well as citizens' collective expectations" than to federal appellate courts.[26]

The states have ensured impartiality through various mechanisms. These include recusal rules and judicial canons, in place in almost every state. Over a dozen states currently permit litigants "peremptory" challenges to judges.[27] Nearly every state that holds judicial elections has in place contribution limits.[28] Some states, such as Alabama, have tied recusal rules to campaign contributions.[29] Proposals exist for publicly financed judicial elections.[30] The West Virginia legislature has even proposed amending the state's constitution to put in place a three-member "Judicial Recusal Commission" to issue binding decisions on "whether a . . . judge [or] justice should be recused from hearing, deciding or participating in deciding" a given case.[31]

A state's remedy against an unwanted but not unconstitutional appearance, should it want one, is in recusal canons more rigorous than due process requires; there need not be a due process violation for West Virginia to have a remedy.[32] Ironically, West Virginia's proper remedy is provided in the words of Justice Kennedy:

[26] Brief of the States of Alabama, Colorado, Delaware, Florida, Louisiana, Michigan, and Utah as Amici Curiae in Support of Respondents, Caperton v. A.T. Massey Coal Co., Inc., No. 08–22, 129 S. Ct. 2252 (2009).

[27] See Richard E. Flamm, Judicial Disqualification: Recusal and Disqualification of Judges 789–822 (2d. ed. 2007).

[28] See American Judicature Society, Judicial Campaigns and Elections: Campaign Financing, http://www.judicialselection.us/judicial_selection/campaigns_and_e-lections/campaign_financing.cfm?state (visited August 9, 2009).

[29] Ala. Code §§ 12-24-1, -2 (2008).

[30] Deborah Goldberg, Public Funding of Judicial Elections: Financing Campaigns for Fair and Impartial Courts, Judicial Independence Series, available at https://www. policyarchive.org/bitstream/handle/10207/8737/publicfundingofjudicial. pdf?sequence=1 (visited August 9, 2009). "In direct response to the controversy surrounding Justice Benjamin's non-recusal . . . West Virginia amended its campaign finance laws related to judicial elections. See 2005 W. Va. Acts, Ch. 9. The new law requires [Internal Revenue Code] §527 groups to register and disclose their financing, and further, establishes a $1000-per-election cap on individual contributions to §527 groups operating in West Virginia." See Brief of the States, *supra* note 26, at 17. Any contribution limit, it is worth mentioning, would likely be unconstitutional. See California Medical Assn. v. FEC, 453 U.S. 182, 201 (1981) (Blackmun, J., concurring); North Carolina Right to Life v. Leake, 525 F.3d 274 (4th Cir. 2008).

[31] H.R. J. Res. No. 104, 78th Leg. Sess. (W. Va. 2008).

[West Virginia] may choose to have an elected judiciary. It may strive to define those characteristics that exemplify judicial excellence. It may enshrine its definitions in a code of judicial conduct. *It may adopt recusal standards more rigorous than due process requires,* and censure judges who violate those standards. *What [West Virginia] may not do,* however, is censor what the people hear as they undertake to decide for themselves which candidate is most likely to be an exemplary judicial officer.[33]

West Virginia "cannot opt for an elected judiciary and then assert that its democracy, in order to work as desired, compels the abridgement of speech."[34] Similarly, the state cannot opt for an elected judiciary and then assert that judicial impartiality can occur only in the absence of speech.[35]

Despite the fact that rigorous recusal standards were the more workable remedy—and the one more in line with the Court's jurisprudence—the Court instead chose to stretch its due process jurisprudence beyond recognition.[36]

---

[32] See, e.g., Ashwander v. Tenn. Valley Auth., 297 U.S. 288, 347 (1936) (Court need not "formulate a rule of constitutional law broader than is required by the precise facts to which it is to be applied") (citations omitted).

[33] White, 536 U.S. at 794 (Kennedy, J., concurring) (emphasis added).

[34] *Id.* at 795.

[35] Justice O'Connor has suggested that a "State's claim that it needs to significantly restrict . . . speech in order to protect judicial impartiality is particularly troubling. If the State has a problem with judicial impartiality, it is largely one the State brought upon itself by continuing the practice of popularly electing judges." White, 536 U.S. at 792 (O'Connor, J., concurring).

[36] Massey Coal, in a brief opposing certiorari, mentioned that if, under operation of a rigorous recusal canon, "lawyers and litigants knew that their contributions or [independent] expenditures might force a judge's recusal, then they could be chilled from exercising their First Amendment rights." Brief of Respondent in Opposition to Certiorari at 22, Caperton v. A.T. Massey Coal Co., Inc., 08-22, 129 S. Ct. 2252 (2009). But this is incorrect. The interest of the citizen who runs independent expenditures in judicial elections is in convincing his fellow citizens of the better judge(s) to sit on the bench in his state. He has no interest or right in having a particular judge hear his case, just as a judge has no right to hear a particular case. Just as a litigant possesses no right to have his case heard by a particular judge, see Sinito v. United States, 750 F.2d 512, 515 (6th Cir. 1984) (collecting cases), see also 46 Am. Jur. 2d Judges § 25 ("litigants have no right to have, or not have, any particular judge of a court hear their cause"), and a judge possesses no right to hear or decide a particular case unless it is assigned to him pursuant to the standard procedures used in his jurisdiction. As the Court said in passing over 80 years ago, "In [being recused from a case] there is no serious detriment to the administration of justice nor inconvenience

Stretching the Bias Standard

Generally speaking, "bias" offends constitutional due process, thus requiring judicial recusal, in two instances. The first occurs when an adjudicator has a "direct, personal, substantial, pecuniary interest in reaching a conclusion against [a litigant] in [the] case."[37] "Bias" also occurs in special cases, such as contempt proceedings, where the adjudicator has "been the target of personal abuse or criticism from the party before him."[38]

Justice Benjamin did not have a direct, substantial, pecuniary interest in Blankenship's independent expenditures. Nor was Benjamin the target of personal abuse or criticism from Harman Mining when it appeared before him in the underlying appeal. The record shows no relationship or interest between Blankenship and Benjamin other than lawful $1,000 contributions to Justice Benjamin's campaign committee by Mr. Blankenship[39] and Massey's PAC,[40] which even Caperton conceded are not evidence of bias on the part of Justice Benjamin.[41]

Nothing in the record suggests that Blankenship handpicked Benjamin to run against Justice McGraw, either directly or through an intermediary. Benjamin chose to campaign to be a justice of the West Virginia Supreme Court independently of Blankenship and with no promises or even discussions of support. Likewise, Blankenship chose to run independent expenditures independently of Benjamin,

---

worthy of mention, for of what concern is it to a judge to preside in a particular case; of what concern to other parties to have him so preside?" Berger v. United States, 255 U.S. 22, 36 (1921).

[37] Tumey v. Ohio, 273 U.S. 510, 523 (1927).

[38] Withrow v. Larkin, 421 U.S. 35, 47 (1975). For a detailed explanation of due process, the bias standard, and the infirmity of any so-called "appearance of bias" or "probability of bias" standards, see Brief of Respondent, *supra* note 12 at 15–27.

[39] See Brief of Center for Competitive Politics as Amicus Curiae in Support of Respondents at 2, 6, Caperton v. A.T. Massey Coal Co., Inc., No. 08-22., 129 S. Ct. 2252 (2009).

[40] *Id.*

[41] See Brief of Petitioners at 16, 26, Caperton v. A.T. Massey Coal Co., Inc., 129 S. Ct. 2252 (2009) ("It is not the case that recusal is constitutionally required whenever a judge receives campaign support from a litigant . . . especially where that support represents only a small fraction of the total support for the judge's campaign.").

and may have done so regardless of the identity of McGraw's opponent.[42] There is no suggestion that Blankenship coordinated his independent spending with Benjamin or with any member of his campaign.[43] Blankenship's independent spending did not go to Benjamin personally, or even to Benjamin's campaign account, beyond the $1,000 contributions that petitioners conceded raised no due process issue.[44]

The actual facts of *Caperton,* as opposed to the hyperventilating press accounts, are easily distinguished from the Court's line of due process cases, which require a "direct, personal, substantial, pecuniary interest" on the part of a judge or adjudicator before constitutional due process is offended.[45] For example, *Tumey v. Ohio* involved a mayor, sitting as judge in Mayor's Court, who earned a percentage of every fine he assessed bootleggers.[46] *Aetna Life Ins. Co. v. Lavoie* involved a state supreme court justice who would receive damages in a pending bad-faith claim against his insurer only if he first upheld the constitutionality of bad-faith claims against all insurers.[47] *Mayberry v. Pennsylvania* involved a judge who had a personal stake in protecting his reputation from a litigant that attacked him in court, personally and repeatedly, calling him a "dirty, tyrannical old dog," and a "dirty sonofabitch."[48] And in *Ward v. Village of Monroeville*, by fining more traffic offenders, the mayor sitting as magistrate in Mayor's Court would directly—and with certainty—further his responsibilities for revenue production and law enforcement.[49]

---

[42] See *id.* at 2.

[43] See *id.* at 17 (arguing that "Justice Benjamin['s] . . . debt of gratitude in this case is not diminished by Mr. Blankenship's use of independent expenditures, rather than direct contributions"); see *id.* at 34 (acknowledging that "Justice Benjamin['s] . . . 'campaign was completely independent of any independent expenditure group,' including And For The Sake Of The Kids") (citation omitted).

[44] See *id.* at 7 ("Mr. Blankenship had donated $2,460,500 to And For The Sake Of The Kids" and "spent another $517,707 of his personal funds on independent expenditures").

[45] See, e.g., Tumey v. Ohio, 273 U.S. 510, 523 (1927).

[46] See generally Tumey v. Ohio, 273 U.S. 510 (1927).

[47] See generally Aetna Life Ins. Co. v. Lavoie, 475 U.S. 813 (1986).

[48] Mayberry v. Pennsylvania, 400 U.S. 455, 456–57 (1971).

[49] Ward v. Village of Monroeville, 409 U.S. 57 (1972).

Whether Justice Benjamin would have won but for Blankenship's actions, on the other hand, is highly speculative. Setting aside any actions by Blankenship, Benjamin raised over $800,000 for his campaign. Other groups and individuals besides Blankenship made hundreds of thousands of dollars in independent expenditures. Every daily newspaper in the state save one endorsed Benjamin for the office. Moreover, having been elected to office with no quid pro quo or even vague understanding owed to Blankenship, Benjamin could not be at all certain that his reelection more than eight years hence would result if he ruled for Massey Coal—particularly if Blankenship were the unscrupulous and ruthless character, lacking in loyalty or fair play, that the press and Caperton himself portrayed. The idea that Justice Benjamin would obtain a "'direct, personal, substantial, pecuniary'" benefit by finding for Massey Coal is at best "highly speculative."[50]

Despite the press reports suggesting otherwise, Brent Benjamin did not "get" $3 million. The most that can be said that he "got" was elected, though this was necessarily the result of many factors, not the least of which were the intervening decisions of hundreds of thousands of West Virginia voters. While candidate Benjamin could control contributions made directly to his campaign account (and had the ability to refund them), he had no control over independent expenditures made by third parties, and no ability to refuse or refund them. Nothing in the record supported the conclusion that Justice Benjamin's ruling was a payoff for Blankenship's spending. And as the independent expenditures—made two years before this case ever reached the West Virginia Supreme Court—could not be undone, Blankenship could neither withhold nor demand refund of the $3 million he had spent had Justice Benjamin ruled against Massey in the underlying appeal. As it is said in contract law, more in recognition of reality than as an aspiration, "Past consideration is no consideration."[51] That statement is at least equally true when, as in *Caperton*, there was not even the allegation of an agreement between the Blankenship and Benjamin.

---

[50] Lavoie, 475 U.S. at 822 (citation omitted), 826.

[51] See, e.g., Murray v. Lichtman, 339 F.2d 749, 752 n.5 (D.C. Cir. 1964) (citing Glascock v. Comm'r of Internal Revenue, 104 F.2d 475, 477 (4th Cir. 1939) and 1 Williston on Contracts § 142 (3d ed. 1957)).

Furthermore, if reelection or defeat were all that was at stake for Justice Benjamin eight years hence, Benjamin's actions, the resulting media firestorm, and anger throughout West Virginia and many quarters of this nation, may far from ensure his reelection but rather damage his prospects for it. In short, Benjamin's failure to recuse in *Caperton* may actually make him vulnerable at reelection time.[52]

---

[52] See, e.g., Allan N. Karlin & John Cooper, Editorial, Perception That Justice Can Be Bought Harms the Judiciary, The Sunday Gazette Mail (Charleston, W. Va.), Mar. 2, 2008, at 3C ("It is time to say publicly what attorneys across the state are saying privately: Justice Brent Benjamin needs to . . . step down from hearing cases involving Massey Energy and its subsidiaries. His continued involvement in Massey litigation endangers the public perception of the integrity of the Supreme Court of Appeals."); Editorial, Finally, Register Herald (Beckley, W. Va.), Feb. 18, 2008 ("Benjamin clearly was aided by Blankenship's multi-million dollar campaign against incumbent Warren McGraw and even[ ] though the justice has stated unequivocally he isn't influenced by Blankenship, it just doesn't look good."); Editorial, Bravo, Charleston Gazette (W. Va.), Feb. 16, 2008, at 4A ("Benjamin remains the only Massey-connected justice still presiding over Massey cases. Clearly, for the sake of impartiality, he should . . . recus[e] himself from all Massey cases."); William Kistner, Justice for Sale, American RadioWorks (2005), available at http://americanradioworks.publicradio.org/features/judges ("One of [Justice Benjamin's] major backers was the CEO of Massey Energy Company, the largest coal producer in the region. The company happened to be fighting off a major lawsuit headed to the West Virginia Supreme Court. That prompted many in these parts to say that Massey was out to buy itself a judge."); Cecil E. Roberts, Editorial, Blankenship's Hollow Rhetoric: His Money Defeated McGraw, Now He Must Help Miners, Charleston Gazette (W. Va.), Dec. 13, 2004, at P5A ("Give us a break, Don. . . . The real reason you bought the state Supreme Court seat is because Massey will soon stand before that court to try to rid itself of a $50 million jury penalty for putting . . . Harman Mining, out of business."); Edward Peeks, Editorial, How Does Political Cash Help Uninsured?, Charleston Gazette (W. Va.), Nov. 9, 2004, at 2D ("[T]hese voices raise the question of vote buying to a new high in politics. . . . It's a new day in political campaign financing for party, candidate and message by any and every means. . . . [T]he U.S. Supreme Court has said spending one's money on a political message is a right of free speech."); Brad McElhinny, Next Court Race Could Be Just As Nasty: Justice Larry Starcher Could Be a Target in 2008 If He Seeks To Stay on Bench, Charleston Daily Mail (W. Va.), Nov. 4, 2004, at 1A (quoting former West Virginia Supreme Court Justice Richard Neely as stating: "It's an absolute disaster for the judiciary. . . . Now every seat on the Supreme Court is for sale. . . . Judges will be required to dance with the one that brung them. . . . When someone like Don Blankenship offers you $3 million, you can't turn it down."); Carol Morello, W. Va. Supreme Court Justice Defeated in Rancorous Contest, Wash. Post, Nov. 4, 2004, at A15 (quoting Beth White, a coordinator with West Virginia Consumers for Justice, a group that ran pro-McGraw ads during the campaign, as stating: "It proves that West Virginia Supreme Court seats were for sale."); Cf. Adam Liptak, Judicial Races in Several States Become Partisan Battlegrounds, N.Y. Times, Oct. 24, 2004, at A1; Paul J. Nyden, Coal Companies Provide Big Campaign Bucks: Brent

Justice Benjamin was almost certainly aware of this at the time he heard the Massey matters, both on the merits and in recusal motions. As Justice Sandra Day O'Connor has stated while criticizing the election of judges generally, "[e]lected judges cannot help being aware that if the public is not satisfied with the outcome of a particular case, it could hurt their reelection prospects."[53] For years, in the face of numerous studies that have found that campaign contributions play no statistically significant role in legislator behavior,[54] those favoring restrictions on political speech in the form of campaign contributions and independent expenditures have argued that the influence to be feared comes in issues outside the limelight.[55] If, however, there was ever a judicial "issue" of high public interest, the *Caperton* case was it. Justice Benjamin will face a tough reelection contest for his alleged role in the Massey affair and his failure to recuse—and he knew it at the time he decided not to do so.[56] If we are to presume a bias or a "probability of bias," it would as likely have been to rule *against* Massey in the underlying action, not for it.

In reaching its decision, the Court stepped well beyond its pecuniary-interest and contempt-proceeding precedents to broaden due process violations to ill-defined areas.

Caperton's Effects on Campaign Finance

For all the problems the Court's opinion may create for due process jurisprudence and judicial credibility, the remaking of due process

Benjamin Raking in Heaviest Contributions, Charleston Gazette (W. Va.), Oct. 15, 2004, at 1A.

[53] White, 536 U.S. at 789 (O'Connor, J., concurring).

[54] See Stephen Ansolabehere, John de Figueiredo, and James M. Snyder Jr., Why Is There So Little Money in U.S. Politics?, 17 J. Econ. Perspectives 105 (2003); see also Stephen Ansolabehere, Rebecca Lessem & James M. Snyder, Jr., The Orientation of Newspaper Endorsements in U.S. Elections, 1940–2002, 1 Q. J. of Pol. Sci. 393, 394 & n.2 (2006) (collecting citations and data from a number of studies, and observing that a "range of studies of aggregate election results, survey data, and laboratory experiments find that when endorsements occur they typically increase the vote share of the endorsed candidate by about 1 to 5 percentage points").

[55] See e.g., E. Joshua Rosenkranz, Faulty Assumptions in 'Faulty Assumptions', 30 Conn. L. Rev. 867, 879 (1998) (arguing that studies showing that campaign contributions have little effect on a legislator's behavior should be disregarded because the influence of contributions is found in "stealth issues . . . on which public attention is not focused").

[56] See Brief of Center for Competitive Politics as Amicus Curiae in Support of Respondents at 11, Caperton v. A.T. Massey Coal Co., Inc., No. 08-22, 129 S. Ct. 2252 (2009).

jurisprudence may be the less interesting dynamic at play in the *Caperton* case. Indeed, we believe that the real issue in the case, for much of the press, for the American Bar Association, and certainly for some amici, was to chip away at judicial elections in general and at constitutional protections for independent expenditures for all elections in particular.

Caperton argued in the Supreme Court that "[t]he likelihood that Justice Benjamin harbored, and sought to repay [a] debt of gratitude ... is *not diminished* by Mr. Blankenship's use of independent expenditures, rather than direct contributions, to furnish his financial support."[57]

Since *Buckley v. Valeo*,[58] however, the Court has repeatedly held that independent expenditures, such as those made by Blankenship in the Benjamin-McGraw race, cannot be limited by the legislature.[59] Contribution limits "prevent[ ] corruption and the appearance of corruption spawned by the real or imagined coercive influence of large financial contributions on candidates' positions," says *Buckley*, "while leaving persons free to engage in independent political expression and to associate actively through volunteering their services."[60]

Further, the *Buckley* Court noted that, "Unlike [direct candidate] contributions, ... independent expenditures may well provide little assistance to the candidate's campaign and indeed may prove counterproductive."[61] As the Court explained, the "absence of prearrangement and coordination of an expenditure with the candidate or his agent not only undermines the value of the expenditure to the candidate, but also alleviates the danger that expenditures will be

---

[57] Brief of Petitioner, *supra* note 5, at 17 (emphasis added).

[58] 424 U.S. 1 (1976).

[59] The single narrow exception to this statement, so-called "corporate-form corruption," is not applicable to this case. See Austin v. Mich. State Chamber of Commerce, 494 U.S. 652, 660 (1990) (identifying the "corrosive and distorting effects of immense aggregations of wealth that are accumulated with the help of the corporate form and that have little or no correlation to the public's support for the corporation's political ideas" as "a different type of corruption").

[60] 424 U.S. at 25, 28.

[61] *Id.* at 46.

given as a quid pro quo for improper commitments from the candidate."[62] The Court's analysis retains its validity today. For example, Professor Roy Schotland has documented numerous instances in which independent expenditures in state judicial elections have backfired against the preferred candidate.[63] Judicial elections are elections, no less so than any other. "The difference between judicial and legislative elections" is "greatly exaggerate[d]," and "the First Amendment does not permit . . . leaving the principle of elections in place while preventing . . . discussi[on concerning] what the elections are about."[64]

Therefore, even under a "probability of bias" standard to determine whether judicial recusal was mandated by the Fourteenth Amendment's Due Process Clause, independent expenditures should not create a "probability of bias," just as independent expenditures do not create "corruption" or even the "appearance of corruption." The *Buckley* Court held that "large independent expenditures . . . do[ ] not . . . appear to pose dangers of real or apparent

---

[62] *Id.* at 46–47. In his brief to the Supreme Court, Caperton mischaracterized and attempted to rely on a statement from Federal Election Commission v. Wisconsin Right to Life, Inc. (WRTL II), 127 S. Ct. 2652, 2672 (2007), to assert that "there is no reason to believe Justice Benjamin is any less likely to feel a debt of gratitude to Mr. Blankenship because . . . his financial support was provided through" wholly independent, rather than direct, means. See Brief of Petioners, *supra* note 41, at 34 (quoting WRTL II, 127 S. Ct. at 2672). In *WRTL II,* Chief Justice John Roberts wrote: "We have suggested that this interest [in preventing corruption] might also justify limits on electioneering *expenditures* because it may be that, in some circumstances, 'large independent expenditures pose the same dangers of actual or apparent *quid pro quo* arrangements as do large contributions.'" 127 S. Ct. at 2672 (quoting Buckley, 424 U.S. at 45). Chief Justice Roberts, in turn, was quoting *Buckley,* which stated: "First, assuming, *arguendo,* that large independent expenditures pose the same dangers of actual or apparent *quid pro quo* arrangements as do large contributions, [FECA's expenditure limit] does not provide an answer that sufficiently relates to the elimination of those dangers." 424 U.S. at 45. So what the Court has really said on the topic is not the unequivocal statement that "in some circumstances, large independent expenditures pose the same dangers of actual or apparent *quid pro quo* arrangements as do large contributions," but rather the equivocal statement that, *for the purpose of argument,* the Supreme Court has *suggested* that the interest in combating corruption *might* justify *some* limits on expenditures because it *may* be, in *some* circumstances, that they pose a risk of corruption. And then this Court proceeded to strike down expenditure limits in FECA.

[63] See, e.g., Roy A. Schotland, Comment on Professor Carrington's Article "The Independence and Democratic Accountability of the Supreme Court of Ohio," 30 Cap. U. L. Rev. 489, 490 (2002).

[64] See generally Republican Party of Minnesota v. White, 536 U.S. 765, 784–88 (2002).

corruption comparable to those identified with large [direct] campaign contributions."[65] So long as a state chooses its judges by popular election, those elections must include the speech of independent speakers. The "'power to dispense with elections altogether does not include the lesser power to conduct elections under conditions of state-imposed voter ignorance. If the state chooses to tap the energy and the legitimizing power of the democratic process, it must accord the participants in that process ... the First Amendment rights that attach to their roles.'"[66] According participants the free speech and association rights that attach to their roles in judicial elections is no violation of due process, for history shows that "[j]udicial elections were generally partisan during" the 19th and early 20th centuries, with "the movement toward nonpartisan judicial elections not even beginning until the 1870s."[67]

Caperton argued, however, that Blankenship's, "strong personal and professional interest in the outcome of the case ... created a compelling reason for Justice Benjamin to [have and] repay [a] debt of gratitude to Mr. Blankenship by casting the deciding vote in Massey's favor."[68] In short, Caperton argued that candidate Benjamin "benefited" from Blankenship's spending, was "grateful" for it, and, thus, was *compelled* to repay Blankenship for it.

Before *Caperton*, the U.S. Supreme Court had explicitly rejected the argument that Congress may restrict the funding of independent activity that merely "benefits" a candidate.[69] The related argument—

[65] Federal Election Comm'n v. Nat'l Conservative Political Action Comm., 470 U.S. 480, 497 (1985) ("In *Buckley* we struck down the FECA's limitation on individuals' independent expenditures because we found no tendency in such expenditures, uncoordinated with the candidate or his campaign, to corrupt or to give the appearance of corruption. For similar reasons, we also find [the current] limitation on independent expenditures ... to be constitutionally infirm.").

[66] White, 536 U.S. at 788 (quoting Renne v. Geary, 501 U.S. 312, 349 (1991) (Marshall, J., dissenting)) (citation omitted).

[67] *Id.* at 785.

[68] Brief of Petitioner at 17, Caperton v. A.T. Massey Coal Co., Inc., No. 08-22, 129 S. Ct. 2252 (2009).

[69] See, e.g., McConnell v. Fed. Election Comm'n, 540 U.S. 93, 156 n.51 (2003) ("Congress could not regulate financial contributions to political talk show hosts or newspaper editors on the sole basis that their activities conferred a benefit on the candidate.") (emphasis in original) ; see also *id.* at 354–55 (Rehnquist, C.J., dissenting). That the independent groups addressed were members of the institutional press is of no constitutional significance. "[The] purpose of the Constitution was not to erect the press into a privileged institution but to protect all persons in their right to print

that Justice Benjamin's alleged "gratitude" for Blankenship's independent expenditures caused Justice Benjamin to be unconstitutionally biased on behalf of Massey—would prove too much. Its logic can be extended to find "bias" in any of a range of other independent political activity, in multiple forms and from multiple actors, long recognized as vital to democracy. A group of community organizers that work to get out the vote in neighborhoods that disproportionately support a candidate would "benefit" that candidate and may make him "grateful." But would it violate due process to have those organizations appear in a case before him? What about the community members who lead or participate in the organization?

Candidates may enjoy disproportionate popularity among environmentalists, or women, or union members, or residents of a certain geographical area, etc.; the votes of such interest groups are also valuable to the candidate. Does it violate due process for a judge to sit in a case where these organizations, or their members or supporters, appear before him?

Millions of dollars were spent by non-profit organizations in West Virginia opposing candidate Benjamin. One independent opponent organization, West Virginia Consumers for Justice, received approximately $2 million in contributions, including approximately $1.5 million from members of the plaintiffs' bar, as well as $10,000 from Caperton himself and $15,000 from the law firm that represented him.[70] There were other independent groups besides those supported by Blankenship that opposed McGraw. Citizens for Quality Health Care, funded in part by the West Virginia Chamber of Commerce, spent nearly $370,000 on anti-McGraw advertisements.[71] Citizens Against Lawsuit Abuse also ran critical ads.[72] Would it violate the

---

what they will as well as to utter it. '[The] liberty of the press is no greater and no less' than the liberty of every citizen of the Republic." First Nat'l Bank of Boston v. Bellotti, 435 U.S. 765, 802 (1978) (Burger, C.J., concurring) (quoting Pennekamp v. Florida, 328 U.S. 331, 364 (1946) (Frankfurter, J., concurring) (internal quotation marks and citation omitted)).

[70] See John O'Brien, Caperton Was Anti-Benjamin From the Start, W. Va. Record, Jan. 24, 2008, available at https://wvrecord.com/news/206942-caperton-was-anti-benjamin-from-the-start.

[71] See Paul J. Nyden, Coal, Doctors' Groups Donated to Anti-McGraw Effort: Massey President Donald Blankenship Remains Largest Donor, Charleston Gazette, Jan. 7, 2005, at P5A.

[72] See Juliet A. Terry, Benjamin Hopes to Shine Light on Justice, State J., Nov. 5, 2004, at 4.

Fourteenth Amendment's Due Process Clause if Justice Benjamin—
or Justice Warren McGraw had he won—were to hear a case involving any of these parties? Or heard a matter involving any of their
contributors, members, volunteers, or supporters?

Judicial candidates and officeholders often feel gratitude toward
media outlets that endorse their candidacies. Studies of the electoral
effects of newspaper endorsements indicate that such endorsements
are typically worth between one and five percentage points to a
candidate.[73] Again, by this logic media outlets could not be permitted
to appear before the West Virginia Supreme Court—or, for that
matter, any elected bench—against another party while they continue their tradition of judicial candidate endorsements, lest the
media outlets open the door to "bias" or its "appearance."

Evidence, suggests, however, that the public does not perceive
"gratitude" or an "appearance of gratitude" to be the pervasive
problem asserted by Caperton. A survey conducted by Rasmussen
Reports in 2008 found that, "55% believe media bias is more of a
problem than big campaign contributions" while just 36% disagree.[74]
The survey also found that just "22% believe it would be a good
idea to ban all campaign commercials so that voters could receive
information on . . . campaign[s] only from the news media and the
internet. Sixty-six percent (66%) disagree and think that . . . it's better
to put up with an election-year barrage of advertising rather than
rely on the news media."[75]

Nonetheless, Caperton asserted that "if a litigant's or attorney's
campaign support for a judge generates an objective probability of
bias in favor of one of the parties to a case, due process requires the
judge's recusal."[76] In one sense, this assertion merely begged the

---

[73] Stephen Ansolabehere, Rebecca Lessem & James M. Snyder Jr., The Orientation
of Newspaper Endorsements in U.S. Elections, 1940–2002, 1 Q. J. of Pol. Sci. 393, 394
& n.2 (2006) (collecting citations and data from a number of studies, and observing
that a "range of studies of aggregate election results, survey data, and laboratory
experiments find that when endorsements occur they typically increase the vote share
of the endorsed candidate by about 1 to 5 percentage points").

[74] Rasmussen Reports, 55% Say Media Bias Bigger Problem than Campaign Cash,
Aug. 11, 2008, available at http://www.rasmussenreports.com/public_content/
politics/election_20082/2008_presidential_election/55_say_media_bias_bigger_
problem_than_campaign_cash.

[75] Id.

[76] Brief of Petitioner, *supra* note 41, at 27.

question: does independent campaign support, "generate[ ] an objective probability of bias"? The Court's campaign finance jurisprudence would seem to say no. Moreover, the assertion had already been addressed and rejected by the Court in *White*, when it ruled that, "if . . . it violates due process for a judge to sit in a case in which ruling one way rather than another increases his prospects for reelection, then—quite simply—the practice of electing judges is itself a violation of due process."[77] But clearly the practice of electing judges is not a violation of due process. Indeed, it is no violation of the federalism principles embodied in the U.S. Constitution.

Another problem with the Court's decision can be found in considering what would have occurred had Justice McGraw won reelection. Whatever recusal standard would apply to Justice Benjamin would presumably apply equally to his opponent, for in a system of winner-take-all elections, whether the $3 million was spent independently to support the judicial candidate or to oppose him matters little to the perceived impartiality of the judge. The flip side of spending for Benjamin is spending against McGraw; the flip side of "gratitude" is anger and revenge; of "benefit," harm. Surely if Justice Benjamin's involvement created an appearance of bias, so would that of Justice McGraw, the target of Blankenship's expenditures—only the bias would then have been against Massey Coal instead of for it. Caperton and his amici argued that Blankenship set out to "change the composition" of the West Virginia Supreme Court that would hear Massey's appeal.[78] Beyond the implied suggestion that this was somehow an illegitimate goal, it should be apparent that under the Court's due process and recusal theory, Blankenship would have been guaranteed success in this endeavor, as his independent speech would have rid him of incumbent Justice Warren McGraw in either case! Under the Court's ruling, either recusal will be a one-way street, or the Blankenships of the world will know how to rid themselves of their Justices McGraw.

Caperton argued that "the timing of Mr. Blankenship's campaign support strongly suggests that it was intended to influence the outcome of this $50 million appeal."[79] One may certainly conclude that

---

[77] White, 536 U.S. at 782.

[78] Brief of Petitioner, *supra* note 5, at 1.

[79] *Id.*

Blankenship *intended* to defeat incumbent McGraw, or even that Blankenship *intended* that his spending would result in the election of a judge more likely than incumbent Justice McGraw to overturn a verdict in the Massey case. This is, after all, the "intent" of any independent speaker in any election campaign: to defeat one candidate for office and elect another, and many such speakers often "intend"—or at least hope—that after an election the policy or approach of one public official will end and that another will take its place. But historically, the Court has held that "a speaker's motivation is entirely irrelevant to the question of constitutional protection."[80]

The Supreme Court in *Buckley* has "already rejected an intent-and-effect test for distinguishing between discussions of issues and candidates."[81] It should have rejected a test that measures the intent of speakers acting wholly independently of an adjudicator to decide which recusal motions must be granted or rejected under the Fourteenth Amendment's Due Process Clause. Chief Justice John Roberts argued in his plurality opinion in *Wisconsin Right to Life II,* a test focused on the speaker's intent could lead to the "bizarre result" that identical ads aired at the same time would be limited for one speaker, but not for another. Similarly, if intent of the spender matters to the due process analysis, identical ads costing the same amount would cause no bias and require no recusal for one group of litigants, but would create bias and demand recusal for another.[82]

If Independent Expenditures Can Cause "Bias" in a Judge, Might They Cause "Corruption" in a Legislator?

"Corruption," as defined in *Buckley,* is the danger of quid pro quo arrangements.[83] "Bias," as delineated in this Court's opinions, seems strikingly similar. For example, in *Tumey v. Ohio,* bias was found when an adjudicator earned a percentage of the penalty upon finding bootleggers guilty.[84] In *Aetna Life Ins. Co. v. Lavoie,* the Court mandated recusal where a judge upheld the constitutionality of bad-faith claims against all insurers *for* damages while he had pending

---

[80] WRTL II, 127 S. Ct. at 2665–66 (citation omitted).

[81] *Id.* at 2665 (citing Buckley, 424 U.S. at 43–44).

[82] *Id.* at 2666.

[83] See 424 U.S. at 26–27.

[84] 273 U.S. 510 (1927).

his own bad-faith claim against his insurer.[85] Bias has also been found where a judge found a man guilty *to burnish* his reputation as a one-man grand juror,[86] or fined a defendant *to burnish* his reputation as the municipality's revenue generator and law enforcer.[87]

But the activity captured in the "bias" standard is more acute or insidious than the activity captured by the "corruption" standard because bias requires a direct, substantial, personal or pecuniary interest in reaching a conclusion against a litigant in the case.[88] Campaign contributions, however, *cannot* convey a direct, personal, or pecuniary interest in the legislative candidate—campaign finance law forbids it.[89] Bribery, the sale of votes for personal benefit, covers legislators and is already illegal, as the *Buckley* Court acknowledged when it held that limiting campaign contributions serves a compelling state interest that goes beyond bribery statutes.[90]

Independent expenditures, on the other hand, have historically not been found to pose a threat of "corruption" or the "appearance of corruption"; the *Buckley* Court was clear about that when it said that "[u]nlike contributions, . . . independent expenditures may . . . provide little assistance to the candidate's campaign and . . . may prove counterproductive."[91] Therefore, we are left with the following propositions: (1) Independent expenditures in legislative elections do not pose a threat of "corruption or its appearance"; (2) the "corruption or its appearance" standard must mark activity short of conferring personal benefits on the legislator supported, for the reasons discussed above; but (3) "bias" in the judiciary, *does* require a direct, personal, pecuniary benefit to judge once elected; and yet, after Caperton, (4) independent expenditures cause "bias or its probability" in a judge.

The holding in *Caperton,* and the resulting jumble of propositions, suggests that if independent expenditures create the probability of

---

[85] 475 U.S. 813 (1986).

[86] In re Murchison, 349 U.S. 133 (1955).

[87] Ward v. Village of Monroeville, 409 U.S. 57 (1972).

[88] See, e.g., Tumey, 273 U.S. at 523; accord Lavoie, 475 U.S. at 822.

[89] Federal campaign finance law prohibits the use of contributions for the personal benefit of any person. See 2 U.S.C. § 439a.

[90] 424 U.S. at 27–28.

[91] 424 U.S. at 47.

bias, they must also create at least the "appearance of corruption," that is, the possibility that political actors will respond to the wishes of donors rather than constituents.

Indeed, it would seem that if independent expenditures can create "bias" or its "probability" in a judge, then the edifice the Court has painstakingly erected to shelter independent political speakers from the threat of government-imposed limitations would collapse. For if independent expenditures would create the greater, more direct, personal, substantial, pecuniary benefit necessary to a finding of "bias," then independent expenditures must always create the lesser potential benefit necessary to a finding an "appearance of corruption," leading inexorably—if taken seriously—to the overruling of *Buckley,* as well as of *Federal Election Commission v. Massachusetts Citizens for Life, Inc.* (MCFL),[92] and of *Randall v. Sorrell.*[93]

The difference between the judicial and legislative functions is a weak distinction for finding that independent expenditures that cannot create a threat of quid pro quo in a legislator *must* create a direct, personal or pecuniary interest in a judge. While it is true that a judge has absolutely no interest in the outcome of the dispute on the specific parties before the bench, in fact judges are increasingly called upon to interpret statutes and constitutional provisions in ways that broadly affect public policy. At the same time, in an age of legislative earmarking, where benefits are granted or denied to specific members of society after intense lobbying and deliberation in much the same way that victory or defeat is given to parties arguing before a court, a tribunal may infer that independent expenditures that would cause bias in a judge must cause corruption in a legislator.

While the Supreme Court has never "assert[ed] nor impli[ed] that the First Amendment requires campaigns for judicial office to sound the same as those for legislative office,"[94] we must recognize that if

---

[92] 479 U.S. 238 (1986) (contribution limits on independent expenditures funded by individuals unconstitutional).

[93] 548 U.S. 230 (2006) (expenditure limits on candidate speech unconstitutional). Moreover, should independent expenditures become limited or prohibited on such a basis, *Buckley's* holding regarding limits on contributions to candidate campaigns must be reexamined, for that holding relied in part on the idea that First Amendment burdens were minimized because speakers could still make independent expenditures. Buckley, 424 U.S. at 28.

[94] White, 536 U.S. at 783.

the mere existence of an independent expenditure campaign in a judicial election creates an unconstitutional threat of "bias" or its "appearance" in a judge, then courts are likely, over time, to infer that the mere existence of independent expenditures in legislative elections must create the threat of "corruption" or its "appearance" in legislators. The *Caperton* Court should have avoided the confusion and the unavoidable weakening of protections for core independent political speech that would flow from such a holding under the Fourteenth Amendment's Due Process Clause.

We think it fair to suggest that for some of the amici that supported Caperton, this case was less about due process than about getting the Court to overrule *sub rosa Buckley*'s protections for independent expenditures in election campaigns[95] despite the Court's repeated

---

[95] We cannot help but suggest that petitioners' amici are champing at the bit for any finding in the affirmative, to the eventual detriment of the line drawn consistently by the Court since *Buckley*. Such amici have participated in most any and every effort to impose or further campaign expenditure and/or contribution limits for independent speakers. See, e.g., Davis v. Fed. Election Comm'n, 128 S. Ct. 2859 (2008) (Democracy 21, Campaign Legal Center, Brennan Center for Justice, and Public Citizen Amicus Br.); Federal Election Comm'n v. Wis. Right to Life, Inc., 127 S. Ct. 2652 (2007) (Brennan Center for Justice Amicus Br.); Randall v. Sorrell, 548 U.S. 230 (2006) (Brennan Center for Justice Amicus Br.) (Campaign Legal Center, Democracy 21, and Public Citizen Amicus Br.); McConnell v. Fed. Election Comm'n, 540 U.S. 93 (2003) (Brennan Center for Justice, Campaign Legal Center, Democracy 21, and Public Citizen for Intervenor-Defendants Br.) (Center for Responsive Politics Amicus Br.) (Common Cause and AARP Amicus Br.); Federal Election Comm'n v. Beaumont, 539 U.S. 146 (2003) (Public Citizen, Common Cause, Democracy 21, Campaign and Media Legal Center, and Center for Responsive Politics Amicus Br.); San Jose Silicon Valley Chamber of Commerce Political Action Comm. v. City of San Jose, 546 F.3d 1087 (9th Cir. 2008) (Campaign Legal Center Amicus Br.); Duke v. Leake, 524 F.3d 427 (4th Cir. 2008) (Campaign Legal Center Amicus Br.); North Carolina Right to Life, Inc. v. Leake, 482 F. Supp. 2d 686 (E.D.N.C. 2007) (Campaign Legal Center and Democracy 21 Amicus Br.), aff'd in part and rev'd in part, 525 F.3d 274 (4th Cir. 2008); Real Truth About Obama, Inc. v. Fed. Election Comm'n, No. 3:08-CV-483, 2008 U.S. Dist. LEXIS 73551 (E.D. Va. 2008) (Campaign Legal Center and Democracy 21 Amicus Br.), appeal pending, No. 08-1977 (4th Cir. notice of appeal filed Sept. 12, 2008, briefing completed Nov. 12, 2008) (Campaign Legal Center and Democracy 21 Amicus Br.); Ohio Right to Life Society, Inc. v. Ohio Elections Comm'n, No. 2:08-CV-492, 2008 U.S. Dist. LEXIS 79165 (S.D. Ohio 2008) (Campaign Legal Center and Ohio Citizen Action Amicus Br.); SpeechNow.org v. Fed. Election Comm'n, 567 F. Supp. 2d 70 (D.D.C. 2008) (Campaign Legal Center and Democracy 21 Amicus Br.); Committee on Jobs Candidate Advocacy Fund v. Herrera, No. C 07-3199 JSW, 2007 U.S. Dist. LEXIS 73736 (N.D. Cal. 2007) (California Clean Money Campaign, California Common Cause, Campaign Legal Center, and Center for Governmental Studies Amicus Br.).

rejection of their overtures in *Randall, MCFL,* and *California Medical Association v. Federal Election Commission,*[96] all the way back to *Buckley.*

As one of these amici in *Caperton* breezily said to the Court, "*distinctions* between contributions and expenditures have only marginal salience when it comes to the fundamental fairness concerns at the core of due process," and that "[t]his case ... allows the Court to resolve the due process issues *without any need for inquiry* into the permissibility of restrictions on expenditures supporting a candidate vis-à-vis contributions to a candidate."[97]

But the distinction is an important one, even in matters of due process. And, if the question of protections for independent speech arise in the future, we would expect these amici to cite *Caperton* for the proposition that independent political expenditures enjoy less constitutional protection.

Can *Caperton* Be Cabined?

The Court began with a broad "standard" in *Caperton*:

> We conclude that there is a serious risk of actual bias ... when a person with a personal stake in a particular case had a significant and disproportionate influence in placing the judge on the case by raising funds or directing the judge's election campaign when the case was pending or imminent. The inquiry centers on the contribution's relative size in comparison to the total amount of money contributed to the campaign, the total amount spent in the election, and the apparent effect such contribution had on the outcome of the election.[98]

Kennedy, who wrote the majority opinion in *Caperton,* has stated that "[j]udicial integrity is ... a state interest of the highest order."[99]

See also Brennan Center for Justice, If *Buckley* Fell: A First Amendment Blueprint for Regulating Money in Politics (2000).

[96] 453 U.S. 182, 203 (1981) (Blackmun, J., concurring) (contribution limits on independent expenditures funded by individuals unconstitutional).

[97] Brief for the Brennan Center for Justice at NYU School of Law, The Campaign Legal Center, and The Reform Institute as Amicus Curiae In Support of Petitioners at 23, Caperton v. A.T. Massey Coal Co., Inc., No. 08-22, 129 S. Ct. 2252 (2009) (emphasis added).

[98] Caperton, 129 S. Ct. at 2263–64.

[99] Republican Party of Minn. v. White, 536 U.S. 765, 793 (Kennedy, J., concurring).

At the same time, Kennedy has been one of the Court's strongest voices for free speech in the realm of campaign finance.

Thus it is almost certainly no accident that Kennedy's *Caperton* opinion struggles to define the case as an outlier that should have no broad precedential value. Interestingly, the *Caperton* opinion did not describe Blankenship's spending as what it was: "independent expenditures." Instead, it repeatedly referred to Blankenship's spending as "contributions." This use of nomenclature may allow the Court to escape the logical problems for the protection of independent expenditures that seem to have been created by the ruling in *Caperton*. Justice Kennedy's opinion for the majority shows every sign of attempting to side for Caperton and Harman Coal while saving the Court's traditional distinction between independent expenditures and contributions in the campaign finance realm.

For openers, as noted, Kennedy goes along with the popular press descriptions of the facts and some of the briefs supporting Caperton. These descriptions, as we have noted, routinely describe Blankenship's activity in terms of "contributions," "contributed," etc., and Justice Kennedy's opinion likewise calls Blankenship's expenditures "contributions." Collapsing the distinction may reflect poor draftsmanship or even a poor understanding of the facts. It may even reflect a willingness to abandon the contribution/expenditure distinction at the center of post-*Buckley* campaign finance law. But we are inclined to believe the possibility that it is intentional, accepting the plaintiff's legally inaccurate description of the facts in order to avoid doing damage to the Court's traditional protection for independent expenditures.

It is also worth noting that the majority opinion has no concurrences from the Court's liberals—not even from Justice John Paul Stevens, who has long criticized the contribution/expenditure distinction from a pro-regulatory viewpoint. None wrote to say, "This is the problem with independent spending in campaigns." Perhaps, even, Justice Kennedy would not have allowed it.

Whatever the reasons for accepting the language of "contributions" rather than the factually correct language of "expenditures," Kennedy works valiantly to describe the case as a one-of-a-kind endeavor. Eight times he refers to the facts as "extreme" five times he references their "extraordinary" nature, and his opinion eventually notes that the *Caperton* case is one a kind, a *Bush v. Gore* of due process law: "The parties point to no other instance involving judicial campaign contributions that presents a potential for bias comparable to the circumstances in this case."[100]

Whether Kennedy's effort to limit *Caperton* to its "extreme" facts will succeed may depend on the interpretation given the case by lower courts and the first few, if any, "*Caperton* motions" to reach the Supreme Court. If the case is interpreted narrowly, *Caperton* motions may be a brief phenomenon, though sporadic cases can be expected to test the limits of *Caperton* over time. As Chief Justice Roberts noted, *Caperton* raises many more questions than it answers.[101] And Justice Antonin Scalia is correct that the *Caperton* majority runs into trouble by believing every perceived injustice can be cured by constitutional law.[102] But if *Caperton* motions are regularly granted, they will become a normal weapon in legal practice, and over time each such motion will argue for a racheting down of the type of factual situation requiring recusal.

While due process will never take a backseat to other constitutional considerations, judicial elections, even as we have known them, seem relatively safe for now. *White* makes clear that the standard for speech in judicial elections is strict scrutiny,[103] and there is little reason to think that *Caperton* will drive the Court to invalidate the states' power to choose judges by elections rather than by appointments. Nevertheless, if the Court were ever to accept greater limits on speech in judicial elections, the seed of such a decision will have been planted in *Caperton*.

As to whether *Caperton* marks an intention or a willingness to undermine the Court's campaign finance jurisprudence, we may soon know. Despite its choice of nomenclature—"contributions" instead of "expenditures"—the risk with *Caperton* is that it will cast doubt upon the constitutionality of independent expenditures in judicial, legislative, and executive elections. If independent expenditures can cause bias in a judge, why can't they cause corruption in a legislator?

---

[100] Caperton, 129 S. Ct. at 2265 (emphasis added).

[101] *Id.* at 2267.

[102] *Id.* at 2275.

[103] Republican Party of Minnesota v. White, 536 U.S. 765, 774–75 (2002).

This term, in *Citizens United v. Federal Election Commission*,[104] the Court took the unique step of ordering reargument and supplemental briefing on the questions of overruling *Austin v. Michigan Chamber of Commerce*[105] and the part of *McConnell v. Federal Election Commission*[106] that upheld a ban on pre-election advertising paid for by corporations and unions that was premised on *Austin*. Citizens United ran a video-on-demand documentary criticizing then-presidential primary candidate, Hillary Rodham Clinton. The FEC pulled the plug on *Hillary: The Movie* because the film ran over satellite television too close to a primary election and was paid for with corporate funds. In other words, independent communications were banned, despite their independence.

If the Court takes the opportunity to overrule *Austin*, as we believe it should, it would have to do so based on the independence of the communications made by Citizens United: other rationales in *Austin*, such as the "corrosive and distorting effects of immense aggregations of wealth" obtained via the corporate form currently support contribution bans, rather than the contribution limits upheld in *Buckley*.[107] Therefore, if *Austin* falls, *Caperton*'s potential to damage protections for independent communications will be neutralized. If, on the other hand, the *Citizens United* Court retains *Austin*, the potential will remain that *Caperton* may one day be cited to remove constitutional protections for independent political speech. That this may occur over Justice Kennedy's objection will be small solace to those who seek to protect free speech in political campaigns.

---

[104] Citizens United v. FEC, 129 S. Ct. 2893 (2009).

[105] Austin v. Mich. State Chamber of Commerce, 494 U.S. 652, 660 (1990).

[106] McConnell v. FEC, 540 U.S. 93 (2003).

[107] 494 U.S. at 660.

Looking Ahead: October Term 2009

*Jan Crawford Greenburg**

When David Souter testified before the Senate Judiciary Committee in 1990, the White House lawyers who had prepped him for his confirmation hearings quickly began getting a collective sinking feeling. Instead of hearing the solid "strict constructionist" George H.W. Bush had portrayed him to be, they listened as Souter—their nominee, their unknown but presumably conservative nominee—talked an awful lot like a liberal.

On question after question, Souter surprised. He heaped praise on the iconic William Brennan, the justice he was replacing. He defended the rulings of the Warren Court. He even distanced himself from Antonin Scalia's legal theories.

In the committee room, Senator Charles Grassley, the Iowa Republican, grew increasingly impatient. On Souter's first day of testimony, Grassley had asked him the kind of friendly questions nominees tend to get from senators who support their president.

There was, for example, this softball: What does Souter think about the liberal view that "the courts, rather than the elected branches, should take the lead in creating a more just society?"[1]

Souter knocked it out to left field: "Courts must accept their own responsibility for making a just society. The courts are going to be forced to take on problems which, sometimes, in the first instance, might be better addressed by the political branches of government." And if the other branches refuse to address a "profound social problem" raising a constitutional issue, Souter said, "ultimately it does and must land before the bench of the judiciary."[2]

---

* Legal Correspondent, ABC News, and author of Supreme Conflict: The Inside Story of the Struggle for Control of the United States Supreme Court (2007).

[1] A Hearing on the Nomination of Judge David Souter to be an Associate Justice of the U.S. Supreme Court before the S. Comm. on the Judiciary, 101st Cong. 142 (2009) (Questioning of Souter by Sen. Grassley).

[2] *Id.*

"The law of nature and political responsibility, constitutional responsibility, abhor a vacuum," Souter told Grassley.[3]

Pennsylvania Senator Arlen Specter, then a Republican, sounded amused by the entire exchange, telling reporters during a break: "I don't think you'll find a more liberal statement anywhere. It was out of Brennan's left pocket."[4]

Conservatives were baffled, and on Souter's second day of testimony, Grassley wasn't as friendly. Referring to their earlier exchange, Grassley told Souter his testimony "seems to me more the terminology likely to come from a judicial activist."[5]

"If we are going to have a Supreme Court that thinks it can fill vacuums every time there is a perceived problem, then ... you are going to be a very busy person," Grassley continued, "because democratic self-government does not always move with the speed or the consensus or the wisdom of philosopher kings who might best fill those vacuums."[6]

But Souter didn't back off, leaving the Republicans to wonder just who the untested New Hampshire jurist really was. Surely, some thought, Souter was just playing along to get confirmed. Surely he didn't really mean it.

And sure enough, in his first year on the Court, it appeared Souter, who sailed through to confirmation 90-9, hadn't meant it after all. He eased those concerns with solid conservative votes, standing alongside Chief Justice William Rehnquist. The collective sinking feeling in the White House became a collective sigh of relief.

But a justice's first term can be misleading, as conservatives would quickly learn.

By the end of his second year on the Court, Souter was voting more in line with his testimony, casting decisive votes on issues

---

[3] *Id.*

[4] Linda Greenhouse, Filling in the Blanks, New York Times, September 15, 1990, at 11.

[5] A Hearing on the Nomination of Judge David Souter to be an Associate Justice of the U.S. Supreme Court before the S. Comm. on the Judiciary, 101st Cong. 240 (2009) (Questioning of Souter by Senator Grassley).

[6] *Id.*

ranging from abortion to school prayer. He saw numerous "profound social problems" in his tenure on the Court, and he often stepped into fill the vacuum, whether on the death penalty or civil liberties or voting rights. He may not have been the "judicial activist" Grassley worried about, but he sure wasn't the "strict constructionist" George H.W. Bush promised, either.

In fact, David Souter's greatest legacy may be what he was not: a key fifth vote for conservatives.

Nineteen years after David Souter's confirmation, his replacement will step into her first term on the bench, facing an array of difficult issues while also learning how to work with eight colleagues who aren't exactly lacking in confidence about their respective jurisprudential approaches.

It's too soon to say whether the 2009 term will end up as a blockbuster—like Anthony Kennedy's first term, as well as the first terms of Clarence Thomas and Samuel Alito. Of the 46 cases granted thus far, there is one major showdown: a frontal assault on campaign finance laws. There also is a potentially divisive constitutional challenge to life sentences for juveniles, a widely accepted practice in the states, but one condemned internationally. And there are important cases that go to the heart of constitutional structure and power.

But the docket, which obviously will nearly double by the end of the year, has yet to reflect the kind of divisive issues that Kennedy, Thomas, and Alito had to grapple with in their first terms—cases on issues like abortion and race. The 2009 term is as notable, at this point, for the change in the membership of the Court as for the panoply of cases the justices will confront.

A New Justice Arrives

Since we've all taken to heart the old saying that a new justice makes a new Court, all eyes will be on Sonia Sotomayor in her role as the new junior associate justice. Reporters will analyze her questions at argument for clues about her leanings. Professors will scour her opinions to discern her philosophical approach. Legal analysts will look for new coalitions and voting blocs, the kind that emerged when Justice Thomas joined the Court, again after Justice Stephen Breyer went on board and, most recently and vividly, after Justice Alito took Sandra Day O'Connor's place.

Will Sotomayor find a comfortable home with the so-called liberal wing (something O'Connor never managed to do with the conservatives)? Will she help persuade swing justice Kennedy (as Breyer did with O'Connor)? Or will she help solidify the conservative majority by pushing Kennedy further to the right (as the famously charming William Brennan did with O'Connor in her first term, when he wrote "the bloom is off the rose" in a dissent to one of her first opinions for the Court)?

Questions, we all have questions, and the 2009 term will provide some hints. But if history is any guide, it's best to wait a year or two before making bold proclamations or answering with any degree of confidence.

Consider the confusing picture that has emerged thus far of Sotomayor—one that is, in some ways, as confusing as the images that emerged of David Souter at his confirmation.

When President Obama introduced Sotomayor as his first Supreme Court nominee, conservatives seized on her speeches and immediately painted her as a liberal activist who would rely on her heart and feelings when deciding cases, not the law. Souter got similar treatment from liberals when George H.W. Bush tapped him to replace William Brennan. (Abortion rights groups had issued flyers that proclaimed: "Stop Souter Now or Women Will Die.")

There are other parallels. Sotomayor's confirmation hearing—like Souter's—stirred concerns about her philosophy among those who had expected to extend full support. Even with friendly questions from Democrats, she refused to engage. This was a relatively new experience for liberals, who haven't suffered the kind of crushing disappointments that conservatives have endured with nominees who ended up surprising them. Ruth Bader Ginsburg, a women's rights advocate before joining the bench, was more direct in her testimony. Stephen Breyer gave a fascinating, accessible seminar on liberal jurisprudence.

Sotomayor was different. She didn't "pull a Souter" and paint herself in entirely different ideological stripes than expected, but she didn't embrace liberal jurisprudence either. She was an enigma.

At times she sounded as conservative as Chief Justice John Roberts, who clearly articulated a conservative judicial philosophy in his confirmation hearings (much as Breyer had done for liberals in the previous decade). Here's just one example of Sotomayor parroting boilerplate judicial conservatism: "The great beauty of this nation is that we do leave . . . law-making to our elected branches and that we expect our courts to understand its limited role."[7]

At times she sounded like a coy liberal nominee, hiding the ball on questions about, for example, international law. This was a particularly striking exchange with Republican Senator John Cornyn of Texas, which suggests she's right there with Scalia, Thomas, Roberts, and Alito on disdaining the use of foreign law:

"Foreign law cannot be used as a holding or a precedent or to bind or to influence the outcome of a legal decision interpreting the Constitution or American law that doesn't direct you to that law," she told Cornyn.[8]

But let that answer settle in, and then process this subsequent response, which suggests she really stands with Ginsburg, Breyer, and Kennedy:

"In my experience, when I've seen other judges cite to foreign law, they're not using it to drive the conclusion," Sotomayor said. "They're using it just to point something out about a comparison between American law and foreign law. But they're not using it in the sense of compelling a result."[9]

And at times she was, well, nonsensical. When asked by Senator Lindsey Graham of South Carolina whether the Constitution was a "living, breathing, evolving" document, she responded:

> The Constitution is a document that is immutable to the sense that it's lasted 200 years. The Constitution has not changed except by amendments. It is a process—an amendment process that is set forth in the document. It doesn't live other than to be timeless by the expression of what it said. What changes is society. What changes is what facts a judge may get.[10]

That was a chance to put forth the case for liberal jurisprudence, with no risk to the nominee—a decisive Democratic majority in the

---

[7] A Hearing on the Nomination of Judge Sonia Sotomayor to be an Associate Justice of the U.S. Supreme Court before the S. Comm. on the Judiciary, 111th Cong. ____ (2009) (Statement of Judge Sonia Sotomayor).

[8] *Id.* (Questioning of Sotomayor by Sen. Cornyn).

[9] *Id.*

[10] *Id.* (Questioning of Sotomayor by Sen. Graham).

Senate meant that, as Graham remarked candidly, short of a "melt-down," her confirmation was assured going in.[11] Instead, she inexpli-cably danced around an issue that a first-year law student who has skimmed Stephen Breyer's book[12] could have slammed out of the park.

Contrast her answer to Breyer's response, at his confirmation hear-ings, to a general question about whether the Constitution can change as society changes. (In 1994, we hadn't seen the term "living Constitution" become a popular way of distinguishing between judi-cial liberals, who embrace it, and judicial conservatives, who prefer the "dead" version.) Here's Breyer back in 1994:

> I think that in applying the Constitution in general, one looks, of course, to the conditions of society. I think the Constitution is a set of incredibly important, incredible valuable princi-ples, statements in simple language that have enabled the country to exist for 200 years, and I hope and we believe many hundreds of years more. That Constitution could not have done that if, in fact, it was not able to have words that drew their meaning in part from the conditions of the society that they govern. And, of course, the conditions and changed conditions are relevant to deciding what is and what is not rational in terms of the Constitution, as in the terms of a statute or in any other rule of law.[13]

Sotomayor also explicitly distanced herself from Obama's approach to judging in an exchange with Arizona Senator Jon Kyl:

> KYL: Let me ask you about what the President said. He used two different analogies. He talked once about the 25 miles— the first 25 miles of a 26-mile marathon. And then he also said, in 95 percent of the cases, the law will give you the answer, and the last 5 percent legal process will not lead you to the rule of decision. The critical ingredient in those cases is supplied by what is in the judge's heart.

---

[11] *Id.* (Statement by Sen. Graham).

[12] Stephen Breyer, Active Liberty: Interpreting our Democratic Constitution (2005).

[13] A Hearing on the Nomination of Judge Stephen Breyer to be an Associate Justice of the U.S. Supreme Court before S. Comm. on the Judiciary, 103rd Cong. (1994) (Statement of Judge Stephen Breyer).

Do you agree with him that the law only takes you the first 25 miles of the marathon and that that last mile has to be decided by what's in the judge's heart?

SOTOMAYOR: No, sir. That's—I don't—I wouldn't approach the issue of judging in the way the President does. He has to explain what he meant by judging. I can only explain what I think judges should do, which is judges can't rely on what's in their heart. They don't determine the law. Congress makes the laws.[14]

Sotomayor's testimony was too much for some on the Left to take. Georgetown law professor Mike Seidman declared himself "completely disgusted" by her testimony. Seidman, who clerked for liberal icon Thurgood Marshall, wrote in an online debate:

If she was not perjuring herself, she is intellectually unquali-fied to be on the Supreme Court. If she was perjuring herself, she is morally unqualified. How could someone who has been on the bench for seventeen years possibly believe that judging in hard cases involves no more than applying the law to the facts?[15]

A clearer picture of Sotomayor will begin to emerge when she takes the bench this fall. Despite her testimony, she is unlikely to disappoint liberals as nominees like Souter (and Kennedy and O'Connor) have disappointed conservatives. But it's nonetheless a mistake, as Souter's case shows, to read too much into a justice's first term, even when the new justice is an experienced and presum-ably liberal federal judge like Sonia Sotomayor.

In Justice Kennedy's first full term, for example, he voted with Rehnquist 92 percent of the time, more than any other justice. He cast decisive conservative votes on discrimination, abortion, and the death penalty. His vote with Rehnquist, Scalia, and White in *Webster v. Reproductive Health Services*, a four-justice opinion that proposed a different way of analyzing abortion cases, convinced people on both sides he would eventually agree to overturn *Roe v. Wade*. The

---

[14] A Hearing on the Nomination of Judge Sonia Sotomayor to be an Associate Justice of the U.S. Supreme Court before, 111th Cong. (2009) (Questioning by Sen. Kyl).

[15] Mike Seidman, The Federalist Society Online Debate Series: The Sotomayor Nomi-nation, Part II, available at http://www.fed-soc.org/debates/dbtid.30/default.asp.

Washington Post pronounced him "at least as conservative" as Robert Bork would have been.[16]

But those early votes were deceiving, and over the next few years, a more lasting image would emerge: Kennedy was a winnable vote for liberals. He would change his mind. He could be persuaded. He just couldn't say "never," especially on those "profound social problems" like abortion.

Even a justice's demeanor can change after his or her first term on the Court. Sotomayor, for example, has a reputation as a fierce questioner. Perhaps she'll step up and go head-to-head with Chief Justice Roberts and Justice Scalia. Perhaps she'll assume Souter's role of stepping in and assisting lawyers who struggled to answer withering questions from Scalia.

But if she shows reticence in her first year, it may not tell us much. When the experienced appeals court Judge Alito became Justice Alito, he made a conscious decision to ease into his new role. In his first term, he was deferential and reserved. He asked few questions, deliberately opting to first absorb the routines and rhythms of the Supreme Court bench at argument.

Alito has since emerged as one of the Court's most effective questioners. He is probing and focused, often homing in on pragmatic consequences, but still grounded in law. He often gets the attention of key swing vote—Kennedy, who is not reluctant to jump in at argument and demand that lawyers answer Justice Alito's questions.

Bottom line: it may take a while for us to understand the kind of justice Sonia Sotomayor will be.

Campaign Finance

In any event, the new justice has hit the ground running, thanks to the Court's decision to return to the bench nearly a month early, on Sept. 9, for re-arguments in a major campaign finance case, *Citizens United v. Federal Election Commission*.[17] At issue is whether *Hillary: The Movie*, a feature-length, relentlessly critical film of presidential candidate Hillary Clinton, was an "electioneering communication" and, as such, regulated under the 2002 Bipartisan Campaign

[16] Al Kamen, Kennedy Moves Court to Right: Justice More Conservative than Expected, Washington Post, April 11, 1989, at A1.

[17] Citizens United v. FEC, 129 S. Ct. 594, reargument scheduled, Citizens United v. FEC, 129 S. Ct. 2893 (2009).

Reform Act. (That law also is known as "McCain-Feingold," after Senate sponsors John McCain, the Arizona Republican, and Russell Feingold, the Wisconsin Democrat.)

Before BCRA, campaign finance issues were governed by the Federal Election Campaign Act, which prohibited corporations and unions from spending their general treasury funds on "election-related activities." In *Buckley v. Valeo* in 1976, the Supreme Court interpreted the FECA's "election-related activities" to encompass only those activities that amounted to "express advocacy," such as a direct call to "Vote for Me" or "Don't Vote for Her."[18]

After *Buckley*, however, corporations and unions started running so-called "issue ads" to get around the law's restrictions on express advocacy. They weren't a direct plea to "Vote for Me," but instead typically criticized the opponents' stands on the issues.

Part of BCRA was designed to close that loophole with restrictions on "electioneering communications." Those communications are broadcast on radio or television 30 days before a primary election or 60 days before a general election, and feature candidates for federal office. According to BCRA's Section 203, corporations and unions are prohibited from spending their general treasury funds on those advertisements. BCRA also contains disclosure requirements identifying the person or committee funding the advertisements.

A broad array of groups challenged BCRA, but the Court upheld key provisions, including a facial challenge to Section 203, in *McConnell v. FEC* in 2003.[19] *McConnell* also reaffirmed *Austin v. Michigan Chamber of Commerce*, where the Court upheld limits on corporate financing of "express advocacy" because of the "corrosive and distorting effects [that] immense aggregations of [corporate] wealth" could have on elections.[20] In *McConnell*, the Court said "issue ads" also could be limited because most were the "functional equivalent of express advocacy."[21]

The Court again waded into campaign finance restrictions in *Wisconsin Right to Life v. Federal Election Commission*, which made two

---

[18] Buckley v. Valeo, 424 U.S. 1, 47 (1976).

[19] McConnell v. FEC, 540 U.S. 93 (2003).

[20] Austin v. Mich. State Chamber of Commerce, 494 U.S. 652, 660 (1990).

[21] McConnell, 540 U.S. at 206.

different appearances in the Court.[22] The case involved advertisements taking aim at Senators Feingold's and Herb Kohl's votes to filibuster judicial nominees. The group argued those ads were not the "functional equivalent of express advocacy," and the justices allowed the as-applied challenge to Section 203 to proceed in the lower court.[23] After the lower court found the ads were, in fact, the functional equivalent, the case headed back to the Supreme Court.

In the second go-round, the Court ruled that *McConnell* could not apply to those types of advertisements.[24] Three justices—Kennedy, Scalia, and Thomas—argued that Section 203 was unconstitutional and said *McConnell* and *Austin* should be overruled. Roberts and Alito joined in a more narrow controlling opinion, holding that BCRA barred only ads that were the "functional equivalent of express advocacy," which it defined as ads in which there "no reasonable interpretation" of anything other than an advertisement expressly supporting or opposing a candidate.[25] Because the ads targeting Feingold and Kohl didn't mention character or fitness for office, they could be interpreted as something other than an express ad against them. As a result, they were not covered by BCRA, the Court held.[26]

The case now before the Court came about after Citizens United tried to distribute *Hillary: The Movie* through a "video-on-demand" service, in which cable subscribers could get the movie for free.

The Federal Election Commission took the position that the movie, which was funded with corporate money, was an "election communication" and could not be paid for with corporate funds. Citizens United sued, and the Court heard arguments in the case in March.

The justices then upped the ante, deciding in the last week of the term to hold over the case and directing the parties to brief whether the Court should overturn *Austin* and a portion of *McConnell*. Overturning those decisions could pave the way for corporations to use

---

[22] Wis. Right to Life v. FEC ("WRTL I"), 546 U.S. 410 (2006), FEC v. Wis. Right to Life ("WRTL II"), 551 U.S. 449 (2007).

[23] WRTL II, 551 U.S. at 412.

[24] *Id.* at 481.

[25] *Id.* at 455–504.

[26] *Id.* at 456.

their general treasury funds to advocate the election or defeat of political candidates.

A recap: In *Austin*, the Court held that corporations may be prohibited from financing express electoral advocacy with funds from their business activities. In *McConnell*, the Court upheld BCRA's ban on corporate treasury funds being used for express advocacy or the functional equivalent of express advocacy. The Court in *McConnell* also upheld the law's definition of "electioneering communication," which had been attacked as facially overbroad.

The Obama administration is arguing the case is a "particularly unsuitable vehicle" for reexamining either *Austin* or *McConnell*, because Citizens United is a nonprofit corporation with an expressly ideological purpose—both of which make it a "distinctly atypical corporation."[27] The administration also argues the broad constitutional question was not properly raised in the case because Citizens United abandoned efforts to assert a facial challenge to BCRA's Section 2003 and did not argue that either *Austin* or *McConnell* should be overruled.

On the merits of the constitutional questions, the administration argues that a reversal of those decisions "would likely invalidate federal legislation that has restricted corporate electioneering for over 60 years, as well as similar legislation enacted by many states."[28]

"Overruling *Austin* and *McConnell* would fundamentally alter the legal rules governing participation of corporations—including the Nation's largest for-profit corporations—in electoral campaigns, and would make vast sums of corporate money available for overt electioneering," the administration argues.[29]

The argument marks Solicitor General Elena Kagan's first appearance before the justices. She squares off against former solicitor general Theodore Olson, who once defended the very laws he now asks the Court to overturn—as well as another former solicitor general, Seth Waxman, who will be arguing on behalf of BCRA's congressional sponsors, and famed First Amendment attorney, Floyd

---

[27] Supplemental Brief for the Appellee at 2, Citizens United v. FEC, No. 08-205 (July 24, 2009) 2009 WL 2219300.

[28] *Id.* at 1.

[29] *Id.* at 2.

Abrams, who represents Senator Mitch McConnell (who was BCRA's leading opponent and is now Senate minority leader).

In his supplemental brief, Olson homes in on the March argument of Deputy Solicitor General Malcolm Stewart, who was defending the FEC's position that *Hillary: The Movie* was an "election communication." The argument got away from Stewart when he asserted, under sharp questioning, that the law could also be interpreted to ban campaign-related books if funded with money from general corporate treasuries.[30]

"Enough is enough," says Olson in the Citizens United brief. "When the government of the United States of American claims the authority to ban books because of their political speech, something has gone terribly wrong and it is as sure a sign as any that a return to first principles is in order."[31]

"It would be anomalous, according to the government, if it did not have the power to prohibit all corporate and union communications that constitute the functional equivalent of express advocacy because the government already makes it a felony for corporations and unions to make any communication that includes express advocacy—even 'a newsletter,' 'a sign held up in Lafayette Park,' or a '500-page book' that includes 'vote for X' as its last three words," Citizens United argues in its brief.[32]

Religion and Speech

After the *Citizens United* appetizer, the Court formally returns the first Monday in October to kick off a sitting that includes two other compelling First Amendment cases, both of which are likely to garner a significant amount of public interest and provide clues on how the Court's newest justices will approach critical issues of free speech and standing.

---

[30] See especially Transcript of Oral Argument at 27–30, Citizens United v. FEC (March 24, 2009) (No. 08-205), 2009 WL 760811 (series of questions by Justices Alito and Kennedy and Chief Justices Roberts, culminating in Stewart's admission that if the publisher didn't comply with campaign finance regulations, "we could prohibit the publication of the book").

[31] Supplemental Brief for Appellant at 2, Citizens United v. FEC, No. 08-205 (U.S. July 24, 2009), 2009 WL 2219301.

[32] *Id.*

In *Salazar v. Buono*, the justices will rule on a challenge to a religious cross that is displayed on the 1.6 million-acre Mojave National Preserve in southeastern California.[33] After a legal challenge, Congress passed legislation that transferred the speck of land where the cross was displayed to a private buyer. There are two issues in the case: Whether Frank Buono, a former employee at the preserve, has standing to challenge the cross, and whether Congress can avoid a constitutional challenge by transferring the land to a private entity.

The controversy over the cross has raged for more than a decade. It was erected in the preserve nearly 75 years ago as memorial to veterans who died in World War I, and has been replaced several times. It now is made of white metal pipes and is about five feet tall, making it visible to anyone who drives on by a remote road in the preserve.

The controversy began when a man asked the National Park Service for permission to erect a Buddhist shrine nearby. The Park Service rejected the request and indicated it was planning to remove the cross. Local officials protested and Congress eventually swapped the one-acre parcel of land where the cross is located with other land privately held in the preserve.

Buono argued in his suit that the government could not pick and choose among religious symbols—that if it allowed the cross, it must also allow other religious symbols.

The government argues that Buono has no standing to sue because he is not seeking "to redress a personal injury, but instead to vindicate a view of the Establishment Clause" that public lands where crosses are displayed should also include other symbols, if the public wishes.[34] It says Buono has only a "policy disagreement," which is not grounds for the lawsuit against the government.[35] Buono replies that his objection is not an abstract one, but stems from his "direct and unwelcome contact with a government-sponsored religious display or practice."[36]

---

[33] Buono v. Kempthorne, 527 F.3d 758 (9th Cir. 2008), cert. granted sub nom., Salazar v. Buono, 129 S. Ct. 1313 (2009).

[34] Brief for the Petitioners at 13, Salazar v. Buono, No. 08-472 (U.S. June 1, 2009), 2009 WL 1526915.

[35] *Id.*

[36] Respondent's Brief at 19, Kempthorne v. Buono, No. 08-472 (U.S. July 27, 2009), 2009 WL 2365232.

If the Court recognizes that Buono has standing, it must then decide whether Congress could duck the constitutional challenge with the land swap.

Also in October, the justices will decide whether the government can ban videotapes of dog fighting, or whether those depictions of animal cruelty are protected speech under the First Amendment. At issue in *United States v. Stevens* is a 1999 federal law prohibiting animal cruelty, which prosecutors invoked to charge a Virginia man, Robert Stevens, with selling videotapes of pit bulls participating in dog fights.[37]

Stevens operated a business called "Dogs of Velvet and Steel" and a website called Pitbulllife.com, through which he sold videos of the dog fights. The videos include scenes of "savage and bloody dog fights and of pit bull viciously attacking other animals" and are narrated by Stevens. He was convicted and sentenced to 37 months in prison.

The U.S. Court of Appeals for the Third Circuit struck down the law, holding that it would not create a new exception to the First Amendment in order to prohibit depictions of animal cruelty.[38] The last time the Supreme Court said an entire class of speech could be prohibited was in 1982, when it ruled in *New York v. Ferber*[39] that child pornography was unprotected by the First Amendment, and the en banc appeals court said it would not create a new category of unprotected speech absent "express direction" from the Supreme Court.

The appeals court also rejected a proposed analogy to child pornography. Although it acknowledged that, as with child pornography, all 50 states have laws prohibiting animal cruelty, and that the offenses are difficult to prosecute, it held that the government interest was not as compelling. Animal cruelty is not "of the same magnitude as protecting children," the appeals court wrote.[40] It applied strict scrutiny and invalidated the statute on its face.

---

[37] United States v. Stevens, 533 F.3d 218 (3d Cir. 2008), cert. granted, 129 S. Ct. 1984 (April 20, 2009) (No. 08-769).

[38] *Id.* at 220.

[39] New York v. Ferber, 458 U.S. 747 (1982).

[40] Stevens, 533 F.3d at 228.

Three judges dissented, arguing the law regulates only a "narrow subclass" of depictions of "depraved acts committed against an uniquely vulnerable and helpless class of victims."[41] The dissenters said the First Amendment does not protect those depictions, because the government has a compelling interest in preventing animal cruelty, and the depictions are "no essential part of any exposition of ideas."[42]

The Justice Department makes a similar argument, noting that the law applies only in rare cases, where the depictions are illegal, created solely for commercial gain, and lack "serious religious, political, scientific, educational, journalistic, historical or artistic value."[43] "Like child pornography," the government continues, "the material here depicts the horrific maltreatment of helpless victims, which society long has deemed reprehensible."[44]

Stevens's brief attacks the government's relativism regarding constitutional speech protections. "If the First Amendment meant to permit such a balancing test, then the First Amendment would read more like the Fourth Amendment, proscribing only 'unreasonable' prohibitions on speech."[45] The Cato Institute echoes this sentiment in its supporting brief, arguing that "[t]he 'categorical balancing' proposed by the Government for identifying categories of proscribable content is an open attempt to end-run—and even subvert—the Court's traditionally rigorous scrutiny of content-based restrictions on speech."[46]

Life Sentences for Juveniles and the Relevance of Foreign Law

The justices also will grapple with a number of high-profile criminal cases, including a constitutional challenge to life sentences for juveniles that also could be a good barometer for measuring the

---

[41] *Id.* at 247.

[42] *Id.* at 236 (quoting Chaplinsky v. N.H., 315 U.S. 568, 571 (1942)).

[43] Brief for the United States at 15, United States v. Stevens, No. 08-769 (U.S. June 8, 2009) 2009 WL 1615365.

[44] *Id.* at 36.

[45] Brief for the Respondent at 14, United States v. Stevens, No. 08-769 (U.S. July 20, 2009) 2009 WL 2191081.

[46] Brief for the Cato Institute as Amicus Curiae in Support of Respondent at 16, United States v. Stevens, No. 08-769 (U.S. July 27, 2009), 2009 WL 2331221.

newest justice and her approach to criminal law—as well as international law.

This question is a natural outgrowth of the Court's 2005 decision in *Roper v. Simmons*, in which it struck down the death penalty for juveniles.[47] The argument is essentially the same: that a life sentence for a juvenile crime is basically a death sentence, and therefore violates the Constitutional prohibition against cruel and unusual punishment.

The cases, *Graham v. Florida*[48] and *Sullivan v. Florida*,[49] both involve life sentences for juveniles who committed non-homicide crimes. Terrance Jamar Graham was 17 when he received life without parole for a series of robberies, which violated his probation for an earlier armed burglary. Joe Harris Sullivan was given life without parole for committing sexual battery when he was 13.

The cases raise slightly different questions, and the Court could resolve them differently. Graham directly confronts the specific question of whether the Eighth Amendment prohibits a life sentence for a juvenile. Sullivan's case also injects his young age of 13, suggesting he is entitled to greater Eighth Amendment protection than a 17-year-old like Graham. But Sullivan's case has a wrinkle: He was sentenced nearly 20 years ago.

Unlike in the juvenile death penalty context, when the court found growing societal opposition, life sentences for juveniles are more commonplace. More than 2,200 juveniles now are serving life sentences in the United States, and not a single state has a per se rule rejecting the use of life sentences for juveniles in every case.

The case also gives the justices another opportunity to wade into the issue of using foreign law to interpret the Constitution, which factored into the *Roper* decision as well—and, as discussed, in Justice Sotomayor's confirmation hearing. As with the juvenile death penalty, the international community frowns on life sentences for juveniles, the state court noted in *Graham*. The court observed that outside the United States, only a dozen juveniles are serving life sentences,

---

[47] Roper v. Simmons, 543 U.S. 551 (2005).

[48] Graham v. State, 982 So. 2d 43 (Fla. Dist. Ct. App. 1st Dist. 2008), cert. granted sub nom. Graham v. Florida, 129 S. Ct. 2157 (May 4, 2009) (No. 08-7412).

[49] Sullivan v. State, 987 So. 2d 83 (Fla. Dist. Ct. App. 1st Dist., 2008), cert. granted sub nom. Sullivan v. Florida, 129 S. Ct. 2157 (May 4, 2009) (No. 08-7621).

and the United Kingdom recently barred them. The state court concluded that while the weight given the international community was "persuasive," it does not counter the "individual rights of the state to impose its chosen sentencing scheme if that scheme is not held to be otherwise unconstitutional."[50]

Miranda **Revisited?**

The criminal docket also will involve the justices in the familiar issue of *Miranda* warnings, which will raise broader questions about *stare decisis*. In *Florida v. Powell*, they will decide whether standard *Miranda* warnings that advise a defendant he has a right to "talk to a lawyer before answering any of our questions" are adequate.[51] The Florida Supreme Court ruled that those warnings were deficient, affirming a lower court decision that threw out the conviction of Kevin Dewayne Powell, who had confessed to owning a firearm after Tampa police read him the warnings off a standard form. Powell's confession provided the basis for his conviction as a felon in possession of a firearm.

Ruled the Florida Supreme Court:

> [T]o advise a suspect that he has the right "to talk to a lawyer before answering any of our questions" constitutes a narrower and less functional warning than that required by *Miranda*. Both *Miranda* and article 1, section 9 of the Florida Constitution require that a suspect be clearly informed of the right to have a lawyer present during questioning.[52]

The issue sharply divided the lower Florida courts, much as it had society. Although conservatives have long been critical of the *Miranda* as a blatant example of judicial lawmaking, the Supreme Court in *Dickerson v. United States*[53] seemed to put the issue to rest in 2000. Chief Justice William Rehnquist wrote the majority opinion rejecting a constitutional challenge to *Miranda*, saying, whatever the merits of the original holding may be, principles of *stare decisis*

---

[50] Graham, 982 So. 2d at 51.

[51] State v. Powell, 998 So. 2d 531, 532 (Fla. 2008) cert. granted sub nom. Florida v. Powell, 174 L. Ed. 2d 551 (U.S. June, 22 2009) (No. 08-1175).

[52] State v. Powell, 998 So. 2d 531, 542 (Fla. 2008).

[53] Dickerson v. United States, 530 U.S. 428 (2000).

counseled against overruling it. Justices Scalia and Thomas dissented.

Crime and Federalism

Another criminal case before the Court this term raises pressing questions of federalism, giving the new justices a clear opportunity to embrace (or reject) the Rehnquist legacy, which put clear limits on congressional power.

At issue in *United States v. Comstock* is whether Congress had authority to pass a statute that allows the government to place in indefinite civil commitment "sexually dangerous" persons.[54] The issue has divided trial courts across the nation, and the U.S. Court of Appeals for the Fourth Circuit ruled the law exceeds the limits of congressional power and intrudes on the powers reserved to the states.

Congress enacted the civil commitment provision as part of the Adam Walsh Child Protection and Safety Act of 2006. It establishes a national Sex Offender Registry, increases penalties for federal crimes against children, and strengthens existing child pornography prohibitions. The only provision at issue authorizes the federal government to commit a "sexually dangerous" person to the custody of the Bureau of Prisons, even after the person has completed his prison sentence.

Graydon Comstock, who pleaded guilty to receiving child pornography, was certified as a sexually dangerous person six days before the end of his 37-month prison sentence. He remains incarcerated more than two years later. Several other men filed similar challenges after they, too, were certified as sexually dangerous and held in prison after their sentences expired. (The appeals court noted that the attorney general has certified more than 60 people as "sexually dangerous" in the Eastern District of North Carolina alone, all of whom remain in prison.)

The government argues that Congress had authority to pass the statute under the Necessary and Proper Clause (which the appeals court flatly dismissed) and under the Commerce Clause.[55]

---

[54] United States v. Comstock, 551 F.3d 274 (4th Cir.), cert. granted, 129 S. Ct. 2828 (2009).

[55] *Id.* at 281.

For decades, courts rarely questioned congressional authority, assuming everything was, in some way, connected to commerce. *United States v. Lopez* changed that. In that case, the Supreme Court held that federal laws prohibiting possession of a gun in a school zone exceeded Congress's Commerce Clause power, since it was not regulating either commercial or interstate activity.[56] Then, in *Morrison v. United States*, the Court struck down a provision in the federal Violence Against Women Act that had created a federal civil remedy for sexual assault, holding those crimes do not substantially affect interstate commerce.[57]

The appeals court said *Morrison*'s rationale for rejecting Commerce Clause authority over civil sexual assault crimes applied with equal force to civil commitment statutes.

"Federal commitment of 'sexually dangerous persons' may well be—like the suppression of guns in schools or the redress of gender-motivated violence—a sound proposal as a matter of social policy," the appeals court wrote. "But policy justifications do not create congressional authority."[58]

The court concluded that the power claimed by the civil commitment statute, authorizing "forcible, indefinite civil commitment," is among "the most severe wielded by any government."[59] "The Framers, distrustful of such authority, reposed such broad powers in the states," the court wrote, "limiting the national government to specific and enumerated powers."[60]

Sarbanes-Oxley and the Separation of Powers

The Court also will take up another major constitutional powers case when it grapples with whether the Sarbanes-Oxley Act violates separation-of-powers principles. The case, *Free Enterprise Fund v. Public Company Accounting Oversight Board*,[61] is significant on a number of levels, and gives the justices an opportunity to establish key

---

[56] United States v. Lopez, 514 U.S. 549 (1995).

[57] United States v. Morrison, 529 U.S. 598 (2000).

[58] Comstock, 551 F.3d at 280.

[59] *Id.* at 284.

[60] *Id.*

[61] Free Enter. Fund v. Public Co. Accounting Oversight Bd., 537 F.3d 667 (D.C. Cir. 2008), cert. granted, 129 S. Ct. 2378 (2009).

guideposts on presidential power and separation of powers concerns.

At issue is a challenge to the constitutionality of the Public Company Accounting Oversight Board—whose acronym, PCAOB, is cutely pronounced "peek-a-boo"—which enforces the Sarbanes-Oxley regulatory scheme. Challengers contend the appointment of PCAOB's officers violates the Constitution's Appointments Clause.

The Appointments Clause gives the president exclusive power to appoint government officials, but the PCAOB's officers are appointed by the SEC, which has limited power to remove or supervise them. That gives the PCAOB's officers broad authority and puts them in a different league than other similar authorities, such as the IRS Commissioner and governors of the Federal Reserve—all of whom must be nominated by the president and confirmed by the Senate.

The U.S. Court of Appeals for the D.C. Circuit said PCAOB members were different, so Congress could dictate the "power of removal as it deems best for the public interest."[62] The Free Enterprise Fund, along with other groups challenging the PCAOB—including the Cato Institute as amicus curiae—say that gives them too much power and insulates them from political accountability.

The Erosion of Property Rights

Another sweeping and divisive constitutional question is at issue in *Stop the Beach Renourishment v. Florida Department of Environmental Protection*.[63] In that case, the justices will return to the question of property rights, in an appeal of a Florida Supreme Court decision that a beach erosion control statute did not unconstitutionally deprive landowners of their property.

*   *   *

So the justices will take their seats with the table more than half set in terms of cases. They will continue adding cases throughout the fall, but the lineup already suggests the 2009 term will be an

---

[62] *Id.* at 683 (quoting United States v. Perkins, 116 U.S. 483 (1886)).

[63] Walton County v. Stop the Beach Renourishment, Inc., 998 So. 2d 1102 (Fla. 2008), cert. granted sub nom. Stop the Beach Renourishment, Inc., v. Florida Dept. of Envtl. Protection, 129 S. Ct. 2792 (2009).

important one, with several difficult and important constitutional principles at stake. One pending cert petition could ratchet up the stakes. It would inject the court into a contentious issue that snagged Sotomayor in her confirmation hearing: Whether the Second Amendment is incorporated against the states—and if so whether that would be through so-called "substantive due process" or via the resurrection of the Fourteenth Amendment's Privileges or Immunities Clause.

With its rich constitutional questions—even those that aren't publicly explosive—October Term 2009 also will start the process of understanding new Justice Sotomayor. It should as well provide a greater understanding of Roberts and Alito, who will be grappling with issues they've not yet confronted at the High Court.

But keep in mind these principles as the Court goes through the 2009 term with its newest member: First impressions can be dead wrong. Speculation can be uninformed and off base. (Just ask Justice Thomas, the subject of ludicrous and grossly inaccurate news articles in his first term that he was somehow Justice Scalia's "lackey.") And justices can take a year or two to find their footing, as well as their philosophy.

Contributors

Randy E. Barnett is the Carmack Waterhouse Professor of Legal Theory at the Georgetown University Law Center, where he teaches constitutional law and contracts. After graduating from Northwestern University and Harvard Law School, he tried many felony cases as a prosecutor in the Cook County States' Attorney's Office in Chicago. He has been a visiting professor at Northwestern and Harvard Law School. In 2008, he was awarded a Guggenheim Fellowship in Constitutional Studies. Professor Barnett's publications includes more than eighty articles and reviews, as well as nine books, including *Restoring the Lost Constitution: The Presumption of Liberty* (Princeton, 2004), *Constitutional Law: Cases in Context* (Aspen, 2008), and *Contracts: Cases and Doctrine* (Aspen, 4th ed. 2008). His book, *The Structure of Liberty: Justice and the Rule of Law* (Oxford, 1998), has been translated into Japanese. His opinion pieces appear regularly in such publications as *The Wall Street Journal*. In 2004, Professor Barnett argued the medical marijuana case of *Gonzalez v. Raich* before the U.S. Supreme Court. He delivered the Kobe 2000 lectures in jurisprudence at the University of Tokyo and Doshisha University in Kyoto. He also appears on such programs as the CBS Evening News, The News Hour (PBS), The Glenn Beck Show (FNC) and the Ricki Lake Show. In 2007, Professor Barnett was featured in the documentaries, *The Trials of Law School* and *In Search of the Second Amendment*. He also portrayed an assistant prosecutor in the independent film *InAlienable*, which stars Richard Hatch, Courtney Peldon, Marina Sirtis, Erick Avari, and Walter Koenig.

Mark Chenoweth is a Washington, D.C. attorney and a senior fellow in legal studies at the Pacific Research Institute. He has championed asbestos reform, overcriminalization reform, and numerous tort reform initiatives in a dozen or more states and at the federal level. He also has significant experience counseling clients regarding federal and state ethics, lobbying, and political contributions compliance matters. As counsel for legal reform at Koch Industries, Inc., from 2004-08, he authored the Reliability in Expert Testimony Standards Act and led the national corporate effort to promote the *Daubert* standard for the admissibility of expert evidence in state courts. Prior to joining Koch, Mr. Chenoweth served as an attorney advisor in the Office of Legal Policy at the U.S. Department of Justice, where he vetted potential judicial nominees and drafted violent crime anti-recidivism legislation. Before joining DOJ, he practiced law at Wilmer, Cutler & Pickering and clerked for the Hon. Danny J. Boggs on the U.S. Court of Appeals for the Sixth Circuit. Mr. Chenoweth serves on the board of directors of the American Tort Reform Association. He previously served as chair of the sound science subcommittee for Lawyers for Civil Justice, chair of the expert evidence subcommittee for the Civil Justice Reform Group, and as a private sector member of the American Legislative Exchange Council's Civil Justice Task Force. Mr. Chenoweth received his B.A. in Ethics, Politics & Economics from Yale University and his J.D. from the University of Chicago Law School, where he co-founded the Institute for Justice Clinic on Entrepreneurship, became a Tony Patiño Fellow, and served as Associate Editor of the University of Chicago Legal Forum.

Roger Clegg is president and general counsel of the Center for Equal Opportunity, where he writes, speaks, and conducts research on legal issues raised by the civil rights laws. The Center for Equal Opportunity is a conservative research and educational organization based in Falls Church, Virginia, that specializes in civil rights, immigration and assimilation, and bilingual education issues. Mr. Clegg also is a contributing editor at *National Review Online*, and writes frequently for other popular periodicals and law journals. From 1982 to 1993, Mr. Clegg held a number of positions at the U.S. Department of Justice, including Assistant to the Solicitor General, where he argued three cases before the United States Supreme Court, and the number-two official in the Civil Rights Division and in the Environment Division. From 1993 to 1997, Mr. Clegg was vice president and general counsel of the National Legal Center for the Public Interest, where he wrote and edited a variety of publications on legal issues of interest to business. He is a graduate of Rice University and Yale Law School.

Robert Corn-Revere is a partner in the Washington, D.C. office of Davis Wright Tremaine LLP, specializing in First Amendment and communications law. He has been active in FCC proceedings and in various court challenges to FCC enforcement actions governing broadcast indecency, including *CBS Corporation v. FCC*, involving the $550,000 fine for the 2004 Super Bowl halftime show. Among his other cases, Mr. Corn-Revere argued *United States v. Playboy Entertainment Group, Inc.*, in which the United States Supreme Court struck down Section 505 of the Telecommunications Act of 1996 as a violation of the First Amendment, and *MPAA v. FCC*, in which the United States Court of Appeals for the District of Columbia Circuit invalidated FCC rules mandating "video description" of television programs. Mr. Corn-Revere writes extensively on First Amendment and communications-related issues and has provided expert testimony before various congressional committees and the FCC. He is co-author of a three-volume treatise entitled *Modern Communications Law*, published by West Group, and is editor and co-author of the book, *Rationales & Rationalizations*. He formerly served as Chief Counsel to FCC Chairman James H. Quello, and previously was Commissioner Quello's legal advisor on mass media issues. In 2003, Mr. Corn-Revere successfully petitioned Governor George E. Pataki to grant the first posthumous pardon in New York history to the late comedian Lenny Bruce.

Daniel Crane is professor of law at the University of Michigan and counsel at Paul, Weiss, Rifkind, Warton & Garrison LLP. He has was previously professor of law at the Benjamin N. Cardozo School of Law, Yeshiva University, a visiting professor at NYU Law School and the University of Chicago, and a Fulbright Scholar at the Universidade Católica Portuguesa. He received his B.A. from Wheaton College, Illinois and his J.D. from the University of Chicago, where he was member of the Law Review. His primary scholarship is in antitrust and law and economics. His work has appeared in many leading law journals, including the *University of Chicago Law Review, Michigan Law Review, California Law Review, Cornell Law Review*, and the *Texas Law Review*. He is co-editor (with Eleanor Fox) of *Antitrust Stories*, a collection of chapters by leading antitrust authorities on significant antitrust cases and has a book entitled the *Insitutional*

Structure of Antitrust Enforcement forthcoming with Oxford University Press. Professor Crane is an editor of the *Antitrust Law Journal* and a member of the advisory board of the American Antitrust Institute.

Patrick Garry is professor of law at the University of South Dakota School of Law. He has published ten books, the most recent of which are *Wrestling With God: The Courts' Tortuous Treatment of Religion* (Catholic University of America Press) and *An Entrenched Legacy: How the New Deal Constitutional Revolution Continues to Shape the Role of the Supreme Court* (Penn State University Press). Professor Garry is also Director of the Hagemann Center for Empirical Legal Research at the University of South Dakota, and has directed every research project since the Center's inception. In acknowledgement of his scholarship and research accomplishments during his tenure at USD, Garry received the President's Award for Research Excellence, the University's highest award for scholarly research accomplishments. Professor Garry is also an invited contributor to *The Oxford Companion to the United States Supreme Court, The Encyclopedia of the U.S. Supreme Court,* and *The Encyclopedia of the First Amendment.* He received his Ph.D. and J.D. from the University of Minnesota.

Jan Crawford Greenburg is an ABC News legal correspondent based in Washington, D.C., covering the Supreme Court and national legal issues. She provides legal analysis for all ABC News platforms. Ms. Greenburg has secured recent interviews with five of the Court's justices. In his first network television interview, Chief Justice John Roberts discussed the Court and his life since he became Chief Justice. She later sat down with Justice John Paul Stevens for his first-ever television interview, in which he discussed the man who appointed him to the Supreme Court in 1975, former President Gerald Ford. Ms. Greenburg interviewed Justice Clarence Thomas about his life, his bitter confirmation hearings and his views on the law. She also sat down with Justices Stephen Breyer and Antonin Scalia for a conversation about their respective legal approaches. Ms. Greenburg's book on the Supreme Court, *Supreme Conflict: The Inside Story of the Struggle for Control of the United States Supreme Court,* was published in 2007 by Penguin Press and was a *New York Times* bestseller. Before joining ABC, Ms. Greenburg was the national legal affairs reporter for the *Chicago Tribune* and the Supreme Court correspondent for The NewsHour with Jim Lehrer on PBS. She is a graduate of the University of Alabama and the University of Chicago Law School.

Stephen M. Hoersting is vice president and co-founder of the Center for Competitive Politics, a non-profit organization dedicated to promoting free speech in election campaigns. He served as general counsel to the National Republican Senatorial Committee under its chairman, Senator George Allen, during the 2003–2004 election cycle. He advised 51 Senate offices and 34 campaigns, including candidates, vendors, pollsters and consultants in the first election after the passage of McCain-Feingold, and helped win seven of eight open seat races for U.S. Senator. As a former counsel to then-Vice Chairman Bradley A. Smith of the Federal Election Commission, Mr. Hoersting has a detailed understanding of campaign finance law, its jurisprudence, and the enforcement and regulatory processes of the Federal Election Commission. He has published on campaign finance issues for the Cato Institute, the *Election Law Journal, The Washington Times, Roll Call,* and *National Review Online*; has appeared on C-SPAN's Washington Journal, and offered expert testimony on Capitol Hill. Mr. Hoersting earned a J.D. from Capital University Law School, cum laude, in 1996, and a B.A. in Economics from The Ohio State University in 1990. He is an alumnus of the Institute for Humane Studies, and served as the Federalist Society's Publications Chairman for the Free Speech and Election Law Practice Group.

Erik Luna is a professor of law at Washington and Lee University School of Law. He graduated summa cum laude from the University of Southern California and received his J.D. with honors from Stanford Law School, where he was an editor of the *Stanford Law Review.* Upon graduation, he was a prosecutor in the San Diego District Attorney's Office and a fellow and lecturer at the University of Chicago Law School. In 2000, Luna joined the faculty of the University of Utah College of Law, where he was named the Hugh B. Brown Chair in Law and was appointed co-director of the Utah Criminal Justice Center. Luna has served as the senior Fulbright Scholar to New Zealand, and he has been a visiting professor with the Cuban Society of Penal Sciences in Havana, Cuba, and a visiting scholar at the Max Planck Institute for Foreign and International Criminal Law in Freiburg, Germany. Luna is an adjunct scholar with the Cato Institute and a member of the U.S. Chamber of Commerce's Working Group on Criminal Law Issues.

Kenneth L. Marcus holds the Lillie and Nathan Ackerman Chair in Equality and Justice in America at the Baruch College School of Public Affairs, City University of New York, and is director of the Initiative on Anti-Semitism and Anti-Israelism in American Educational Systems at the Institute for Jewish & Community Research in San Francisco. Before joining Baruch, Marcus served as staff director at the United States Commission on Civil Rights. For this work, Marcus was named the first recipient of the Justice and Ethics Award for Outstanding Work in the Field of Civil Rights. Shortly before his departure, the *Wall Street Journal* observed that "the Commission has rarely been better managed," and that it "deserves a medal for good governance." Earlier, Mr. Marcus was delegated the authority of Assistant Secretary of Education for Civil Rights, served as a Commissioner on the U.S. Commission on *Brown v. Board of Education*, and was the General Deputy Assistant Secretary of Housing and Urban Development for Fair Housing and Equal Opportunity. Before entering public service, Mr. Marcus was a partner in two major law firms. Mr. Marcus now publishes and speaks widely in the areas of constitutional, civil rights, and education law. In 2010, Cambridge University Press will publish his book on anti-Semitism in American higher education. Mr. Marcus is a graduate of Williams College, magna cum laude, and the University of California at Berkeley School of Law (Boalt Hall).

Michael E. O'Neill is an associate professor of law at the George Mason University School of Law, where he specializes in criminal law and procedure and constitutional law. He received his B.A., summa cum laude, from Brigham Young University and J.D. from Yale Law School, where he served as an essays and book reviews editor of the *Yale Law Journal.* He is presently finishing a masters degree at Johns Hopkins University. Following law school, Professor O'Neill clerked for Judge David B. Sentelle on the U.S. Court of Appeals for the District of Columbia Circuit and Justice Clarence Thomas on the Supreme Court. O'Neill previously served as Chief

Counsel and Staff Director for the U.S. Senate Committee on the Judiciary during the confirmation hearings of Chief Justice John Roberts and Justice Samuel Alito. He was also confirmed to serve as a Member of the U.S. Sentencing Commission and worked as General Counsel to the Senate Judiciary Committee, as a Special Assistant United States Attorney for the District of Columbia, and in the U.S. Department of Justice's Criminal Division, Appellate Section, where he was responsible for drafting appellate briefs in the courts of appeals and working on government merits briefs and certiorari petitions before the Supreme Court.

Roger Pilon is vice president for legal affairs at the Cato Institute, where he holds the B. Kenneth Simon Chair in Constitutional Studies. He is the founder and director of Cato's Center for Constitutional Studies and the publisher of the *Cato Supreme Court Review*. He is also an adjunct professor of government at Georgetown University through The Fund for American Studies. Pilon's work has appeared in the *New York Times, Washington Post, Wall Street Journal, Los Angeles Times, Legal Times, National Law Journal, Harvard Journal of Law & Public Policy, Notre Dame Law Review, Stanford Law & Policy Review, Texas Review of Law and Politics* and elsewhere. He has appeared, among other places, on ABC's Nightline, CBS's 60 Minutes II, National Public Radio, Fox News Channel, CNN, MSNBC, CNBC. He lectures and debates at universities and law schools across the country and testifies often before Congress. Before joining Cato, Pilon held five senior posts in the Reagan administration, including at State and Justice. He has taught philosophy and law and was a national fellow at Stanford's Hoover Institution. Pilon holds a B.A. from Columbia University, an M.A. and a Ph.D. from the University of Chicago, and a J.D. from the George Washington University School of Law. In the 1989, the Bicentennial Commission presented him with the Benjamin Franklin Award for excellence in writing on the U.S. Constitution. In 2001, Columbia University's School of General Studies awarded him its Alumni Medal of Distinction.

Ilya Shapiro is a senior fellow in constitutional studies at the Cato Institute and editor-in-chief of the *Cato Supreme Court Review*. Before joining Cato, he was Special Assistant/Advisor to the Multi-National Force-Iraq on rule of law issues and practiced international, political, commercial, and antitrust litigation at Patton Boggs LLP and Cleary Gottlieb LLP. Shapiro has contributed to a variety of academic, popular, and professional publications, including the *L.A. Times*, *Washington Times*, *Legal Times*, *Weekly Standard*, *Roll Call*, *National Review Online*, and from 2004 to 2007 wrote the "Dispatches from Purple America" column for *TCS Daily.com*. He also regularly provides commentary on a host of legal and political issues for various TV and radio outlets, including CNN, Fox News, ABC, CBS, NBC, Univision, Voice of America, and American Public Media's "Marketplace." He is an adjunct professor at the George Washington University Law School and lectures regularly on behalf of the Federalist Society, The Fund for American Studies, and other educational and professional groups. Before entering private practice, Shapiro clerked for Judge E. Grady Jolly of the U.S. Court of Appeals for the Fifth Circuit, while living in Mississippi and traveling around the Deep South. He holds an A.B. from Princeton University, an M.Sc. from the London School of Economics, and a J.D. from the University of Chicago Law School, where he became a Tony Patiño Fellow. Shapiro is a native speaker of English and Russian, is fluent in Spanish and French, and is proficient in Italian and Portuguese.

Bradley A. Smith is the Josiah H. Blackmore II/Shirley M. Nault Designated Professor of Law at Capital University Law School in Columbus, Ohio. His works on campaign finance and election law include the critically acclaimed *Unfree Speech: The Folly of Campaign Finance Reform* (Princeton University Press 2001) and articles in the *Yale Law Journal*, *University of Pennsylvania Law Review*, *Georgetown Law Journal*, *Ohio State Law Journal*, *Harvard Journal of Legislation*, *Stanford Journal of Law and Policy*, *Cornell Journal of Law and Public Policy*, *Election Law Journal*, and many others. He has also published in the *Wall Street Journal*, *Washington Post*, *Los Angeles Times*, *Chicago Tribune*, *New York Daily News*, and numerous other leading papers and journals, and is a frequent guest on national television. In 2000 Professor Smith was appointed by President Clinton to fill a Republican-designated seat on the Federal Election Commission, serving until 2005. He served as vice chairman of the Commission in 2003 and chairman in 2004. He has served on the Advisory Committee to the American Bar Association's Standing Committee on Election Law, on the Executive Committee of the Free Speech and Election w Practice Group of the Federalist Society, and on the Advisory board to the Institute of Politics at the University of Minnesota School of Law. He is also on the Editorial Advisory Board of the *Election Law Journal* and the Advisory Board to the *Harvard Journal of Law and Public Policy.* In 2005 he co-founded, with Stephen Hoersting, the Center for Competitive Politics, and has served as its chairman since its inception. He is a graduate of Harvard Law School and Kalamazoo College.

ABOUT THE CATO INSTITUTE

The Cato Institute is a public foundation dedicated to the pri ited government, individual liber kets, and private property. It takes its name from *Cato's Letters*, pop. tarian pamphlets that helped to lay the philosophical foundation American Revolution.

Despite the Founders' libertarian values, today virtually no aspect of life free from government encroachment. A pervasive intolerance for individua. rights is shown by government's arbitrary intrusions into private economic transactions and its disregard for civil liberties.

To counter that trend, the Cato Institute undertakes an extensive publications program that addresses the complete spectrum of policy issues. It holds major conferences throughout the year, from which papers are published thrice yearly in the *Cato Journal,* and also publishes the quarterly magazine *Regulation* and the annual *Cato Supreme Court Review.*

The Cato Institute accepts no government funding. It relies instead on contributions from foundations, corporations, and individuals and revenue generated from the sale of publications. The Institute is a nonprofit, tax-exempt educational foundation under Section 501(c)(3) of the Internal Revenue Code.

ABOUT THE CENTER FOR CONSTITUTIONAL STUDIES

Cato's Center for Constitutional Studies and its scholars take their inspiration from the struggle of America's founding generation to secure liberty through limited government and the rule of law. Under the direction of Roger Pilon, the center was established in 1989 to help revive the idea that the Constitution authorizes a government of delegated, enumerated, and thus limited powers, the exercise of which must be further restrained by our rights, both enumerated and unenumerated. Through books, monographs, conferences, forums, op-eds, speeches, congressional testimony, and TV and radio appearances, the center's scholars address a wide range of constitutional and legal issues—from judicial review to federalism, economic liberty, property rights, civil rights, criminal law and procedure, asset forfeiture, tort law, and term limits, to name just a few. The center is especially concerned to encourage the judiciary to be "the bulwark of our liberties," as James Madison put it, neither making nor ignoring the law but interpreting and applying it through the natural rights tradition we inherited from the founding generation.

CATO INSTITUTE
1000 Massachusetts Ave., N.W.
Washington, D.C. 20001